BY MEN OR BY THE EARTH

A Corporate Lawyer Walks Out on Law, Love, and Life, and Walks
Across America With His Adopted Dog

By
Tyler Coulson

The Walkout Syndicate LLC
Chicago

The Walkout Syndicate LLC
Chicago, Illinois

walkout@thewalkout.com
thewalkoutsyndicate@gmail.com

www.thewalkout.com

© 2012 by Tyler Coulson

Walkout Syndicate and design are trademarks of The Walkout Syndicate LLC.

Book design and cover photo by Tyler Coulson.

Cover design by Jenna Bragagnolo.

ISBN 978-0-9856119-0-3

Library of Congress Control Number: 2012908403

May, 2012

To the Reader:

This is BY MEN OR BY THE EARTH, and it is about a man, a dog, the law, and a long walk. It is made of three smaller books:

Book I: THE MOMENTS THAT TURN US, which takes place between March 11, 2011 and November 8, 2011;

Book II: FEEL THE SELFISH FURY, which takes place between August, 2005, and March 10, 2011; and

Book III: ...AND THE MOON SAYS HALLELUJAH, which takes place between December 24, 2011, and January, 2012.

I wrote each book, broke each into small sections, and then shuffled the sections of the three books together into BY MEN OR BY THE EARTH. So three stories are told simultaneously within BY MEN OR BY THE EARTH. Each section titled with a fragment from *The Rubaiyat of Omar Khayyam.*

This book is as true as I could make it, but some things had to be changed. I changed names. I made up some stuff and some composite characters, like Rosie and Celio in Book III, and compressed the chronology of a few things. I left out a lot of things.

I wrote this thing in Chicago, in San Pedro, Ambergris Caye, Belize, and along 3500 miles of North American highways.

Many people deserve thanks. Among them, I would like to thank Heidi J. for walking and talking with me and loaning her car to the cause; Sir John McGuilicutty auf Ulm for his generosity, without which I may have ended the Walk in Iowa; Sajal and Joe for taking me in when I had nowhere to go; and Tom Coulson, Joan Coulson, George N. Coulson, and Thelma Coulson for everything they did to make my life possible and to give me the chance to make something of myself.

This book is dedicated to Mabel and to every other dog who has been there when needed.

I hope you like it, and I hope it has a happy ending.

Tyler Coulson
Chicago, Illinois

Myself when young did eagerly frequent
Doctor and Saint, and heard great Argument
About it and about: but evermore
Came out by the same Door as in I went.

With them the Seed of Wisdom did I sow,
And with my own hand labour'd it to grow:
And this was all the Harvest that I reap'd-
"I came like Water, and like Wind I go."

From FITZGERALD, EDWARD,
The Rubaiyat of Omar Khayyam of Naishapur (First Edition).

BOOK I: THE MOMENTS THAT TURN US (A)
AWAKE!

I woke on the Atlantic seastrand south of Rehoboth Beach, Delaware. The sky and sea were stormy gray, but ribbons of white clouds ringed patches of pale blue sky. Sky and sea blended in the east into an upturned bowl of churning gray. Salted wind off the ocean rustled the tips of my beard and rustled the dry stalks of dune grass behind me. Wind carved blonde waves into Mabel's bright auburn hair and churned up whitecaps on the stormy Atlantic.

"I have never been here before," I said to Mabel. Mabel glanced at me, wetted her nose with her tongue and then looked back into the upturned bowl where the sea and sky connected. She and I hardly knew each other. Mabel came to me from a shelter in a distant state. I didn't know who had abandoned her or why, and, if she knew why she'd been abandoned, she didn't say. She had been torn suddenly away from everything she knew and was standing on a Delaware beach with a man she had known for only a little over a month. She and I watched day break behind the clouds, brighten the clouds, and separate the sea from the sky on the horizon. Waves crashed on the beach in front of us. I was 32 years old.

I come originally from that Midwestern ocean of land where waves are made of green corn and winter wheat, and I can watch ocean surf for hours and never stop wondering. But to the west I was daunted. I may have waited too long, gotten too old and soft. Five thousand miles on foot. Twelve states. The Allegheny Mountains and the Sierra Nevada. The Rockies. The Tall Grass Prairie and the Great Plains. The Mojave Desert. Bears and mountain lions. Tornados and heat waves. And people! Meth heads and grifters and criminals and drivers on cell phones. Crumbling highways that ribbon westward from the Atlantic to the Pacific.

Mabel was anxious to start moving but I was daunted. There were so many risks and so many uncertainties. I was an attorney (or had been two weeks earlier) and attorneys are soldiers in a War Against Risk and Uncertainty. From $170,000/yr to being homeless on a beach. I suppose there is some risk in that; there is some uncertainty there. Mabel wagged her tail.

I had imagined this Moment for a long time, and had dreamt of it constantly for the last year—ever since I had decided on a beach in San Diego that "Damnit, I could walk across this continent and be happier than I am now". In my dreams, it had looked just like this, had smelled just like this. And there had been daydreams, too. Back in Chicago, I had been several times caught staring out the window of my 26th floor office, dreaming of standing homeless on that Delaware beach. I had woken many nights in a 17th story penthouse apartment from a dream of being on that exact beach. And in my stupid dreams, blue-suited men barricaded me on the beach. Men in blue suits with accordion files and bankers' boxes stuffed with documents and with vibrating Blackberries.

"I have never been in this spot before," I said to Mabel again.

In my dreams, I had never actually stepped off that Delaware beach. In my little dreamy dreams, I had paced back and forth between the blue Atlantic and the men in blue suits, and each time I built up the gumption to just-do-it-already those men in blue suits blocked my way. And, when the dream became so frustrating that I could not take it, I would rush headlong to burst through the line of men in blue suits. Like red rover red rover. I would wake in a terror as I felt myself swallowed up by their interlocked arms. But there I was.

It was March 11, 2011. I wasn't dreaming.

I could feel the real weight of the heavy pack on my back. This was 90 or 100 pounds of gear and water. In my dreams, the pack had never hurt like this, my feet had never sunk into the sand under the weight of the pack, and Mabel had never been there. Mabel had never nudged my left hand with her wet puppy nose.

"Have you been here before?" I asked Mabel. Mabel has big hazel eyes, and I almost know what she is thinking when she looks at me. Or I can almost imagine what she is thinking. She was thinking: "We need to go. You need to start moving."

But I couldn't move because I was afraid. The pack and my feet were heavy. I was soft, weak, and fat after almost six years behind a desk and behind casebooks. I was insolvent. I was unsure of everything and I was scared. And that first step! I couldn't settle myself on that first step because I had built in my mind a map of "firsts" all across the country: first step, first mile, first state, and on and on. It would be a *process,* I told myself, and it would all make sense and be easy to analyze. And I cannot be daunted by an analytical process.

I wanted so badly to call my girlfriend, Isra, and say ""we aren't doing this; we are moving in with you today". Walking across the United States is a ridiculous idea. It was stupid, wasn't it? I had an education, great parents, and the most wonderful girlfriend. I wanted to marry her. And she said that she wanted to marry me! So why put all that off for at least five months, maybe six? I should be off somewhere working, making money to pay off my student loan indenture. I thought for a moment that I was too weak and too scared, that I would call it all off.

But Mabel nudged me again. She sat and then stood and then sat again and wiggled.

"Let's go," she thought.

"Let's call this off," I said. "If I start, don't I have to finish? Can't I call this off and go home to Isra? We can do everything *now*! I don't need to wait until D.C. to ask her and I don't need to walk across the country before we get a life started! But what kind of life could I even start?"

Mabel didn't have anything to say to that. She wetted her nose again and flitted her gaze around at the beach.

"And what do I do if we fail, Mabel?" She thought about the question. "And I will probably fail. How far do I have to walk before I can fail without

2

being embarrassed in front of all these people? All of these attorneys who are watching me? Do I have to make it to Ohio? To Illinois? We can't make it." Mabel scowled.

"You have to. Move. Shift," she thought. "I can help you."

She stood again and tugged on the lead. She puts all of her 45 pounds into that leash when she needs to, and she tugged hard enough to pull me off my center of gravity and I fell, walking, toward the inland of the continent.

I took my first step.

BOOK II: FEEL THE SELFISH FURY (A)
INTO THIS UNIVERSE, AND WHY NOT KNOWING, NOR WHENCE.

Think of me this way: a 27-year-old man ready to beat the world in khakis and a button down shirt. I was young, strong, and eager when I walked into the University of Iowa College of Law as a first year law student, a "1L". I had it in my head that people like me *should* go to law school; that I should do it because I had the *mind* for it. I was excited by the intellectual challenge, the competition, the rigor of the thing. I have heard that among people who drop out of law school, the most common reason is "it just wasn't what I expected it would be". That's the most common reason for thru-hikers to quit the Appalachian Trail or the American Discovery Trail, too. Or so I hear.

But that wasn't going to happen to me. I was going to whoop it and go on to a rich and fulfilling life.

Law school began with orientation and introductions. I was an angry man and held my cold eyes low under my brow; I grinned with masked derision and anger at the right-out-of-college kids who had no idea what to expect. And I was immediately embarrassed for myself, too, for having flung myself into school after so many years of being *out* and for having so many dreams of what I could become—it's funny and embarrassing to think back on how I thought I might change the world or become rich. We probably all thought we would change the world or get rich, thought we knew the days and nights of law students and of lawyers. We all knew everything.

No one knew anything.

We all had a first day. The doe-eyed scared ones and the driven ones with cold or wild eyes. Those students who were more cynical than I, or who knew more about the workaday world of the law, already shared a sense of apprehension. Some became defensive from day one. See the tall girls who smiled and stared at the floor; the thin boys with thousand yard smiles who saw that, even in this new world, "I will never fit in"; the rubes and country hicks (like me) who tried so hard to make "sophisticated" first impressions. Some folks closed up entirely and I never talked to them after the first day. The first day overwhelmed a lot of students because so many of the personalities at law school are so big and so abrasive. New law students often actively avoid becoming friends with their classmates.

3

The Boyd Law Building at Iowa is a clinical, uninviting thing built in a 1980s vision of hyper-modernism. We called it the BLB. It is circular and built into the side of a bluff over the Iowa River. There is nothing natural or warm about the BLB. The classrooms have pew-style seating as if we were all in church. The glass-fronted face of the thing opens onto a concrete mezzanine, and a small patch of grass with a Burgher of Calais statue permanently frozen in a "WTF?" gesture, forever casting a motionless and confused glance into the law school. *Les Bourgeois des Calais* is a sculpture by Rodin depicting an incident in French history when the British King, Edward, laid siege to Calais; he agreed to spare the city if six of its wealthiest, most powerful citizens would surrender and be executed. Six burghers surrendered, and one is immortalized in the sculpture at Iowa Law. None were executed. Over the course of three years, most Iowa Law students wondered more than once: "Is the Burgher confused because we wouldn't let him into the club, or is he confused because he did get in and can't remember why he applied?"

On the whole, the Iowa Law student body was a lot like every other law school body in the history of legal studies. We were mostly middle-of-the-road white guys—guys who would never do anything genuinely fascinating or interesting, but who would fill our lives with slightly above average achievements; most of us were smart and capable, I think, and some of us weren't quite as smart, not quite as capable. We were never great at sports or math or anything, really, but were always really, really passable at everything we attempted to do. Most of us had probably already reached a point in our lives where everyone who knew us had wondered: "Why hasn't he done more? He is *soooo* smart and talented." There were several minority students at Iowa Law, and on average they seemed just as smart and capable, of course, but not as outgoing as we desperate white guys. (Every now and again, someone would suggest, or hint, or outright *say* that the minorities, especially black students, were there because of affirmative action. Some affirmative action program might have had an impact on admissions—I don't know—but regardless of any standardized test scores or undergrad grade point averages, the minority students I knew at Iowa were absolutely as smart, as capable, and as qualified as anyone else.) The women at Iowa law were mostly smart, too, often dangerously smart, and usually were either not quite attractive enough to have ever been taken seriously in life or were too attractive to be taken seriously in law school. There is a deep bitterness—a *mahat*[1] sadness—in the hearts of most women in law school.

And there I was.

So, sometimes think of me this way: 27, single, no kids, no savings, nothing really. Nothing. I had never accomplished anything. When I started law school, I had $23 in the bank. I was a fool sitting in the first section meeting of Contracts I with the most infamous Socratic Method professor in the law school. We'd all heard horror stories about law school, and most had probably watched or read *Paperchase*, with its monolithic antagonist

---

[1] "Mahat" means great, big, or grand in Urdu and Hindi. In Sanskrit, it can also mean the complete material existence.

4

Professor Kingsfield. We probably all expected Kingsfield to walk through the door, and we were all impatient and nervously formatting and re-formatting note templates we'd created in Word. But Kirkland walked through the door.

BOOK III: ...AND THE MOON SAYS HALLELUJAH, 12.24.11

(5.5 hrs) Drive from parents' house in rented car; drive until 9 or 9:30, gravel around rural hometown; stop car idling, outside town, dead end gravel near interstate. Cry. Research gun on passenger seat, under red sweatshirt, roommate's .45, liberated from under his bed. Note gun is illegal in Chicago, roommate doesn't care. Analyze issue, uncontrollable; grow concerned. Phone call w/good friends (Carrie & Heidi). Research re: uncontrollable, physical thought; determine odd, like someone else's; conclude not scared of finality; fear powerlessness. Wait for thought to get too big; call w/Carrie re: "I'm not doing well"; call w/Heidi re: "I'm scared of myself a little." Feel shame and embarrassment. Feel shame and embarrassment. Research re: Have I got more friends to call?; conclude no more people to talk to. Research re: "How heavy is that gun?"; determine is heavier than it looks, like all guns. Note grip was comfortable, but gun not balanced well. Breathe. Research re: "What's that sky look like tonight?"; determine sky clearest, emptiest had seen since Utah. Analyze calm feeling; lift gun.

(.3 hrs) Discover police lights behind car; see Sheriff arrive. Conclude was still not scared; feel shame and embarrassment. Hide gun. See Sheriff approach car, hand on his gun. Determine Sheriff looked nervous or confused. Recognize sheriff, was sheriff when I lived here. Research sheriff: Former Navy Seal, good guy, big Irish-Catholic family, figured he'd run for congress, never did. Hand ID out window.
Sheriff: "What's the problem?"
T: "Nothing."
Sheriff: "Wisconsin license plates? Long ways from Wisconsin."
T: "My name is Tyler. I'm from here. It's a rental car."
See Sheriff smile; determine he recognized me.
Sheriff: "Haven't seen you in 10 years."
T: "I've been around."
Sheriff: "What the Hell are you doing out here?"
T: "Hiding from my family. It's..."
Sheriff: "What are you doing?" Still holding my ID.
T: "I, uh, well, I just tried to walk across the country with my dog."
Tell sheriff we'd been on long walk. Respond to information requests: how long walking, how was weather, was there traffic, what about water.
Sheriff: "Back to the real world."
T: "Yeah." Refrain wailing. Hold shoulders low/close over chest. Feel shame.
Sheriff: "You ok?"
T: "I think I am."

Sheriff: "You ok?"

T: "I think I am." Receive ID.

Sheriff: "I was on the interstate and saw your car over here. Aren't but two cars use this road. Had to check. It's hard to come back. Take all the time you need."

T: "Is this a county road or a private road?"

Sheriff: "I think it belongs to the county. But if anyone gives you any trouble, tell them you talked to me. Take all the time you need."

T: "Thanks, Man."

Sheriff: "I have to go or they will panic and send officers out here. Be safe. Take *time*."

(.3 hrs) Watch Sheriff leave, was alone. Believe that Sheriff understood me; note that he was the first person to interact with me the right way since the end of the Walk. Consider fear again; feel relief to be scared. Research re: "Is being scared better than the alternative?"; conclude yes. Text w/high school friend, Everett: "You around? Want to ride around all night? I am not doing well." Text from Ev: "What's up?" Respond: "Suicidal." Ev: "Ready now. Pick me up."

(3.2 hrs) Drive three hours w/Ev, same gravel roads. Listen to radio. Remember stories. Drive until couldn't hold eyes open. Drop Ev off at his sister's house. Discuss issue w/Ev, re: powerlessness of thoughts and actions. Discuss Ev's conclusion, i.e., "It's some fucking brain thing, man, from being outside so much; it'll pass. I mean, you're not, like, actually *depressed*, right?" Respond: "I'm not *sad*." Ev offers: "Yeah, dude, I was actually *depressed* for a while. And it's different than what you've got. You just need time to calm down, Man. And some sleep."

T: "I haven't slept much in two months."

Everett: "How much of this is because of what happened with Isra?"

T: "Not much, I don't think. I'm just a little fucked up. My brain isn't working right." Refrain wailing, feel sleepy.

Everett: "You ok?"

T: "Yeah. I think so. I'll be all right. Thanks."

Everett: "Your roommate Sirinder is right; you need sleep. Go to Belize. Get some sleep. Have some time where, you know, Mabel isn't depending on you, where no one is depending on you. Get your head on straight."

T: "I will. Thank you." Refrain wailing.

Everett: "No problem. Keep on chooglin', Man."

(3.3 hrs) Arrive home. Sleep three hours.

BOOK I: THE MOMENTS THAT TURN US (A)(i)
FOR ALL THE SIN WHEREWITH THE FACE OF MAN IS BLACKEN'D.

Mabel and I stepped off the sand and headed toward Rehoboth Beach, south of the eastern terminus of the American Discovery Trail at Cape Henlopen. The weight of the pack hit deep in the bones of my feet and in my knees and my hips. My back and legs strained and I leaned heavily on my walking stick through whole strides. I told myself that I was just out of shape and that it would get easier, because it had to get easier.

I was over packed but I didn't know that. I am a strong enough fellow and had decided to hike with a traditional pack rather than lightweight or ultra-light. I could have recited the contents of my pack from memory at that time.[2] The thing about walking across the country is that you can't know how to pack for a trip like that until you do it because it is not a "trip"; it's a lifestyle. As out of shape as I was, it was difficult to walk under the strain of 90 or 100 lbs.

Mabel and I had walked pretty well together from the beginning. Back in Chicago, she had learned quickly to walk on my left side. We had gone on walks around the block or to the Grant Park dog park and Mabel was pretty good about walking with me. But Mabel is a strong-willed, red-haired dog. She *knew* not to pull on the leash but would sometimes pull until I corrected her with a "heel!" and she would be embarrassed. I was scared to clip her lead to my hip belt at first because I did not want her to pull me off my center of gravity or, worse, to pull me over a cliff or into traffic. So I clutched a walking stick in my right hand and her lead in my left hand.

We were not fast enough. I could estimate our speed at about two m.p.h when we started in Delaware. I figured the math during that first mile. At two m.p.h., that's a maximum of 20 miles a day? Maybe 24? That was too slow, I thought, because I could not depend on 10 hours on the road every day. I started figuring distances and days, when I might be where. *That* was the urge to plan and to control everything, to know it *all*, and to know what will happen before it happens. To "unpack" every problem to constituent issues and to kill each issue with attention and logic. To catalogue your day in six minute intervals like a biglaw attorney who must account for 2000 hours a year. I was breathing pretty heavily as we turned westward in the beachfront center of Rehoboth Beach and headed into the continent. I had mapped out the one-mile mark ahead of time so that I could take a picture of it. We walked on the sidewalk along the left side of the road. Rehoboth Beach is a pleasant beach town, the first Atlantic beach town I had ever seen north of the Carolinas. All beach towns are similar in texture and attitude, and Rehoboth Beach seemed laid back and comfortable.

---

[2] My pack contents were something like: Dry bag (contents: extra pair pants, extra hiking shirt, 2 pair long underwear, 8 pair of mixed weight socks, 4 pair silk sock liners, t-shirt, 1 pair khakis, 1 polo style pullover shirt), dry bag with sleeping bag, dry bag with 3 days' food (including ghee, or clarified butter), water filter, hatchet, length of rope, journal, phone and charger, Mabel's records, map, flashlight, headlamp, multi-tool, rain jacket, stocking cap, several cigarette lighters, flint and steel, tinder, gaiters, solar panel and battery, first aid kit and blister kit, fleece jacket, half zip pullover, gloves, 2 gallons of water (at 8 lbs a gallon!), toiletries (toilet paper, toothpaste and brush, safety razor, camp soap, skin lotion for chapping), 3 changes of batteries for the flashlight, dog food (6 lbs), tent (about 5 lbs), sleeping pad, MSR Whisperlite Internationale camp stove, one 20 oz can of gasoline, a 2-pot cook set and frying pan, two 20 oz. cans of bear spray, tarp, and an emergency supplies kit. (The emergency supplies kit was basically an ultra-light hiking kit and contained a tarp for shelter, fire starter, signaling mirror, emergency poncho, and emergency blanket.) I also carried a copy of Edward FitzGerald's translation of *The Rubaiyat of Omar Khayyam*, which was my grandfather's favorite poem.

I smiled when I could see the one-mile mark. Milestone. First step, first mile, first state, and so on. This was all part of the *process* that I had created in my little dreaming mind. I was *seeing* the first mile, but my eyes were on the Rocky Mountains. Three obstacles above all others on an east/west thru-hike can best a hiker: the Rockies, the desert, the Sierra Nevada. The goal must be to cross the Rockies late enough in the year to avoid late winter weather, but early enough to reach the Sierra Nevada before the year's winter. You must train your eyes on a distant land from the first step.

I turned my phone on through the mesh of a pocket on my hip belt so I could snap a picture at Mile One. Mabel knew I was excited and pranced along beside me. We could no longer see the ocean and were only a few blocks from turning on to a long stretch of strip malls and fast food joints. We walked beside an open lot ringed by a chain link fence, and someone was driving a Bobcat skid steer loader in the open lot.

Mabel took a fright and jumped when she saw the Bobcat. She zipped behind me and then in front of me because she was afraid to be pinned between the fence and me. In her fright, she wrapped her chain lead around my left foot and the chain also wrapped around my left ring finger; she bolted again and the lead pulled my left foot up off the ground. The hiking stick was in my right hand with a leather thong fastening the stick to my right wrist. I tried to balance on my right foot with Mabel skittering manically on my left and 100 pounds on my back.

Then the weight shifted in my pack and the pack seemed to jump over my center of gravity. Falling is a serious concern for backpackers. Falling causes more injuries than bears or snakes or criminals or anything. It's easy to fall and break a rib that punctures your lung, to fall on your face and bust up your nose or your cheekbone. A fall could have ended the Walk quickly and I knew that I would fall. A great number of thoughts went through my mind in a scintilla of time.

I thought about how I couldn't get my hands free to break my fall because my left hand was tangled in a chain leash and my right hand was bound at the wrist to an ironwood walking stick. I thought about how I couldn't spin around to limit the chance of broken bones or death because my left leg was up off the ground tangled in the lead and had pulled me too far over already.

I thought about Steve Fossett, the multi-millionaire adventurer who, on his first attempt to travel around the world in a hot air balloon, crashed a few miles from his launch. Fossett could survive that embarrassment because he had a million billion quadrillion dollars to fund another, better adventure. But I didn't have Fossett's money. Even Fossett with his limitless access to money still met an inevitable death in the Sierra Nevada. My death was about to be a little more embarrassing.

Then, as I was falling, I thought that I had always heard that the hardest bone in the human body is right at the top of the forehead. That is why you should never punch someone in the forehead, and why a head-butt can break a nose or a jaw. And, because I could not free my hands or spin around, I decided to break my fall with my forehead. I leaned forward, and dove toward the pavement. The sidewalk got bigger and bigger, and I thought about that old thought experiment where the mathematician bounces a ball against a wall from 10 feet away, then from five feet away, then 2.5 feet away, then 1.25 feet away. Because you can halve numbers into infinity, the mathematician never reaches the wall. The conundrum there is that the ball does reach the wall, every time.

My forehead drove into the pavement. I don't think I lost consciousness, but may have because I did not hear my head hit the pavement, and I didn't hear the snap of my left ring finger, which I am sure must have made noise when it broke because I could not bend my finger for weeks and it swelled up like a sausage and throbbed with pain all the way to D.C. The pack slid forward on my back and slammed into the back of my head and neck. The momentum from it transferred to my head and pushed my head skidding along the sidewalk. I crumpled on the sidewalk.

I wiggled my toes in my boots before I tried to get up to make sure I wasn't paralyzed, and then moved my fingers to free them from the chain leash and walking stick. Mabel whined and snuck in close to lick my forehead. I unbuckled myself from the pack, rolled out of it, and sat up. I touched my right pocket for the outline of a ring I was carrying, then I touched my right hand to my forehead. There was blood. My hand was covered in bright red blood and the blood dripped off my hand and head into puddles on the pavement. I could smell and taste the iron in the blood.

"Are you alright, Buddy?" Two huge black men in dark suits jogged up the sidewalk toward me. I looked at them and Mabel sat, wiggling and excited. They looked like Jehovah's Witnesses. "Are you alright?"

"Can you see my brain?" I asked. I thought that was a funny question under the circumstances, and I was worried because neither of the men laughed.

"Nah, I can't see your brain but you scarred you self," he said. "You scarred you self." He had an accent, and I could not tell for sure if he was saying "scared" or "scarred". Either would have been appropriate.

The Jehovah's Witnesses sat with me and gave me a roll of paper towels to sop up the blood. There was a great deal of blood, but I didn't think any bones were broken in my head. My forehead had slid across the pavement, so instead of a broken head I had about 15 three-inch lacerations running up my forehead above my right eye. The cuts weren't deep, but one probably could have been stitched and they all bled like a river. The Jehovah's Witnesses were patient and concerned. They offered several times to give me a ride to a hospital, but I didn't think I should use my health insurance in a country where so many people don't have access to health care services. And I didn't want to bleed in their car. Instead, I sopped up the blood and wiped the wounds and used some of the water they gave me to clean myself up.

After I got to my feet, I took a picture of the cleaned wound and then I bandaged my head with a handkerchief and thanked them. I took some reading materials from them and said I would read them. Mabel and I walked on. Blood ran out from underneath the handkerchief and covered half of my face. Warm blood coagulated and became sticky; it cracked on my face. I walked like that for a few miles and people gave me strange looks.

I stopped at a gas station on Coastal Hwy and hid with Mabel behind the building where I could put down my pack and have the room and time to clean my wounds. But the manager came out of a back door to have a cigarette and found me there. He seemed concerned, probably that I would die in his parking lot. He told me to use the bathroom inside. I cleaned my wound with water and tincture of iodine in the bathroom of the gas station. The manager of the gas station asked me if I needed an ambulance, but I promised him I was fine. There was a motel a few blocks down the road.

I checked in to the motel and tried not to sleep because of that old wives' tale about sleeping with a concussion. Plus, I emailed pictures of the injury and a description of the accident to Dr. Cravath—a doctor friend of mine from my old law firm—and he told me that it looked like I would not die, but that sleeping would be a bad idea. I had to wash blood out of my beard and the motel sink turned pink and revolting with my blood, so I used a dab of gasoline to clean the porcelain. My face swelled and my right eye began to swell shut. My head and neck hurt. I emailed a picture of the injury to Isra, and she responded "Ouch, that looks horrible" but did not call me. I turned on the TV, sat on the bed, and read the Jehovah's Witness tracts.

Mabel gave a grand sigh and went to sleep on the bed.

BOOK I: THE MOMENTS THAT TURN US (A)(ii)
FOR 'IS' AND 'IS-NOT' THOUGH WITH RULE AND LINE, AND 'UP-AND-DOWN' WITHOUT, I COULD DEFINE.

I was stuck in that motel another day because my right eye swelled shut. I burned with frustration. To finally get started on something so big and so rushed and then have to sit around a whole day doing nothing but watching TV and watching Mabel get anxious and rambunctious drove me mad. It is hard to stay still when everything in your legs and heart tells you to go-go-go. But my head and neck still hurt, my left ring finger was in bad shape, and my eye was swollen shut.

We started out for California again the next day. I thought of it that way, like we were just "walking to California", as if it were just a goal or a thing or a destination. It was none of those things, but I wouldn't understand that for a long time. Mabel and I hiked a serpentine path toward Milton, which was about 17 miles, according to Google Maps, where my American Discovery Trail map told me there were places to camp and a motel and/or bed and breakfast. It was good that Mabel and I had a destination and a plan, because it was our first real day of the trip, and it takes a while to get used to the idea of having no definite place to stay. It was one of the most difficult days of the trip because the pack was heavy and I was in horrible shape and it was a long walk.

We started out with difficulty getting out of the city. Rehoboth Beach and Lewes are not pedestrian friendly; most American cities are not. So on our first day on the road after I recovered a bit from the pavement dive, we were quickly stopped on the roadside at or near the junctions of several busy city streets. My right eye was still shut and our way was blocked on the left shoulder of the road. Mabel and I had to cross the intersections of two roads very near the intersection of three other roads at or near the same time in order to get to the right side of the road because we could not pass on the left side. There were no crosswalks and no stoplights. Our only options that I could see were to cross there or to hike backward about a mile to a crosswalk, wind around a residential district, and emerge again on the other side of this road. I could not accept the latter option—it was too early in the trip to do any backtracking. Backtracking would have hurt my morale and shaken Mabel's confidence in me. And I had no way of knowing how many miles the detour would add or if it would be any easier, so there was too much risk and uncertainty. I had to cross.

The traffic was consistent, if not heavy. When spaces opened in the southbound lane, the northbound lane was full; in the rare cases where the main road seemed to open up, then traffic would often feed in from the additional roads. Crossing the road shouldn't be too tough, especially not for a highly trained legal mind. So I started thinking about this problem like an attorney would think about the problem. After almost six years of legal training, both in law school and in practice, I could approach problems *only* as an attorney would approach a problem.

> **Issue**: How best can Tyler cross the road?
> **Rule**: One should look both ways and then cross, obeying all traffic control devices.
> **Application**: Tyler looked both ways, and there was still traffic. There were no traffic control devices.
> **Conclusion**: We need more research.

I tried to "unpack" the problem by identifying all the sub-issues. I had good authority that there is an accepted method for crossing the road, that one should find a crosswalk, look both ways, etc. Previous personal experiences had all proven those authorities more-or-less accurate.

Ah, but this situation can be distinguished! Generally, there are not so many inflows of traffic. Generally, a person crosses *one* street, or perhaps an intersection of two streets. But here there are four or five streets in close proximity. There usually are traffic control devices to aid the pedestrian-errant, but not here. In many cases there are crosswalks or pedestrian bridges. Not here.

Well now, there is an argument from public policy that this is a flawed intersection, and if you view this problem through the lens of critical race theory....

Now, what the hell is wrong with this situation? I'm not a physicist, but I'm not a complete idiot. I am educated. And I've been competent in most things for most of my life. And yet I cannot cross a road? I'd heard speeches about the "legal mind" and "learning to think like a lawyer" when I was in law school. I read *Paperchase*. I get it. I had a "legal mind". But crossing the road shouldn't be a time consuming exercise in nuance. I didn't have time to argue about the definitions of "road" or "cross" or "intersection", or to think of a new and novel way to look at the issue of road-crossing, or to approach road crossing from a critical race theory perspective. (Which, ironically, is a legitimate perspective on the broader road-crossing problem.)

The "legal mind" is a surgical tool: powerful when deployed in appropriate situations. Tunneling into rabbit holes is simply what the legal mind does. After sufficient training, the legal mind looks at problems not from every reasonable angle, but from every conceivable angle. Too often, the legal mind creates problems that do not exist; we make simple problems far more complex. We recognize and implement arguments not only for the correct proposition, but for *any* proposition. White is black. Rich is poor. Then people pay you to make those arguments and then you buy expensive televisions.

But sometimes you need to use a blunter instrument.

Mabel can make decisions. She often makes bad decisions, sure, but she isn't afraid to commit. She wasn't bothered by this road-crossing problem. Cross or go around! She didn't care which. But I couldn't stop thinking about the options, weighing potential costs and benefits of crossing versus going around. I would convince myself to cross, and then think "ah, but the potential costs are so high!" I would convince myself to go around and write off a few hours from the day, but then I would think "no, there is too much uncertainty! Who knows how long it will take to snake our way through that residential district!" To Mabel, though, this was simply a contest between Man and Road. It wasn't the end of the world. Almost nothing is the end of the world. So you face some danger, so you lose some time, so this and so that. "Just relax," Mabel thought, "You aren't very important."

So we crossed, and here is how we did it: We waited until there were no cars, and then we crossed the road.

I was re-learning how to think.[3]

BOOK III: ...AND THE MOON SAYS HALLELUJAH, 01.03.12[4]

Drop Mabel off with law school friend in Chicago; pack small bag; travel to O'Hare airport. Arrive Belize, Central America, cloudy skies, air thick and warm, smelled of diesel and asphalt, wind sounded like cracking palm fronds. Want to snorkel, work on book. Remember everyone saying I "need to get away for a while", need "to get my head on straight". Taxi to shore through blown-out Belize City; note poverty, people living in hovels, shacks.

Water taxi to Caye Caulker, island off the coast. Research Caye Caulker: tiny; walk length of it in about an hour. Meet Kendra Booth at her rental condo.

K: "Where are you staying?"

---

[3] Later in the year, after upgrading the mapping and satellite imaging features on my phone, I found that the intersection in question had posed much less of an obstacle than it looked like from the ground. There were a number of ways I could have walked around it, but I could not see them from the ground.

[4] Incremental time entries omitted for remainder of Book III.

T: "I didn't make reservations. I found a room at the Barefoot Caribe up the road. On the third floor. The door doesn't work well. The German couple next door asked me not to come home too late because the door slamming will wake them up."

Dinner w/Kendra; eat fish on the islands, only eat fish on vacation. Have several drinks.

T: "I haven't slept in 44 hours."

K: "Jesus."

T: "I didn't sleep well in November or December."

K: "Jesus. Why?"

T: "I was on the phone a lot."

K: "Are you ok?"

T: "Of course. But I should go back to my room."

Return to hotel; find room hot; open window, no screen. Shower; look in mirror; catalogue what I see. Review timesheets from November/December; compare what I saw then: man w/beautiful puppy, unemployed, probably unemployable, lives on friend's couch, much debt. Consider Caye Caulker: pretty at night, not much happens, dogs mill around. Turn on TV; check Iowa Caucus results. Put manuscript on chest to review. Draft story:

I was excited to go to Belize. I'd never been to Central America and I think people were right that I was desperate for a vacation. About 80% of the decisions I've made in the last six or seven years I made out of sheer desperation. No way to live a life, really. So I was desperate for a vacation. Desperate, at any rate. In the old days, when I hung around with white, middle-class inheritor poets who dressed down, drank coffee, said "that's so meta", and did open mic SLAM poetry, they would have probably written me a haiku that read:

Tyler falls apart.
Schadenfreude in the flesh.
Right in front of us.

"Schadenfreude." That was a popular word a few years back. Mostly with those poet types who dressed down, drank coffee, and said "that's so meta". It makes me happy that that word isn't so popular anymore.

Wake two a.m.; see German woman from next door had broken into room, stood in corner by door. She said: "Be cool, Man." Consider killing her out of self-defense; decide to ask her what was up. She said: "Came in through the window to turn off your TV"; she and fiancé couldn't sleep next door. Make new friend, her name is Bea. Trash story from earlier in evening.

Wind blows in off the sea and clouds gather over the tiny island.

BOOK III: ...AND THE MOON SAYS HALLELUJAH, 01.04.12

Wake on Caulker; snorkel. Have drinks with Canadian girls, one girl could not stand well for the rum, was on vacation, intensely.

Imagine snowflakes the size of kittens' paws falling in Chicago.

BOOK II: FEEL THE SELFISH FURY (A)(i)
ALL THE SAINTS AND SAGES WHO DISCUSS'D OF THE TWO WORLDS SO LEARNEDLY.

Kirkland walked unsteadily and held a stack of books in unsteady arms. He dropped the books heavily on the lectern, then ran his finger down a hidden class roster. This was our introduction to the Socratic Method. "Mister...." he trailed off, then: "Adams. What is a contract?"

"Um, well, it's a *promise or set of promises that a court will enforce,*" Adams said, and it was unclear whether he had read directly from the definition in the casebook or whether he had memorized it. Adams was a good looking young man in a button down shirt (more-or-less like mine) with neatly trimmed hair and an eager, serious smile on his face. His teeth were perfect, of course.

"Yes, that is the book's definition of a contract. But what does it *mean?* What *is* a contract? What is a promise?"

"Well, it's when someone promises to do something," Adams answered.

"But do people always do what they promise they will do? You promise that you will kill me," Kirkland said. "Is that a contract?"

"Well, no."

"But it's a promise?" he asked.

"Yes."

"Then why is it not a contract?"

"I just...I'm not sure. I mean, I don't think a judge is going to force me to kill you."

"Mr. Adams, I promise to give you a million dollars. Do we have a contract?"

"Uh...well...I mean, that would depend."

"On what would that depend, Mr. Adams?" Kirkland asked.

"Well do you *really mean it?* If you don't really mean it..."

"Oh, you really mean to kill me. I really mean to give you a million dollars. But then I don't. What happens to your promise?"

"Nothing, I guess," Adams answered.

"Why not?"

"Because it wouldn't be fair?"

"I'll ask the questions," Kirkland said. "That's how this works: I ask questions and you answer them. Why wouldn't it be fair?"

"Because I didn't do anything for the million dollars," Adams answered.

"Ah...because there was no *consideration?*" Kirkland asked. Adams said yes. "So a contract is not enforceable...it's not a real contract...unless both sides get something?"

"Yes."

"Ah. But what about...."

This back and forth went on for an hour. Each answer got another question. Sometimes Mr. Adams would fire off an answer that he thought was good, and you could tell from his tone of voice that he felt as if he'd

14

reached an ultimate answer, but Kirkland would come back with some other, more pointed question. Nothing was right. Nothing was correct, nothing was complete. These questions aimed at the fundamental step of *defining* a contract—a definition that one would assume would be necessary in a class on contracts. We did not even discuss that day's assigned cases. It seemed like Kirkland was picking on Adams, and we all grew uncomfortable, especially Mr. Adams. At the end of his hour, Adams looked demolished and his hands shook like a little child or a scared puppy. Most of us in the classroom hated Kirkland right then, I think, because we all knew that each of us would get the same treatment eventually. The hate dissipated as slowly we realized he was among the best professors any of us had ever had. (The same cannot be said for all law professors who use the Socratic Method.)

That was our introduction to law school and to the Socratic Method: Professor Kirkland grilled a young student for 50 minutes. He spoke with no one else during class. And because *everything* is a personal attack to the unenlightened law student mind, we hated him. And we were ashamed of our ignorance.

Later that week, another professor teaching another course used the Socratic Method. But in that class, the professor called on a student and asked him for the "facts of the case". The student did not know the facts of the case, and said so. Rather than move on to another, more prepared student, the professor stayed with that frightened little kid, asking him over and over again for the facts of the case as the frightened kid tried to read the facts of the case from the casebook in front of him. The professor stayed with this student for about half of the class, asking him over and over again questions that he could not possibly answer because they were questions that had absolute answers—the kid hadn't read and didn't know the facts. (With Kirkland, earlier in the week, by contrast, the questions he asked had no absolute answers.) When that was all finished, the professor then gave us a short speech on how we should "come prepared to discuss the case material". All the while the rest of us in the class (and that frightened kid) had missed out on a half an hour of lecture time that we were paying expensive tuition for the privilege of not hearing.

Everyone knows that this overly aggressive, adversarial method isn't pedagogically useful in most instances, but most professors use it...just because! It's the way we learned, damn it, and it's the way you'll learn! Law school is not "taught", in the traditional sense, where one would get a textbook and read the material to learn it and be tested on it. Instead, law school uses the "case method". In the case method, law students read hundreds of judicial opinions—some cases are hundreds and hundreds of years old—and extract legal rules, facts, and procedural rules from the opinions. It is argued (and generally agreed) that the case method develops in students a "legal mind" by re-training students' ability to use critical reasoning, analysis, and argument. It works.

Law schools traditionally follow the same basic 1L curriculum: property, contracts, torts, criminal law, civil procedure, and a constitutional law course dealing with the structure of our federal system of government rather than the Bill of Rights (which is covered later).

I met a few hundred people the first week, including most of my class. Iowa law uses a section system—the class of about 200 people is broken up into small "sections". Students usually have one or two small section classes, and a couple of larger lecture classes. I had small section Contracts and Property, but Torts and Criminal Law were larger affairs, each with maybe 100 students. The small section writing model potentially provides deeper learning in small section courses, and can build a sense of camaraderie within the section as well as competition among the sections. At Iowa Law at that time, certain small sections were chosen to be writing-intensive; my writing section was Property I with Kaye Traurig, one of my favorite professors. I was quick to make friends with most of the people in my section—was equally quick to pick out students who I knew I would dislike. And my first impression was wrong about quite a few of the people I met. My class was a smart group of talented and driven people, and I imagine that the first week of meeting all of those future world-beaters intimidated a lot of the new students. I could not afford to be scared or intimidated by a few 24-year-old kids with egos—I was already too scared by the debt that I was taking on. It wouldn't be possible for me to get out of law school without at least $100,000 in debt. So doing well and landing a high paying job were necessary. Failure really was not an option. It was a scary commitment, capable of tracking and trapping me. I think we all felt anxiety about our decisions to attend law school, and I think we all suspected that we had made the decision without having enough information to make an *informed* decision.

But the demands of law school on my time quickly overcame the initial fear and anxiety. I had no time for fear, anxiety, or for second-guessing the decision I had made—I was "behind schedule" the first day! After the scrutiny that Adams got in contracts it was clear to me (or I thought it was clear to me) that I had not understood the case material as well as I should have. I was directly off to the coffee shop downtown after class to re-read that day's materials more closely. I felt as if I had a learning deficit constantly for a while—not only did I have the next day's material to prepare for, but I had to re-learn what I had not understood from that day's material. I fretted and read and re-read and took almost verbatim notes of class lectures, constantly wondering if I understood. Was I "getting it"?

Wednesday night of that first week was the first "Law Night", the semi-official weekly law student social event at a bar. Most law school student bodies have a version of law night, usually with some witty name, like "Bar Review". I went to a few Law Nights while at Iowa, but only two are worth noting and only one was important. On the first Law Night of my first year, I talked with new students and some 2Ls at a bar in downtown Iowa City. Students got very drunk that night—like high school drunk. There was something distant and desperate about the night and the drunken law students. The event shocked me not in a "moral" way, but in a "maturity" way. (Don't get me wrong, I've been known to get uproariously drunk, and did so on several occasions during law school.) Most of the students were just kids and they all seemed scared and desperate and lonely. Or, who knows, maybe that was only me? I heard more than a few conversations that night where these new students were bragging–*already bragging*–about some answer they had given in some class.

I had thought that Law Night was a chance to meet my colleagues and to "network". That wasn't really the case. For example, I spoke briefly with a mischievous looking girl sitting alone on a railing and watching everyone. She looked at me over her puffy smile like she wanted me to introduce myself.

"I'm Tyler," I said to her. "Havin' a good time?"

"Not really," she said, and gave another puffy grin. She bit at the lip of her plastic cup.

"Alright. Well, sorry to hear that."

"Look," she said. "I'm not looking for a relationship."

I was confused, as she clearly was not having the same conversation I was having.

"Ok. Noted."

"I'm just looking for sex," she said, and gave me that same puffy, sly grin.

"Noted," I said again, and walked away. There was a clear and real distinction between the younger students and the older students. There was another clear and real distinction between the "non-traditional" students– those in their late 30s or 40s–and *everyone else.*

The only important Law Night that I attended was a year away.

During the first week, I talked outside the building with a kid in my section named Mark Lee. He was an impeccably dressed kid with frosted tips in his hair. He had a questionable quality, and he was an evangelical Christian who stood outside the building and smoked before classes. The first time I met him, he said:

"I've got a bit of an edge. I've been in academia already. Yeah, I have a master's degree from [a respected school] and before that I was in the grad program at [another respected school]. So I've got a bit of an edge."

"Think so?" I asked.

"Yes, I know so. I'm going to finish first in the class."

"You are?" I asked. "Well, maybe it's a good thing we met. Maybe you can get me a job when this is all over."

He laughed, but I was serious.

"We'll see," he said. "But I am going to do it. I'm serious about it."

Conversations like that, and after having seen Mr. Adams torn apart in Contracts, and having listened to other professors harangue other students in other classes, and then to hear 23-year-old frat kids bragging about some answer they had given! It was a strange week and I began to suspect that something might be odd about the law culture. So I pulled aside a few of the people I had met that week and who I knew I was bound to get along with and asked them to go on a canoeing trip in northern Iowa.

We drove to northern Iowa that weekend, camped, and floated. We called ourselves the Iowa Law Students Canoe Consortium. We sat beside a northern branch of the Iowa River, watched the flicker of a dying fire and felt cool autumn air roll over the heat of the summer; we talked about the next day's float trip. We had beers and veggie burgers, and Gabriela ran the MSR stove and cooked for all of us. The fire was hot and the river made gurgling noises and we all went to sleep in warm tents. We were all very young, though we didn't feel it just then, and pretty soon it would all be over. We drank cold beers the next day and we floated down the river in canoes. Amrita, a petite little Indian girl from Africa, rode in the front of my canoe. She was very proper in manners and had perfect posture, so I thought she had probably had etiquette training. She made paddling gestures up front but really was just along for the ride, and when we reached the end, Amrita said "well that was lovely" and Adam Zimmerman put a foot on the river bank and said "terra firma once again". Then we were all back into cars and back to Iowa City to get on with the business of being law students. And it *is* a business.

BOOK I: THE MOMENTS THAT TURN US (A)(iii)
MANY KNOTS UNRAVEL'D BY THE ROAD.

Once Mabel and I were safely out of the congestion of Lewes, she and I made up some time. Our pace was too fast, in fact. She and I made 12 miles in three hours. That's a *really* fast pace when you are carrying 90 or 100 lbs and are out of shape, but the excitement of finally being out there revved me up. I pushed too fast. Soon, I started to feel all blown out, like I had been beaten to a pulp. I had to stop a lot and I leaned on the walking stick, or I put the pack down and sat cross-legged on the roadside with Mabel. I made up excuses to stop, like "I need to call this or that friend", or "I need to consult the map". All lies. I was stopping because I was all blown out.

It got scary at about 12 miles. Each step felt like my whole body was a foot and it was all broken; I was pretty sure my feet were broken. My shoulders tensed up and started to give out—shoulders and feet are the first to go on a long hike. I hadn't trained appropriately for the Walk, and that was part of the challenge. I had no choice but to keep us walking, though, and my thoughts went to a bad place. There was so much pain in my feet that I doubted whether I would make it even to Milton, let alone California.

When Mabel and I were a few miles from Milton, I mumbled to myself "help me, help me" with each step. I don't know what kind of help I wanted, or from whom, but I know I wanted my feet to not give out on me. It felt like they might. And I pleaded with my feet, too: "Don't give out, don't give out, don't give out." I couldn't feel what was going on with the rest of my body because the pain in my feet overcame my nervous system, and that oversight would rear up and kick my ass in short order.

It was a bright and clear late winter day, and it wasn't that cold, but I was bundled up and Mabel's coat kept her warm in the middle of nowhere outside a small, Delaware town. I imagine that passing motorists were unsure what to make of us: I was a bearded vagabond with a dog and a walking stick mumbling "help me, help me" to myself as I walked. They must have wondered what I carried in my big pack, the way I'd wondered when I had seen hikers before I became one. I wondered if they could see on my face how desperate I was, how much pain I was in. If 17 miles was so hard—and it *was*—then how could I hope to do 5000?

"Help me, help me, help me."

A lady in a pickup truck stopped on the county highway just as the Milton water tower came into sight above a dense growth of trees.

"You need a ride, Guy?" the woman in the pick-up truck shouted.

"Nope, I'm good," I answered. It was a knee jerk reaction. No, of course I'm fine! I got this! I still muttered "help me, help me, help me" as she drove away, confused as to why this freak wouldn't jump in the back of the truck. I wanted nothing more than to jump into that truck and take a ride into a nice place to sleep, but I said no. I don't know what I was thinking.

Most likely, I was reveling in the self-imposed pain and torture. That's a trait of mine, and of many lawyers. It keeps a law student studying 18 hours a day, every day. It's what keeps a lawyer billing 3000 hours a year (or, hell, even 2000!) There are a million ways that people torture themselves. Of course, a lot of people are like this; it isn't unique to the legal field. It felt to me at the time like it *meant something* that I was putting myself into that situation, experiencing that pain, and still going on despite it all. I don't know.

But we made it into Milton and found that there was no place to camp, there had never been a motel, and the only bed and breakfast in town was closed and had not been dog friendly even when it was open. I stopped at a local bar and left Mabel clipped to my pack outside the door. I asked inside the bar for any sort of ideas about where Mabel and I could stay, and the bartender was unable to help me, but she spotted me a beer and that was quite a nice thing. I drank the pint and was back out the door. I had to struggle, twisting and contorting, to put the huge pack on my back and then Mabel and I shuffled to a gas station down the street.

I dropped the pack outside the station and hurried in to buy two Cokes and three Snickers bars. I started to think that there was something wrong with my legs while I was buying the snacks. It was unclear whether or not I would ever be able to stand again if I sat down. My legs felt like misfiring machines, disconnected from my body and broken down.

"Do you mind if I sit outside and eat this?" I asked.

"What?"

"I just walked here from Rehoboth Beach," I said. "Can I sit in the parking lot and eat this?"

"Oh yeah. Sure. No problem at all."

I sat down beside Mabel and tried to cross my legs. I knew I was in a bad situation as soon as my ass hit the ground. I ate the Snickers and drank the Cokes quickly, hoping that the sugar would do something. And the sugar might have done something, but not enough. Not soon enough. I could not stand up. My legs did not work. I couldn't even *feel* my legs, although I knew they must be in pain. They were pointless things, worthless hunks of flesh good only for sitting on. Mabel was a little tired, too, and she curled up next to me in a ball and snuggled close.

This was a strange and worrisome moment. I could neither stand nor walk, and was stranded at about 6:00 p.m. in a Delaware town without a place to camp or stay, and I looked and smelled pretty bad. It was getting dark quickly and I had no idea what to do. I had set off that morning thinking that everything would work out because the information I had indicated I could find a place to stay in Milton. But I fought the urge to be angry with myself, or feel like I was "unprepared", or any of that. Because why the hell waste your time blaming yourself for being stranded half a continent away from everyone who cares about you and stuck with a tired dog in the parking lot of a gas station? I mean, come on! That's the good stuff, right there.

I made a few phone calls around town and asked everyone I talked to if they knew of a yard where I could camp or a campground or *anything* nearby. No one I spoke with would let me camp on his or her yard and no one knew of a place to stay. Of course, I didn't blame anyone for not letting me camp—yard camping is a delicate matter, and it usually can't be negotiated over the phone. To secure yard camping, it is important that the homeowner sees and talks with you, so that he/she knows you are on the level.

After exhausting what I thought were all my options, I looked up the phone number for the nearest police station. I thought it would be best to call the local police and say something like this: "Hi. I am a cross-country hiker and my legs don't work. I don't want to get arrested, but need a place to stay. Any suggestions?" I have never had a good relationship with police officers, in general, but I have found that when *I* reach out *to them*, it sets the tone for the conversation and they are much more likely to actually help. Not a certainty, but more likely. So I dialed the number and as I was going to hit "send" on my phone, the strangest thing happened: A taxicab pulled into the parking lot. This was not a yellow cab or a checkered cab, mind you. This was an old Ford Aerostar van with something like "Mike's Taxi Service" spray-painted on the side. When the driver finished pumping gas, she walked toward me at the gas station door.

"What are you doing there?" she asked, before she even reached me. "You look beat." She could hardly look directly at me, probably because my face was so banged up.

"I can't stand," I said.

"You need a ride?"

"I think so," I said. "But I don't know where. I'm walking across the country and there is no place to stay here in Milton."

"Across the *whole* country!? You're almost done!" She had a big, chubby smile on her face.

"I just started," I said. "Going the other way."

"Oh," she said, and her smile turned into a scrunched up question mark under her nose. "Why?" People are interested in *what* you are doing for about five seconds, I would learn, and then all they care about is *why*. It's the *why* that people want, or need. Unless otherwise noted, every person who I met on this trip asked me why I was doing it.

"Eh, you know...." I said. I couldn't tell her why.

"Still. No place to stay here, not anymore."

"My map says there is a...."

"Yeah, well, used to be. Closed down, maybe 2005. 2004? Long time. You need a ride? Look, I can give you a ride to the nearest motel. I can even come get you in the morning, bring you back right here."

"Really?" I said.

"Yeah, motel's on my way home."

"Where is it?"

The driver's name was Karen, and she had a powerful smoker's voice. She helped me to stand and, once she had me on my feet, I could stand and could walk, but not well. The Snickers and Cokes hit and I started to feel a little better. I could amble painfully. Gravity is tough sometimes. Karen drove me back the way I had come, and I was humbled at how quickly we covered the ground it had taken me all day and a lot of pain to cover. The motel was almost all the way back to Lewes. It was an independently owned thing in the middle of nowhere north of Lewes.

I stepped out of the van at the toilet of a motel and almost passed out from the pain in my feet. I was stoic because I didn't want to wince or cry out in front of anyone. I limped over and leaned my pack against the motel and clipped Mabel to it, then said goodbye to Karen and got her phone number so I could let her know about the morning pick-up. Checking in was a nightmare—not because of my feet, but because the place was run by a couple of 15-year-old Jerry Springer kids.

The room was horrible. Everything was broken, the TV didn't work, and the toilet was full of feces. The room smelled deeply of stale cigarette smoke and the windows would not lock. I didn't have the energy to argue or to complain, so I flushed the toilet and got my sleeping bag out of the pack and laid it out on the bed. I cleaned and re-dressed the wounds on my head in the main area of the motel room because I thought that would be "cleaner" than doing it in the bathroom. I ordered pizza and took my shoes off. I wanted so badly to use the camp stove because carrying a stove for 17 miles instills a compulsion to actually use the thing. But I settled for a pizza and leaned back on the bed to wait for the pizza and to watch my feet swell once the boots came off. It was like watching water flow into flesh colored balloons. I was pretty certain they were broken.

The pizza arrived, and I shouted out in pain when my feet touched the ground. Then I ate the pizza in the dark while Mabel snuggled up against me. I called Isra, but she didn't want to talk, so we just said little boyfriend-girlfriend things and then hung up. I fell asleep that night feeling very tired and a little alone. Mabel was there, though, and she sat near me and watched me breathe as I slept.

The next morning I woke up with my feet and right eye still swollen, but my eye was opening up. Walking was not really an option. So there it was: two days off out of the first four days walking. I was ok with that, though, because taking time at the beginning to heal would have (or should have had) a great payout later, because I would be stronger, uninjured. So Mabel and I sat around doing nothing all day, waiting for Isra to call, writing in the journal of the trip, and emailing people who had started following along on the trip online. I *knew* that my farewell email was good—it had taken a year to draft—but I had no idea it would resonate with anyone outside Sidley and I had no idea so many lawyers were so profoundly unhappy as I had been.

All the time off right at the beginning was not a bad thing, though it felt like it at the time. Anyone who starts a long hike like this should go slowly at the beginning—slower than I went, even. My problem was that I never started slowly. From the beginning I had two speeds: as fast as I could go or not moving at all, and that is no way to live a life.

BOOK I: THE MOMENTS THAT TURN US (A)(iv)
IN A BOX WHOSE CANDLE IS THE SUN.

Karen drove us back to Milton on the second day. Mabel was running low on food because we had started a day late and we had lost days to injury, so we stopped at the grocery store in Milton. It was the first time on the trip that I had to leave Mabel leashed to the pack and out of my sight, while I went inside a building for a little of the Ol' Commerce. I bought some dog food in a seven-pound bag and got breakfast for myself. I ate breakfast outside the store with Mabel and a few people stopped to talk with me and to pet Mabel.

"Seriously? Walking *all the way* across the country?"

"Yup," I'd answer.

"Well, you're almost done!"

"Nope. Just started."

"Oh. Why?" They always asked me why.

Then Mabel and I were on the road again. I felt very weak. My feet were still swollen a little from the first long hike, and each step sent a shooting pain up through my knees. Shortly outside of Milton, my left shoulder and arm began to hurt. It was a sharp pain and there was a *constant* feeling of pressure in my chest, so I thought I must have been having a heart attack. Mabel and I stopped alongside the road so I could take some aspirin, and I called Isra to tell her that I loved her and was thinking about her. Then we trudged on, heading for Redden State Forest. Including all of our detours and the errands in Milton, our road was about 15 or 16 miles that day and I barely made it to Redden State Forest.

Redden was our first night camping and I was excited to see how Mabel would handle sleeping in a tent. I had been keeping a pretty keen eye on the weather, and the nighttime low was supposed to be about 38 degrees Fahrenheit that night. That is chilly, but not dangerously cold if you are well prepared, and I thought Mabel and I were prepared. I registered us with the forest ranger, and there was no fee to camp there. There were several campsites cut into the forest, each with a fire ring. There were no other people camping there at that time of year, so the forest was empty. The lady at the ranger's station gave me directions and told me we could fill up our water bottles from the spigot on the building that night or in the morning. Mabel and I were both pretty beat from the day hiking, so we were quick about getting into the forest, finding a camp, and setting up the tent. Mabel didn't help much, but she ate and drank and watched.

I had a Mountain Hardwear tent. On a long hike, you want to have a light tent. Manufacturers make tents lighter by using lightweight materials and by making the tents smaller. The tent was very small, and it was not freestanding, which meant that the tent could not stand up unless it was staked out in the ground. (It was a mistake to get a tent that wasn't freestanding, but I didn't know that yet.) The tent weighed about five pounds, which didn't seem like much when I bought it, but felt heavier and heavier as the miles piled up. The tent was very difficult to get into and out of and there was very little room inside. To get in, I had to lean down and put my hands in a push-up position, enter the tent backwards, feet first, and then roll into the thing. It was cramped and uncomfortable and the tent was too low profile for me to sit up once inside. Once inside with the sleeping bag, sleeping pad, minimal nighttime gear, and Mabel, not enough room remained for me even to roll over. Now, this is the type of thing you should really know *before* you begin a cross-country hike. I had set the tent up before the Walk, of course, and had gotten into it and learned about it before we started out, but I hadn't tried it out in a realistic situation with my nighttime gear and Mabel in it with me. Had I done that, I probably would have returned the Mountain Hardwear tent for something a little roomier. But there I was.

I gathered wood and twigs from the forest floor for kindling. I carried a bag of dryer lint and a tub of Vaseline to use as tinder—the lint is tinder, anyway, but with the addition of Vaseline as an accelerant it is very easy to start a fire. I had a couple of cigarette lighters with me, but I decided to start the fire with a magnesium and flint fire striker that I had because it would feel a little more rugged. Rugged!

I made dinner over the fire—rice and beans—and Mabel and I ate. The Sun went down and she and I got into the tent for the night. It was not clear from my research, nor from the forest ranger's answers, whether there were any wildlife in the area that would bother us that night, so I put my pack (with the food in it) on the other side of the trail about 300 yards away from the tent site. I didn't think there were bears in Delaware, but there are always raccoons and I didn't want them riling up Mabel in the middle of the night. Anyway, it is best practice to place the food and materials away from the tent. I should have kept at least my clothes bag with us in the tent, though, because it got very cold. It dropped below 40 degrees before we got into the tent, and at midnight I woke shivering in my sleeping bag with Mabel trying frantically to get into the sleeping bag with me. Ice covered the inside of the tent from Mabel's and my breath condensing and then freezing. The thermometer that I kept in my tent read 21 degrees. My sleeping bag was rated only for 35 degrees. I am an extremely warm sleeper, but, like an idiot, I had not put on enough extra layers of clothes before sleeping, so my warm clothes were in my pack far away in the dark, cold night and I was shivering to death. Mabel was fine, but was frustrated because she could not get into the sleeping bag with me to warm me up. I zipped open the bag and a wall of frozen air hit me, and then Mabel clawed her way into the bag and put her side against my chest and stared at me. She licked at my face, then rested her head on her paws and watched as I went back to sleep, still shivering a bit but much warmer than I had been. I was warm and safe when I woke the next morning in the tent and the sleeping bag, and Mabel was still there, still staring at me.

I doubt Mabel saved my life that night, but she made the night safer and warmer for me. From that point on, I caught her all the time waking up to check on me. At night, thinking I was asleep, she would sniff around and put her paw on my sleeping bag to find cold spots, and that's where she would lay. It could be that she was just looking for a cold place to sleep, but I like to think she was looking out for me. In the next month, she probably saved my feet from frostbite a dozen times.

When Mabel and I struck camp and walked out of Redden State Forest it was our first day hiking without any idea of a place to stay. In Milton, I had at least thought I knew of a place to stay ahead of time, even if I had been wrong. I was anxious about the uncertainty of it at first but Mabel wasn't fazed a bit, I guess because she had faith in me. Soon, following her lead, I stopped feeling anxious as we walked along the blacktop country roads. I tested out different ways of looking at the problem of being quasi-homeless. Instead of saying "I am staying here", I said to myself "I am staying somewhere", but there is a lot of uncertainty in that statement. Then I said to myself "I am staying anywhere". That was a liberating thought. Then I said to myself "I am staying anywhere I can stay", and I stuck with that. As the trip went on, I worked my way deeper and deeper into that attitude. "Tonight I will stay anywhere I can stay." This attitude, as much as anything, made this hike so much different than some of the more popular epic hikes like the Appalachian Trail. This hike would not be only a relationship between "nature" and me like it would have been on the AT. Instead, the Walk would be a relationship among Mabel and me, nature, laws, and humans.

We got a rather late start, which would become pretty common for us, but we had gone a few miles by 11 a.m. It was a cool day but it was sunny and clear and there was very little traffic on Delaware's back roads. I had a black stocking cap and gloves on, but only one layer of fleece that I zipped when we stopped moving but kept open when we were walking.

We stopped a few miles into the day's walk beside an empty road to drink, to rest, and to review the map. I leaned on my walking stick and Mabel sat patiently beside my pack. There were very few houses along the left hand side of the road, spaced at about quarter or half mile intervals, and to the right were open fields bounded by trees and brush.

A gas company pick-up sped past us, then screeched to a halt and reversed. The man in the truck rolled down then window and shouted out at us.

"Are you on the Trail?" he asked.

"I am," I said. I was leery of the man because we were several miles from the nearest town, and he was the first person to stop his car right alongside of us.

"That is great! Wait here. Can you just wait here a minute?"

"I can," I answered.

"That is great. Won't be more than 10 minutes."

The man drove the truck into the driveway of a house about 100 yards behind us and he let the truck idle there. I drank a little more water and checked the weather forecast. The weather report called for rain late that night or into the morning. We didn't have to wait for the man for very long and soon he pulled back onto the road, drove back to us, and parked his truck beside the road.

His name was Cary Garmon and he worked for the gas company as a regional sales manager. He asked us questions about where we had been, where we were going, and why we were hiking the ADT. He smiled non-stop and said "great" and "that is great" in his slow voice whenever he was tickled by one of my answers. He had traces of a slow Virginia accent that could make even bad news sound like "everything is gonna be fine".

"Mabel," he said when I introduced them. He sounded out her name slowly and petted her behind the ears. He sounded like he was tickled to have discovered Mabel's name. Mabel put her front paws on the truck to stand up and lick Cary and I had to pull her down. "Mabel. That is just great. You know, we had a gal stay with us named Rachel. She was walking the Trail but was coming the other way. Know her?"

I said I did not.

"This was about 10 years ago. She started in California but she had to break over the winter somewhere out west and then she got back at it the next year or so. But this is just great."

We talked for about 20 minutes and he smiled the entire time even though Mabel pulled and jumped and fought with me throughout the conversation. He gave me his card and he wrote his cell and home numbers on the back of the card with a little sketch of where his house sat off the Trail.

"If you don't find a place to stay...well it is almost noon. And you've already gone, what, five miles. Probably won't make it to our place tonight. But tomorrow night."

"How far are we talking?" I asked.

"Oh...12 miles. Maybe 13. Well, you have my number. Call if you need something or if it gets to be dark and you don't have a place to stay."

Mabel and I were packed up and back on the road before Cary was out of sight. We did not stop walking again for almost three hours, and then only for a short break to drink. It was cool, though, so Mabel hadn't even been panting and she didn't drink much water. I paid very close attention to Mabel's drinking and breathing very early on in the trip because I was still learning about her. Another mile or so and she and I came to a crossroads by an old church with a soda machine on the porch. The soda machine didn't work and so we sat for a while on the porch and watched as clouds began to form.

We hit the road again and had to stop in another half an hour. Then we walked again and I had to stop again in 15 minutes. I was pretty well cashed for the day, but I wanted to keep going so we walked for five minutes and rested for one minute, over and over for another hour or so. The last several miles we hiked were tough for me, if not for Mabel. The pain of each step started in the balls of my feet, then surrounded my foot and, at half stride, shot up through my leg and into my lower back. It worried me how closely the pain of that day resembled the pain I had felt on the way into Milton. I wanted to be making constant physical improvement, but worried that I wasn't.

We made it to Cary's home at almost 6:00 p.m. He, his wife, and his daughter lived in a beautiful two-story house set back from the road by a long driveway. They had a playhouse near the main house and behind the playhouse was a sheep pen with about 15 sheep that I could count. I stopped halfway into the driveway to call Cary; it is courtesy to call ahead.

Cary was surprised that we had made it and were standing in his driveway. He was off somewhere picking up his daughter from a high school sports practice and was on his way back to the house. He thought Mabel and I should wait where we were until he could warn his wife that he had invited me to stay there. So I dropped the pack and we waited about halfway up his driveway for Cary to come home. It was a relief to take the pack off and know that I wouldn't have to strap it on my back again that night. I felt so light, like I could jump for miles, and my gait was all bouncy and funny as I walked around to loosen up my legs and hips.

Cary let us stay in his daughter's old playhouse that night. He apologized several times for not letting stay in the house, but, because it was just he and his wife and daughter, he thought it would be uncomfortable for them to have a strange man sleep in their house. He didn't need to apologize but it was a nice gesture in a series of nice gestures from Cary. The playhouse had become a storage shed after his daughter had outgrown it, but there was a futon in the shed. Before I settled in, Cary and I sat outside the playhouse on lawn chairs and talked for over an hour. He brought out food for Mabel, pancakes and sausages for me, and a hot cup of tea. I took off my shoes and, as my feet swelled like footballs, we talked about Delaware and Virginia, Joe Biden, and the traffic that comes in from D.C. in the summer. He told me how he and his wife had met at college and how he had come to live in Delaware. When I stood and could hardly stand for pain in my feet, he offered me ice or a heating pad but I politely refused.

I called Isra that night and we spoke for about five minutes. I was too exhausted and my feet hurt so badly that I could not stand to even be on the phone talking without grimacing and whining.

"We shouldn't talk anymore," she said.

"What?"

"We shouldn't talk while you're on this trip. It's all about you, anyway."

"What?" I asked.

"This is your thing. It's your trip. It's about your discovery and all of that. If that's the way it is, then we shouldn't talk."

I didn't understand what she was saying, really, because she often said things that didn't make much sense. So I shrugged it off, saying that she misunderstood what the whole trip was about and said "Uh, you know what this is about. We talked about this". But I didn't have the energy to discuss it anymore with her, so I just verified the weekend that we would meet in D.C., again, and went to sleep. I asked her if we could push the D.C.

weekend back a week, but she said it wasn't possible because she had plans in D.C. that weekend.

I slept like a rock that night in Cary's daughter's old playhouse with Mabel curled up in a ball between the back of the futon and me. It was raining when I woke in the morning but Cary or his wife had left breakfast for me outside the door of the playhouse with another thermos of hot tea and a note that I should feel free to wait out the rain. The rain cleared by 10 a.m. and Mabel and I were back on the road bound for Maryland. (Cary called me every few weeks during the Walk, and his first questions were always where I was and how Mabel was doing.)

We were pretty quickly into Maryland. Delaware had been only 44 miles, but had taken us four days. I felt as though I'd accomplished *something* when I saw the Maryland state line sign, but mostly it felt like a punch line to a very short joke. I called my mother and Isra and some other people, but only to chuckle about the fact that I had crossed a very small state on foot. It is funny to be proud of crossing a flat, 44-mile stretch of Delaware when somewhere up in the distance you have the expansive prairie, the Rocky Mountains, and the endless southwestern deserts.

On the day we reached Denton, Maryland, I remember sitting beside the road at 5:00 in the afternoon beside a sign that read "Denton 6 miles". The ADT directions, which were not 100% accurate due to typos, had given me incorrect mileage that day (or I had figured the math wrong), and when Mabel and I strode around our last right hand turn before Denton and saw that sign, my heart sank. Six miles. *Six miles.* It was late in the day and we'd already done more than 10 miles. Six more!? The sign may as well have said 16 or 160. I did not believe there was a chance in the world that I could walk six more miles in that kind of pain. There was nowhere in the immediate vicinity to camp, and I was pretty sure we'd not find a place to stay before Denton. Having no choice is a pretty strong motivator.

That day's hike was the first that was as much mental as physical. Every day had been difficult, but that day was different. I was exhausted physically, and was feeling emotionally low. Isra wasn't talking much with me. I was unhappy with my pace and my progress. Each step hurt so much. But we had to do it, and Mabel was fine. She is a good dog. She lapped at some water and we set off. She pranced in her way for the whole six miles and had no idea what a struggle it was for me. I was very proud when I made it into Denton that day.

BOOK III: ...AND THE MOON SAYS HALLELUJAH, 01.05.12(1)

Pack; talk to Germans before leaving Barefoot Caribe; learn they will never travel through U.S. again; they say "U.S. airports are like Gestapo".

Water taxi to Ambergris Caye, also small island, bigger than Caulker. Land, San Pedro. Determine clothes still smelled bad from Walk; remember roommates had washed them several times, told me: "These all smell like shit, Dude." Resolve to get new shirt. Note Kendra looked relaxed, billed about 3000 hours last year, busy attorney, vacation necessary.

Research re: hostels on Ambergris; discuss "Pedro's Inn" w/taxi driver; conclude is likely acceptable. Arrive Pedro's Inn by foot.

Barefoot locals walk briskly along cobbled streets. Tourists and Belizeans and ex-pats drive golf carts.

Research Pedro's Inn: combination hostel/hotel/bar/poker room/pizzeria/animal hospital/Jagermeister-appreciation-society just south of San Pedro's old town, off gravel road, down gravel side street, white-fenced compound. Research hotel: three stories, looks like old tuberculosis sanatorium, inside and out. Meet w/Rosie, office manager; research Rosie: about 22-years-old, black hair, Caucasian-ish, perfect diction. Research Pedro: white-haired English ex-pat named Peter, no patience for idiots, buys rounds of Jager for everyone in bar without warning. Rosie says: "Don't be loud after 10 if you're at the pool. Peter lives up there and he *will* come out and shout at you if he is sleeping. He's usually not sleeping." Learn hostel full of Germans, Aussies, Canadians, some Dutch. Learn hotel has room; take room.

Survey picnic table by office, tables by pool; determine good place to work. Review manuscript; drink two beers. Travel up road to store; buy Cuban style shirt for vacation.

Bells ring out on faraway islands and a man plays the harmonica behind a tin shed on a Caribbean island, thinking no one can hear him.

BOOK II: FEEL THE SELFISH FURY (A)(ii)
CAUGHT BETTER THAN IN THE TEMPLE LOST OUTRIGHT.

The 1L year is a hazy thing in memory. Aside from the first week and the canoe trip, most of my 1L year is lost in a fog of memories of smells, of faces, of words, and only a few clear memories. To a certain degree, law school is like that phrase about the 1960s: If you remember it, you weren't there. Certainly if you do well your first year, then you likely won't remember it in any great detail. You will remember rules, case names, and some funny anecdotes, but that's about it.

I spent most days at the Java House in downtown Iowa City. I lived up on the hill across from the basketball stadium, and would usually walk downtown to study. I remember spending time in between classes in the BLB, studying on the benches or in the basement studying on a couch. I liked to loiter out around the building with other students talking about "outlines".

"You mean you haven't *started* your outline yet?" someone would ask. And another student would say:

"My outline is up to date except for this week's cases."

And someone would say: "I don't even know how to write an outline" or "what is an outline?"

The outline is the holy grail of each law school class. None of us yet knew how to build one, or what should be in it. It's a pretty easy thing, though.

None of us yet really knew anything, though, and so we sat around talking about how we were going to organize our outlines. We traded jokes and gossip about other law students because there were always jokes and always gossip to share. I even started to *care* about the gossip. There was always gossip because we were always there. Every law student except those with families at home spent most of his or her time at the law building or studying somewhere with other law students. Through the gossip and the shared experience these people were becoming like extended family to me.

I sat outside in front of the law school on the warm days on a concrete wall that separates the Burghers' grassy patch from the road. I sat cross-legged on the wall in the Sun and read the casework for that day or for the next day. I was diligent enough, but was usually behind the syllabi. A few of the other students liked to be outdoors, and we struck up friendships out there. I met Sirinder, a smart and funny Indian fellow who was always, always dressed to the nines and who always seemed to have just had a party at his house the weekend before. We started hanging out together on the weekends. Amrita and Gabriela, both veterans of the canoe trip, liked to stop and study out there and we became friends. Amrita, especially, liked to stand around the wall with me and talk and laugh. She got a kick out of me and I got a kick out of her. She was very petite and pretty, wore enormous satellite shaped earrings, and had a lovely accent and called things and people "lovely" all the time. "Well she is a lovely person," she would say. Or: "we had a good time together. It was lovely. Perfectly lovely." My friend Julie Camp, who is a true Iowan, once said: "Oh my God! I want to put Amrita in a little box and give her to my mother! That sounded awful." But Amrita was viciously cynical, and hardly ever believed in anything good or positive. Amrita and I became very close for quite a while and I enjoyed her company a great deal.

The 1L relationship that I remember the best (maybe aside from that with Amrita) is the student-teacher relationship I had with Professor Kirkland. Kirkland put me in the hot seat on the third or fourth day of class. And it was challenging, but I held my own, I think.

The deal with the Socratic Method is that every student gets *one* day on the hot seat, and no more. Several weeks into the class, he put me in the hot seat *again*. That was an embarrassing and awful experience because I was not prepared. (Usually people stopped preparing after they'd had their turn in the chair, because the deal was that you were only supposed to be called on once.) I cannot think of another time in my life when I felt so hopeless, so inexperienced, so vulnerable, and so weak as when Kirkland demolished me because I was not prepared. Unlike Mr. Adams, who was unlucky enough to be picked on the first day, I had no excuse for being unprepared. I sounded like a fool and a moron in front of my peers and colleagues.

I was convinced that there was some sort of animosity between Kirkland and me. I convinced myself that he hated me and that he wanted to embarrass me and to deflate me in front of my classmates. Whenever he spoke with me in class, there was mockery or derision in his voice. And he put me on the hot seat twice! Why!? I needed to know *why,* as if there had to be a reason. With friends, I began to refer to him as "The Fascist", because in class he argued as a right-wing demagogue would argue.

Then, much later in the semester, he put me in the hot seat again...for the *third* time.

"Mr. Coulson," Kirkland said nonchalantly at the beginning of class. There was a gasp from a few of my classmates, because they knew I had done this twice before and they knew that I felt the animosity from this guy. My classmate to my right even whispered to me: "Why is he picking on you?"

"He's had his turn," someone said.

"What?" Kirkland said. "Oh, yes, you have, haven't you Mr. Coulson? Well, I should find someone else."

"I'll do it," I said. "I got the time."

And I *killed* it that day. I was ahead of him on every question. I led the discussion as much or more than he did. I *knew* the game by then. After each of my answers, I knew *exactly* what question would come next—sometimes I even asked and answered the follow-up before he could get the follow-up question out of his mouth. My head was high when I left that class and I *hated* that man.

Later, my friend Gabriela told me that she'd talked to Kirkland about perhaps working for him as a research assistant and she had mentioned me.

"You know Tyler?" he asked, and she said his eyes lit up.

"Yeah, we're friends."

"Good choice," he said. "He's a smart kid."

But when she told me that, I didn't react the way a law student *should.* I was happy that he thought I was a smart kid, I guess, and I started to suspect that he was not a right-winger—he was an incredibly talented lecturer who was playing a part, that's all. I felt bad that I had been so wrong about him, but I didn't feel any sense of fulfillment or pride at living up to this guy's expectations. I came to understand later, both in law school and in practice, that many law students and lawyers define their whole lives based on satisfying others' expectations—like making up for some missing fatherly affection. I've known law students and lawyers who would work themselves to death for scraps of praise. I don't have that need or desire.

By the end of the semester, I understood Kirkland's methods. He was a very talented lecturer who understood theatrics, and who understood how the Socratic Method *should* be used. In his class, we learned about the law *and* we learned how to discover. I had dinner with Kirkland a couple of times at his house much later, and he is the sweetest man with the sweetest wife and daughter. I have been wrong about a million things in my life, but I have very rarely been so wrong as I was about Professor Kirkland when, during those first months of my first year, I hated him. It is tradition that students clap to show their approval when a class finishes for the semester—it's a silly thing because now it is so standard that it has become almost a meaningless gesture. A few professors, however, like Kirkland, really deserved a round of applause—he had worked very hard for us and taught us all a lot. But Contracts was the first class that our section finished for the year, and we were unclear whether or not to clap. I started to, but when no one else joined in I felt that maybe "we don't do that sort of thing at Iowa", so I stopped. When we clapped at the end of Criminal Law and Torts, I knew we had done something very wrong to Professor Kirkland, and I emailed him an apology. I think it meant something to him; his response was heartfelt and warm—he thanked me greatly and told me that he had been bothered all that week because no class had ever rejected him like that before. I had been very wrong about him.

But law school made me wrong about a lot of things....

BOOK III: ...AND THE MOON SAYS HALLELUJAH, 01.05.12(2)

Sit at picnic table in shade by office; edit manuscript. Analyze weather: nice. Email w/Kendra re: Potential bicycle tour of island later in afternoon; determine should work before potential bicycle ride, while have time. See Rosie appear, looks younger than the day before.

R: "Hello."

T: "How's it going?"

R: "My day was going great but now I can't get my milk to froth and this is kind of ruining my day."

Note Rosie has mischievous smiles, emotionless eyes. Learn everyone on Ambergris has accent except Rosie. Discuss expensive espresso machine in inexpensive office; learn Rosie cannot work machine; ask Rosie to make coffee in Mr. Coffee in corner.

T: "Heartbreaking. But coffee is better than nothing."

R: "I'm not going to make coffee. I want a cappuccino."

T: "Coffee is better than nothing."

R: "It's motivation. If I can't figure out this expensive machine, I am not going to use the simple one, either. Motivation."

T: "Heartbreaking."

R: "I know. Are you a writer or something? What are you working on?"

Cool breeze off the Caribbean shakes the palm fronds and kicks up waves of long black hair.

BOOK I: THE MOMENTS THAT TURN US (A)(vi)
WHO IS THE POTTER, PRAY, AND WHO THE POT?

We made slow progress over the next few days. The pack was far too heavy and it cost me a lot of time. To begin with, I lost a lot of time eating. My calorie needs went through the roof while carrying that heavy pack—I was probably eating a minimum of 3000 calories a day, and had several days where I ate 10,000 or 12,000 calories, and that simply takes a lot of time. (Despite the enormous amount of food, the extra pounds I'd put on in Chicago dropped away and were replaced with muscle in my legs.) Obviously, the pack slowed my pace due to the weight of it, but breaks were the largest time sink. To maintain a steady pace, it is vital to take breaks, and it is vital to learn *how best* to take breaks. But breaks killed my progress in those early days with the heavy pack. It was time consuming to remove the heavy pack, and then I would sit alongside the road for five or ten minutes waiting for my back to loosen up and for the spasms to stop. Only when I could stand straight up would I think about putting the pack back on. But putting the pack on was time consuming, too. After five miles or so, the thought of putting that thing back on after a break was horrible. So little breaks, which should have been three or five minutes, often stretched into 15 or 20. But we were still on schedule to meet Isra in D.C., and that was what was really important.

One cost of the extended breaks was that it was often late in the afternoon or early in the evening by the time I reached a given town, often far too late in the day to ask for a place to camp. People generally don't get strange men walking up to their door and asking to tent on the lawn, and I was uncomfortable doing that, anyway. At night? No, I don't think that would have worked so well. Look, a thru-hiker with a dog is quite a strange looking fellow, scraggly and bearded and stinking. I knew that I would appear dangerous or strange. Going in to the Walk, for example, one thing I told myself *very strongly* was to stay the hell away from children. That is, of course, almost impossible when you have a dog as cute as Mabel.

Once, in Maryland, I was several miles from anything and was suffering for a Coke and a sandwich pretty badly. A farmer in the middle of nowhere told me that there was a farm store that also sold candy bars and the like right up the road a few miles. But I found no store when I got to the intersection he described. Instead, I found a house on the corner with a couple of little children playing on the back yard swing set. I didn't know whether to take the right or go straight at the intersection, but I thought straight. So I went straight. The little girl from the house across the street came running as fast as she could across her yard toward Mabel and me. I put my hands up over my head and shouted: "Don't talk to strangers!" I probably could have handled that better. The girl stopped and yelled back at me: "Don't worry Mister, I won't. What's your dog's name?"

I laughed. Five or 10 seconds later, I saw that the girl's mother had come to the door and I waved at her to let her know I was ok, but she didn't wave back. I asked the little girl about the gas station, and I asked her *very loudly* so that her mother could hear but I don't think her mother could hear. The little girl told me that I'd gone the wrong way, and so I turned around. But once I got around the corner, the girl came running around the house and shouting at me.

"MISTER! Mom says I was wrong. The gas station is *that* way!" and she pointed back the way I'd come with a grand flourish. So I thanked her and turned back around. I saw her mother in the doorway again and I waved at her. This time she waved back, and I felt good about that.

Mabel and I walked on and when we found the gas station I ate a 12-inch sub, a six-inch sub, a chocolate shake, a Coke, and a half a gallon of water—all in about 45 minutes. I had been more or less starving and I decided I had to pay more attention to my calorie needs—I would start eating more during the course of the day, and would carry a lot of easy to eat, easy to digest food like trail mix. I stopped again to relax on the other side of a four-lane highway from the gas station, and a long-haul trucker pulled up alongside us but didn't get out of the cab of his truck.

"Where are you headed?" he asked. He had a long, thin face and a little bit of a moustache.

"California."

"Whew. That's a long way. Hitching?"

"No," I said. "We're hiking."

"Going through Ohio?" he asked.

"Not for a long time," I said.

"I'm going through Pennsylvania and Ohio if you want a ride. I can get you to Ohio."

"I don't want a ride, but thanks for offering," I said.

"I've got soup," he said. "Be a nice warm ride. And I've got plenty of cans of soup. I'd feed you the whole way there."

"We're walking," I said. "Not hitching."

"I like dogs. It'd be no problem. You and your sweet little puppy. I'd like that. I'd like the company," he said. "And I've got soup or we could stop and I could get you a sandwich."

"No thank you," I said. He started to talk about cans of soup again, and I got Mabel up and put the pack on. "Have a safe trip," I said to him. He followed us in his truck for about a quarter of a mile and then overtook us and drove on.

Mabel and I stayed in a couple of motels in Maryland, and we did our first stealth camping. We hiked across the eastern shore of Maryland to the Chesapeake Bay Bridge. I was in pretty brutal shape by the time we reached Kent Narrows, Maryland, so we checked into a motel at the base of the bridge and took a needed day off. The earlier zero days had made sense, because of the injuries and overwork. But I took a day off in Kent Narrows only because I was *tired.* I concluded that I needed to re-tool quite a bit. My boots were not working, for example. My feet hurt so badly at the end of each day that sometimes I could not even stand, and the nightly swelling was off-putting. Plus, my boots were starting to feel too small even at the beginning of a day before my feet had swollen. And my pack felt like it was *actually* killing me. There had been several instances over the course of the short trip that I had thought I was having a heart attack due to the intense pain in my left hand and arm, but I had slowly (after many days of popping aspirin) realized that the pack was pinching a nerve in my shoulder and that I wasn't having a heart attack. So I decided that my first priority—even ahead of making it to D.C.—was to re-tool my equipment. I searched on my phone for the nearest outfitters; there was an REI (an outdoor activities outfitter that is, ostensibly, based on the co-operative ownership model) in College Park, Maryland, just north of D.C., and I set College Park as our number one priority.

The Bay Bridge is 4.3 miles long and is on the official ADT despite the fact that it cannot be hiked. Instead, the ADT suggests that people get a ride over the Bay. (The other alternative, swimming, is probably ill advised.) There is a man, John Arundel, who lives nearby on Kent Island and who volunteers for the ADT; he will give thru-hikers a ride over the bridge if they need one. I called him and scheduled a ride for the next day.

John was a great fellow, very personable. We talked about old cars, which were his passion. His son, he told me, went to work for the Pacific Crest Trail 10 years earlier and that had spurred his interest in epic hikes, so he had contacted the ADT to volunteer to shuttle people across this bridge. He carried a cane with him because he had recently had hip surgery, but he looked to be about 20 years younger than he told me he was. He loved Mabel, of course, and he refused to drop us off in Skidmore on the other side of the bridge.

"Are you a strict traditionalist?" he asked.

"About what?"

"About this hike."

We were on the bridge and I stared at the blue water and over the blue water to the green trees and some shimmering glass and steel over by Annapolis.

"Nope," I said. "I am not a strict traditionalist about anything."

"I gave Jack Planck a ride about three weeks ago," he said. "Do you know him?"

"Just through email," I said, and thought to myself that "ah...he's got three weeks on me now; he's gained about three days". Jack Planck was a young kid from Maine who was out thru-hiking the country, too.

"He's a really nice kid," he said. "He's not a traditionalist, either. I dropped him off just outside Annapolis. I *could* drop you off by Skidmore, or over by Arnold, but then you have another bridge to get over before Annapolis. And with Mabel, it might be hard for you to get a ride."

"I'm just thankful for *this* ride over *this* bridge," I said. "So whatever you think is best is absolutely fine with me."

He took us across the bridge, and then across a little peninsula and another bridge and onto the western shore of Maryland. Maryland's eastern shore was almost wholly rural and looked much like my home county in Illinois except it was flatter than my home county, the homes were somewhat nicer, and there were a lot more horses. But Maryland's western shore is urban: more traffic, more towns, far fewer chances for camping safely, stealth or otherwise. The ADT goes through College Park, and I would re-tool at the REI, which would save me from begging a ride from someone in D.C. to get to another outfitter.

We hiked out of Annapolis on back roads, and over the next couple of days we hiked through Crofton and into Bowie, all the while thinking about how I would re-tool in College Park. I knew I would need boots and a new pack, but I wasn't sure how I could make my pack lighter.

Outside of Bowie, Mabel and I reached a metal bridge over the Patuxent River. The bridge was "paved" with grated metal panels instead of a solid pavement. Mabel and I both could see right through the bridge to the water below us about 40 feet down. The spacing in the grates of the bridge was big enough that Mabel could not walk on it because her little paws might have slipped right through. It was not a very big river, but we could not walk across it. There would not likely have been much need for a bridge if we could have walked across the river.

I was pretty sure that Mabel's paws wouldn't fall through the grating on the bridge and, once I was sure that crossing the bridge was no physical danger to her, I tried to coax her out onto it. But she would not come out onto the bridge. She stopped at the end of the pavement, where it met the grated bridge, and would move no farther. When I called for her to come out and gave a little tug on the leash, she would raise one paw and move it out over the bridge, but as soon as her paw was over that uncertain bridge, she would pull her paw back to the pavement and shift uneasily between her four paws. She looked down at the water below the bridge and then back at me, then she would try again but again would pull back her paw and shift uneasily. She knew that we were headed across that bridge and she knew that I was *definitely* heading across the bridge, and she began to whine because she thought I would leave her. Having Mabel with me was a great responsibility.

I walked her back away from the bridge to the edge of the metal guardrail extending from the south side of the bridge. There, I wrapped her leash around the guardrail and secured it there with a biner so she could neither run away nor run into traffic, and then I walked across the bridge. Mabel began to yip high-pitched, panicked barks as soon as I was maybe three or four steps onto the bridge. It was painful to hear her yipping like that, because she was certain that she had been abandoned there. There is not a person in the world who could have heard that yipping and howling and not broken near to tears by the sound of it, so full of sadness and fear. But there was no choice in the matter, so she went on howling and I went across the bridge. On the other side, I dropped my pack and the walking stick alongside the road and walked back across the bridge. Mabel stopped her raucous when I was about halfway back over the bridge and instead she stood very erect, tail wagging, and her eyes absolutely fixed on me. She exploded in energy, jumping and pulling at the leash and wagging her tail when I got about 10 feet away from her. I knelt beside her and she nuzzled up against me, licking my face and leaning against me. I unlatched her and lifted her up into the cradle of my arms. She was too big to carry like a baby, but that was the only way to carry her, and as soon as she was up and in my arms she relaxed and looked at the bridge as if she knew exactly what had been going on the whole time. She kept her eyes trained forward as we walked onto the bridge, but about halfway across she scanned over the side and down below the bridge, and then turned to look me in the face. And she looked me in the face all the way across the rest of the bridge. She seemed to be puzzled, relaxed, and happy. I think she knew at that moment that I would never leave her behind.

BOOK II: FEEL THE SELFISH FURY (A)(iii)
MY HONOUR IN A SHALLOW CUP.

I spent hundreds of hours in the Java House and drank gallons of coffee. The baristas were friendly and I often got free refills or free espresso shots or a free pastry. They were always quick to chat, and the place was filled with characters like the lip-ringed barista who had the most ridiculous hairdo, all puffed up in the back in the shape of a big blue peacock tail. She must have spent an hour or two every morning getting that hair in that shape, and that gave me strength to carry on—if she could devote that much time to a hairdo, then I could at least study for an extra half an hour. So the Java House became my study spot, and I sort of held court there. I sat in the back of the coffee shop, at their big wooden tables with Tiffany style lamps, and would put my nose down into a casebook or I would re-work the almost verbatim notes I took in class on my laptop. Mostly I watched Homestar Runner videos and read metafilter.com. I studied and worked on my outlines all day and all night, and left the Java House at close—right around midnight—to walk home with my clothes thick with the smell of exotic coffees from Guatemala, Peru, and Africa. And I thought about *nothing* on the walk home except the walk home.

Law students knew that I was always there, and students who I barely knew would say "You're always at the Java House, right?" when I would meet them almost for the first time in the hallways of the BLB. Students who I knew well and who I barely knew at all showed up at the Java House and often came to me to discuss issues or questions they had with law school problems. It made me feel like a superstar. People came to *me* for help and for instruction, and it made me feel superior. Superior is not fully the right word, but it is close and, anyway, I was being *trained* to feel superior. Law school often forces students either to feel superior or, worse, to feel inferior. Iowa, like almost all law schools, graded on a forced curve—a curve that often results in almost arbitrary distinctions between similarly skilled law students. People who knew the material and who could apply the rules and who owned a class would get lower grades, sometimes very low grades, simply because *that's the way it is.* You are superior or you are inferior and there are no shades of gray.

The difference between an A, which can get you a job, and a C, which can cost you a job, can be as little as a few points. So I was trained to feel superior when people came to me because they could not understand a particular rule or, more often, could not understand the doctrinal relationship among a set of rules. And when I could explain it, I knew that I really understood it. They came to me for contracts, for property, for torts. They came to me with questions about everything and, as often as not, I could help them. I felt superior for the first time in my life and it went to my head.

And I loved law school because it made me feel good about myself. It just was not that hard for me. I could understand the game well enough that other students even came to me with criminal law questions—and I could answer them usually with a quick glance at the book or the model rules we studied, *even though I had neither read nor studied that class all semester.* (Rather than spread myself thin studying my three important classes *and* the gargantuan reading assignments in criminal law, I focused on the classes that I felt were important and that I believed I could kill. I was not the only student to do this, and for a very good reason.) I felt like I was teaching my fellow students, but I wasn't. They were teaching *me*, and we were teaching each other.

Let me make this clear, even if I do put too fine a point on it. Law school is a commitment of three years' of time and three years' of student debt. Many law students—such as myself—come from lower socio-economic standing, either "lower class" or what is still called the "middle class" but is essentially a slightly more affluent lower class with generally low social mobility. (I had no debt from undergrad, for example, but had about $120,000 in student loan debt when I left law school.) You find yourself staring down the barrel of six-figure or high five-figure debt, and at about the same time you realize that the only grades that matter, or that *really* matter, are 1L grades. That is a lot of pressure, and it breeds a competitive and sometimes violently self-destructive environment. It's a culture that is unhealthy, and a culture that it is hard to unlearn.

And I was *good* at it.

At the end of the first semester, students began to break off into more exclusive cliques based on perceived intelligence. People chose study partners and would rant on and on to others about how their study partner "is a genius. He just *gets it.* Yeah, you know him, he's...so and so". There is a sheer, blind admiration for a few students who seem to "get it", and the other students pick their champion and are sure that their champion will help them through this or that class. Students began to make predictions about who would and would not do well when first semester grades came in. (Individually, everyone predicted their own failure—loudly and sometimes obnoxiously. That is a defense mechanism, a risk management tool. These high achievers suddenly found themselves in a new and different world and had realized that here, in the BLB, they might *not* be high achievers. Someone must be below average, after all: It's not an average if everyone's above it.) When people told me that I would "kill the curve" in this or that class, I demurred and said that I would be lucky to get a C-. But, truthfully, I knew I was going to do well. I had no choice but to do well.

From my observation, unhealthy behaviors began in earnest by November in others and in myself. Late October and early November is about the time the pressure started to weigh too heavily on too many young kids: On the weekends, you could not avoid running into blind drunk law students; in day-to-day life, it became impossible to maintain meaningful friendships with any of the other law students. Otherwise well-adjusted young men and women got blind drunk or drugged, then ran off into the night with their car keys to go home to study rather than to let someone drive them home. Friendships with women turned into meaningless sexual things that were ultimately destructive, and friendships with men dissolved entirely because I wouldn't study with them or because they wouldn't study with me. Socially and personally, the end of that first semester was a strange time.

And the guns came out academically. Desperate students who felt that they *didn't get it* but who absolutely did "get it" went searching for answers and found hornbooks and treatises. Then the hornbooks and treatises started to go missing from the library, mis-shelved "accidentally" or missing outright. Students fought among themselves and said increasingly nasty things about one another. Students who hardly knew each other, or who hated each other in real life, hooked up on the weekends or weeknights or weekdays, *sometimes in the law building.* In short, the culture went from being a culture of high ideals in August and September, to a culture of amorality in October, to a culture of immorality in November.

People became "gunners". "Gunners" are those kids who work superhuman hours, memorize all the minutiae of every case in the casebook, and hope to go on to bill 3000 hours a year at top firms. They are gunning for that top spot. Hands always raised, constant yapping and spouting nonsense opinions and questions, complete domination of class time. Some of the gunners—the ones who we all knew, or should have known, were not going to do well—became outspoken in class about policies and social justice. Eyes and noses in casebooks, but ever eager to pull themselves out of that book to talk to you about how well they understood the policy. But the kicker is that "getting" law school is about understanding the minutia of rules and applying them to *specific* fact sets—and policy doesn't matter. If you can see the forest, then you aren't looking closely enough at the trees. But the gunners worked the longest hours and lorded over everyone how vast their outlines had become. They bragged about how late they worked on their outlines and how they had bum rushed this or that professor about an issue during office hours. They made disparaging comments to other students, and "jokingly" told other students "maybe you should just drop out".

"I just don't ... I can't get my head around causation," one would say. "I just can't see the difference between but-for causation and proximate causation."

"You don't understand proximate causation?" the Gunner would say, his or her voice rising in utter and total disbelief. "Well, I think that means you've probably already failed. Maybe you should just quit?"

And then everyone would laugh. Oh, hahahaha. It was funny. But it wasn't funny, because there are people who just *do not get it.* There are very smart people who work very hard and are completely unable to understand the law school game. I tried very hard not to be derisive and mean like those awful gunners. The funny thing is that the gunners were often the people who did not do well when grades rolled around. I tried to not be like them, but wasn't always successful. Sometimes I lost my temper.

At the end of the first semester, most folks broke into study groups. I don't know how everyone chose whom they would study with, but most gunners handpicked their study groups. The really smart kids who also "got it", didn't bother so much—they either didn't want study groups or they had already identified one another and had been studying together the whole semester. But gunners picked their study groups and the lesser students were happy to be invited. One gunner who I mentioned earlier, Mark, asked me to meet with his study group once—just *once* of course, on a "trial basis". They were going to go over torts before the exam, and because I was in his section (or he was in my section) he thought I might want to join. I reluctantly agreed, mostly because I didn't want to offend anyone. The study group started off well enough, but it pretty quickly devolved when we, as a group, tried to answer an essay question about a negligence tort. In the facts of the hypothetical question, a speeding motorist strikes a bicyclist on a busy street. Now, the proper way to analyze a hypo like this is to first identify what the potential tort is—here, the tort of negligence—and then to identify what elements must be shown to prove the tort. In this case, the elements of negligence are 1) the tortfeasor owes to the victim a duty to abide by an appropriate standard of care, 2) the tortfeasor breached that duty, 3) the breach caused damages, and 4) there were damages. In short form, the tort of negligence is "duty, breach, causation, damages". After arguing what the appropriate duty of care was and whether or not it was breached, the student then should analyze the issue of causation. When analyzing causation, the student must argue whether or not the tortfeasor's negligence *actually* caused the damage (known often as "but-for" causation) and whether the negligence was the *legal* cause of the damages (known as "proximate" causation) because there will be no liability for negligence that is not the legal cause of damages. One issue in our hypothetical worth discussion was the issue of *negligence per se*. And when we began to discuss it, Mark led the group through a misguided 45-minute argument about *negligence per se* and causation. At first, only a couple of us disagreed with him, but then almost all of us disagreed with him. Worse, almost no one could explain *why* we disagreed with him, but we knew he was wrong. The argument dragged on and I became angrier and angrier because each minute wasted on an argument like that is a minute not used actually preparing to answer an essay question. And my minutes *mattered* to me because, unlike the gunners, I intended to maintain a regular life even during finals. (I failed at that, too, of course.) Eventually, it became clear to me and to some others that Mark— who is a very, very smart fellow—simply did not get it. He thought that the driver's speeding *was* the tort. But speeding is not a tort; hitting a cyclist is *perhaps* a tort. Mark had, I believe, confused the proof of negligence with the assumption of causation. In retrospect, I believe he confused *negligence per se* (which proves negligence) with *res ipsa loquitur* (which sometimes allows a court to infer negligence), and with causation. His misunderstanding of those building blocks had confused his analysis of the problem and he couldn't understand why he was wrong. Without the basic understanding of the duty, breach, causation, and damage, he could not put together a coherent response to an essay on the tort of negligence. I got very frustrated after 45 minutes and said something like:

"I don't have time to waste studying with a stupid fuck who thinks speeding is a tort," and removed myself from the table. As I walked away, I heard him say:

"Yeah, we'll see when grades come out."

I feel badly about that whole scene now. I feel awful about how selfishly and stupidly I reacted. I didn't feel badly about it at the time.

I was not surprised when my first semester grades came in. They were high. I knew I was in the top 10% of the class. And it had been easy for me. I stressed out over the finals, and studied harder than I'd ever studied before—in itself, that was no feat, as I had never really studied before. Many law students have never studied before, because law school attracts those people who have never had to study, which is ironic, because studying is a very large part of practicing law. Everything in academia had come so easily for most of us. All my stress was self-imposed and I taught myself to work better and more efficiently under stress. Soon enough, I could work *only* under stressful conditions.

BOOK III: ...AND THE MOON SAYS HALLELUJAH, 01.05.12(3)

Sip coffee. Resolve to answer Rosie's question.

T: "It's a book. I went on a really long walk with my dog. People tell me I should write a book about finding myself."

R: "Did you find yourself?"

T: "I found some stuff."

Two Dutch girls check out. Rosie returns.

R: "Not much of a vacation. People like you come to Belize for vacation. And then they don't have any fun."

T: "It's a working vacation. I'm here to work and to snorkel. I love to snorkel."

R: "We have great snorkeling. But I haven't been snorkeling in over a year. I'm too busy."

T: "Too busy with what?"

R: "I work here. I have four other jobs. And I got my own candle business. And I'm in medical school."

T: "You are busy. And I want to see Mayan ruins."

R: "We have them! I can set all of that up for you, if you want. You should see the Mayan ruins at Lamanai."

T: "We will. My friend and I are renting bicycles today, though."

R: "Will that be in your book?"

T: "Doubtful."

R: "Will I be in your book?"

T: "Doubtful. It's over already."

R: "Oh. What happened in it?"

Belizean couples embrace on the dirt road, and grains of earth slip away into the sea.

BOOK I: THE MOMENTS THAT TURN US (A)(vii)
AND THEN NO MORE OF THEE, AND ME.

The first truly long day of the trip was a 25-mile hike into Greenbelt, Maryland. Greenbelt city limits touch the College Park city limits, but I intended to camp in a national park in Greenbelt. The first serious rain of the trip was coming in the next few days. Mabel and I saw almost no one during most of that walk. It was long, the weather was nice, and the roads followed gently rolling hills. The route went way out of the way, and we ended up hiking a triangle instead of a straight line. We walked by a few government properties with big signs reading that we could not enter, and we walked by a couple of gun clubs where people were inside shooting off their guns. We entered Greenbelt from the north and stopped at a gas station at a large, soft bend in the highway.

"Some kind of Movement or something?" the man behind the counter asked.

"What?"

"Saw another one of you guys three weeks ago. You walking across the country, right?"

"I am," I said.

"Another of you about three weeks ago. You're right on his tail."

"I have a dog," I said.

"Ah. The owner here loves dogs," he said.

"Can I sit outside and eat these M and Ms?" I asked.

"Yeah. If the owner sees you, he'll bring some treats for your dog."

Mabel and I sat in the parking lot for quite a while. I ate M & Ms, and Mabel ate some treats. And then we walked the last few miles into the Greenbelt National Park, including about 1.5 miles *into* the park. In National Parks and, indeed, in almost every park in the country that offers camping, the campsites are usually as far into the park as possible. They are all accessible by car, it seems, but difficult to reach on foot. It was a difficult thing to have hiked so far and then to have to hike so much *farther* and *uphill*—I had budgeted us at about 21 miles that morning, but we ended up around 25 miles. (Months later, I mentioned Greenbelt Park during a phone call to fellow thru-hiker Jack Planck. "I hate that freaking park," he said. "It was *so far* in to the campgrounds!") But Mabel and I beat the rain by the skin of our teeth and set up camp. It rained a bit that night and may have snowed a little. It was our first rain while in camp, but it wouldn't be our last. The next day we hiked out of the park and I stopped at the main office to pay for the camping I'd done. You should always pay your fair share with public resources like the national park system.

It was a brief walk from there to College Park.

In College Park, I took a motel room to hide from the rain and to have a base of operations to get over to REI and to the post office. An REI employee re-sized me for a pack and I learned that I had been wearing the wrong size pack. I had been sized for a pack a couple of years earlier, and the guy back then was pretty sure that I was a medium. But it was clear as a bell that day that I needed a larger pack for broader shoulders and a longer torso. I got a replacement pack that was essentially a larger sized version of the same pack I had before. I got a pair of Vasque hiking boots that were 1.5 sizes larger than my previous boots. The weight of the pack over the last week had made my feet almost two sizes bigger. I also got a lighter, more compact sleeping bag—rather than pay for a technically advanced bag, I got a bag with a higher temperature rating because I thought (wrongly) that the cold weather was mostly behind me. And I got a smaller gas can for the MSR stove because every little ounce counts. I mailed the old stuff all home to my parents' house in Illinois.

Mabel and I left for D.C. after a day off in College Park to re-tool. It was one of the few well spent zero days early on in this trip because I could immediately feel the difference in the larger, lighter pack. It fit better, and the nerve pain in my shoulder never came back, and my feet absolutely sang with the comfort of the new boots. It was a good feeling to be so close to D.C. because I had chosen D.C., almost arbitrarily, as the terminus of the first "leg" of the walk. It was the first of only a handful of genuinely urban cities I would visit on this hike.

I was about to walk on my own two feet into the nation's capitol—and not from a suburb, or from a home on the outskirts of the city, but from the Delaware seashore on the Atlantic Ocean. Mabel and I had hardly even started, in the grander scheme of things. But to Mabel and me, it felt like quite an accomplishment to have made it to within striking distance of D.C. We would stay in D.C. with a law school friend, Kendra Booth, who I had not seen since graduation. I was excited, too, because Isra was visiting D.C. that weekend from her new home, and I was desperate to see her. I was anxious to see if Mabel would remember her. I had my doubts that she would, because Mabel...well...she doesn't give the impression that she is a genius. She lopes around and chases her tail and always seemed to have an empty, silly smile on her face when we walked. If Mabel didn't remember her, I thought that it would probably be a bit of a blow to Isra's ego and that worried me.

That was our first day walking through a low-income, high crime neighborhood and we had no problems, at all. Mabel and I got some funny looks, and the funny looks we got were justified—I was, by that time, a funny looking guy with a pretty big beard and a walking staff. As for Hyattsville and the surrounding area, despite its reputation, Mabel and I did not feel unsafe or threatened. I cannot say the same for every low-income neighborhood we walked through on this trip.

We entered Rock Creek Park on the northwest side of D.C. Mabel and I followed the main park road, occasionally dropping off onto bike and foot trails. The Rock Creek is a clear creek that runs swiftly over exposed rocks, and it has cut a valley into what is now the District of Columbia. The park was empty except for a few runners and every now and again a car went by and the driver honked or waved, or both. Some drivers honked and waved and seemed to indicate that they knew who I was. D.C. is a city of lawyers, after all, and I'd had a little publicity, so I imagine some of the drivers were lawyers who guessed I must be that stupid lawyer they'd read about. They probably all thought I was crazy; I wasn't crazy back then.

Mabel and I crossed a pedestrian bridge over the creek near the south end of the Park and I met two older ladies who walked together there every day.

"Where are you two off to?" one of the silver haired ladies asked.

"California," I answered, and stopped to lean on my walking stick. "We came from Delaware."

"Well," she said, "maybe *this* is sanity."

We all laughed and that got Mabel excited. I liked these ladies' worldview, and we talked for a while. One of the ladies was born and raised in D.C. and the other had been there for 30 years. We talked about one lady's daughter, who is a human rights attorney in D.C. Her human rights attorney daughter loved every day of her job and her only fear was having to retire one day.

"That's the way to do it," I said. "I'm jealous of that."

"But she doesn't make very much money," the lady added with a smile and a shrug.

The ladies wished me luck and Mabel and I headed out of the park. Mabel and I exited Rock Creek Park a few blocks from Kendra's neighborhood, and after a quick consultation with my map (and directions from the nice ladies in the park) Mabel and I were on the right track. Kendra, being young and hip and professional, lived at the junction of the Adams-Morgan and DuPont neighborhoods of D.C. Mabel and I had made superb time that day and I knew we would have quite a wait until Kendra could tear herself away from her office and let us into her apartment.

Washington D.C. is not very big, especially if you have just walked from Delaware. I was actually very near to where Isra was staying with a friend of hers—a half a mile or less from Kendra's apartment. We were in no hurry, so I stopped beside the road and called Isra. It was a pretty brief call. She was busy downtown somewhere with her friends, so we couldn't get together. I hadn't seen her for a month and had just walked about 200 miles, and rushed the last week so that I could see her. But she wouldn't see me. Then she said she would be busy all day and night on Friday, but that we could get together on Saturday. My hand went to the ring in my pocket. I knew something was very, very wrong.

She had been so supportive of the Walk, and we had made plans for me to move in with her as soon as the Walk was over. But as soon as the Walk actually started, she had started to sound distant on the phone. I tried to put her out of my mind. It was a beautiful day—one of the few beautiful days we would have that spring. So Mabel and I walked on.

Just a few blocks later we climbed a hill, and on top of the hill we could see through a clearing in the buildings and there was the Washington Monument. It was a sublime moment. The monument was great and huge and beautiful, like all monuments should be, but also appeared almost quaint and endearing. I had walked there from the ocean. There had been some difficulties and setbacks, like the head injury, but every day it had gotten easier and easier. Every day I had learned better and better how to ignore the pain in my feet and shoulders, and every day I had felt my body getting stronger. Seeing the top of that obelisk in the Sunlight, I felt like there was very little I could not do if I set my mind and body to the task. On the C & O Canal, I could start making some long days and really get in shape to float across the Midwest. Mabel and I walked quickly, and I got a lot of funny looks from people because of the stupid smile on my face.

Mabel and I sat in Kalorama Park near Kendra's apartment. Kendra works at a big, prestigious firm in D.C., and I knew the kind of hours she must work. So I assumed it would be 7 or 8 p.m. before she could drag herself away from her office. Anyway, there is nothing more pleasant than to wait in a pretty little shaded park. Mabel and I sat on a bench in the shade, and talked to a few people who asked where we were headed or whether we were homeless. After a while, we would move out into the Sun and rest there before returning to the shade.

Mabel and I walked over to Kendra's apartment building, about six blocks away, around 6:30 p.m. She lived on a pretty tree-lined street and the trees were beginning to think about showing green buds. Mabel and I sat on the sidewalk outside the apartment building and waited. Residents of the building started coming home in waves, and many of them looked like attorneys but they didn't give us any grief for sitting right outside their security door. Many stopped and talked to us for a little bit and got a kick out of the fact that we had walked from Delaware.

I was a little nervous about meeting with Kendra. She had been one of the real kids in law school who *got it*, and everyone called her a "gunner". A lot of folks had considered me a gunner in law school because I did pretty well—but I wasn't a gunner, I was just good at the law school game. I hardly studied at all. But Kendra was the genuine article—a smart person who "got" the game and who worked superhuman hours. You could tell that she loved it, and I think she finished at or near the top spot in our class.

So I knew she would be the type of third year associate that got the big bonuses, that worked the long hours, and that talked constantly about legal issues and office gossip because the office would have become her entire world. I imagined she must have been bringing home about 250K a year after her bonus, and probably was dating either an attorney at her office or an attorney at another big shop in D.C., or maybe, even, a Supreme Court clerk. (Or no one at all, as so often happens to successful female attorneys.) And I was nervous to talk with her. I was no longer in her social class. I was not a highly paid attorney anymore. I was a guy with a dog. She spent her days on nuanced, high-level legal issues for prestigious clients, and I spent my days wondering whether I could find a good camp and fuel at night. I guess I was embarrassed, and a little insecure.

But it was good to see her when she turned the corner and started walking toward her apartment. She looked like an attorney walking home on a Thursday or Friday night—light and happy, but reserved enough because there are no real weekends. Mabel could tell from my reaction that this was the person we were waiting for and she started wagging her tail. Kendra said "Hi Mabel!" and Mabel totally lost it. I tried to restrain Mabel, because I didn't want her jumping all over Kendra in her slightly above business-casual attire. Kendra and I tried to say hello and welcome and all of that, but Mabel was jumping and whining, and then she would drop down and sniff at Kendra's crotch and Kendra said "Wow. She's friendly". I tried to feign embarrassment but I really thought it was all a funny scene.

After I got Mabel calmed down, Kendra walked us up to her third floor apartment.

Now, Kendra is quite a lovely looking gal. There is this term: "law school hot". It refers to women or men who are average looking, but because of how insular and bizarre the law school experience is, the law of proximity makes these people appear extremely attractive within the law school community. (The law of proximity states that a woman's level of attractiveness is inversely proportional to how far away the nearest other woman is. I imagine the same is true for men.) But the thing about Iowa Law—and Iowa City in general—is that everyone there is *beautiful*. You've never seen anything like it. So when I say Kendra is a lovely gal, I don't mean law school hot. She is objectively attractive. (I, by comparison, had always looked forward to going to law school and to being "law school hot". However, because Iowa City is such a beautiful place, I was even *less* attractive, relatively, in law school than I had been in the real world. C'est la guerre.) She hung around with a hybrid clique of gunners and cool kids during law school. I would have picked Kendra as a kind of yuppie, consumer, Starbucks-drinking, vapid kind of thing when we were in law school. She ran all the time and was very slim and healthy, and wore exercise clothes, and she had long blonde hair and was a social butterfly type who nevertheless studied all the time.

Kendra's apartment and her lifestyle shocked me, completely. She was absolutely nothing like I had imagined.

Kendra works all the time and spends very little time at home. Most attorneys I know who had faced the same sort of situation had poured money into their living arrangement: They bought houses and furniture and big screen TVs and sound systems. It's a common reaction from people who don't get to spend a lot of time at home—they want to suck every last bit of joy possible from their few moments at home. But Kendra had adopted the same approach I had when I was an attorney. She had a single couch, which she told me was a third-hand thing she had picked up in undergrad. The back of it was missing because it wouldn't fit through the hallway of her current apartment with its back on. Solution: cut off the back of the thing. She had a futon, too, which seemed to me to be about 30 years old. Her TV was an old small-screened boxy thing and all of her cable and wireless Internet paraphernalia were sitting on the floor in the corner. She had a single can of beans in her pantry and her refrigerator had a can of Bud Light, a can of Miller Lite, a can of Miller High Life, and several condiments, but that was all.

"I mostly eat out," she said and laughed.

"Looks like it!"

I let go of Mabel's lead and she went sniffing around the couch and the door to the bathroom. Kendra giggled.

"I keep saying that this is the year I have to turn this into a big-girl apartment."

Kendra did some work in her home office/bedroom, and I took a shower. When I was finished, she came back out to deliver a few more excuses for her lifestyle, which were unnecessary.

"I am NEVER here," she said. "Why would I spend a bunch of money on things I never get to use? That is crazy. Crazy!"

"Having great furniture that you don't use is silly," I said.

"It's the physical worst," she said.

"I agree. I didn't have any furniture, either."

"Right on," she said. "Right on. So there are some decent places to grab dinner around here...." She had a lot of work to do over the weekend, but she told me she was planning on putting it all off until Sunday. So when I came back with dinner and a couple of cans of beer, I ate and she talked to me about her life and her work and everything in between. She loved her work, but she didn't like a lot of the bullshit that goes along with working at a big firm. But even if she didn't love it, she would continue to do it because she made so much money and that allowed her to travel—New Zealand, Mexico, Japan, Alaska. She was planning a July vacation to Greece, and I was jealous. We talked about her undergrad days and reminisced about law school. She complimented my beard and told me that she suffered from some genetic affinity to beards as a sign of strength and virility in men, although she never wanted to have children. She told me about the hiking and running and climbing that she had done. Then she disappeared into her office/bedroom and I updated my journal while reclining on her futon and ignoring the TV. When the journal started boring me, I had to figure out how to use the remote controls to her TV because she didn't remember how to use them.

Kendra left early for work the next day and Mabel and I hung around her apartment and the neighborhood just walking around and eating. It rained a little, but it wasn't so bad. That night I called Isra and we talked a little bit, but she had plans that night so we would have to wait until Saturday to talk. Kendra worked all night and Mabel and I did a load of laundry and turned in early.

Kendra had a lot of work to do on Saturday, and so did Mabel and I. We had a great day.

Washington, D.C. is an interesting town to walk around in. There are a lot of trees and green space and it is pedestrian friendly in the government/tourist sections. The buildings are staid and respectable, and there are plazas—not huge, surprising plazas like you might find in a European city, but plazas still. And there are monuments and statues. We found the Casimir Pulaski monument, for example—a man for whom I always got a day off of high school in Illinois. He has his own statue of him on a steed leading some battle or another.

If the statues and monuments are any indication, D.C. is a monument to war. The Vietnam Memorial, the African American Civil War Memorial, Iwo Jima Memorial, Korean War Veterans Memorial, and on and on. The D.C. War Memorial. The Washington Monument, for a President who led in a time of war. Lincoln Memorial, another war leader. (Jefferson's Memorial is small and out-of-the-way, by comparison.) Then there is the Air Force Memorial and the Navy Memorial. There is a separate monument for the women in Vietnam, and there is a Holocaust Museum. There is a World War II Memorial and a Pentagon Memorial. Then, of course, there is Arlington Cemetery—a monument to war and death so base and sad, but yet, although not even in D.C., so many people tell me I "must see".

I tried to imagine what a foreigner might think upon seeing D.C. for the first time, or to imagine that I were an alien from Mars who had to form an impression of the whole of the U.S. from this one town. I was left with the notion that, if I didn't know any better, I would think this town served as the capitol of a nation dedicated to perpetual war. Mabel and I looked at the

White House and the Washington Monument. We saw the Lincoln Memorial and the Jefferson memorial. We walked along the National Mall and looked at the Capitol. We walked by the United States Treasury and the United States Supreme Court. Some of Washington's famous cherry blossoms were blooming, but the whole symphony of white and fragrance hadn't yet begun in earnest. Still, some streets and walkways were lined with the white flowering trees, and it was a pleasant thing to walk with Mabel among the granite buildings between flowering cherry blossoms. I took pictures of Mabel beside many of the monuments so that I could always remember our trip. I took pictures of Mabel beside the White House, the Lincoln and Washington Memorials, and the Jose Artigas Memorial statue.

People from all nations stopped us to pet Mabel and to scratch behind her ears. Thin foreign tourists spoke a million different languages; they wore different clothes, or clothes that were cut a little differently than they would be in the U.S. But it doesn't matter who you are or where you come from, Mabel is intensely precious and needs to be scratched behind her ear. Little Japanese kids squealed and tried to grab Mabel's tail.

Later in the afternoon, after Mabel and I had seen all of the tourist sites that we "needed" to see, we headed back up toward Adams-Morgan to meet with Isra.

Lots of things in life are very difficult. I loved Isra very much. We met in law school, and we had a long, awkward time getting together; it was a challenge for us to work through what separated us. I am a poor, white kid from a farm town, and she was a first generation American. I was an atheist, and she came from a Chicago-area Muslim family. She was five years younger than me, which was enough to matter. So it had taken us about a year to get over and through all the nonsense that made us different. We were really good together, and extremely happy for a while and we had lived together in Chicago. She had taken a job in another state shortly before I started the Walk. She liked the job quite a bit, and I visited several times. We had planned that I would move in with her after the Walk and we would get married. She was supportive of the Walk, and she even got Mabel for me and planned on meeting me at a few different places along the trip.

Then we met in D.C. after I had been on the road for about two weeks. I called her as I walked toward the address she had given me, and she came out onto the sidewalk with the phone still to her ear. She was so beautiful to me, but I could see in the way she walked and the way she looked at me that our relationship was over. On a sidewalk on Florida Avenue, she told me she thought we shouldn't be together. She had good reasons—didn't want to wait for me, thought it was unfair that she was "putting her life on hold" waiting for me to live my dreams, that kind of thing. We had been through things like this before, but had always gravitated back together, even if neither of us really wanted to. She told me all the things she always told me: there was no one else, she hadn't cheated on me or anything, and then she even said: "Look, I'm not even going to see anyone for a long time. I need time to myself, Tyler. I need to find myself and find out what it means to be me. Who I am." I could relate to that.

I could have "talked it out" with her, I think. But I was in no position to "talk it out". And I didn't want to have to talk it out, anyway. She always got what she wanted. So I swallowed hard, turned around and Mabel and I walked away from her. I wondered if I would ever see her again in my lifetime.

People I met always asked me "Why"? When you tell people that you are walking across the country, they care *a little bit* about *what* you are doing, but what they really want to know is *why* you are doing it. I never, or very rarely told anyone *why* I was walking across the country. I had three reasons, three "Whys". The first was that Isra and I weren't happy—I wasn't happy with most things in my life and so Isra wasn't happy with me. She wanted to move and then when she did move she wanted me to move with her. But it isn't easy for attorneys to up and move. I could practice only in Illinois without taking another state's bar exam, and it is hard to find a job *before* you've taken the bar exam. So moving to a different state is difficult without taking an enormous gamble, packing up and moving there and then taking the bar and *then* looking for work. And it was difficult to leave a very high paying job, no matter how unhappy I was, because I had student loans to pay and I wanted to be able to provide financial stability for Isra and me. So I thought that walking across the country might be a good way to segue into a new life somewhere else. It would give me a new skill set—one that I'm more interested and invigorated by. It would give me some sort of jumping off position to look for work in related fields, and it would set my resume apart from others'. I'm not a fool: I knew people would notice. I knew it would raise a few eyebrows. I figured that it could get me a couple of interviews—people would read "Cross country thru-hike" and think "Yeah, let's talk to this guy". And I thought there would be some benefit from that, and that maybe Isra and I could use that to set up and settle down. And I could never have even started the trip without Isra's support—I started this thing because I knew she would support me through it and would be there for me when it was over. So I told myself that our relationship was one of the "reasons" for the Walk, and then one of my reasons for the Walk died right there on Florida Avenue. That was disconcerting. I thought for a second that I would quit and go home. Later I would admit that our relationship wasn't a reason for this Walk, it was only a justification.

Back at Kendra's, I watched TV and tried to not let my voice crack when I spoke. Kendra and I talked about all the things Mabel and I had done that day, and all the things we had seen, and each time I spoke I thought "oh, my voice is going to get weak or waver just a little and then Kendra will know I am heartbroken". But I guess I must have held it all together, because Kendra never mentioned a thing. I was glad she was there to talk to and to take my mind off of everything. And the thing is, Kendra is a genuine, sweet, and good person. You don't meet too many like that.

In the heart of Georgetown, itself in the heart of Washington, D.C., there is a canal, and you might not even notice it if you are not looking for it. I imagine that hundreds or thousands of people every day drive over the canal and are never the wiser of the resource right there. I had done some reading about the history of the Canal, though, and the story of Justice Douglas's campaign to save it. The Chesapeake and Ohio Canal was a marvel of human achievement—a monumental earthwork project fueled by monumental greed, a monumental failure of engineering and economics, and eventually a monument to the National Park system. The Canal runs about 185 miles along the Potomac River from Washington D.C. to Cumberland, Maryland; its purpose was to provide a cheap waterway to transfer the coal wealth of Pennsylvania and West Virginia to D.C. (If there is one thing D.C. can do, it is facilitate the transfer of wealth, usually from poor to rich.) Thousands of Canal workers whose names I will never know dug a ditch on the ridge alongside the Potomac and engineers built locks and dams to fill the thing with water. A hard-pressed gravel towpath about 12 feet wide runs along the entire length of the Canal; donkeys towed barges of coal down the Canal. The Canal served its purpose for a while in the 1800s, and gave rise to a canal culture along its shores. But by most accounts, the Canal was an abject failure. Construction began just as the railroad ascended, moving goods faster and more cheaply than the Canal could. Despite its 74 locks and dams, and 11 aqueducts, it was subject to flooding from the Potomac. The cost of the Canal, too, was a staggering miscalculation. For example, the Paw Paw Tunnel runs nearly a mile, took 12 years to build, bankrupted a number of companies, and was finally completed at 500% over budget. The Canal fell into disrepair for many years; it was a novelty of the 19th Century, half forgotten in the national memory. But folks who lived near the Canal, especially on the Maryland side of the Potomac, used the Towpath as a place to stroll through the wilderness. And those few D.C. residents who felt the inexhaustible pull of the woods would sneak away from their Capitol Hill lives for weekend walks along the Potomac, watching it change from a tranquil stream into a raging, mighty river—an ideal hike for city folks: a soft, sylvan trail affording fleeting glimpses of deer or wild turkey, innumerable turtles and herons, and, occasionally, the furtive black bear. So Congress wanted to pave it when highways replaced rails. Supreme Court Justice William O. Douglas, an affirmed lover of the great Western outdoors and an environmentalist, loved the Canal and Towpath. He believed the path should be preserved as a park for the enjoyment of all Americans. He hiked the entire towpath to build public support for its preservation. The Chesapeake and Ohio National Historical Park is now dedicated to Justice Douglas. Mabel and I were about to walk in the footsteps of giants.

Mabel and I dropped down onto the Towpath in the heart of Georgetown, not really sure what to expect. In Georgetown, the Canal is full

49

with water and bounded on both sides by urban development. Where we entered, at the very beginning of the Canal, the Towpath is on the right side of the Canal, and it looks like a well-kept gravel road.

I welcomed the soft crunch crunch of gravel under each of my footsteps. The Towpath is a great deal softer than asphalt or concrete roads, and I knew my feet would last longer each day and the gravel path reminded me of when I was a kid in rural Illinois. When I was 10 or 12 or so, friends and I would hike a few miles down a combination of gravel roads and railroad tracks to get to a dirty little set of waterfalls. All of our little hearts would beat so powerfully, excited by all the fun that might be possible out there, even though the fun rarely materialized so splendidly as it did in our imaginations, and even though almost no one ever got up the gumption to jump off the train bridge into the pool of dank, brown water below.

I think Mabel and I felt a little bit of that same type of excitement when we first hit the Towpath. That is when the Walk really began, and I had no idea what to expect. "Adventure" rarely happens when you know what to expect. Some folks get a kick out of *danger*, of being close to mortality, like skydivers and spelunkers. But all those folks know what to expect—they know their gear and they have done it all before. But I had no idea what was ahead of us. I no more knew what kind of animals and plants we would see than what the weather would do in two weeks' time. I didn't know how people would react to us, or if we would even see people at all. I knew there would be risks, but I had no idea what those would be. That is adventure. And that is dangerous.

As an attorney, the worst sin of all is to walk willingly toward unknown risk and uncertainty.

On the first day on the Towpath, Mabel and I caught up to a large, slow-hiking man with a stark white beard. His name was Paul and he was from Long Island, so I thought of him as Long Island Paul. He and I sat together at a campground and talked about hiking and about other things. He looked to be about 50 years old. Paul had hiked almost all of the Appalachian Trail in sections and had hiked the C&O Canal before. He was a helicopter mechanic, but had recently decided to change jobs and had found himself with time on his hands. So his wife drove him into New York City and he took the train down to D.C. to hike the Canal. She was scheduled to pick him up in a few weeks up in Cumberland at the end of the Towpath. But he was now thinking that he might just hang a right in Cumberland and hit another trail he knew that would take him back toward New England where he could walk back to a train station.

Long Island Paul took a more lightweight hiking approach than I did—his pack was much smaller and lighter than mine. His tent was a Tarptent brand thing that weighed next to nothing, and his two trekking poles doubled as tent poles. His pack had such a low profile that I could hardly see it over his shoulders. He was dressed warmly and had a stocking cap on, as I did. I hiked a lot faster than he did, though, so once we started back on the trail I left him behind pretty quickly.

There is no word for the peace that exists in walking on a nice wooded path, all alone except for Mabel. A lot of experiences in life are beyond words and those are the experiences people get stuck trying to write about. There are transcendent things in the world, I think, immeasurable in words because they are transcendent things. Even that close to D.C., blue herons sometimes landed in the shallow waters of the Canal and zoomed out and over the great Potomac on my left. The trees were still winter-black and skeletal and through them I could see up to the edge of the ridge on our right and could make out the outline of homes on the ridge. Still, it was quiet and felt primordial out there, and there were no sounds except the birdcalls, the rustling of tree branches, and the crunch of gravel beneath my feet. Several times Mabel saw deer far up on the trail or across on the other side of the Canal and she would perk up and try to give chase. It was still chilly out, and Mabel did not even pant. She and I walked together through the calm wood.

And I began to experiment with the rhythm of my breathing and walking.[5] The first trick was to learn when my walking stick should make contact with the ground. I divided my steps into groups of 4—left foot, 1; right foot, 2; left foot, 3; right foot, 4. The walking stick hit the ground between 4 and 1, again between 2 and 3. Then I cued my breathing on the stick's contact with the ground, and over a few days I worked out how my breathing rate would change with my pace. There are mile markers on the Towpath so I could always estimate where I was and could measure my pace accurately. Before too long, I could estimate my speed by my breathing rate, so long as I maintained my breathing rate cued to the stick. I discovered that breathing rate was key to maintaining an even pace. Even out-of-shape and awful at walking, I was able to maintain a good pace so long as I regulated my breathing. A few times on the Canal, despite the 90 lb pack, Mabel and I managed to do 15 miles in five hours, almost to the minute, without stopping, slowing, or speeding up. If I wanted to speed up, I would count my steps in 3s instead of 4s and count the walking stick in 2s (or, I guess, would count steps in 6s and the walking stick in 4s).

I was re-learning how to breathe.

We stopped that night at a campsite along the Towpath. It was a beautiful spread of flat ground covered in soft, green grass—all the greener because the Potomac and Canal had flooded a few weeks earlier and a few days of brilliant weather had followed the flood. I cooked dinner beside the river and the Sun set in the west so brilliant and golden that I thought of a discussion I'd had only a month earlier with an attorney friend of mine named Wendy, about that "Moment". Wendy and I had met for lunch at Hannah's Bretzel in Chicago and, in a last ditch effort to sell her on the idea of *joining* the Walk, I told her to think of the Moment when you crest a hill or brush aside a bush and there is the Pacific Ocean! Like Wendy, I'd thought that the Moment would happen when I saw the vast Pacific Ocean spread out before me. We thought there would be a shining moment of enlightenment. But here was something very much like the Moment happening right in front of me. I took a picture of that Sunset and shared it

---

[5] The breathing experiments went on for many days on the Canal, but I have condensed them here to better explain the process.

51

with my Twitter followers and emailed it to Wendy with the caption "This is a Moment".

Think of the innumerable circumstances and conditions that had to occur in order to find me there to see that Sunset! All the mistakes and the missteps. Law school. Isra. Law school! Isra! Sidley! That day in Debra's office when I "declared my preference" of practice groups! All the moments that had *impacted* my life, and there I was in that moment. I had nothing to show for all the mistakes except for that Sunset and Mabel begging to lick the pot of leftover beans and rice. I thought of all the other great Sunsets I'd seen. For all that pain and heartache and frustration, I'd seen a lot of great Sunsets and Sunrises. Each had probably been Moments just like that one, but I was too wrapped up in myself to notice them at the time. That is a great shame.

The Sun set and Long Island Paul lumbered into camp. He asked if I minded that he camped there, and I did not mind. Company is good, even if it is another quiet man. Long Island Paul loved long hikes and, as a veteran of many, he had very little faith that I would make it across the whole continent. I didn't have much faith that I would make it, either.

Mabel and I were awake early the next morning, but Long Island Paul had already woken up, eaten, packed, and hit the trail. I knew I would catch him later that day, and I wondered if we would stay in the same camp again that night. The company would be nice.

BOOK I: THE MOMENTS THAT TURN US (B)(i)
A CHEQUER-BOARD OF NIGHTS AND DAYS.

Mabel and I made good time and caught Long Island Paul after only a few miles. He looked to be in good form, and told me he was feeling pretty good about the day. I was worried, though, because the weather forecast called for a lot of rain later that day and for the next two days, coupled with a pretty steep drop in nighttime temperatures.

"It was chilly last night," he said. "How did you two do?"

"Ok," I said. "But it's supposed to get really cold again."

"You'll make it," he said. "Don't wait up for me. Hike your own hike."

So we hiked our own hike. Mabel and I rushed ahead to the next campsite. We rushed that day only because I had a lot I wanted to add to the journal. And it wouldn't hurt to beat Long Island Paul to the camp because we could scan the place for the choicest campsite. Mabel behaved very well. She and I hit our campsite with plenty of daylight remaining. The campsite was better than some, but not ideal. It was up at grade with the Towpath, so flooding was no serious threat, it had an intact fire ring and a picnic table, and there was some firewood lying around on the ground to be used as fuel if we needed a fire. The campground was mostly exposed dirt and mud but there were two thin patches of grass, one about 40 yards from then picnic table and the other about 50 yards from the picnic table. Both were on a slight slant, which would provide drainage in the event of standing or running water—it is better to let gravity move the water away from your tent rather than to wake up in a puddle.

I quickly unpacked my cooking gear on the picnic table and cooked my dinner. I always take up a lot of space when I cook and so I wanted to be done by the time Long Island Paul got there, if he ever got there at all. He had been in good form when we passed him, but he wasn't moving all that fast. I boiled water and poured in a packet of prepared cheddar broccoli rice. I opened a can of tuna with the old fashioned can opener on my multi-tool and poured it in, oil and all. I fed Mabel and I ate the rice and tuna directly from the pot. Mabel finished her meal in seconds and then sat and stared at me while I ate. When I finished, I gave what little was left to Mabel—she always ate whatever was left over and cleaned the pot for me. Long Island Paul limped into camp just as I finished eating—and it was a good thing I had finished eating when he got there, because I would have lost my appetite directly.

We said hello to each other and he sat at the picnic table.

"I might be in a spot," he said. He wore his camp shoes—Croc sandals—instead of his hiking shoes.

He peeled the sock off his left foot. All the skin on the front half of his foot had loosed, ripped away from his foot, and was bunched together in white, fleshy ribbons on the sides of his foot. The muscle and sinew was all revealed in bright maroon and purple like the rabbits we dissected in high school biology after we had cut away the skin and we could see the muscles exposed. The torn skin was white and wrinkled.

"Jesus, Man," I said. There wasn't much more to say.

"My shoes," he said. "They aren't working. I had to stop and switch to these sandal things." He fiddled with the wilted skin around his foot, and talked about having his wife mail to him a pair of broken-in sneakers for him to finish his hike. I offered to him the pair of Garmond boots that I had forgotten to mail home in D.C., and his first reaction was neither to say yes or no, but to admonish me for still carrying the shoes.

"You are carrying two pairs of shoes?"

"Just for a bit," I said.

"And that brick of a battery I saw you with? No wonder you're in so much pain. How much does that pack weigh?"

"It's heavy," I agreed. I had not told him about the pain I'd been having in my feet, but I think he could tell. "But I have a lot of stuff for Mabel. Don't worry about my pack, though. Worry about your feet. Here." I lent him my multi-tool and he used the cuticle scissors to cut away the wilted skin from his foot and then he took off his other sock. The right foot was just as bad, and he cut away that skin, too. This is the kind of injury that ends hikes. Paul told me that he had never before had to cut short a hike because of foot problems.

"I might have to hike into town tomorrow."

"I think you should," I agreed.

"Just what I don't need is to have my feet go septic and to die out here. My wife would never let me live it down."

I gave Paul extra triple antibiotic ointment and a roll of bandages for his feet. He had Neosporin, but not enough to treat his large wounds. I was over-packed and could spare it. Paul had planned to zero the next day, as Mabel and I were planning to do to wait out the rain, but it would be better to trudge the eight miles or so into Poolesville and make sure his feet wouldn't get infected. It depressed him a little, because it is frustrating to be forced off the trail.

I tented up for bed early that night. Paul took the less desirable spot closer to the picnic table, so Mabel and I were about 50 yards from the picnic table. It started to get cold soon after we got inside the tent, but I knew the cold wasn't keeping Paul awake because I could hear him snoring from 30 feet away. I lay on my back with Mabel curled up on my feet until I drifted to sleep.

Mabel and I woke with a start around midnight to a horrible racket. Light flashed back and forth over the tent and the light filtered through the rain fly and lit up everything in the tent in an eerie green glow. I heard loud, terrifying shrieks with human shouts above the shrieking, and because I was still half asleep I couldn't really process all the input—I thought I was in an X Files episode and Mabel and I were about to be taken up. But then the fog of sleep cleared and I threw open the tent. The cold woke me and I began to understand what was going on.

The shrieks were the far off barking of dogs and the horrible whinnying of a horse on the Towpath. The horse reared mightily and screamed and the rearing set spinning the lantern fastened to the horse. The pitching and swaying lantern cast blinding light and pallid shadows that, in the tent, had made me anxious. A man on the Towpath tried to calm the horse.

"Sorry!" I shouted. "I have a dog over here!"

"I'm huntin' with dogs!" the man shouted. "This horse isn't afraid of dogs."

My voice seemed to calm the horse, as if it might have been me that spooked it and, once I was revealed to be a man with a man's voice, there was nothing more for it to fear. The lantern stopped swinging and the man, now almost behind the bright light, waved several times and said over and over that he was sorry for having woken me up. I heard Long Island Paul stirring as I walked back to my tent, but I don't think he was awake.

It wasn't easy to fall back to sleep in the tent. I had an unsettled feeling as if there could be something bad afoot that I couldn't quite identify. There was the cold, of course, and some kind of critter nosed around the outside of the tent and Mabel growled. Hunting dogs barked and bayed in the far off distance and I figured they must have had a coon in a tree as I fell asleep.

Long Island Paul was already up and eating breakfast when Mabel and I rolled out of the tent the next morning. It was nice to sleep in, in spite of and because of the cold. The temperature had dropped below 30 degrees the night before. So it was nice to wake up, smell the cold, and then decide to stay curled up in the sleeping bag with Mabel's warm body on my feet. When we finally climbed from the tent, I made a quick line to the picnic table to feed Mabel and to make myself a hot cup of tea. I made a lot of mistakes on the front end of this trip, but one thing I did right was to bring tea. There are few things in the world better than hot tea on a morning like that one, or at the end of a cold hiking day. That hot cup of tea and a hundred others like it were worth their weight in the water I carried. I poured the hot tea into a water bottle and held the bottle in my trembling hands. I boiled a water bottle's worth of water and put the piping hot bottle into a dry sack with a fleece and my icy feet. My feet warmed and I saved the water to drink later. Then Mabel and I walked down the steep embankment to the river. The walking warmed me up and Mabel loves to sniff around anywhere where there has been wildlife.

Mabel was beside herself at the river. There were tracks carved and smudged all over in the mud beside the river; they looked almost like dog tracks but larger, and Mabel couldn't get enough of them. Her tail was up, then down, then wagging, and then down again. She sniffed around the tracks, but not on the tracks, and then she looked at me and whined. That is what she does when she wants to play with a puppy we see or when she wants to attack a deer on the trail. The many tracks were all smudged in the mud and, because of how smudged they were, it looked like some dogs had come through in quite a hurry. I assumed they were from the hunter's dogs the night before. Then Mabel's tail went down, she stopped whining and started doing the low "whoof" she does when she wants to warn me that something or someone is nearby. Long Island Paul was stirring.

Long Island Paul was not a tea drinker, so he made more oatmeal and grumbled about his feet. He moved slowly and had decided for sure to hike off the trail to tend to his feet. We talked for a bit about the horse incident from the night before and I told him how the light and the whinnying made me think there was an alien abduction going on.

"Did you have something pawing on the tent last night?" he asked, and I nodded. "Any trouble with the cold?"

"It was a little rough," I said.

"Unseasonable," Paul said. "I was a little worried about you two. It was cold last night, and you said you had already had some trouble with the cold. It is going to be worse tonight."

"I know. We are going to zero out today and dodge the rain."

"Good plan," Paul agreed. "It would be pretty cold for Mabel in the rain. Take some candy bars into your tent tonight. Little secret. If you are cold in the middle of the night, do some sit-ups in your sleeping bag and eat a candy bar."

"I normally try to keep food out of my tent," I said, "but tonight I think I will take your advice."

It is an absolute, bright-line rule that you *do not take food into your tent* when you are in bear country. In bear country, you don't even take scented toilet supplies into the tent—no toothpaste, no scented toilet paper. In *real* bear county, you don't even take into your tent the clothes that you wear when you cook. But I had researched the area ahead of time, and we were *not in* bear country. The Maryland Department of Natural Resources web page and all the other sites I read were clear that there *were no bears that far south or east along the Canal*—there were bears only in the four westernmost counties of the state, with the odd lost yearling bear who wandered off into eastern Maryland to scare Baltimore suburbanites. Long Island Paul, for example, took all of his gear and food into the tent with him every night to keep them dry and never once worried about bears. There was *certainty* that there were no bears there.

Paul plodded out of camp on torn up feet around 8 or 8:30 in the morning. I watched him walk away and I winced every time he took a step. He was gliding or shuffling instead of walking, and he looked to be going about one mile an hour. At that rate, it would be six o'clock at night before he made it into town. But he had to hike his own hike. I hoped that he could make it to town before the rain started coming down in buckets.

I packed my pack, put it on the picnic table and fastened my blue tarp over the pack. There is no way to guarantee you will keep your gear dry. Nothing is waterproof, no matter what the advertising says. Mabel and I were back in the tent by 10:15 a.m. and cold rain began to fall. Mabel and I were safe and dry—each raindrop hit the rain fly with a smack like falling on a snare drum. It was cold, but it would get colder that night. I set an alarm for 6:00 p.m. because I could not be sure whether I would fall asleep during the day. I must have fallen asleep, because the alarm went off in what seemed to be the next instant. So at 6:00 p.m., I took Mabel out of the tent and fed her, then re-fastened the tarp over my pack. Back at the tent, I put on all the clothes I could so to stay warm through the night. I wore silk long underwear, quilted long underwear, and pants; a long sleeve base layer top, a long sleeve shirt, a poly-blend pullover, and a fleece; three pairs of silk sock liners and three pairs of thick, wool socks; gloves, and a balaclava that I wore as a stocking cap. At 6:30 or so, I tucked myself back into the sleeping bag and Mabel curled up in a ball beside my shoulder.

I woke up around 10 that night. I don't know why I woke up then, but I imagined it was because I had been in the tent almost non-stop for 12 hours and had been asleep for at least 8 of those hours. Mabel was already awake when I opened my eyes. She was always awake before me. I gave Mabel a few loving pats on the head, and scratched her behind her ear, and then she curled up in a ball on my legs like she does on cold nights. I took a picture of her curled on my legs and it was the last picture I would take of that tent. Shortly after 10 o'clock, I reclined on my back with my arms stuffed down into my sleeping bag, and couldn't move around very well. I was about to have one of the worst nights of my life.

BOOK III: ...AND THE MOON SAYS HALLELUJAH, 01.05.12(4)

Sit at picnic table; meet Celio. Research re: Celio: Portugese, about 30 years old, lives in Pedro's Hotel, in Belize to fly for Tropic Air, will be pilot after he builds hours, smokes Belizean cigarettes, is probably in love w/Rosie. Welcome Celio at picnic table with me.

R: "He's a writer. He's writing about taking his dog for a walk."

C: "That interests me."

Observe Celio's accent is like Russian accent; remember he is Portugese; note my confusion.

C: "Tell us your book, Friend. How have you named it?"

T: "Not sure. I was going to call it *Feel the Selfish Fury*, but now I'm probably going to call it *The Moments That Turn Us*."

C: "Ha! What a title. Why do you call it like that?"

T: "Lots of reasons."

C: "You don't have to tell me the story, if this is an uncomfortable thing."

R: "Oh, Celio, he'll tell it if I ask him to. Won't you? Tell it?"

T: "It's autobiographical. Makes me nervous to tell it. Makes me feel selfish and silly."

C: "Everyone is selfish and silly. Look at Rosie! Selfish and silly."

R: "I'm not selfish. I am silly. Tell it?"

T: "It's long."

C: "We have time, Friend! Everyone on this island has time. This is an island where...pfft...there is very little but time. Coconuts. Rum. And time."

T: "Ok."

R: "It's about you?"

T: "Sort of. It's about me, and a dog, and the law."

C: "How does it start?"

T: "How *does* it start? Good question. I don't know yet."

C: "You must have a starting, Friend. If there is nothing to hold on to at the the starting, then pfft."

T: "Well...think of me this way...."

The Ocean breaks in white-capped waves a mile out to sea along the reef that runs the length of Belize.

BOOK I: THE MOMENTS THAT TURN US (B)(i)(a)
LIFT NOT THY HANDS TO IT FOR HELP.

A beast walked by the tent.

Mabel perked her head and her ears went back and down against her head. She and I stared at the nearly opaque left side of the tent where the beast had walked. It was a bear. I didn't have to see the animal to know it was a bear. It sounded big, not like a raccoon or a beaver or opossum. I could hear the thump of each of its feet hitting the ground and knew it was an animal of 200 or more pounds. There were four feet making four footfalls, which meant it couldn't be a human. I heard the shuffling, horrid cadence of the beast's feet falling on the wet ground. Over that cadence, we heard the beast's ghastly insistent breathing. Mabel looked at me and I looked at her, and I saw that she was scared. She did not bark—not even the low woof she does to warn me of an approaching animal or person. I don't think she even dared to take a breath and I know that I didn't breathe until I knew the beast had gone out of the range of its paws' swipe. Mabel situated herself in the cubbyhole of the tent beside my shoulder.

I knew the bear was probably at the picnic table tearing at my pack to get at my food store. We had been rained in for quite a while and the forecast called for more rain, so running out of food was not an option of us. I had to save our food from the bear. I zipped open the tent as quietly as I could and rolled out of it into my hiking boots as I stood up. I held my breath for some reason and tried to be quiet, as if sneaking up on a bear were a good thing. I told Mabel to stay in the tent and I turned toward the picnic table. I had the long ironwood hiking stick in one hand and a can of bear spray in the other, and I had a knife attached to the waist of my pants. I did not know what I intended to do, but I knew I had to do something—it would be bad national park stewardship if I were to allow the bear to become accustomed to human food. So I clicked on my headlamp and walked slowly toward the picnic table. It was about 30 degrees. The rain was cold and I could see little silvery streaks of rain in the light from my headlamp.

When I was about a hundred feet out from the picnic table, I saw the bear and stopped where I stood.

The bear was up on its hind legs at the end of the picnic table, and used its front paws and snout to try to get underneath the blue tarp and at our food. It looked to me at the time to weigh 2000 pounds—immense, ponderous, and muscular. The beast struggled to get its snubbed, snorting snout under the tarp and it fumbled with its massive paws the size of tennis rackets. I watched for infinite moments as the rain soaked my clothes, my stocking cap, my thick black beard; rain soaked the bear's black coat. I was catatonic like a buck deer in headlights. I was not afraid, and my heart beat steadily. I did not move for what felt like a long time. I stood there until the bear looked at me.

It turned its broad face toward me, did a slow double take, and steadied its eyes at me. I could not see the bear well from that distance in that rain, and its tight black eyes were hidden in the blackness of its brow, but I knew it was looking at me. There was a flash of light brown on its snout, and the light brown flash disappeared behind the eternal blackness of its nose when it stared at me. Its face was as emotionless and cold as mine. It didn't look startled, or angry, or peaceful, or anything—it was just a black bear face, as stoic as if I'd stumbled into its office on a Wednesday morning with a few documents for him to take a look at. Still, there was something dark and powerful about its face and my own thoughts began to roll back into my brain; I could feel that I was back in control of my body. My instinct was to turn and run away as fast as I could, even though I knew the bear could outrun me. My legs almost started me in the other direction several times each second, but I restrained myself because some calculator part of my brain said: "This bear could kill you, and it will if it wants to, but you have bear spray and a large stick and a knife. You can make this a very bad day for the bear right before it kills you."

For some reason, that was enough for me.

And I could almost see the bear's thoughts as it stared at me. It was thinking: "I can kill this guy if I want to. But he has a stick and he's one of the two-legged things. He could make this a very bad day for me right before I kill him."

I put my arms up in the air, breathed deeply, and walked toward the bear. And I said loudly, but did not shout: "I will fuck you up, Bear. Get goin', or I will fuck you up."

The bear didn't move at first as I walked toward it; it stared at me from the deep blackness of its brow. Kept walking. "Hrah!" I shouted. "I will fuck your world up."

Then the bear dropped its paws from the table, huffed or coughed a little, then jogged off into the darkness in the other direction. I walked on toward the bear's retreat, and stopped at the picnic table to investigate. I tightened up the blue tarp, but the bear had not actually loosened the tarp much. With food secure and the bear gone, I walked back to the tent. Mabel had her head stuck out of the tent and, I suppose, had watched the whole thing. I got back into the tent with Mabel and she and I curled back up together against the cold. Mabel was still scared or anxious, though, and so she stayed up in the cubbyhole area beside my shoulder.

I was a bad ass. I was 10 feet tall. No man and no bear could touch me because I was unstoppably powerful and dynamic. There was nothing that I could not have done in that moment because I had stared down the bear and I had not wavered. Cowered by the force of my humanity and the fierceness of my masculinity, the bear had tucked its tail between its legs and run for its dear life.

"I am an American hero!" I whispered to Mabel, and scratched behind her ear. "Did you see that? Did you? How lucky are you to be on this grand adventure with such a powerful and unstoppable man?"

My heart swelled in my chest with pride and power because I had experienced something real, something barbaric. As close as will ever be possible for me to taste a state of nature. And I won! I beat the bear. Those anemic twerps I had known as attorneys—*they* would have run. They would have given up their food to the bear, and would have given up their camp to the bear. But not me. I was stronger.

I lay there for 10 or 15 minutes, scratching at Mabel and feeling proud of myself and reliving in my mind that fateful moment when I had bested my brother the bear. We were secure there, knowing that no other bear would dare to bother us—and that particular bear would never have the guts to show its face in any human's camp again because I had humbled that bear.

Then, from about 30 or 40 feet away, I heard the bear huff and chuff loudly and stamp its feet against the wet ground, the signs that it was considering charging the tent, and I was a scared little boy again. This would be a long night.

BOOK I: THE MOMENTS THAT TURN US (B)(i)(b)
THE ANGEL WITH HIS DARKER DRAUGHT DRAWS UP TO THEE.

Mabel and I stiffened up in the tent at the sound of the bear haruffing. The big, throaty calls of the bear sounded like "cha ha roof ruff", and the bear slapped the wet ground with its huge paws. At the sound of it, Mabel's neck straightened and she stared intently toward the source of the sound. I sucked in a giant breath and then stopped breathing, and my heart stopped beating, and the whole world stopped around me. I was certain that the bear would charge, barrel through the tent with its teeth and long claws. There was no doubt in my mind that I would soon be torn apart, that I would feel the bear's teeth tearing my muscles from my bones, would hear the unholy, moist gnashing of the bear ripping my muscles and tearing my skin to eat my liver, and I would smell its hot, sour breath as my heart stopped beating and I died.

My heart raced again and beat against my ribcage and my fingers and jaws clenched. Mabel rumbled a low growl. We waited.

We waited.

We waited.

But nothing happened. And as minutes passed, my heartbeat slowed gently and my jaw began to unclench. Mabel's neck relaxed and twice she set her chin on my shoulder before lifting her head up again, to be sure. And the blood flow returned to normal in my body and I felt sort of a warm flush roll over me as each of my muscles relaxed one by one. My breathing calmed and, several minutes later, I was able to close my eyes and try to sleep.

And then: CHA HA ROOF ROOF!

This time from the right side of the tent, maybe 30 or so feet away, but definitely closer than before, and the bear swatted and broke branches with loud snaps. Mabel spun around in the tent, almost standing straddle across my body, and my heart stopped again. This time, I knew it was certain: The bear would charge, and we would die. But again, nothing. Slowly, patiently, we grew accustomed again to the silence and the safety of the night and the soothing, repetitive cadence of the rain striking the rain fly. Five minutes passed, and then 7 minutes, and then 10.

And then: CHA HA ROOF HOOF ROOF HOOF.

Angry paws smacked the ground and snapped branches from the trees—the bear was behind us now. I clenched my white knuckles tightly around the can of bear spray. Mabel's eyes widened, scared and furious. She looked at me, and then back at the tent, like through the tent to the source of the sound, and then back at me, and then back and then back. Each time, I knew she was looking at me for direction or explanation. But I could neither comfort nor calm her. I could only lie there on my back waiting for inevitable death at the paws of a merciless bear. I hoped that it would get me first so that Mabel would have a chance to run away. I had no chance of defending myself against a rampaging bear, but my chances were better than Mabel's. Mabel could always find a new home with a new family—a better master, a better friend, who wouldn't take her on some fool's errand across the country. But, slowly, the calm returned.

And then: CHA HA ROOOOF.

Over and over again the bear threatened to charge the tent, each time working Mabel up into a greater and greater rage, and each time taking a year off my life for the fright. The bear seemed to be toying with us, like it had grown up watching those horrible 1980s horror movies where the killer is never quite seen, and never quite strikes, until you cannot take another second of suspense and only then does the killing start. I imagined that the bear might any minute call my cell phone and say "the bear is coming from inside tent".

I was nearly hyperventilating. My heart beat so hard and so fast, and there was so much tension and fear filling the tent, that anyone standing nearby, including the bear, could have counted my heart rate by the pulsing of the tent. The tent had turned into a heaving, lifelike pod of fear and death. On and on the bear threatened, and, with trembling fingers, I turned on my cell phone to text my friends and family.

"Bear in camp. I love you."

It was nearly midnight. The bear had been torturing us for almost two hours. The temperature continued to drop and the bear tormented us into the early morning hours. Again and again the bear threatened, then let us relax, then threatened again. And the bear circled closer to the tent with each threat—closer and closer with each bluffed charge.

Closer and closer.

Cha ha roof. Hoof. Haroof.

The bear circled us over and over again, sending Mabel spinning around in the tent to keep her eyes on the source of the sound. Then, calm. Then: Cha ha roof! This went on another two hours.

Then I remembered that I had brought several Snickers bars into the tent. Half from my own fear of the cold, and half from the urging of Long Island Paul, I had stocked my tent with fuel to help warm me through the cold night. It was nearly 2:00 a.m., and the bear would not give up and go away. On and on it threatened, driven by lust for human food that I had brought into the tent. And I had checked ahead of time—there were not supposed to be bears there. There were no bears there! But there we were. And I whispered an apology to Mabel, quietly, as if making any sound at all would further agitate the beast outside.

"I'm so sorry, Sweetie," I whispered. "I'm so sorry."

Closer. Closer.

The hair on Mabel's back and neck went up. Except for the pattering rain and my beating heart it was total silence. But Mabel's hair stood up, and her teeth began to bare, almost involuntarily in twitches. And she repositioned herself to squarely face the left side of the tent. Silence.

Mabel stared out with single purposed intensity; her hair bristled. My lesser human senses could not see or smell or hear, but Mabel knew that the bear had stopped negotiating. It was right outside the tent, but I could not hear it or see it. Silence.

Then, almost simultaneously, the bear huffed and smacked its paw beside the tent and Mabel, pushed beyond the limits of patience by animalistic fear, let loose a horrible, thunderous growl with her teeth bared fully—but without barking—and leapt across my supine body, snapping her jaws, gnashing and fighting with an enemy she could not see. She attacked so powerfully across my body that, when she hit the left side of the interior of the tent, we both went careening and rolling into a tangle of nylon and netting. Tent poles snapped. The netting and nylon of the tent ripped and pulled, and tent pegs pulled loose from the ground. I shouted what must have been a blood-curdling thing and, with the tent all mangled and torn, I was able to sit up, more or less, and fight to restrain Mabel.

But the bear was gone. In the melee, I think the bear may have swiped once or twice at or near the tent, but neither Mabel nor I were hurt. And I imagine the bear was scared to death—after four hours stalking the tent, the tent fought back. I pulled myself together and Mabel and I got free from the mangled tent. The gravity of the situation hit me immediately. It was 30 degrees and raining and we had no tent. The bear incident had been unsettling, of course, but we were now in a life or death situation.

It was 2:30 a.m. or so, 30 degrees out, there was a cold rain falling steadily, our shelter was destroyed, and somewhere out there in the shadows an angry and humbled bear stalked us. We were sitting on the ground, close together, in a mess of ripped and torn nylon and uprooted tent stakes. That was not a good situation. For a brief flash of time I think I was afraid of the situation, but I cannot be sure. As soon as any emotion passed through my mind, it was immediately gone and replaced with a single, all-consuming thought: Fire. In fact, I cannot really remember *doing* or *thinking* anything else for the next half an hour of that night. There must have been thoughts in my brain because there were signals sent out to my legs and to my hands to do this or that, or to move my body in this or that direction, and surely there were other thoughts in there like "It is really cold" and "I hope we don't die", but I cannot remember a single thought other than Fire. And it was not even the word—it was the idea. My mind centered on a sole notion, the idea of a fire. I know that I got out of the tent mess, but I cannot really remember doing it. And I know that I leashed Mabel under a picnic table out of the rain, but I cannot really remember doing it—I can remember only that it was done, and all the while my brain thought only "fire fire fire fire fire fire fire fire fire...."

The rain was steady and light, but not so light that it would be easy to start a fire. And it had rained all day, soaking every piece of wood in the area, from the small pieces I might use as kindling to the bigger fuel logs. I always carried a big bag of drier lint to use in a pinch as tinder and a tub of Vaseline to use as an accelerant. I must have taken those out of my bag, but I don't remember doing it. I had about 18 oz of gasoline, which is a great accelerant if you have the right sized kindling and logs to take the flame—I know I used all of that gasoline, but I hardly remember doing it. I struggled over the fire pit, burning Vaseline and lint and gasoline, but no wood would take a light. There were a lot of fallen, soaked branches laying about, and I spent at least a half an hour feathering branches out with my knife, exposing the drier wood inside. But that was wasted energy and wasted time, because there had been so much rain that the wood was all soaked through to the core. Even with the gasoline there was almost no hope of building a fire, and the longer I spent trying to build a fire, the colder and wetter I got.

So as suddenly as fire had overrun my brain, it was overrun by the idea of away. Just go, just get away. Get the Hell away and go, go, go. A single idea: Away.

I could have died from exposure without fire or shelter. Without a fire, there was nothing to keep that bear away. The bear would come back. He wasn't so afraid of Mabel or of me that he wouldn't come back for Snickers and ghee. The Beast was probably just out of my line of sight somewhere, probably as few as 80 or 100 feet away, crouching in the trees and surveying my campsite. Without a fire, it was death by cold or mauling by bear. We chose to get out and hike.

I packed up the site as well as I could with rapidly numbing hands and guided only by the faint white glow of the headlamp. Mabel sat patiently under the picnic table and tarp, and alternated between staring at me and glancing around the perimeter of the camp. Her ears perked the whole time. My hands hurt while I stuffed the sleeping bag deep into the bag, and they hurt when I tried to tie off stuff sacks and stuff them into the pack. And all the layers of clothes greatly impaired my range of motion but I thought that my core temperature more or less held steady.

I did a few things that, in retrospect, were probably great decisions but at the time I did without any conscious thought. With my pack stuffed to bursting, I unloaded our food and water on the picnic table. I removed the ghee from the food bag and set it on the picnic table. Of the four Snickers I had squirreled away with me in the tent, I quickly ate three. Then I spread a small handful of ghee on the picnic table, rubbing the butter fat into the wet wood. I opened a Snickers bar and set it at the head of the picnic table on that film of ghee. I had plenty of water—I think probably two gallons—and I drank as much of it as I could, then filled only my 20 oz water bottle and poured out the rest. The pack was noticeably lighter.

I unzipped the top of my rain jacket to let out perspiration and threw the pack on my back and then we were off into the blackness of the Towpath. It was about four in the morning, and we did not really know where we were heading. Mabel walked very close to my side, because my body and the pack deflected some of the rain and kept her a little drier than she otherwise would have been. But the Towpath was soaked with near-freezing puddles and more rain fell on us as we walked and I was worried for Mabel's safety. We walked as fast as we could, but with the cold and the darkness surrounding us we made slow time. The further we got from the camp the more my head opened up to what was going on around me, and then I worried that Mabel was in danger from the cold. I *knew* I was in danger, but that didn't concern me at the time. We hung right onto a paved county road in the middle of nowhere and hoped for a ride. But there was no traffic at all at that hour, and only later as the Sun came up did some cars speed by us, spitting up rooster tails of dirty water that splashed all over us. We hiked on. My vent-less rain jacket heated up like a sauna and my sweat soaked through all several layers of tops under the plastic shell. My teeth chattered and my hands went numb. Mabel trudged on, and tried to pull me ever faster and faster toward Poolesville. Very few cars passed us on the road into Poolesville, and the few that did pass us did not slow down, much less stop. I wondered, as I walked, how Long Island Paul was doing with his skinless feet.

We entered Poolesville on a wide residential street. The rain still fell lightly, and so I could not get my cell phone out to check the map and find out where exactly we were heading. Getting into a town is only part of the problem, because then you have to know where something/anything is. Luckily, the road emptied us out at a T-intersection into the parking lot of a grocery store and a CVS pharmacy. We headed straight for the CVS. I tied Mabel up to the pack and petted her on the head. Her whole body was wet and shaking from the cold, and I went quickly into the CVS to get something warm to drink and something to dry Mabel off with. But the CVS did not have coffee or a microwave or anything hot to drink, so I got a bottle of milk; the CVS didn't have any towels, oddly, so I got three t-shirts on sale for about $10 to dry Mabel. At the register, the cashier looked at me with horror in her eyes and I knew that I didn't look good. My nose was discolored, and there were probably icicles in my beard, and my face was a cold, ashen, pale hue.

"Are you ok?"

"I think so," I said. "My dog is cold."

"What happened?" she asked. I was nervous about answering. Bear encounters are rare, and from my research ahead of time I had been under the impression that there were no bears that far south on the Canal. But I chewed on my lip and looked her in the eyes, and said:

"There was a bear in our camp?" I said, with a questioning tone, not sure if she would believe me or if I should even believe myself. "My dog and I are hiking on the Canal."

"Oh my!" she said. "How big?"

"It looked like a thousand pounds," I said. "So maybe 200."

"Young one," she said.

"It was small."

"Still a bear," she said. She put my purchases in a bag, and my hands could hardly close down around the handles of the plastic bag. "The thing about a small bear is that it is a bear."

"Hey," she said as I began to walk away from the counter. "My husband runs the restaurant in town. They don't open until 11, but he's down there getting ready for the day. I'll call him. You head up there and he'll let you in to get warm in their atrium."

"Seriously?"

"I think you should," she said, and was already dialing the number. "You need to get a hot cup of coffee and warm up."

I went outside and dried Mabel off with the t-shirts, but she still shivered. We were only a few blocks from the restaurant, though, so I tossed the pack back on and we hiked toward Bassett's restaurant in Poolesville, Maryland. I found a dumpster and threw away the tent and some other ruined equipment and cursed it all.

The manager met us at the door and ushered us in through the dining room and into the atrium on the side of the building. We talked briefly, and although he was a nice and genuine fellow who might have wanted to talk more about the hike, he was busy getting his restaurant ready for the day so he left us in the heated atrium. I drank several cups of coffee and petted Mabel. As the color and warmth started to build back up in my hands and face, I took stock of our position.

We were not really in a good place. We had no shelter, and the rain didn't seem to be letting up. The cold and rain had chilled us to the bone that morning, and we really needed to warm up—and that kind of warming up takes a while. Everything I owned that hadn't been in a dry-sack was soaked. And, to repeat, we had no shelter. The manager said I could plug my phone in, so I did and looked for the nearest place to get a new tent. The nearest outfitter was in Harper's Ferry, about 30 miles away, two days' hike from Poolesville along the Canal. We had a tarp, which we could use as shelter in a pinch, but with the ground as soaked as it was and with the temperatures as low as they were, it wasn't possible for us to hike safely without a tent.

I talked with the manager about bumming a ride from someone. Our chances were pretty slim. Not too many people would head for Harper's Ferry, he said, and it would take a long time to find a ride, probably too long for me to hang around in his parking lot.

"Nothing I'd like more than to give you a ride, or have my wife give you a ride, but we're swamped today. I don't know anyone who is free today!"

"That's ok," I said. "You have both been really kind."

"We didn't want you to die on the side of the road," he said. "You two aren't in very good shape. You should get into Harper's Ferry and get warmed up. Get a motel room. Do you have money for a room?"

"I do," I said.

"Well, I think you ought to get a cab. There's a cab company that will come out here."

I called the cab company and had to explain the situation—I'm a guy, with a dog, and a pack full of equipment, and I need a ride. The operator told me it was up to the driver as to whether a dog could come along, and shortly thereafter a cab driver called me and asked me, in his thick South Asian accent, whether my dog was well behaved.

"She hardly moves," I said. "She is awful tired right now."

We made it to Harper's Ferry by noon, and checked into a motel on the south side of the town, about two miles away from the Outfitter's at Harper's Ferry, which is where I would need to shop for new supplies. When we walked into our new room, Mabel went crazy, running in circles and jumping from one bed to the other. I stripped off six layers of wet clothing until I was naked and felt light and cold and clammy. I ran a warm bath, careful to not let it get hot, but even lukewarm water hurt against all my cold skin when I got into the bathtub. I lay there for about an hour, periodically adding warmer and warmer water until I started to feel normal again. Mabel waited patiently on the carpet outside the bathroom door, staring at me as I soaked. After a little over an hour in the bath, I got out and toweled off, then strung out all my equipment and clothes all over the room so that it would all dry out as fast as possible, then I sat down on the bed with my phone to call my friends and loved ones to tell them I was ok. But I was asleep before I made a call, and didn't wake up until late that night.

BOOK II: FEEL THE SELFISH FURY (B)
THEY TALK OF SOME STRICT TESTING OF US.

The gunners hit it hard when finals came around—harder than you can imagine unless you have been to law school. The singular focus on which law students train their considerable energies is a thing of wonder. In the two or three weeks before finals, law students vanished into mysterious internal places. Students were not at the BLB, not at the coffee shop, and sometimes not at home. Folks materialized to ask me questions at the Java House and then slinked back into shadowy nothing. Folks who I'd been hanging around with didn't return phone calls until they were freaking out and needed someone to talk with. I did the same thing.

Two weeks before the first finals week, it got cold and I drove to the Java House instead of walking. It snowed about three inches that morning, and my truck was worthless in the snow. I lived at the top of two hills, so I couldn't drive it home for the snow! A young lady who worked at the Java House offered to let me park in her driveway behind her apartment downtown and wait out the snow, and I did. Then I forgot where she lived. And so over the next few days it was uncomfortable every time I saw her— she would say something about how the truck wasn't a problem and I could leave it there for as long as I wanted, and I would say I was about to come and get it. But I had no idea where it was.

And I didn't care.

All I cared about was the Restatement (Second) of Contracts and the Uniform Commercial Code. I cared only about the elements of 1st degree murder, the elements of the tort of negligence. I cared deeply about the theoretical standard of care that a person owes to a stranger (but I didn't seem to care too much about that in practice). What I cared about was the Rule Against Perpetuities. I cared about the calculation of tort damages in accordance with the Coase Theorem. That was all I *could* care about, because the alternative was too horrible to consider. The alternative was to not do absolutely everything in my power to succeed at the law school game, to not do everything in my power to put me on a road to some sort of financial success to pay back my student loans. The alternative was failure.

And this is a conundrum of legal training: They convinced me (or I convinced myself) that no word, no idea, no concept in the world has a singular meaning, they trained me to argue that black is white and rich is poor, they developed in me the analytical tools I need to redefine the entire world for the convenience and needs of a client. But not with failure. And not with success. Success and failure are monolithic, and they cannot be redefined. If you succeed, you will have a great life. If you fail, you are indentured to your student loan overlords for the next 80 years and you end up chasing ambulances in Nowhereseville, Anystate, population You. I learned that there is *no* single truth anywhere, ever, at all, except the truth of success and failure. I was trained that *my life* is black and white, and yours is not.

We had our last small section Property I class on the last Friday of the semester. Now, almost every law school has a reading week before finals, a week in which there is no class so students can prep for finals. Iowa, on the other hand, spreads the exams out over two weeks and does not give a reading week. Professor Traurig closed our last Property class with a little pep talk about finals.

"Now, I know you all are probably freaking out," she said. "But don't. You know this. You all have your outlines, you know the material, and you have reading week."

"We don't have a reading week," I said.

"And you have a reading weekend," she said, without missing a beat. There were rounds of nervous laughter.

But most of us had probably already been spending time as if it were a reading week. In the two or three weeks before finals, people skipped classes because their time was better spent studying than wasting an hour on a lecture. The students who "got it" understood how much there was to learn and to apply on each exam and, more importantly, they *understood* what the forced curve could mean: It could mean the *potentially* arbitrary elevation of one exam over another, it could potentially open or potentially close the doors to future employment. It meant there was a chance that one single sentence on one archaic issue or another may cost you an A+, may cost you an A, may cost you a job and a career. And for the law student, the only rational response to that situation is to study, study, study. Harder. Longer. Faster. More efficiently. All day. All night. All the time if you have to. Because "arbitrary" cannot exist. There is no "arbitrary". There are rules and there is order and there is a process to things. Process.

PROCESS.

There is a process!

Look at these rules. Look at this system of rules for ordering the goings-on of Mankind. My God, you tell yourself, this has been going on for 10,000 years! Longer! I am a point on a line of men and women that stretches from this point in time back to the first dispute settled not by sheer force but by an outside arbiter. What are these 10 or 20 thousand years worth if not the death of the arbitrary? I *am* a part of the Anglo-Celtic-American legal system—and there is nothing arbitrary about it. I have to study! That's all. Nothing is arbitrary. And *even if it is arbitrary* in general, it won't be arbitrary for me! Let those other sons of bitches get lucky on their exam or get unlucky. Won't be like that for me. I will know everything in here. I will kill that fucking curve, and destroy those fools.

I was so lost.

After the last final of each semester students ran, sometimes *actually* ran, away from the BLB to their homes and cried or danced or drank or whatever it was they liked to do. Some of us loaded our cars to get the hell out of town, often back to see our parents and family, and some of us went out one last time for an end of the semester bash. I always went out one last time and then ran home to my family because I had not seen them or talked to them in quite a while and because I was sick to death of law students. It's like everything in your mind is telling you "Away! Away!".

BOOK I: THE MOMENTS THAT TURN US (B)(ii)
MYSELF WITH YESTERDAY'S SEV'N THOUSAND YEARS.

We were several days in a motel on the outskirts of Harper's Ferry under appalling weather, cold and rainy. I decided that we needed some ground rules, or "rules of engagement". I decided that we would not walk if it was 45 degrees or colder with a forecast of rain, or if it was colder than 40 degrees with or without rain in the forecast. I could always put on more layers, or lay up in the sleeping bag if it got dangerously cold. But I felt that the cold and rain were too dangerous for Mabel; I could not keep her dry. So we were stuck there in Harper's Ferry for a few days waiting for the rain to clear and the Sun to come out.

I reorganized my pack during that time. Through trial and error, I found better ways to organize my equipment so that the pack would be better balanced and so I would have easier access to often used items. Most importantly, I created a "tent bag", which contained the minimum essentials I would need through the night so that I could pitch the tent and dive in it with only one bag of essentials: flashlight, toilet paper, fire starter, length of twine, water purification tabs, bear spray.

That was the first time on the trip that I felt lonely. I had felt alone plenty of times, but I began to feel lonely in Harper's Ferry. There's a difference between loneliness and aloneness. Aloneness is being alone, but loneliness is a longing to not be alone. Isra had left me, I knew no one for hundreds of miles, and all of my friends were attorneys who couldn't stop their day and talk to me on the phone. It was clear that many of my old friendships and relationships in the legal world were dying of attrition—out of sight and out of mind. If Mabel and I failed, I knew that those attorneys I had known would have nothing to do with me. We hung around in the motel watching TV and scribbling nonsense into my travel journal. There were these "admirers", or whatever they should be called, who had heard about the Walk and who had sent me emails. So I answered those, and started email conversations with strangers.

A girl named Heidi, who I had met once at a party and who had gone to high school with an ex-colleague of mine, emailed me and asked about hiking across Indiana with me. I said "yes" immediately. But for the most part I was alone with Mabel in an awful motel room. I wasn't just alone. I was lonely.

On the second day in Harper's Ferry, we walked the couple of miles into town to the Outfitter's at Harper's Ferry. The owner, Laura, worked the shop that day and she was a lot of help to me. She is an energetic woman, healthy and slim and always smiling. She beamed when I told her that we were on the ADT trying to go all the way across the country.

"Oh my, the ADT! You have to sign in to my book! Do you know Jack?"

Laura keeps a book of thru-hikers' signatures, and a lot of thru-hikers come through Harper's Ferry. The Outfitter's is located at the halfway point on the Appalachian Trail and at what I would guess is the most common drop out point on the ADT. I told Laura about my pack, what I was carrying, and she took me into the big room upstairs to look at stoves and rain gear. She asked me again:

"Do you know Jack?"

My phone rang, and it was Jack Planck. I had never spoken with Jack before, but I knew him a little by email. Jack had started the ADT about 2.5 weeks before me from Cape Henlopen and was already pretty far ahead of me due primarily to the bad weather and setbacks that Mabel and I had already run into.

"You won't believe this," I said to him, "but I am at the Outfitter's and Laura *just now* asked me about you. Let me call you back when I get done getting a tent and stuff."

"A tent?" he asked.

"Yup. My tent was destroyed. Bear incident."

"I know, Dude! That's why I called, because I saw it on Twitter. I *have* to hear about it. Make sure to get a freestanding tent."

I told Laura that Jack had called, and she smiled.

"How is he doing?"

"I don't know," I said. "He sounds good. He's doing well."

"Good," she said. "He was not doing well when he came through here. He had foot problems all the way from Delaware...blisters...and he just wasn't in a clear frame of mind; he wasn't in a good place, so I didn't think he would make it...not like you: You're all smiles, aren't you?"

"The whole thing is funny," I said. "I'm feeling pretty good, but I'm mostly amused."

"What is funny?"

"The whole thing," I said. "The whole thing."

I picked out new gear with Laura's help. It was the first real assistance I had taken regarding the hike. First, I got an alcohol stove—basically a very small metal pot that you pour denatured alcohol into and light the alcohol. The stove weighed next to nothing and I could pick up fuel in almost any gas station. The best fuel to use is HEET in the yellow bottle, or any other non-branded fuel line anti-freeze in yellow bottles. Red bottle will work, too, or even rubbing alcohol, but both have a higher water content and will burn cooler and create a lot more soot on your equipment. The other weight advantage of the alcohol stove is that you can carry denatured alcohol in any plastic bottle, but gasoline must be carried in heavier metal containers. Laura gave me a used 24 oz Coke bottle filled with denatured alcohol.

"If you are cooking for a lot of people," she said, "or if you are way up in the mountains or need to melt snow for water, then stick with the MSR stove. But for what you are doing right now, the alcohol stove is better."

"I tried to make one," I said. "Before the trip, I tried to make an alcohol stove out of soda cans."

"Yeah. You can do that, but...."

"Exactly," I said. "It doesn't work that well and isn't very strong."

I got rain gear, which I had learned the hard way was something you shouldn't skimp on. I got a bright yellow rain jacket because we would be spending so much of our time near highways. The jacket was vented, but even with the vents, Laura warned me, "this thing will *stink* before too long". I also picked up a few pairs of socks because it never hurts to have clean, warm socks.

Laura strongly advised me to get the Big Agnes Fly Creek 2, which she said is *by far* the most popular tent on the Appalachian Trail. The Fly Creek 2 is a two-person tent, but it would be pretty cramped for two people. It is easy to set up and it is freestanding. A freestanding tent can be set up anywhere without staking the tent out. My other tent, by comparison, would not stand up if it could not be staked out. If you find yourself needing to set up a camp on a slab of concrete or in gravelly or rocky ground, you can lose a lot of time trying to stake out a tent—or you could be unable to stake it out at all—so the freestanding Big Agnes was a big improvement. Most importantly about the Big Agnes, it weighed two pounds 10 oz. That meant weight savings of a little over two pounds, and trimming pack weight is key to long distance hiking. The price tag on the Big Agnes was pretty steep, but the new tent would be my home for the next few months. So I bit the bullet and spent about $500 at the Outfitter's.

In all, I got a new tent, some socks, a new rain jacket, an alcohol stove, and a bear bag to hang my food and scented items in. It was a good day for Laura at the Outfitter's at Harper's Ferry.

When we started our walk back up the hill through quaint Harper's Ferry, I talked on the phone with Jack Planck for about two hours. He was almost to Ohio. We talked about his foot problems, which had been pretty painful he said, but he thought Laura had maybe exaggerated about how badly he'd suffered. He had done some research on blistering, and apparently there are people who tend not to blister; rather, their skin tears off and cuts. I told him that I might be that type, as I had very few blisters. His closest call so far had been falling pretty hard on a bridge outside a little West Virginia town.

"I was *so* embarrassed, Man!" he said. "These people were looking at me, and thinking 'Who the hell is this guy?' You know?"

"I do," I said. "I know what it is like."

We stopped on the front step of the headquarters of the Appalachian Trail Society so that I could focus on talking with Jack. He is a lot younger than I am, and we had never talked before, but we talked like old friends. It was the first time that either of us had talked to a fellow thru-hiker, and even though neither of us was very far along on the trip, we both had been affected by it already. We talked about the weather and the loneliness, how the idea of a cold Coke could get you through another mile and how an actual Snickers bar could get you through three hours of walking. We talked about girlfriends; his had left him, too. He warned me that he thought I could not do some portions of West Virginia safely, not with a dog—he told me there were mountain descents that had been unsafe for him even without a dog. We talked about a thousand things that I can't even remember now. We just talked.

I wished him luck and told him I was jealous of his progress, but he assured me I would catch him at any time. He was probably three weeks ahead of me. But it was clear to both of us at that time that I would be doing longer days than he would. That turned out to be sort of true, but it also turned out not to matter because of the amount of zero days we took.

We got off the phone when Jack was about to get back on the road—he was walking under good weather, unlike Mabel and me, and his lunch break was over. We headed back to the motel and Mabel sniffed around as we walked. It was another cold day, but it would have been a good enough hiking day had I not had errands. That was frustrating because we wanted to get back on the road. The conversation I'd had with Jack was a nice change, but it got me thinking about things. It dawned on me that very few people would ever be able to understand what I was doing, and even fewer would ever understand the experience. Not like Jack, who already understood and just *knew*. It struck me that, no matter how this walk turned out, people would talk to me about it and think "oh, what a great adventure" or "that sounds like so much *fun!*" and they would never be able to understand what it was really like. And it struck me that I was on the front-end of a very lonely few months.

"Come on, Mabes," I said. "We have to get going or else we'll just stop and die. Ohio, Mabel. We have to get to Ohio."

BOOK II: FEEL THE SELFISH FURY (B)(i)
WHAT LAMP HAD DESTINY TO GUIDE HER LITTLE CHILDREN?

The stress of first semester finals never went away because we started hustling for jobs as soon as our grades were in. We were about to become "rising 2Ls" and most of us wanted a paid first year summer associate position with a firm. The money was good if you could land a summer gig, but firms rarely hire rising 2Ls for paid positions. We all put probably 30 or 40 hours into paper-thin resumes awash with trite phrases designed to make us sound somehow qualified for something we were nowhere near qualified for. The search for a paid first summer internship was largely an exercise in understanding failure. But there in the middle of it all was one of the few magical moments of my law school career.

I was running late for an interview in the basement of the BLB and had forgotten completely which firm I was even supposed to be interviewing with. I stopped by the library to review the interview schedule. My resume and transcripts laid exposed at my side as I checked the schedule. Fellow student Adam Zimmerman stopped to chat with me. He glanced around and made some comment to me about hanging out or the canoe trip or something, but he hurried off when he realized I was busy. I was quickly off to the interview. He sent me an email later that day. I am paraphrasing, but it read something like this:

> "Tyler, I really should apologize. When I stopped by to talk with you today, your resume was lying out, and I saw your GPA. Maybe you didn't want people to see that. I don't think I looked at it on purpose, but I saw it. Maybe I did look at it on purpose. Anyway, congratulations on a great first semester. I am really sorry. Adam."

That was the single most stand-up action I saw in law school. Zimerman had come along on the canoe trip, and we'd bought each other a drink from time-to-time, but we hadn't really "bonded". I think we rather did bond at that moment, and we were friends after that. Little gestures like that mean a lot to people when those gestures are performed in ridiculous environments. I knew he was for real after that, and it's hard to be sure with most law students whether they are for real or not.

I got a callback for a summer position in Madison, Wisconsin that season and then maybe I did a stand-up thing, too. I was excited to interview with a leading Madison firm, and two of my classmates got callbacks there, too—Mike, and Amrita. Amrita, however, had no car and no way to get to Madison for the interview; she wasn't too keen on being a firm lawyer anyway, and had decided not to go. "Well, that's silly," I said. We were standing together outside the BLB with a couple of other law students. "You should at least *go*. See if they can schedule our interviews on the same day and you can ride with me." It hadn't crossed her mind that she could get a ride, but she agreed it was a good idea. When she left, another student, whose name I don't recall, so we'll call him Scott Howard, stared at me with a look of horror on his face.

"What?" I asked.

"You're a fucking idiot," Scott Howard said. "How many jobs do you think that firm is going to give out? One? Two?"

"Probably a couple," I said. "Maybe just one 1L summer position, though. I'd bet just one."

"So the less competition, the better. You shouldn't give her a ride."

So, I guess, on one hand you've got stand up guys like Zimerman and on the other you've got cutthroat guys like Scott Howard.

There I was.

Somewhere in the middle, I guess.

BOOK I: THE MOMENTS THAT TURN US (B)(iii)(a)
LEAVE THE WISE TO WRANGLE.

We hit the Canal again after Harper's Ferry. The day was warmer and we were in a fairly heavily trafficked area of the Canal so there were many more people to see briefly and to talk with even more briefly. I was hyper-aware of everyone and I felt a bit like someone was following me. I pulled a few lengths off the Towpath and cowered beside trees when we took our breaks. I constantly looked behind me to see who was following me. Almost always the answer was "no one". Still, I felt pursued. It was probably nerves. I thought back to that conversation that Allen Ellis had always tried to start at our Farmers' Lunch at Sidley: "Do you feel like you succeeded at law school and came to a big firm like this because you are chasing something or because you are running from something?" In between measuring my breaths against the rhythm of my strides and restraining Mabel from chasing after a deer or a turkey, I thought: "Am I chasing or am I fleeing?"

And it was an appropriate thought to have, because outside of Harper's Ferry I met a day-hiker—a lovely lady about 50 years old who was out walking quickly and pumping her arms up and down.

"Where are you headed with all that stuff?" she said through a big, toothy grin.

"California."

She stopped to talk with us, but for some reason I didn't slow down. Instead, I just looked at her and walked on.

"Why?" she called out. And I exhaled deeply because I was sick to death of that question.

"Heartbreak," I said.

"Are you leaving it or headed for it?" she asked.

"Both," I muttered. She was probably already too far behind me to hear the frustration in my voice.

The first night back on the Canal we camped about 15 miles up from Harper's Ferry, and the first thing I did after I pitched the tent and got dinner going, was to pack all of my scented items—food and toiletries—into the bear bag and hang it 300 yards up the Towpath. An old man rode by on a bicycle as I was hanging the bear bag.

"Wastin' your time," he called out, then slowed and almost stopped beside me. The bicycle wobbled because he slowed so dramatically.

"Huh?"

"Wastin' your time. Ain't no bears here."

"My dog and I had a bear in camp just a few nights ago down by Poolesville," I said.

"Well, yeah, they got one down there," he answered. He rode off and I secured the bear bag.

The difference between 10 bears and 11 bears is a *hell of a lot smaller* than the difference between zero bears and one bear.[6] Hanging food and toiletries in a bear bag is best practice. Black bears are, or should be, little threat to humans. They are generally herbivores and very rarely do they instigate any problems with people. Bears become "problem bears" because lazy, inconsiderate people, or people who don't know better, leave food and trash around. Black bears love trash. That is just how they roll. It doesn't take very many half-eaten bags of Cheetos in fire rings or friendly morons tossing Twinkies to bears at a trash dump before an otherwise healthy and safe black bear loses its innate fear of humans. When *that* happens, then you have a problem bear that might kill or maul a person. That's the same reason why some dogs become problems: because humans abuse and/or mistreat them. That is the same reason why some humans become problems.

The next day on the Canal, I met a man wearing a hiking kilt and asked him about it. (Chafing was a problem for me and was getting to a point where walking was very painful, and I thought that a kilt might help.) This

---

[6] Author's Note: I tweeted this conversation, and Elie Mystal from www.abovethelaw.com sent me an email saying, essentially, that the difference between 10 bears and 11 bears is a hell of a lot smaller than the difference between zero bears and 1 bear. I was already thinkin' it, but I should give him some credit for being funny.

guy's trail name was The Kilted Hiker. We discussed hiking kilts and some of his experiences hiking in Yosemite. I told him about the bear incident.

"Where was that?"

"Down by Poolesville," I said.

"Ah! That guy. That's a known bear," he said. The idea of a "Known Bear" bothered me. "There's a Zen Buddhist retreat over there that sits on about 80 acres, I think. Maybe less, maybe more. And that bear hangs around with the Buddhists. Eats their garbage, walks around the edge of their land."

"So he's a 'known bear'?"

"Yeah. People know him," the Kilted Hiker said.

"That's not good."

"No, it isn't. But the Buddhists are a peaceful crew, I think."

The Kilted Hiker was a nice fellow, and I enjoyed his stories about Yosemite. He got stuck in the snow one time in Yosemite and lost the trail, had to spend two nights out there alone, and when he finally found the trail again he discovered that he had been camping on a sheet of ice over a small pond about 10 feet away from the trail. He made it out alive, though, and that's what counts.

"You don't have a trail name?" the Kilted Hiker asked me.

"Nope. Just my regular name," I said.

"You'll probably get one," he said. "If you hike long enough, someone will give you a trail name and it will just stick. Even if you don't like it."

The rest of the Canal was an awful experience. It rained almost every day, with only a few hours of decent weather in the afternoons. The Canal has water pumps at every campsite, but the handles on the pumps are removed during the winter and they had not been put back yet. Republicans in Congress pushed the government to the brink of shut down—as they had done in the 1990s—and so it looked as though the water pumps might never be turned on. Federal employees are the folks who turn the pumps on. So we periodically had to hike off the trail for a few miles to get to a town to re-supply with water because I didn't want to drink from the Potomac unless I had to, even though I carried a Katadyn water filter. I had to carry much more water at all times than I would have liked because I did not have steady access to fresh water.

We saw towns like Brunswick and Antietam, site of the bloody Civil war battle, and we saw homes and bars flying Confederate flags. We stopped at a pub where a sign behind the bar referred to President Obama as a "nigger". It was a bit shocking, I guess, even though Confederate flags and such were not that abnormal where I grew up. I thought about it like this: Imagine five people out hiking together and they desperately need to get about 30 miles down the trail, but one of the hikers is very slow and lags behind. The one that lags will be the loudest, always shouting "Wait up! Don't leave me behind!" That's the Confederate Flag. And, I imagine, one day that will be the U.S. Flag.

We met few hikers along the way, and were soaked and cold most of the time. It was not so cold that I felt we were in danger, most times, but it was uncomfortable and the weather slowed us down considerably. Everything was damp when we camped. The ground was damp and the fallen wood was damp, and my socks were damp and everything I pulled from my pack was damp. I sometimes had to stop to build fires to warm my feet and dry my socks. I stored my clothes in a dry sack, but dry sacks are not 100% waterproof. Moreover, once water gets in there, it ain't coming out. One wet sock in my dry sack and then all my clothes became moist and mildewed in the pack. But we kept going, Mabel happy and prancing, and me with my head hidden in the yellow hood of my rain jacket. We walked by Dargan and Mercersville, and all the other little towns along the Canal. We stopped at locks and looked with awe at how much manpower must have been wasted on this failed Canal. We talked to a few day-hikers when the weather was good, and we asked them for more information on the weather. With all the rain, it began to feel like we were headed into something horrible.

I fought to keep Isra out of my thoughts.

My beard grew longer.

And we left the Canal to get food and water and to see the little towns along the Canal. I began to carry a lot of water, sometimes four gallons, because I knew a storm was coming. The last thing I wanted was to be stuck without water and to have to drink filtered water out of the Potomac River. But we ran out of water only once.

One day, as we headed up the Canal, the people I saw began to say things like: "Thru-hiking this thing? There's a storm coming!" or "You ready for the rain?"

We were not ready for the storm when it came. I checked the forecast on my phone and it was grim. It called for a great deal of rain and storms, chilly but not cold temperatures. That night was supposed to be cold and rainy, but the next night there was a real storm coming. A "be careful" storm. A "get in the basement" storm. Mabel was doing fine on food, but I didn't have much left except protein bars—it's a big mistake to eat a protein-rich diet without a high water intake. Seriously, do not eat a protein rich diet without sufficient water intake. We were doing well on water, but not well enough to outlast a four-day storm. We were too far away from town to hike out before the storm hit that night. So we sped up and pushed on to make the next campsite. Clouds welled, and my demeanor changed. We met a man running on the Canal and he stopped to talk to us.

"Seriously? All the way to California?"

"Yeah," I said. "But this is going to be a tough week with this storm coming on."

"Do you have everything you need?"

"Running low on food, but we should be fine."

"Here," he said, and gave me several candies and a few energy bars. "I have to carry this stuff because I'm diabetic." I asked him several times if he was sure about giving me the candies, but he said that he was almost done with his run and he had plenty of everything he needed. I took the candies and the energy bars and thanked him.

Later, I ran into a group of men working on the Canal with a large earth-moving machine. Men stood around in yellow vests, too, all part of the bicycle patrol of volunteers who monitor, maintain, and clean the Towpath.

I spoke at length with a couple of them, and they expressed some concern about my well being. I promised them that we would be fine, but they were nervous, so they gave me an apple and several different kinds of energy bars. I ate the apple as soon as we were out of sight of the men, and it was one of the best apples I've ever eaten.

My phone lost service a few miles before we camped. There are stretches on the Canal where my cell signal would not travel over or around the steep ridges. I was out of contact with everyone in the world by the time we found a spot to dig in. The rain was on its way and the wind picked up. I rushed to set up the tent and to tarp over some of my equipment. I pitched my tent on a more-or-less flat patch, which was not ideal. But I took extra time to check the trees above us—you should never camp under dead or dying trees with weak branches that might break in the wind and come crashing down on you in your sleep.

I double bagged my food to hang in a nearby tree because the bear bag was not waterproof. We didn't have access to a sheltered picnic table, so a lot of my equipment had to come in the tent with me. It was a tight fit in the tent when we climbed in at one of the last campsites before the famous Paw Paw Tunnel shortly before the storm hit. I believe we were in camp about 4:30 in the afternoon and the rain started shortly after that.

I was physically tired and in pain in most of my joints, even though I was only a few hundred miles into the trip. Most of my clothes and supplies were damp. It was cold. The tent was so crowded that we had little room to move around inside, although I could sit up a bit. We had two gallons of water beside the tent, but were pretty low on food. Most importantly, I had no iPod, no books except the *Rubaiyat*, no Kindle, and my phone didn't have service. When we climbed into the tent that night, not really tired and a bit revved up by the worry of the oncoming storm, it hit me that I would have a hell of a time keeping myself occupied if the rain came and stayed.

And the rain came. It drizzled at first, then poured a steady rain as the temperature fell. Drops of rain hit the rain fly like individual drum strikes in a non-stop roll. Mabel and I cuddled up in the tent and I tried to sleep. I must have fallen asleep because I woke up about three hours later and the rain still fell. I must have fallen asleep again, because I woke up three hours later and the rain still fell. I continued this routine all through the night until I woke up the next morning to a Sunless world of continual rain. And we lay there in the tent; every now and again unzipping part of the rain fly to peek out into the world and verify that, yes, the rain was still falling.

Rain fell all the next day. There were brief breaks when the rain would slow but not stop, and I would let Mabel out or I would sort of slither out of the tent and we would relieve ourselves, and then huddle back into the tent again, always hiding from the rain. I had nothing to do but to listen to the rain and to try to occupy my thoughts. I stared into the stitching of the tent and out at the few blades of grass I could see outside the tent and under the rain fly's vestibule. Mabel repositioned herself on my feet or my legs. I breathed.

On it went through the day and into night, but no thunderous storm came, despite the forecast. We lay there hiding. Not eating. Not drinking enough. We hid in the loneliness and aloneness of the tent. There was no one else in the entire world in those days. No one. In. The. Entire. World. I counted minutes and seconds and counted in an older unit of time that they used to measure time before someone invented clocks. I struggled and fought to *sleep* but I couldn't sleep and eventually I became unsure of whether I was asleep or awake. Then, late the next night or the next (I couldn't be sure of time anymore), the storm came.

The wind tore across the ridge all through the night. Like a freight train, or a wave of traffic on the freeway. Gusts of wind came screaming from a mile away down the ridge, louder and louder until they were almost on top of us and then directly over us, and then they would speed away along the ridge. Our tent hardly moved in the wind because we'd pitched in the lee of the ridge and the tent angled into the wind that screamed down the ridge. The storm raged, deafening and intense. It would have taken only one gust to make it over that ridge and to run instead along the Potomac and Mabel and I would have been in trouble. The Big Agnes, as stout and strong as she was, would not hold up to a wind like that. Rain fell all through the night and the next morning and the wind picked up and fell away, and all through the day again it rained and the wind blew, and we lay there. I lay there so long that my lower back hurt and I was unsure whether I was awake or asleep or whether I was alive or dead. It was so dark and overcast outside, with the clouds hung so low, and the world was silent except for that howling wind, that I thought maybe Hell was real and I was in it.

It was the closest I have ever come (and hopefully will ever come) to solitary confinement. Twice on the Canal I was rained into a tent for a stretch of at least three days. It was an inhuman existence. Solitary confinement is not a *human* punishment.

There was a brief break in the rain around five o'clock one day, but it was still overcast and misting and cold. We leaned out of the tent at this chance and found ourselves being flanked by a group of maybe 30 Boy Scouts and their troop leaders coming down the Canal from the other direction. They were loud when they set up their camp about 300 yards from me. Pretty soon a bunch of Boy Scouts came over to my fire ring to try to start a fire with wet wood. They probably get a badge for that or something. The Boy Scouts lost focus and instead took turns shooting fire accelerant onto a burning stick and laughing at the big flame it produced. Thankfully, as the boys lost their focus on the task at hand, their troop leader fellows came over and stood beside them drinking coffee and offering suggestions to them on fire starting.

I could no longer stay in the tent.

We got out and I spoke with the troop leaders a bit. They liked hearing about my trip so far. They were impressed that I would do such a thing and asked if I would talk to their Boy Scouts about it when I was done, but I told them that I wouldn't be back, maybe ever. We traded tips on warm weather clothes and I explained to one little fat kid how important it was to keep your clothes dry. He went back to his tent and changed into dry clothes and immediately started having a better time. The Boy Scout leaders had heard that another big storm was coming but were pretty sure they'd missed the worst of it.

"I know," I said. "I was shooting for the Paw Paw Tunnel the other day. Thought I would stay in there away from the storm."

"That's good thinkin'," the man said. "You're about a half a mile from it."

"I know," I said. "But it got late...this was about three days ago? Maybe four? Maybe, I've lost track. I've been in that tent since then."

"You've been in there for four days?" he asked.

"I think so," I said. "I'm pretty hungry."

The storm returned, though not so strong, and they herded the Boy Scouts back to their side of the campground. None of them had successfully started a fire. We retired again to the tent, but I realized that we were out of water. The howling wind on the ridge was immense, and I imagine those boys were quite scared. I would have been, too, if I cared at all whether I lived or died. The storm subsided some around four in the morning, and I walked down to the Potomac with my water filter and filled a gallon jug with water. I drank quite a bit of it directly and then refilled what I had taken. That moment, and once again the next day, would be the only times I used my water filter on the trip and the only times I drank water from natural sources. The water did not taste good, but it was cold and wet and I was very thirsty.

The Boy Scouts packed and left the next morning as I lay in the tent, listening to them laugh. I packed and we were on our way, but my legs and back were stiff and hurt a great deal and I was hungry. We made it only to the Paw Paw Tunnel before I realized that my feet hurt from being cold and wet rather than from use. So we holed up in the tunnel and built a fire to warm my feet and dry my socks. It was no easy task to get the fire going, and we lost a lot of the day and ended up staying in the Tunnel that night. It was creepy in that dark, dripping tunnel all night long.

I was hunched over on a tarp and in a sleeping bag in the tunnel with a tiny little fire burning. My hair and my long beard were matted together. My clothes were dirty—my convertible pants had been off-white when I got them, but by that time they were stained with a million streaks of dirt and soot and clean lines ran through those stains where my sweat had run. My face was dirty and my fingernails were ringed in black. I smelled like sweat and camp smoke and wet dog and bad food.

And I slept in a tunnel.

We woke the next day and hiked out off the Canal and into Paw Paw, West Virginia. I got cell service again a ways up the Canal and had about 35 voice messages. They were mostly from my mother. I found out that the storm we had been in had produced tornadoes south of us in North Carolina, one of which had killed eight people in Raleigh.

I got a good meal and we got set up with more clean water and then headed back onto the Canal. We were close to finishing the Canal and it felt like it had been a harder 185 miles than it should have been. The Canal should have taken us about 10 days but we ended up stuck on or near the Canal for almost three weeks. In that time, I had gone several days without seeing or talking to a person three or four times. I had been rained into two motel rooms, and rained into the tent for more than three days in a row twice. After the last time rained in on the Canal, I hiked into the next, nearest town to get a Kindle—I was afraid that I might go insane if rained in again without something to keep my mind occupied. We trudged on, slowly and uncomfortably, and I had no idea why we kept going. It was during the time on the Canal that something started to happen in my brain, or in my mind, or in my personality. Something started to change, I think, and many things started to die.

I started thinking of "Ohio" before we were off the Canal—Harper's Ferry was the first time I *said* Ohio, but it was a little later that I began to *think* of Ohio as something powerful. Jack was already almost to Indiana, and I told myself that, if not West Virginia, at least in Ohio the road would open up and we would make some time. One thing that people usually don't consider is that when weather slows you down, the delay is not just for a day or so—delays compound. When I lost a day, I also lost a day of *conditioning*. That meant that later, down the road, I was not able to do long, fast days like I should have been able to do. I *did* long days, don't get me wrong, but I suffered for them and my recuperative time was slow.

But Mabel never once suffered any of these glitches, either of her brain or her body. She woke up and walked and then settled in for the night and then did it again. Every day was exciting for her and everyday she saw new and wonderful things. Mabel never seemed to suffer physically and she never seemed to have any emotional issues. She didn't seem to worry that she had no answers for life's questions, and didn't seem to be looking for answers. Mabel took the War Games[7] approach to finding the meaning of life: The only winning move is not to play the game at all.

BOOK III: ...AND THE MOON SAYS HALLELUJAH, 01.05.12(5)

Finish discussion w/Rosie & Celio. Learn sand flies come out every night between 5:00 and 7:00 p.m., bite and drink human blood.

R: "Well law school sounds awful."

Research acquisition of two more cups coffee. Inform Rosie that law school was like that; nod. Agree w/Rosie, it sounds like high school. Note further agreement, but with ashtrays. Concur w/Rosie's finding, high school must be the same everywhere. Note Pedro has been listening from office.

R: "But anyway, you're on *vacation* now. So you should just relax."

C: "Yes, this is an island of relaxation. This is what I've heard. Pfft. You will find other lawyers here, Friend, if you look."

See Pedro appear in doorway; note Pedro's island attire, shorts/t-shirt/flip flops.

P: "Are you an attorney?"

Chuckle at British accent.

T: "Yup."

---

[7] War Games is a 1983 movie starring Matthew Broderick and Ally Sheedy.

P: "Get the fuck out of my hotel!"

Laugh; verify others are laughing; determine correctly it had been joke.

P: "Attorneys are such fucking wankers."

R: "Peter!"

T: "I agree."

P: "Only let you stay here because you looked to be a writer with all those papers. Didn't you see the 'No Chinese, No Lawyers' sign?"

Laugh; note everyone is laughing.

P: "We only give Rosie a pass because she's mostly Welsh."

T: "Hmm."

Research re: Rosie's ethnic ambiguity; conclude is partially Chinese.

P: "Are you a wanker?"

T: "I try not to be."

P: "I'm just another British *wanker* living the dream in Belize. But lawyers...it's a different world. I'd just as soon we get rid of them all."

T: "Are you a lawyer?"

Note Peter laughs, does not answer question; disappears. Research question: Is Peter an attorney? Conclude need more research.

R: "I don't ask Peter anything about his life. I think he's a spy."

C: "Pfft. Peter is an asshole."

T: "Is he Welsh?"

R: "He's British. My father is Welsh."

T: "I've already met more Welsh people here than I ever have before. I think I've met all of Wales except for Catherine Zeta Jones. And Tom Jones. My grandmother was from a Welsh family, so I hear."

R: "Everyone has a Welsh grandmother."

T: "Really?"

R: "It's just a saying. It seems down here like everyone you meet has a Welsh grandmother."

T: "Ah. It's like that with Indians in the States. Everyone's grandmother or great-grandmother was an Indian. People usually say Cherokee. It's all bullshit, though. I guess the Welsh are the Cherokees of the British Isles."

R: "Everyone is everything down here."

T: "Everyone is everything everywhere. No one knows anything. They didn't have paternity tests or Maury Povich in the 17 and 1800s. Who knows? What about you, Celio?"

C: "I am not Cherokee, no. Nor do I know this people."

T: "Yeah, but Welsh?"

C: "Only through my grandmother."

BOOK I: THE MOMENTS THAT TURN US (B)(iii)(b)
WHAT! DID THE HAND THEN OF THE POTTER SHAKE?

We were 24 or 25 miles on our last day on the Canal—a long day for us back then. The Towpath wound through ridges into some highlands and suddenly opened up near the western terminus. There were broad, green lawns on the other side of the Canal, and the forest thinned. There were now many more day-hikers than there had been. We met a blind couple who were walking together along the Canal. They were *both* blind. But they were holding hands and seemed very much in love—when they heard me walking toward them, the man stopped me and asked me to describe for them what the Canal looked like. There is not much of a Canal up there.

"It is a green pathway," I said, "and there are some downed trees in it. It is quite lovely."

"It is the Canal?" he asked.

"Yes."

"But there's no water in it?"

"Not here," I answered. He and his wife had turned to "look" at the Canal. "The Canal is not maintained this far away from D.C. There is water in the Canal further toward D.C."

"But what is that sound?"

"That's water draining from somewhere over there and into the Potomac. I think that is the water that *would* be draining into the Canal if the Canal were maintained up here."

"It sounds beautiful," he said.

"It is."

"Doesn't it sound beautiful?" he said to his wife. She nodded.

"Yes, it is beautiful," she said.

How does a blind couple get out and do so much? That's something to be proud of, not only if you *are* that blind couple, but for all of mankind, I think. They were in love. We walked on. I smelled awful and my beard had gotten very long. I caught up to Long Island Paul about eight miles outside of Cumberland, where the Canal and Towpath terminate.

"I thought you went home!" he called out. I walked into the campsite and sat with him for a while.

"No."

"I met a guy who said he had met a cross country guy, beard, just like you, said that he was giving up and going home."

"I didn't say that," I said. He told me what the guy looked like, and I remembered him. "No, I told him I was done *for the day*. I remember that guy. There was another storm coming that day, and we were done *for the day*. I think near Big Pool. He was heading toward D.C."

"Same guy," Paul said. "How did I get in front of you?"

I told him the story of the Bear and the Rain, and I told him about the weather we'd run into. He had also run into bad weather, but he was much better equipped for rain than I was—he had full rain gear and no dog to take care of—so he had hiked in all the breaks in the weather. He hiked during every bit of clear weather, even if it was only one or two hours, and had progressed steadily from campsite to campsite. I had caught up with him because I did substantially longer days, though fewer. We had been rained into a town along the Canal at the same time that Paul had been. He had stayed in a garage at the bicycle shop in town where they often let C&O hikers camp—which Mabel and I could not do—and because he did not have Mabel to care for, he was able to break out of there in a brief bit of clear weather the next morning while I was still stuck there in a motel.

"Price you pay for takin' a dog with you," he said.

"Worth it," I said.

"Probably is."

His wife would pick him up in Cumberland in eight days. He missed her a great deal, he said, and had decided not to hike back so that he could see her sooner. They were greatly in love, too. We shared a few more stories and I took a picture of Paul with Mabel. But I had to head out pretty soon after that because I was hungry and had no food and was desperate to get off that Canal. About five miles later, with only three miles left until Cumberland, my body quit on me as it had in Milton.

We sat together, Mabel and I, at the water pump at the last campground on the Canal. The handle was on the pump. I was overcome with weakness. I had only two pieces of food left—a can of tuna, and a stick of beef jerky that I got for Mabel a few days earlier. The jerky was in her pack, mixed up with some dog treats that looked and smelled exactly like the jerky stick. I took my boots off so my feet could breathe and I ate the tuna with my fingers. A man and a woman on bicycles rode by and stopped to talk with me. They were on their second cross-country ride. They were not sure how far they would go this time, but they liked to get out and ride together. They had a nice hotel booked in Cumberland. They were very much in love.

I was still weak. So I ate the piece of beef jerky. It was the first time I had eaten beef since 1997. It tasted disgusting, but the calories in it helped me to get up and push on to Cumberland. As I walked the last three miles, it struck me that perhaps I had eaten a dog treat. C'est la guerre.

We walked around a final corner and the world opened up. We could see for a few miles in a green valley with a big, powerful Potomac River to our left and nothing at all of the Canal remained on our right. In the near distance I saw the many church steeples of Cumberland. The weather was beautiful, and smoky haze gathered in the trees of the mountains around Cumberland. We walked into Cumberland and collapsed at the first open business we could find, the Cumberland Trail Connection—a bicycle shop and headquarters of a homebrew association. I staggered in and bought a couple of Cokes and a couple of Luna bars. We sat on a bench outside and drank and ate greedily. I had not reserved a motel room in town because I had been focused on making miles. There were a couple of hotels near there, but they were expensive and the only affordable motel I could find seemed like a long ways away. The owner of the Cumberland Trail Connection (and president of the homebrew association) walked by me on his way into the shop and looked at me quizzically. He was a stout fellow and he wore a leather full-brimmed hat and a jacket that was partially leather and partially denim. I thought he looked sort of mountain man meets urbanite meets rural white guy.

"Are you ok?" he said.

"Yeah."

"Just got off the Canal?"

"Yes," I said. He was across the parking lot from me so we were almost yelling at each other. "Like 25 miles today."

"Do you need wireless? You can use our wireless."

"I've got cell service," I said.

"Do you need something to eat?"

"I already ate about five Luna Bars from your shop," I answered.

"Do you need a beer?"

"Yes," I said.

"Well bring in a couple of these bikes and we'll have a beer."

I rolled a few of his display bicycles into the shop for him and then Mabel and I sidled up next to the work bench in the back and drank a couple of small cups of beer with the bicycle shop crew. They were all homebrewers, and the owner had been the brewmaster for a fairly well known brewery. The beer was very good.

"Look," he finally said, "it'll take you several hours to get over to the motel. If you can even get there. I don't know if you can even walk there from here because of the freeways. And you're beat. I'll just give you a ride."

"Are you sure?" I asked.

"No problem at all. I've got dogs, so the truck is used to dogs in it."

He never smiled at me or laughed, but was very good-natured. I think that he had a lot of things on his mind; everyone does. I threw the pack in the back of his truck and he and I talked about hiking on the way to the motel. He was a hiker, as well, and had done some long distance hikes and mentioned that he was also not a lightweight or ultra-lighter.

"My pack is too heavy."

"Well, I'm not a lightweighter, either," he went on. "I get the attraction, and it would be fun, too, but to me it just doesn't make sense. I want a certain level of comfort and safety when I hike. And I don't mind carrying an extra few pounds to do it. It's not like I'm racing. There's no race."

"I agree. But I think my pack is too heavy."

"Well hike your own hike," he said. "Don't let anybody tell you how to do it." When we got to the motel, he insisted on waiting until I got checked in. There were no problems with getting a room, though, so I was in and back out to the truck very quickly. He had gotten out and was reaching into the bed of the truck to pull out my pack. He grimaced and let out a gasp of air as he hoisted it out and onto the ground.

"Jesus K Rist!" he said. "Are you kidding me?"

"I told you."

"I am not a lightweight guy, and I can tell you I'd take at least 20 pounds off of that."

"You should feel it when I've got water with me."

"We see everyone coming off the Canal," he said. "That's the heaviest pack anyone ever carried up the Canal. You need to lighten it."

"I know," I said. "I've been trying."

He wished Mabel and I good luck and gave Mabel a couple more treats and then he was gone and I was in a motel marking the end of my time on the Canal. Finishing the Canal felt like an accomplishment. Rain and bears and heartache and a pack that was doubly too heavy. No water. Threatened government shutdown. Storms. I believed that Ohio would be—*had to be*—faster and that we would make up time. It was nice to call friends and my parents and say "We accomplished something" instead of "We've had another setback". I ate and talked with people on the phone, then spread out all my equipment on the beds in the motel room to dry it all and to take stock of what I had. Even though I needed to lighten my pack, I invented scenarios to justify keeping it all. But when I sat down on the chair to change out of my hiking clothes to get ready for a shower, I noticed that my socks would not fit over my calves. My calves were so enlarged from carrying the pack that they were the size of thighs. No injury, no swelling, just muscle. I started throwing stuff away and mailing stuff home.

BOOK II: FEEL THE SELFISH FURY (B)(i)(a)
THE VINE HAD STRUCK A FIBRE.

It was easy to fall back into routine when spring semester began—working every weekday and weeknight, all tweaked on coffee and Red Bull, then going out and getting royally drunk one night on the weekend...sometimes two. Sometimes three. When grades come in during the winter break, a student should (and some do) re-evaluate his or her decision to attend law school. Unfortunately, rising 2Ls rarely make rational decisions. They are likely just too confused, and routine is how many students dealt with the confusion.

For many, quitting would have meant leaving behind the only friends and social network that they had left. Law school narrows your social circle, and it is sometimes difficult to rebuild pre-law school relationships. I was completely out of touch with my old friends and family. It is difficult to imagine a socially acceptable subculture that produces as insulating an experience as law school. To succeed at law school, most students have no choice but to sacrifice their personal lives. You either "win" or you "lose" and, be sure, there are students there who *will* give up everything else in life to succeed. So you have to. At Iowa, most successful students had to leave their hobbies, interests, and healthy relationships right at the foot of the Burgher of Calais, whose arms outstretched and confused face said: "*This?* You bring me *this?*"

The confusion caused by the case method, the curve, the competition, the debt, the personalities, etc., is compounded by the fact that students *don't seem to be learning how to be a lawyer.* Law school teaches almost no practical skills.

It is a trade school, but with the exception of a few clinical opportunities, law schools don't teach the trade. This is a great shame, and the only way to correct this is for law schools to provide actual practice experience. Clinics, in which students actually practice law, are expensive for law schools to run and they don't bring in the kind of income that classes do—one professor can teach a class of 20 to 100 paying students, but a single clinical professor can only manage five or ten paying students. So it seems the economics of it make it difficult for law schools to teach practical skills. The result is that most law school graduates know nothing about the actual practice of law upon graduation.

There are no classes on how to file a lawsuit, how to schedule a conference call, or how to create a meeting agenda. Law grads have almost no training on how to talk with a client who wants you to advocate a legally or morally unsound position. No classes teach the mechanics of running a case or of responding to or managing a discovery request. There is simply very little practical about law school. Imagine a school for electricians that spends 98% of the coursework on the history and theory of electricity and 2% of the time teaching you how to plug in and unplug a washing machine. That's law school.

When I finished my first year of law school, I think maybe five or ten people dropped out...*maybe* five or ten. I considered quitting or transferring to a more "prestigious" school, but I didn't. I stayed where I was, because I loved Iowa City, I loved the Iowa Law faculty, and I loved so many of my fellow Iowa Law students.

And, anyway, the law school experience is not *all* bad. The culture of drinking, drugs (primarily pot and adderall, though I never did either), and sex has some benefits. Drinking and associated behaviors mounted when pressure mounted. The law school community became more prone to drama and infighting as the year went on—often about sex. A lot of the students were young—22 or 23 or 24—and were experiencing real stress for the first time, and felt like they were experiencing it alone. So it led to a lot of strange, self-destructive behaviors.

There is a great deal of drinking and a great deal of hooking up among 1Ls. It just happens. The frequency depends largely on the particular clique you find yourself in. (There are always cliques in law schools—it's an older version of high school with ashtrays.) The hookup rate seemed to be the highest among the "fresh-out-of-undergrad frat/sorority" clique. But it happens all through the class and in a thousand different ways: when one student goes to another student's apartment to study, at night after the bars, after house parties and unexpectedly after final exams, and after spending too much time across a table from someone in the coffee shop or in the library. It happens, and it carries over to the firm culture, too. An acquaintance of mine described it this way: "There definitely is a law school culture. I think it's unhealthy. And I think it transfers to the law firm culture. There's way too much drinking. WAY too much drinking. That definitely carries over to law firms. There's way too much sex. I probably shouldn't say that. Look, it's not immoral, it's amoral. It really does break people. It breaks people's sense of self and self worth."

I had more life experience than many or most law students—27 is not old, by any means, but the majority of law students come directly out of undergrad or after a brief, one-year hiatus. Many or most have never had a real job, or maybe have had one job, and there is no collective conception of the struggles and banalities of day-to-day life, much less of day-to-day practice of law. Because these kids are just that—kids—and because many are failing to meet their expectations for the first time in their lives, *and* because they are so confused and under stress for the first time, there is a desperate energy in the law school culture.

Take, for example, this girl in my class named Loretta. She and I had nothing in common; she was a pretty girl, very smart, but she ran around with the high school clique and there was really no reason for us to be friends. But we happened to be at the same function in downtown Iowa City one night during 1L year and she was very drunk. Out of nowhere, she appeared and sat beside me at a booth along the wall.

"So you've *never* hit on me," she said.

"Not that I recall, no," I said. "Want me to?"

"Every girl wants every guy to hit on her," she slurred. "And every guy in school has hit on me except you. Why is that do you think?"

"Because I think you're a train wreck," I answered. She smiled and laughed.

"Goddamn you are right," she said. "I'm a fucking train wreck! And it's great."

I have no idea what she meant, but I thought that she had come to talk to me to make her boyfriend jealous, because she kept looking over at him. We talked for a little while that night and then she disappeared back into the fog of law school. But after that, we sort of chatted online every now and again and would talk with each other when we saw each other out on the weekends. She told me about her problems with school and with her boyfriend, always in a really self-deprecating way, and once during a very pressured finals season she said:

"My dog just shits in the house. I haven't taken him out in three days because I am too busy studying. I just let him shit and then I clean it up. Or my brother cleans it up. Sometimes we don't clean it up."

And Loretta went to a very prestigious law firm after graduation.

That's law school, right there.

BOOK I: THE MOMENTS THAT TURN US (B)(iv)
AND PITY SULTÁN MÁHMÚD ON HIS THRONE.

The Appalachian Mountains separate the eastern seaboard from the big, green interior of the country. The Appalachians run from Georgia in the south all the way into southern Canada. For the intrepid moron who thinks that walking across the continent is a good idea, it's almost impossible to avoid the problem of the Appalachians without heading far south into the heat of a Dixie summer. For a westbound hiker, the Appalachians are the first and last mountain range before the Rockies. The Allegheny Escarpment is a wall or shelf rising steeply into the rugged Appalachians, and runs along much of the Appalachians. South of Cumberland, West Virginia, the Shenandoah Valley stretches along the Allegheny Escarpment and along the West Virginia portion of the Appalachians, often referred to as the Allegheny Mountains.

In Keyser, West Virginia, we picked up U.S. Hwy 50. The road was flat and straight along the New Creek for eight miles out of Keyser. The weather was clear and crisp, and we felt light and ready for the day—so the day's hike didn't scare me, but it should have.[8] At about eight miles, we turned a blind corner and climbed the first switchback of the trip. The road cornered right then quickly turned back to the left in an incredibly steep incline. The road then climbed five miles that seemed to be directly upward to the top of the Escarpment at about 3000 feet. That stretch of Hwy 50 is narrow and is made to feel narrower because most of the vehicles coming down the mountain are wide coal trucks. The road had some narrow shoulders but in many places had no shoulder at all. Instead, the left side of the road was bounded by a metal guardrail beyond which was a sheer drop down the Escarpment. We should have been scared.

I shortened Mabel's leash and kept her close on my left side between my stride and the guardrail. We leaned in close along the rail and held our breath when the coal trucks sped down the road toward us. I pressed Mabel tightly between my leg and the guardrail so that she could not lurch unexpectedly out into the oncoming traffic. Most drivers coming down the mountain drove safely and seemed to know that we were there and to be concerned for our safety. We trudged upward in the gaps between cars and coal trucks—Mabel had the advantage of four legs, but I felt as if I had to lean over at a 45-degree angle to move forward. The pack, although lighter than before, was a burden while climbing the steep grade. We stopped along the highway or at runaway truck ramps to breathe and to rest and to wonder if we could make it to the top. Mabel didn't suffer like I suffered and didn't seem to appreciate the danger of the traffic.

On our last hairpin turn of that day we came around a blind corner and a tractor-trailer barreled down the mountain probably 20 miles per hour faster than it should have, riding on the shoulder. The driver clearly did not realize he was off the road and he did not see us. My perception of time and speed had changed since I had started the Walk, and time seemed to stop altogether with the tractor-trailer screaming down on us. Strangely, it was almost as though I had all the time in the world to figure out what to do. But there was nothing we could do—to our left were a guardrail and a sheer drop for 100 feet or more. We were just going to die, and there was no alternative. I pushed Mabel against the guardrail and pressed my body as close to the rail as I could get. The driver saw us at the very last instant, broke the truck hard, and swerved back onto the road. He missed my right shoulder by a little under a foot.

We stood there for quite a while and even Mabel seemed to know how close we had come.

That five-mile climb was likely the most difficult five-mile stretch of the trip. I was woefully out of shape to be carrying that much weight up that long, steep climb. My legs could have cramped at any moment or, worse yet, my back could have cramped. Climbing that Escarpment required committing all my available focus to convincing my brain that I was not in pain. At some point during that day, I became so wrapped up in what I was

---

[8] Indeed, I probably should have been scared often on this trip. But I was absolutely fearless after the bear incident. I had no fear response. If I knew then what I know now, I would have recognized that the lack of fear response is not healthy; I would have quit for long enough to get my head on straight.

doing (and the pain I was ignoring) that the weather slipped completely out of my mind. The weather should never slip out of your mind while on a hike like this. By the time we neared the top, we could see a storm rolling in from the distance.

We had seen no place we could even have attempted to camp on the way up the Escarpment. There were no spaces large and flat enough to throw down a tent. I had phone service briefly during a break near the top and I checked the weather. There was an awful storm heading in, and unlike the storms we'd suffered through on the Canal, we had no place to camp as this one came rolling in over us. I decided that we would stop to find a place to camp at the very first chance we got, the very first house we saw. But there simply were no suitable campsites. When we were *very* near the top, but didn't realize how near, a little gravel road broke off to the left down the mountain and into an enclave of three or four small homes. I could not see if the homes were occupied, let alone if anyone was there. It was quite a steep walk down to the little enclave, which meant a steep walk back up if we were unwelcome down there. But we couldn't yet see the top of the ridge, and when you are on the side of a mountain you sometimes feel that it might go up and up forever. So we walked down into the enclave.

I knocked on the door of the first home, a shoddy ranch style with a couple of junk cars in the driveway and kids' toys strewn randomly around the yard. No one answered. So we walked farther, but decided not to knock at the next house because it looked like a rough place. The third of four homes looked inviting and nice and pleasant, and had a well-kept lawn. (The fourth home, off on the right, looked inviting, too, but it was farther.) I left Mabel tied to the pack down by the road and knocked on the door of the third home. A dog barked inside and a woman came to the screen door very quickly. I assumed she had probably seen or heard me coming into their little enclave of homes.

"Hello," I said. "My name is Tyler and my dog and I are walking across the country. We can't really go much farther today, and I was hoping you might let us camp in your yard."

"Walking across the country?" she said. "Well, sure. Do you have everything you need? There's a storm coming."

"I know," I said. "I'm kind of nervous about that and we're really beat from climbing this mountain."

"It's steep," she said. "You walked up it? Carrying that bag?"

"Yes," I said. She asked me why I was walking across the country and I told her that I had disliked my job and wanted to get out in the open. I told her I liked to be outside and I liked to walk, so I decided to see if I could walk across the country. She pointed out a tree in the yard and told me I should set up my tent right by that tree. The woman's daughter, who lived in the trailer back behind the house, showed up with her boyfriend or husband and that guy brought me a lawn chair while I pitched my tent.

"You got water?" the boyfriend asked.

"I have some."

"Well here's a couple cans of soda pop." I took the cans, and decided they would be most of the calories of my dinner. "There ain't no water up here. Gotta truck it all up."

"I hadn't even thought of that," I moaned.

"Yup. Just one of the things about livin' up here. Gotta pay for this view by haulin' in all your own water."

"Well, I've got plenty to make it through the night and tomorrow."

"There's water up there," he said, and sort of waved up the mountain as he walked away. "Up there, there's water at some places. You'll be fine. When this storm hits, though, you can go into the house. She said to tell you that. It's gonna be a rough night in a tent. We get some storms up here, I'll tell you *that* for sure."

Mabel and I climbed into the tent and I worked on the journal and read until I accidentally fell asleep. I was not asleep long, though, and I woke pretty desperate to get out of the tent and to soak up the last few moments of daylight before nightfall. I drank one of the sodas and sat on the lawn chair. The neighbor family milled around and the man of the house was leaving in his pick up truck. He stopped and rolled down his passenger side window.

"Hi there," he said. "My name is Andrew Pancake," and he motioned at me with a plate in his hand. "We just ate dinner and we've got some leftovers."

"Oh!" I said. "Thank you so much!"

"Yeah, Pancake. That's what I said. It's a common name around here, actually. I saw you comin' up that hill," he said. "How far are you going?"

"California," I answered.

"You can't make it without good food. Gotta feed your body and your soul," he said.

"Thank you."

I took the plate, but didn't start eating immediately. I thought for some reason that it would be rude to eat immediately right in front of him. We talked about his odd name, and about living up on the mountain, and about his family and the remodeling they were doing on the house. He warned me that a heck of a "blower" was coming through, and that sometimes it got rough up on the mountainside.

"Mabel and I were out in a storm on the C&O Canal," I said, "and the wind blowing along the ridge sounded like the voice of God."

"It might have been," he joked. "And you're *on* a ridge now. So be careful out here."

"I will."

"I gotta get down there and get some water, or I'd talk to you longer," he said. "What you're doing is great. Amazing."

"Thanks."

"Listen, we try to not let anyone go without at least giving them some scripture." He leaned over and handed excerpts of the New Testament out through the open window. "I don't know what you believe, and I won't preach to you, but we don't like to let people go without offering them scripture."

"Thank you," I said, and took the tracts. I did not tell him I would read them, and I think he knew that I wouldn't, but he didn't care. He wasn't trying to convert me, he was only trying to do what he thought was best for a traveler. He was a rare find on this trip: a Christian who did not actively try to convert me; rather, he made a couple of gifts and was on his way. I imagine he and I would have been a good team working together, or amenable and friendly with each other if we lived in the same community, and we'd chuckle to each other about our differences.

"I gotta get some water. Be careful, and if the storm's too bad, just come knock on the door. And there are no bears here."

We had had such bad luck sleeping during bad weather that I decided Mabel and I should sleep as soon as possible and get in as many hours as possible before the storm. I ate every bit of the food that Andrew had brought me. It was pretty close to the best meal I'd ever had.

The wind blew so hard that night that the tent flattened out in the gusts and the nylon sides of the tent slapped across my face and woke me up. Mabel was already awake, cowering near my feet and staring at me, waiting for me to wake up and make the storm stop. But I couldn't make the storm stop, so instead I called Mabel to the front of the tent where she could snuggle in under my arm with her chin resting on my chest. She felt safer there and soon was able to fall asleep despite the howling winds. I could not get back to sleep for several hours. I watched shadows stream across the top of the tent, and watched from the inside as the wind bent and mangled the tent. I had guessed rightly about the direction of the wind and had pitched the tent in line against the wind, so it was only the great gusts that threatened to knock the tent down. Still, after an hour or so, I got the impression that the tent was starting to float and that perhaps the tent pegs had been ripped out of the ground.

I crawled from the tent the next morning to find a peaceful and clear day and Mabel leapt out of the tent in front of me to run circles around the campsite. The wind had knocked over and moved my backpack, but the tarp had stayed on through the night and everything was dry inside. The tent was dry, too, which confused me because there had been a lot of rain the night before. The Sun had not been up that long, so the fierce wind in the night must have dried the tent. The lady of the house came out shortly and talked with me as I packed.

"Did you make it?"

"I did," I answered and smiled. She was not smiling.

"I hardly slept," she said. "I was worried about you. But we couldn't come get you because we were afraid to go outside."

"I made it," I said. "Was it even that bad?"

She looked blankly at me for about a minute.

"Yes," she said. "It was bad. I'm leaving for work. Do you need anything?"

I said that I didn't, and then I was alone again. Everyone in the little enclave of homes had disappeared or gone to work or gone off to do what normal people do during the day. I packed and we headed back onto the side of the mountain. I was in serious pain from my feet to my shoulders from the hike up the mountain the day before. I couldn't imagine doing it again that day. But we had no choice, so we hit the road and we found that we were maybe a half a mile, probably less, from the top of the Escarpment. We could have made it the day before and beaten the rain, but it would have made no difference—we would still have been tented out in the storm.

At the top of the Escarpment, the road flattened and the roadside opened up in a big green field. We stopped at the top at a privately owned "scenic overlook". It was in a driveway attached to a rickety old building, but there was one of those face-shaped telescopes so it looked legit enough. Someone had put up the face-shaped telescope years ago, I guessed, hoping that there would be some tourist trade. I had packed all of my trash from the day before and was carrying it with me in a plastic bag, and there was a trashcan at the scenic overlook so I thought it would be as good a time as any to get rid of the trash and to check my voice messages. From that vantage, we could see over to Saddleback Mountain, which is where Abraham Lincoln's mother was born. So there was that. But my phone didn't have service, so there was that. I threw the trash away and, already in the garbage, there were an empty bottle of whiskey and a box that read "Do It Yourself Masturbation Kit". I decided we should not stay long at the scenic overlook.

Later, I wrote in my journal that, even though it was not a large mountain, I didn't think I'd ever felt so good as when I crested that thing. I was never one of those people who have a mountain fetish, but that day I understood how it could have happened to me had I grown up in some mountainous place instead of in Illinois. Up there was a different world. It was cooler and the air was cleaner than it had been at the base of the mountain, and the road twisted and it never seemed to be flat for more than a half a mile. Usually the road was straight up or straight down, and walking downhill is no easier than climbing. A few miles later I saw an AT&T sign along the road and decided to give my phone another shot. It worked, and I talked to my mother and some of my friends, and while I was talking to them a man appeared out of the trees and walked toward me. He wore jean shorts and Velcro shoes and a t-shirt that read "Goldberg the Wrestler". He was also wearing an inexplicable pair of clear plastic safety glasses. He had the name "Kenny" tattooed on his arm.

"Walkin'?"

"Yup," I said. "California."

Kenny pursed his lower lip up over his upper lip and nodded.

"Now that's a long way. A long way," he said. He had a mountain accent, or what I assumed to be a West Virginia mountain accent. "I'm Kenny. Got water?"

"I do. Place I stayed last night said there's no water up here. All hauled in."

"Nope," he said. "People got water up here. Not down there on the side, but up here on the mountain. I don't, though. I do, but I don't drink it."

"Oh."

"Chemicals," he said. "I go right down road there. There's a spring comes right out of the mountain. I get my water there. Cleaner. No chemicals."

"Probably best," I said.

"Probably."

"It's great up here," I said. "Gorgeous. I have never hiked through anyplace so pretty."

"It's somethin'," he said. "But it ain't like it used to be. The people aren't as good."

"No?"

"No," he said. "Not by a sight. Now they's all worthless. Don't do nothin' but watch NASCAR."

"Oh yeah? Sounds like my hometown," I said.

"And what the Hell is NASCAR?" he said. I then learned a great deal about Kenny. On NASCAR: "I'd rather eat dogshit than watch NASCAR. Here he comes. He made a left turn. Will he make another? He made another left turn. Dog shit." His views on the weather: "It's gettin' stranger." On his water: "It's all pink with chemicals. Pink. I load mine up from a spring yonder." On basketball: "Who wants to watch a bunch of niggers chase a pumpkin? Dog shit." Once Old Kenny had broken the seal on the word "nigger", he used it pretty liberally, but only when talking about sports. Despite the way he looked, which was decidedly backwoods and would have been scary to me if I had grown up a bit further north in Illinois, he had an easy manner about himself. Frankly, he spoke pretty well, too, even if I didn't much care for some of his word choice.

"Need a place to stay?"

"There's a campground just up here," I said. "Map says so."

"Abrams Creek," he said. "Good. Better get there. There's a ternader warning all day. Big storm comin'. Bigger'n last night."

"Really?"

"Yup. Killed a bunch of people in Arkansas. So those fucking idiots on TV said. Who knows if that's true. They got cabins cheap at Abrams Creek."

"They do?"

"Yup," he said. "They got a fella there named T who runs the place. The place was many years in a state of disrepair, so you know, but T's a good man and has it up and runnin' quite efficient. I do grounds work there sometimes, and T's a good man, good manager. Good to work for."

"Alright," I said. "I'll head there."

I started to walk on.

"Tell T to get in touch with Kenny. It's about time I get up there for some grounds work."

"I will," I promised.

We pushed on to Abrams Creek and were there by one or two in the afternoon. It was not a long day, but I was demolished from the day before. My legs and my back were hurting pretty badly. I had been in a pretty bad storm the night before and, according to both the Internet and Kenny, there was more bad weather coming. So I pushed on to Abrams Creek for one of these cheap cabins I'd heard about. Abrams Creek is a campground down a gravel lane off of Hwy 50. The main office is in a nicer home that was in a pretty intense state of disarray due to remodeling. There was a large green yard behind the home down by the Creek, and there was another home back away from the main home and toward the road. The campground stretched along the creek on winding gravel paths cut into the forest. I tethered Mabel to the pack and knocked on the front door. The man who answered was not large, but he was very well built and had enormous dreadlocks. He was as black as the ace of spades.

"T?" I asked. He contorted his face, probably in response to my contorted face. I was absolutely shocked—Kenny had spoken glowingly of this guy, but *this guy* was black. And it had seemed to me that Kenny was unlikely to speak glowingly of a black guy. Plus, T was the first black person I'd seen since I'd left D.C. The Confederate flags, the word "nigger", the bumper stickers, and all of that—it was a surprise, that's all.

"Yes," he said.

"Hi. Can I camp here?"

He gave a little grunt and called out for someone. He had a few children with him that were probably his younger brothers or nephews or something like that, because they were too old and he too young for a father/son relationship. And you can just tell when a man is talking to his son, and T didn't seem to have that father/son relationship with these kids.

"You're not even done," he said to one of them. "What have you been doing?"

"I'm doing it," the kid said.

"You know, you asked for a job, for some responsibility, and this is it. You've got three rooms to paint, and they won't paint themselves."

"I *will*," the kid said back.

"Say I 'am', not I 'will'. Just do it. This is your responsibility now. It means something."

When T came back he had a clipboard with sign-in paperwork, and I filled it all out while chatting with him.

"I might be stuck here a few days," I said. "I've heard the weather is turning."

"That's what they say," T agreed. "But it's not so bad to be stuck here. We have a great retreat this weekend. We're hosting a yoga and raw foods retreat."

"Really?"

"Absolutely," he said. "I don't know if you're into yoga or raw foods, but we've got some people coming—just real artists. World famous raw foods chefs—it's a hybrid of art and science how these people work with raw food. It will be something to see; something to taste, I guess. And we've got a few yoga instructors coming, and there will be some other events."

"That's this weekend?"

"Yes," he said, and took my registration form and money. "It's going to be a good time."

The trail sloped away from the house and down along the Creek, first beside some tipis and campgrounds and then into the cabin area. The cabins were the small, one-room things that look to be converted storage sheds and that in Illinois are most often used as hunting shacks. Our cabin had a heater, though, and a futon and a writing desk, so it was all I would need. Mabel and I were both asleep by 2:00 p.m. and slept through until the early evening. It was dark and quiet that night and no one was there in the campground to make a sound. When I woke that evening, I took Mabel out and we walked down beside the Creek. It was the first clear night that I could remember, and the stars were out. I wrote in my journal: "It might be that we are at 3000 feet, or it might be that we've gone so many weeks without a clear night sky, but I took Mabel out and the stars were so big and so clear that I thought for a second that they were shimmering fruits that I could have plucked out of the sky and eaten in the moonlight. What would they taste like?"

That was the first night on the trip that I noticed having sleeping troubles. The sleep disturbance may have begun earlier, but I noticed it that night. I could not sleep more than three hours at a time without waking. More importantly, it was difficult to sleep at all and half of the time that I was "asleep" I was actually just "less than awake".

I woke at 6:00 a.m. the next morning, with a Sunrise scheduled for 6:20, but it was frigid cold and windy and the skies were as dark and cloudy as I had seen them on the trip. I felt like I had metal rods running from the back of my knees through my hamstrings and up into my lower back—I could hardly stand up, and when I sat I felt like my lower back would cramp, but I was alright once I was standing. The stiffness may have cleared if I had been able to walk around and get warmed up, but it wouldn't be possible that day. We had a hell of a hike up the hill right in front of us to get to the peak of the mountain and the little town of Mt. Storm and the bulbous black clouds of the storm were parked on top of us—it was clear that it would be another long, cold, and rainy day. All the while, of course, I was aware that a third killer storm headed right for us. It was not supposed to reach us for a few days, but it felt like the storm may have been right there outside the cabin door.

A little after 7:00 a.m., I wrote in my journal: "I just got all packed, then took the dog out and it started raining. It is less than 50 degrees and raining. GODDAMNIT. I have to inquire about staying here another night."

The raw foods retreat was going to start that night, and the entire campground was booked up except for a tipi. So I took the tipi that night and moved my belongings there. T gave me several loads of firewood in what I thought at the time was a friendly gesture. Later that night, I would realize that it was not the kindness of his heart that made him give me so much firewood. I was in the tipi by 8:45 a.m. After I'd moved into the tipi, I stepped out and saw a hulking figure walking toward me, all wrapped up in a blanket with the blanket pulled over his head.

"I never thought I would live to see a day where I would walk across the woods in West Virginia and see a white man coming out of a tipi," the man said. His name was Gregory E. Woods, but he was called Flaco. He called himself a black/Native American "mixed blood", and he was there to run the sweat lodge for the yoga/raw foods retreat. I liked how he used to the term "mixed blood", because I knew he thought that blood meant something—like blood carried history or knowledge. We talked about the recent sweat lodge deaths and how furious he was that people without the necessary training were running sweat lodges in the Southwest.

"We have thousands of years of wisdom from our elders," he said. "The sweat lodge is not something that anyone can just do. It is safe when it is done with the correct spirit and the correct knowledge. A dentist would kill a man if he didn't have the right spirit and knowledge, but they call it training. You should come tomorrow."

We talked for probably two hours. I learned about his family and his experiences. He was about 6'3" and one of the more striking looking persons I have ever seen, with a strong, broad face. Flaco was a "wanderer" he said, following "energy lines" all over the Earth. He had been an illegal immigrant all over in Africa and Asia, a wandering soldier in Europe, and a shaman learning from cousins in South America—cousins removed by thousands of years of evolution and crossbreeding, but cousins all the same.

"Are you staying in this tipi all night?"

"Yes," I said.

"Well, you'll need...is this all your wood?"

"Yes," I said. "T gave me a lot of extra firewood."

"You'll need it. You'll need a lot of kindling," he said. Then he led me around the campsite for an hour, both of us gathering huge armfuls of kindling. "I stayed in this tipi last year at the retreat and I nearly died in the night. Brother, it will be cold in there."

"It's supposed to be cold tonight," I said.

"It will be cold tonight, Brother. And it will be *cold* in that tipi. Unless you have a strong fire all night long. And then you'll have the smoke to deal with."

Flaco helped me gather kindling and Mabel watched us. When we'd gathered stacks and stacks of kindling, we walked together, chatting the whole way, back up to the office. I needed to get connected to the WiFi to send some emails to let family and friends know that I was still alive. I met a nice looking young lady named Siobhani at the office and also two female yoga instructors who were in great shape. And I met Joe, an old black astrologer who would play an important part in the drum circle that night. None of them probably guessed that I am a drum circle nut, but when I inquired about the drum circle a second time they invited me to join.

Mabel and I sauntered back down to the tipi in the cold. I like to talk with people, and I can talk for hours with Kenny the Racist Goldberg Fan, or with Flaco the Mixed Blood Shaman. Sometimes I am too patient with people, but I can't help but think that there is something good in most people. Most people aren't so simple that you should dismiss them out of hand. Take Kenny, for example. It would have been easy to dismiss him the minute he said that basketball involved "niggers chasing pumpkin", but then I would not have heard him speak with so respectfully for this man T, a black man. What does that mean? Can you understand a man like that? And take Flaco: It would have been easy to dismiss him as a hippie weirdo, but then I would never have heard him talk about his social work with underprivileged children, or his belief that the old religions of his people have continuing relevance and significance because they recognize a non-literal transcendent energy consciousness, just like the mythologist Joseph Campbell wrote about. These are real people, no matter how different we are. But so many people can easily turn off the wonder of these people like a garden spigot. I wonder how I became this way, or if maybe I somehow never grew up and ended up a child with an adult body.

I had a lot of time to kill before the drum circle. There was bound to be food there that night that I could have moved in on but, as a show of good faith, I cooked and ate the second to last meal in my food store. Ramen noodles. And I thought about Old Flaco as I ate, and about Old Joseph Campbell, and Old Jesus, Old Muhammed, and Old Andrew Pancake. Time moved slowly in the tipi beside the fire. I imagined myself as one of my Homo Neanderthalensis ancestors 400,000 years ago, and as one of my Homo Sapiens Sapiens ancestors 40,000 years ago. We were out of the wind and the rain, but we could hear the wind shake the tipi. I felt Mabel's heart beat against my hip as she pressed as near to me as she could because I was her World. There we were.

Smoke rose from the fire and steam rose from my hot cup of tea.

Everything smelled of camp smoke and spring.

That night I went to the drum circle and a couple of local Good Old Boys gave me a few beers. These two fellows and one gal with them lived in the white house across from the main office. Power company employees, I think. One of them also gave me some moonshine that he had made, and it was delicious. The Good Old Boys didn't fit in with the raw foods crowd, and I was sort of a translator between the two groups. One of the good old boys, Quinn, wore a union jacket, and that made me feel good. I drank and talked with everyone, but the raw foods people seemed a little put off by the beers. Still, I fell a little in love with Siobhani, the volunteer running the raw foods thing, and then I fell a bit in love with another gal who was dancing with flaming hula hoops as the drum circle raged on. Later that night, I fell much more in love with her. The Good Old Boys warned me over and over that the hike into Mt. Storm would be longer and harder than the hike up from Keyser had been. One of the good old boys, Nick, had come down from Cumberland to work in Mt. Storm, and he got his girlfriend to drive him into Mt. Storm where he got dog food and treats for Mabel.

I joined in on the last few songs of the drum circle, and Flaco and I connected for a bit. I love drumming, and I play all sorts of hand drums in my free time. The thing about drum circles is that most people who take part in them are not really drummers. But it only really takes two "real" drummers: Two legitimate drummers can lock into a groove that everyone can follow and then the real drummers can solo over that groove. And Flaco was old hat at drumming, I could tell. After we'd played a bit, I led the circle into an old Arabic rhythm that I like a lot, a simple thing called the maqsoum, and Flaco went nuts with that one. The flaming hula-hoop girl was pretty fond of that one, as well.

It was a pretty good night.

Confirm Rosie & Celio love story; determine others at Pedro's not so interested. Schedule bike ride w/Kendra, later afternoon; agree to tell story to her. Discuss w/Rosie & Celio re: Law school, love and related matters, food on island. Leave Pedro's; ride bikes around island. Lunch w/Kendra, local food; inform Kendra that I am feeling better.

T: "Slept great last night, too. I haven't slept really in two months. It's better down here."

K: "I know! I absolutely *needed* this. The partner who I do the most work for protected me last month; he told everyone 'you *cannot* give Kendra assignments because she *needs to go on vacation.*'"

T: "Is working at a big firm everything you'd dreamed?"

K: "It's pretty good."

Note that Kendra's hair is mussed, day is windy. Park bike. Cocktails w/Kendra at Palapa Bar up north, fruity drinks over the sea. Calculate bike ride time, several hours. Discuss plans to snorkel next day; agreed to set it up with Rosie at Pedro's. Exit Palapa bar, have work; learn Kendra has reading to do, boyfriend demanded read particular book about Jewish kids growing up or something. Learn her boyfriend is very Jewish; note that she is very Catholic; confirm that they get along, is very sweet.

Return to Pedro's. Edit manuscript. Note stuff missing from story, i.e. "why?" See Rosie brought coffee, sat down. See Celio appear. Resume story. Research re: "Why do people listen to this shit?"; conclude it might be interesting story. Resume story.

C: "She left you after two weeks?"

T: "Yes."

R: "How long had you been together?"

T: "I don't know. A few years. Maybe three or four. Since law school. Whatever. It's her trip, too."

C: "Friend, it may be true that it is her trip, but *two weeks*? And you were yet to walk across the whole of the land?"

T: "That was the plan."

C: "Friend, let Rosie confirm for us, as a woman...what timing could have caused increase in the happiness of this situation?"

T: "None of that matters. It happened. She did what was right, what was best for both of us, really. She's a hero in the story, is the thing."

R: "That is so rough. And you kept going?"

T: "Mabel was there. It wasn't so bad. Mabel is very sweet."

Respond to research questions from Rosie & Celio, re: Were there wild animals?; recount story of bear and rain. See Rosie on edge of seat, her eyes are very big. Hear Celio laughing, re: clearly I am still alive, can't suspend disbelief. Tell about other animals. Respond to research question, re: guns.

Edit manuscript.

R: "Why did she leave you? Because you went on this adventure?"

T: "No. Because I was no good."

R: "Oh!"

C: "You appear to me a nice guy."

T: "People are all different. I think I was a pretty bad guy. She thought I was a bad type."

R: "You can't be sure she thought that."

T: "She told me. She told me that she hated me. That she hoped I would die and that she wanted to kill herself when she thought about how she and I breathe the same air."

Hear laughter; hear laughter stop.

C: "Seriously? Did she tell you this on the street of this story?"

T: "No. Months later. Months later on the phone. Told me that her whole life was ruined and it was my fault."

R: "You don't seem that type."

T: "People are always different with different people. It doesn't matter, anyway. She is a nice gal and it would have been nice had everything gone differently, but it didn't. So here I am."

C: "It must not have been meant to be."

R: "Did you go on the Walk because you didn't want to marry her?"

T: "I don't think so. I don't believe in that kind of subconscious stuff; not for me, anyway. I never tell anyone why I went on the Walk."

R: "Will you tell me?"

T: "No. I won't ever tell anyone."

C: "Your book won't be very good."

Receive email from Kendra: "Thought of title for your book. Call it 'EPLYKFD'." Respond: Not catchy; what does it mean? Email from Kendra: "Eat Pray Love...you know...For Dudes." Tell Rosie and Celio, Rosie laughs, Celio doesn't get it.

R: "So you were broken hearted?"

T: "Sure. Everyone is. C'est la guerre."

C: "I think your book won't be very good, Friend. Not if you won't tell people what it's about."

T: "You think?"

C: "Anyone can walk across a continent. Pfft. I could do that. I could do that with minimum discomfort. Pfft. But I don't! And I know *why* I don't. What I don't know, is *why you did*. I want to know why."

T: "Everyone wants to know why."

R: "He'll tell us. I'll get him to tell me. Want more coffee, Tyler?"

T: "Sure."

Birds sing songs in dense jungle cover and fish jump in northern rivers.

BOOK I: THE MOMENTS THAT TURN US (B)(iv)(a)
AS NOT A TRUE BELIEVER PASSING BY.

And then we got taken for a ride in Mt. Storm, West Virginia. I checked out of the campgrounds and everyone warned me that I should stay another night because there was a "real" storm coming, not like the one that had failed to materialize the night before. The hike up from the campground to Mt. Storm seemed not nearly as bad as I had been told it would be. Maybe it *was* as tough as the hike up from Keyser, but maybe my body had already incorporated the hike up from Keyser and I was stronger.

Mt. Storm is a nothing of a town. It is an old coal town that in the distant past thrived off a seam of coal that ran along Abrams Creek. Now it is an unincorporated community at the top of a mountain. I stopped at the first business I saw, a gas station that had no gas. They hadn't been a gas station for years, the lady said, but the pumps were still there. They had no ATM and accepted only cash, so I spent a dollar of my 10 remaining dollars on a soda pop and headed on down the road. The town is not very big so it wouldn't take me very long to walk the length of it. But there was a nicer home on the left. A man was mowing his yard with his daughter, and he was right out by the road, so I waved at him. He came over to me.

"Hi there," I said.

"Do you need something?" he asked. This man was probably in his forties, and he wasn't in great shape, but he held himself erect and had that sort of vanilla-bland empty look of a police officer.

"I...."

"I am obliged to tell you that it is illegal to solicit rides in West Virginia," he said. "I'm a West Virginia state police officer. This is my day off."

"Well, I will keep that in mind," I said. "But I'm walking."

"Listen," he said. "The Methodist church down there is the only place you can wait. They sometimes will help people find a place to stay or a ride or something, and sometimes people will stop. If someone stops and offers, you can take that ride. But you can't solicit a ride."

"I'm walking across the country," I said.

"Well, then walking out of town is a good start."

"Ok," I said. He could probably tell that I was getting angry. The "lawyer" was about to come out.

"But you can't walk out that way," he said, and pointed to the west, directly along our Hwy 50 route. "You and that dog'd die out there. You can't walk down the mountain. Not alone, not with that dog."

"What?"

"I'm just tellin' you this as a friend," he said. "Straight downhill. Can't see around the corners."

"Is there a shoulder?" I asked.

"No shoulder most of the way. Not on the...well, not on the left side. Which you'd be walkin' on."

"Thanks," I said, and walked away. He called out one last thing:

"Sorry I couldn't help you, but just walk on out of town."

This must have been what Jack was talking about when he told me I could not safely descend the mountain with Mabel. This was the first descent of the trip, and I had no first-hand idea what it would be like. I knew from walking up the Escarpment that there would be blind corners, and there would be places where there was no shoulder. Jack's warning, and the cop's warning, had me concerned because I didn't think Mabel was under sufficient control to risk it. We had no cash, no food, one serving of dog food left, and another storm was coming—this one, they said at Abrams

Creek, would be the "real thing". So I decided to walk up to the next gas station and see about getting cash.

The next "gas station" was something to see, Lister's Gas and Market. There were gas pumps in the front and a service station in the back, so it looked promising. But the closer I got, the more it looked decrepit. Two local boys leaned against the side of the building, smoking cigarettes and doing nothing much of anything. Having come from a small town myself, I knew that these were the folks running the store that day. I have never seen two teenage boys so dour and joyless. The town looked like something out of a science fiction novel about a mysterious plague, or like a tribal third world village in some distant land. I put the pack down and leashed Mabel, and the two boys went into the store directly before I did.

The store shelves were mostly empty, like part of a going out of business sale for many months, or like the store had been looted after a horrible disaster months earlier that left the town empty. It looked like a gas station in Prypiat, Ukraine. The lights were dim and everything had a dusty pallor about it. I picked up a soda and a gas station fruit pie and carried them to the counter. The soda, the pie, and the counter were each covered in a patina of dust.

"Cash today," the boy said as I held out my debit card. "Machine don't work."

"But you have a machine?"

"Yup."

"So you do accept debit cards?"

"Yup," he said.

"But not today?"

"Machine don't work."

I gave him a couple more of my dwindling dollars. I was in a very bad position.

"Is there an ATM around?"

"No ATM," he said. "And the card machine don't work."

"Look," I said, and told him that I was walking across the country. I was in a pretty awful situation, and needed to know how I could get a hold of some cash or a place to stay.

"Motel across the street," he said.

"That over there is a motel? They take a card?"

"I don't know," he said. "Never stayed there." He gave me a wry smile.

"Any other options?"

"You could walk to Grafton," he said.

"I know there will be an ATM in Grafton, but it's like 50 miles."

The kid just shook his head.

I left my pack and Mabel there and walked over to the motel. The motel sat back away from the road, which is why I had not seen it. A fat man was mowing the yard on a riding lawn mower and had a small dog on his lap. Two more dogs bounded out of the house attached to the motel onto the porch and yipped at me. A fat woman came out of the house onto the porch and watched me walk up the driveway. There was no one staying in the motel, and no sign that anyone had stayed there for months. It *looked* structurally sound and relatively clean, but it *felt* abandoned.

"Got a room?" I asked.

"Well, I don't know," the woman answered.

"I'm walking across the country with my dog, and I am stranded here right now."

"We don't take no dogs," she said. I rubbed my forehead. The fat man drove the mower over and turned it off.

"Problem?" he asked, and stroked his dog.

"Need a room," I said. "For one and a dog."

"We cain't have no dogs," he said. "Nope."

"Even with a security deposit?" I asked, which was an odd question, as I had only seven dollars in my pocket.

"Nope," he said, and seemed to be angry. "We cain't help you at all. Go on find some place else to stay."

"Do you have an ATM?" I asked, I don't know why.

"No ATM. No cards. Go check across the street, then find someplace else."

I shook my head a little and stood there for a bit, then turned and walked away. It made no sense to me, at all. There was *no one* there, and this motel clearly wasn't running a thriving trade in the overnight visitor to Mt. Storm industry. They should have been thankful that anyone happened upon their place, even if it was a hiker and his dog.

So I had no food and no money and was 50 miles away from either. No place to stay. No girlfriend. No one I could call. No cell service. With another storm coming. But Mabel had her eyes fixed on me and was wagging her tail because she wanted me to come back to pet her.

Back at the station, the owner arrived in a beat up Chevy S-10.

"My boy called. Said you're stranded," he said.

"I am," I answered. "Need to get out of here. Storm is coming. Think you could give me a ride out of here?"

"I got things to do," he said. "What are we talkin' about here?"

"I'll give you 20 bucks," I said.

"I don't have time for this shit."

He walked away from me, to the back of his station where he was working on the transmission of a 30-year-old pick up truck. So I talked with his son for a while. He and I were leaning against an old Chevy Nova.

"I'd give you a ride," he said. "But I don't think this here Nova'd make it very far. If I believed it would, I'd give you a ride."

"I'll try again with your dad," I said.

I walked to the back.

"I'll give you 30," I said. "And will fill the gas tank."

"That's better," he said. "I'm busy, but I'll do that."

"Ok," I said. "I've only got seven on me, though. So you'll have to get the cash when we hit an ATM."

"I don't have time for bullshit," he said, and ducked back under the pickup.

So I went back to the front of the station, and saw that some folks were messing around outside the Methodist Church. I jogged down.

"Hey there," I said, and waved. The man and woman looked me up and down and looked uneasy. "I'm an attorney, and I'm walking across the country with my dog. But we are stranded here and we need to get to an ATM. Lister down at the station will give me a ride if I can get enough money up front for some gas. So I hate to ask, but, look, I can give you my address and my attorney registration number, and I can send you the money from the very next town."

"Oh, we don't do anything like that," the man said. "No, nothing like that. I just don't know. I'll tell you what, talk to Eugene. He lives right there on the other side of the station. He does most of this kind of thing for the Church."

I thanked the man and his wife and walked up to Eugene's house and knocked on his door. Eugene was probably in his 70s, maybe 80s, and he came out the side door to stand on the porch with me. I told Eugene my story, and then he *interrogated* me—and it was frustrating because not only was the interrogation offensive, it was offensively bad. Half of me wanted to tell him to piss off, and the other half of me wanted to stop him and say: "No, now, Eugene, if you really want to get at the truth of this situation, you should ask me *this* question and then *this* question." But I stood there and listened and answered. He demanded to see my driver's license and then said: "I didn't know it was this easy to make a fake ID." He copied down my driver's license information, and then told me he was going to contact the Illinois Secretary of State. "It's Jessie White," I said, "I used to work for him at the DMV in Champaign, Illinois." Then he said he was going to contact the Illinois bar association, and I said: "If you have Internet access, you can actually search the Illinois bar's website and you'll find my information."

"No," he said, "I don't do internet. I like to talk to the people giving me answers."

After about a half an hour of his slow and poorly worded questions, he pulled a $10 bill from his wallet and handed it to me. I started to write down his address.

"I'll send you this back and a little extra in...."

"No," he said. "Don't write down my address." And he was *scared,* as if writing down his address might grant me some mystical power to control him. Or like I was planning to come back and steal his pot of gold and if I didn't write down the address then I wouldn't be able to find his house. "You're mistaken," he said. "This is an investment, but I don't need a return."

"An investment in my trip," I said with a smile, trying to save a little civility.

"An investment in gettin' you out of town," he said. "Lister should be able to get you out for 17 bucks. If you *really* have seven dollars in your pocket."

I walked away. I didn't even say goodbye or wish him well. I almost didn't take the money, and wouldn't have had I had *any* choice at all. That old man was mean and cold and unjustifiably worried and scared.

Back at Lister's, I said: "Ok. 17 bucks up front, tank of gas, and 33 bucks. Final offer. I got 10 bucks from Eugene."

"I'll do it," Lister said.

And *here* is the twist. Lister then said to his boy:

"Hey, get the S-10 and take Tyler up to the gas station so he can get some cash."

I clenched my face.

"There's another gas station?" I asked.

"Bout five miles up the road that way," he said with a smile and pointed southward behind his station. "My boy'll get you up there and you can get some cash. Then I'll take you to Grafton."

I clenched my face and exhaled deeply through my nose. I didn't even *want* a ride to Grafton—I wanted information, and access to an ATM.

"Don't be too pissed," he said. "You and that dog can't walk down this stretch, anyway. With the way these crazy sons-of-bitches drive? You'd never make it."

That whole damned town scammed me for 50 bucks. But we had a *contract.*[9]

---

[9] Did Lister and I have a contract? Was it an enforceable contract? Can you discuss whether there was an offer to enter a contract and whether there was acceptance of the offer? What were the terms of the contract? What would have constituted material performance of the contract, to the extent a contract had been formed? In this instance, was the contract, to the extent we formed one, founded on a "unilateral mistake"? If I had known there was another ATM nearby, there would have been no reason for me to enter the contract. Lister, *et al*, knew that I was mistaken about the location of the nearest ATM; indeed, they led me to my mistake.

Jurisdictions that interpret unilateral mistake in accord with the Restatement (Second) of Contracts allow for reformation of a contract where one party makes a unilateral mistake and the other party knew about it but failed to bring it to the mistaken party's attention. For example, in *Kish v. Kustura*, 190 Or.App. 458, 460, 79 P.3d 337, 339 (Or.App., 2003), two parties contracted for the sale of real property. The seller and buyer came to an oral agreement for the sale, which was formalized in a letter. However, the buyer later drafted a formal contract containing terms that materially differed from the terms in the letter. The buyer knew that the seller did not speak or write English and assured the seller that the terms were the same as previously agreed to in the letter. The court found this inequitable and reformed the terms of the contract to those in the original agreement, citing the unilateral mistake rule.

See also "The Baseball Card Case," (UNILATERAL MISTAKE: THE BASEBALL CARD CASE, 70 Wash. U. L.Q. 57) involving a dispute between a 12-year-old collector Bryan Wrzesinski and Ball-Mart, a baseball card store in Itasca, Illinois. Bryan had purchased a 1968 Nolan Ryan/Jerry Koosman rookie card for $12, after an unwitting sales clerk misinterpreted the card's price tag reading "1200". The store's proprietor claimed that the card was on sale for $1200, a price in line with its market value, and took Bryan to court to get the card back. The case was settled after two days of trial – the parties agreed to have the card sold at auction with the proceeds going to charity. Presumably, if the judge had come to a decision on the basis of the unilateral mistake rule, little Bryan would have had to give back the card if he knew that the clerk was mistaken about the intended price of the card.

Now, did Lister and I have an agreement, or a contract? Could I have "reformed" my agreement with Lister when I learned there was a nearby ATM? Could I have reformed the contract after I accepted a ride to the ATM?

His name was Ronnie Lister, and he was a character. With Mabel tied into the back of the S-10, and Ronnie and I cramped in the small cab, he drove us down the mountain. Ronnie talked non-stop. He talked about the motel across the street and how he hated that "fat fuck" over there, and how he'd come to learn that lots of small town motels are fronts for running drugs and for prostitution and that's why they stay open even though no one ever stays there. He and the "Fat Fuck" had gotten into a row about a woman a few years earlier, and even though Fat Fuck had been a boxing champion in some underground league, Ronnie had beaten him senseless. I believed that. Ronnie had gotten into a car wreck the week of his high school graduation when he was 17-years-old and half of his face had been ripped off, but an amazing plastic surgeon happened to be in town and that's why he still looked like a human. He turned to face me and pointed at his face so that I could see the light and delicate line where the scar had been.

"Can't even believe it, now," he said. "Half my face. Didn't go to college because of that. Cost a lot."

He talked mostly about his work history and about his current financial condition. When you are an attorney, you hear that stuff a lot. He questioned me about the liability that certain companies or individuals might have to him, and how he could get out of the hole that some state agencies and private actors had put him in. He'd only moved down from Pennsylvania a few years earlier, "For a woman, you know, which is just about the stupidest fucking reason to move anywhere. And Pennsylvania, aw, it sucks, but this place? Goddamn. If I could leave, and if my son were done with school...shit, I'd be gone. You know what I'm sayin'?" I was clear with him that I didn't know the law and that I wasn't his attorney, but agreed with him that he should talk to an attorney because he probably had some actionable claims to get some of his money, expenses, and lost revenue back. He said that he would and thanked me for talking with him. Funny—I was *not* practicing law in Ronnie's truck, but it was probably the best feeling I'd ever had from helping someone with a legal problem.

Then he talked a lot about the business he used to be in, which was concrete, and how he'd put together a crack concrete team made up of the best of the white folks he'd worked with and the best of the Mexicans he'd worked with. "The Mexicans are just harder, you know what I'm sayin'? They ain't smarter, or don't seem it 'cuz they can't talk, but they are harder and faster. They move as slow as grass growing, but Goddamn if they ain't actually faster. Pay 'em with pesos and tacos, practically." And then he told me about how he'd gotten into a concrete pouring race with another guy in Pennsylvania who was black and who "thought his niggers were faster than my boys". And when he said "nigger", he took his eyes completely off the road and stared right at me. I don't know if Ronnie's a racist or not, but to be honest, I really didn't think that he was—I honestly felt like he used that word purposefully to test me, to find out something about me and my limits. It happened a lot on this trip: White dudes would often say "nigger" to test my reaction. It is a powerful word.

He dropped us off near a motel, ATM, and grocery store in Grafton and I gave him his fifty bucks. We had a contract, after all.

It had taken me a month and a half to make it to Grafton. We should have been *well* into Ohio by that time. We had lost days and days and days to the rain and we'd made a pretty poor pace because of the weight of the pack and the awful physical condition I had gotten into by sitting behind a desk for three years. I realized that I'd lost my hiking stick, and I didn't know if I'd lost it during the storm before Mt. Storm, or if Lister had taken it. And then we were stormed into Grafton for a few days while far off in a Pakistani compound, U.S. military forces killed Osama Bin Laden.

On September 11, 2001, I was asleep on my parents' couch when a high school friend of mine called and said: "Turn on the TV, Man, hajjis attacked us. We're at war." He was joking, but he turned out to be right: We were at war, and we still are as I write this. We have always been at war. But in that motel in Grafton, I felt like maybe a chapter in the history of the United States was ending. A bogeyman, of course, but, still, the ostensible justification for two wars of foreign occupation lay dead somewhere at the bottom of the sea. Osama bin Laden had been the mysterious bogeyman of an enemy when I was just out of undergrad, when I was lost out of undergrad, when I was in law school, and when I practiced law. And then he was dead. I remembered the old black women and men who cried and hugged me in the crowd at Grant Park in November 2008. Obama had let us all down, sure, but he was better than the alternative. And he'd overseen the assassination of Osama Bin Laden. That was an important night, and I spent it alone with Mabel in a crappy motel room chatting online with a law school girl somewhere who had gotten a crush on me after reading about my trip on Above the Law and who kept asking to come and visit me that weekend.

There I was.

BOOK I: THE MOMENTS THAT TURN US (B)(v)
THOU ART BUT WHAT THOU SHALT BE—NOTHING—THOU SHALT NOT BE LESS.

The walk from Grafton to Bridgeport was a long, pretty jaunt of about 20 miles along Hwy 50 the entire way, thinking "Ohio" the whole time. If we could just make it to Ohio, we would have enough behind us that we could quit. We would have made enough distance to not be embarrassed, and, anyway, the road would open up in Ohio and we would make better time. The last six miles that day were brutal.

We stopped at a roadside deli about six miles from our destination and I had the best BLT I have ever eaten. I ate the whole thing in about three bites. My brother called and asked how I was doing. I told him that I was fine, because the mountains were behind us and I would have no more hills for quite a while. Of course, right after that conversation, I left the restaurant and found that the final six miles of that day were *all* uphill. Mabel and I were twice nearly killed that day—once by a female driver who was texting while driving and once by a male driver who stared right into my eyes as he swerved at us to scare us. That was the first time on the trip that a driver purposefully swerved at us to scare us, but wouldn't be the last by far. The last mile was a killer, but we made it to the Sleep Inn in Bridgeport by about 6:30 in the afternoon and I was in bed and asleep almost immediately.

The next morning we were up and out before 8 a.m., because we had to make it to Wolf's Summit to meet with ADT trail angel Kay Hunt. She had a young lawyer friend who wanted to meet with me, so I bought a clean t-shirt and body spray at the Walgreen's before we left town.

The Sun was bright but it was not so hot out, and there was a nice cooling breeze but it wasn't cold. It was everything you could want from a hiking day. We walked along pretty open fields, and among small rolling hills and over a grand rise and fall into Clarksburg. Then, on the other side of Clarksburg, we were bum rushed on the side of the road by a pretty young lady named Sandy who was a dog lover. Unlike the previous dog lovers who had left food along the road or what not, this girl unabashedly pulled over and jumped out of her car.

"Oh my God!" she said. "She is *so* cute!" Mabel jumped up and her tail wagged furiously. "She is so cute. I saw you when I was going the other way and I brought you food and water for this cute puppy. Are you two ok?"

"Yes, we are," I said, and told her we were hiking across the country.

"That is *awesome*," she said. She was an energetic thing, and I would have immediately been intimidated by her energy if it were not absolutely clear from the look in her eyes that she was a good person. "I *love* dogs. I work with several of the rescues in the area." Her eyes flashed when she talked about her work with rescue organizations. And that flash seemed to turn almost violent when she talked about the state of the dogs when they come into the rescue and the treatment she had seen before. I shared her sentiments, entirely.

"Look at her!" She said. "You're her *world.* You're her *whole world.*" She said it with a smile and a nod, and stared right into my eyes when she said it. Some people get the human/dog relationship, some don't. She did. She was a big personality in a normal sized body. She left me the food and the water and said she would check on me later. I said it wasn't necessary because I had a rendezvous in Wolf Summit and would have a warm house to sleep in that night, but she winked and nodded and I knew she would be back to find me because she loved Mabel. We walked a little bit faster after that. Sometimes meeting good people made us walk faster.

Mabel and I had gone a ways when an SUV pulled to a stop in front of us on the shoulder and two women stepped out. Sandy was there, and I could tell that the other woman walking toward us was Sandy's mother.

"We come to save you!" the mother said.

"What?" I called out, smiling and shaking my head. I met the women on the side of the road, about 15 feet in front of their car.

"I told Mom about you and she said we had to come and pick you up."

"But I'm *walking*," I said. "Kind of defeats the purpose."

"You can't walk up there," the mother said.

"I said you could, but she says you can't," Sandy added.

"It just isn't safe, Tyler," the mother said. Sandy had told her my name. "There's construction, and they've got those concrete things all along the road."

"But there's a shoulder?"

"Not in some places," the mother said. "In one little stretch, I don't think you even *can* make it. Let alone safe. You'd get hit and get killed and where would little Mabel be then?"

"With me, probably," Sandy said, and laughed. Then she spoke to Mabel and scrunched up Mabel's puppy face with her hands. "Yes you would! Yes you would have to come live with me!"

I protested for a bit, but it was a losing battle: They would absolutely not let me go any farther on foot because they thought it was dangerous. I relented and put my pack in the back of their vehicle and Mabel and I climbed into the back seat.

"Did you come over the mountain?" the mother asked and I told her we had. "Were you safe?"

"We were safe," I said.

"Hmm. Lucky, I think. It's different up there. People are different up there."

"How so?" I asked.

"They are..."

"They're just backward," Sandy said.

"They are backward," the mother said. "They are backward up there, a little. They are a different kind up there, and there isn't as much niceness. There are good, Christian people up there, too. But there are people who are dangerous and just all kinds of backward. My husband, Sandy's father, come from up the mountain."

Sandy and her mother carried me through the "dangerous" part of the highway, which looked to me as though it would have been safe. And once we had gone that far, Sandy's mother decided she would drive us into Wolf Summit. The car was already in motion, so I didn't have much say in that, and it was only a mile or two, anyway. She dropped us off at an insurance agency in the town of Wolf Summit. "Town" is too big of a word for the place—it's a village.

I waited there to hear from Kay Hunt, and the folks who lived in the apartment above the insurance agency brought me a chicken sandwich, some pie, and a couple of cans of soda. So I talked with them for a while about the weather and about West Virginia. They were good folks, and they struck me as pretty similar to a lot of the folks who I had known growing up. I doubt they had very much, but people who have very little often give more than they can afford and after I'd finished my lunch they brought me *another* lunch and I ate it, too. Kay called after a while and told me that she'd contacted the local news and a reporter was *en route* to talk with me. A young cub reporter named Zach showed up after a while and I did an interview with him. How should I answer questions like "Why" or "Do you have any advice for people"?

Well, yes, I guess: Don't let your life get all fucked up like mine. That's what I should have said. I don't remember what I did say, but I'm sure it wasn't quite as honest as that.

Kay set me up with a place to stay in Wolf Summit with her friend, Kyra. I never caught Kyra's last name. Kyra was a very nice lady who had hosted

Jack a few weeks earlier. Her husband and children lived in Pennsylvania, where she spent her weekends, but during the week she lived down in West Virginia in a rented house to be closer to her job. She had to attend a sports function that night, but she took me into her house and told me to make myself at home. Once she was gone, I tied Mabel to the pack in the living room and took a shower in her bathroom in the back of the house. After my shower, I came back into the house all clean and happy and thought: "Jesus, this house *stinks*." Kyra was such a nice person and her house was so nicely kept and decorated, but it smelled awful, and that surprised me. After about a minute I realized that the stench came from my backpack. It smelled like sweat and camp smoke. The night in the tipi had smoked everything I owned, so I moved all of my dirty equipment out onto her porch before Kyra got home.

Kay picked me up to take me to dinner. First she gave me a tour—we saw a rebuilt town of log cabins, one of which her husband had been born in. The museum folks bought it from her husband's family and moved it down off the mountain to put it in this rebuilt frontier town. She took me by a college where a week or so earlier Beyonce and Jay Z had come to see Jay Z's nephew graduate, or something. And she showed me all around the towns in the area. Her lawyer friend had gotten busy and had to cancel, but Kay and I had a nice meal and talked about the hike and the hiking that she and her husband had done. They were avid hikers and *loved* to host thru-hikers. They had hosted Jack, and had hosted infamous long distance hikers like Lion King.

Kyra made breakfast for me the next morning and Mabel and I hit the trail shortly after she left for work, around 7:30. After having followed Hwy 50 for quite a while, we were back on trail on the West Virginia Rails-Trails. The Rails-Trail is a network of reclaimed railway right of ways. There are no tracks or ties anymore, and the trails are wide, grassy, and relatively flat because it was once a railway. The weather forecast was, of course, for more rain, so Mabel and I were in a hurry to beat the weather. The first seven miles or so of the trail that day were muddy and hard to traverse due to some pretty serious flooding in the previous weeks, but we made amazingly good time. We did the first seven miles in about an hour and a half. By two o'clock, we were very near the Shell station where Kay was to pick us up that night. So we stopped a while and napped—Mabel in the shade and I in the Sun. We lay there quite a while in a patch of tall, soft, green grass beside a river. If it were not for the highway off to our right, it would have been as peaceful and pastoral as anything you could imagine. I took pictures of the grass, and I took my shirt off so the grass could scratch my skin. Mabel looked content sleeping in the grass. I lugged the pack back on and we hiked on when I thought we were in danger of getting caught in the storm.

Up trail we crossed a pedestrian footbridge over the river, then walked under a tunnel beneath a different highway, and then the walkway rose up to the parking lot of a Shell station. We beat the rain there, but there was a scheduling issue with Kay and David. They were hours away watching a nephew play baseball and, because of a rain delay, they would not be back to get me until about 10 o'clock that night. So we would have to wait. We hiked up to the Shell and got some food, then went back to the pedestrian tunnel and sat down inside of it to wait out the rain. Kay and David called and told me it would probably be 11 p.m. before they got there. So we relaxed, I read, and we slept in a tunnel under a highway and stayed dry from the rain. It would not be the last time on the trip that I slept under a highway.

Mabel curled into a ball on top of the tarp and I dreamt of Ohio with my head on the cold pavement.

Kay and David picked me up around 11 and took me to their beautiful home somewhere in the countryside near West Union. Their home is spacious and tastefully decorated, and the garage is lined with deer antlers that David had displayed as mounted trophies. The mounts looked like deer sheds to me, but I grew up in Pike County, Illinois, where bucks are legendary and where a rack with fewer than 16 points is no trophy at all—but he wasn't a trophy hunter. Kay teaches high school and David is a retired postal worker, and they are both sweet and kind and pleasant to talk with. I talked with them briefly that night, and I had some ice cream, but I was pretty tired despite the long tunnel-nap I had taken and was pretty quickly off and into bed. I took a shower first and found four ticks on me, though only one had bitten. I could hear Kay downstairs starting a load of laundry as I drifted to sleep and I wondered if she was washing my clothes. She was.

We ate breakfast the next morning and they told me stories about Lion King staying with them, and they told me that Jack had planned on staying with them for one night but had gotten sick and ended up there for three or four days. I had been concerned about getting sick since day one of the trip, but I was not so concerned as I could have been. I had a Blue Cross Blue Shield card in my travel wallet because I had COBRA insurance. Jack, on the other hand, was probably uninsured. Now that would be a different hike, altogether. I hadn't had call to use my health insurance on the trip—or ever— and I was not inclined to do so. So I was thankful that I was still feeling healthy, if exhausted.

Kay dropped us off at the Shell station where she had picked us up and Mabel and I were hiking by 9 a.m. that morning. Our bellies were full and we were well rested after two hosted nights in a row, and my pack had plenty of rice and beans and ramen and Snickers bars. But we didn't get our long day that day. The weather came and sent us hiding in an overhang of an abandoned church a few hundred feet off the trail in a nearly abandoned small town. To kill time, I found a fallen branch from a tree and set to work carving a new walking stick for myself. The wood was light and seemed strong enough, though I would have preferred to have my ironwood staff back—but it was gone, and we could not backtrack. When the weather cleared, we hiked back to the trail and set off hoping for Ellenboro. We didn't make it to Ellenboro.

We made it to the actual town of West Union before the next rain sent us off the trail to a gas station. I got a cup of coffee and we hid under the gas station awning. A middle-aged man who was originally from New Jersey but who had relocated to West Virginia for the "cost of living" was standing there trying to raise money for an animal shelter, and he gave me a sermon on Ron Paul. I did not doubt his good intentions or the sincerity of his beliefs. As it turns out, he told me, the United States is a few years away from food riots because Obama, *et al*, have been planning—some say since 1945 and some say since 1913—to turn the United States into a "Third World Country". He was of the opinion that the machinations had been in place since 1913. I mean, the Federal Reserve! Gold! Food riots! Gold! This was all true, he assured me, because he had researched it all himself. You can't walk across America without running into these Ron Paul conspiracy types, and they make me angry because there probably will be food riots and civil unrest probably is coming—because that's just the nature of things, it happens—and these crazies will claim to have been right all along.

The rain cleared but came back a few miles down the trail. We didn't enjoy hiking in rain, and I had done so much of it on the Canal that I wanted out of it for the rest of the trip. The rain, plus the unexpected long stop in the middle of the day, threw my whole body off. Mabel was fine, but I was feeling tired and drained, and I began to wonder if maybe I had gotten sick while staying with Kyra or with David and Kay. We stopped at an intersection where the Rails-Trail crossed a gravel country road. There was a trailer on the corner, and a nice young man lived there with a friendly dog, so I stopped and talked to him.

"Hey there."

"Hello, Sir," he said.

He was a young and very powerfully built man. I was sure he was only a few years out of high school and out of high school football. He called me "Sir", and that bothered me a little—*cuz I ain't that old*—but "Sir" was a common thing in West Virginia. I guess that's some strain of southern hospitality.

"My dog and I are hiking across the country, and...."

"The whole country? That's awesome," he said.

"Would be if we could do it. We're done for the day, I think. Looking for a place to camp. You know of any place here or up the trail we could camp? Maybe even in your yard?"

"Well, hell, you *can*. You can camp right here in my yard if you want to. But there's a motel just down the hill."

"Where?" I asked. He pointed.

"Right there. Two hundred yards, maybe. Right down there behind those trees. You're more than welcome here, but you'll be a bit warmer and more comfortable down there on a real bed, wouldn't you?"

We talked a bit longer about the weather and about hiking and about sports and about his job. He was a nice fellow and I almost regretted not camping in his yard. But the rain came and the temperature dropped, so Mabel and I tripped on down the hill to the motel. At the bottom of the hill, we could see the parking lot of the motel off to the left and then we could see the motel itself. We were in Greenwood, West Virginia.

The "motel", such as it was, was a rundown looking cash-only place that was run by the owner's middle-aged son and a German Shepherd that looked very mean but that seemed content to lean against the motel and keep watch over things; Mabel was desperate to play with the big dog, but the big dog was having none of it and finally trotted off annoyed. Two of the rooms on the far end were undergoing remodeling, and otherwise all but one of the rooms looked unoccupied. The owner's son walked limply across the parking lot; he was a sickly thin thing with a deeply tanned face and a thin beard.

"Aren't you the guy from the news?"

"Might be," I said. "You got a room?"

"Got a few," he answered.

"Dogs?"

"Sure," he said. "Why not?"

"How much?"

"Forty bucks," he said. "Cash only."

We slept hard that night and I pulled two ticks off of me, one from my head and one from my long beard. I found several ticks dead in the bed the next morning when I woke up. That day was clear, and we pushed through 17 miles to the campsite at North Bend State Park. It was a fee-use campground, but I paid and didn't complain and we had access to a soda machine and cell service, so it wasn't too bad. And we had an enormous open pasture of green grass to camp in, for a change. Finding camping spots had been easy on the C & O Canal, but Rails-Trail had no designated camping. There at the Park the camping was easy and it was nice to lie back down on the Earth where a human should be most comfortable sleeping.

Our quandary that day was that it was 32 miles to Parkersburg and that meant a little over 32 miles to Ohio. OHIO! We could spread it out over two days, but then a line of storms coming our way would be on top of us. In stormy weather (and even in clear weather) it would be difficult to find a place to camp on the Rails-Trail. Or, we could hike to Parkersburg in one day and be asleep in a nice, warm motel in a normal town and have access to a fresh meal and maybe take a day off on our own to really relax. That would be nice, but it would mean a 32-mile day. I had not done anything close to that since the 26-mile day in Maryland, and the big 25er off the C & O, and both had nearly killed me. Thirty-two miles is a long way even without 70 pounds strapped to your back, and every day my feet were killing me at around the 10- or 12-mile mark.

The thing about hiking with a heavy pack is that the more miles you do, the faster the marginal difficulty of each mile increases. For example, the mile you walk between miles two and three is *nowhere* near as difficult as the mile you walk between miles 26 and 27. There is a point—for me, it is about 27 miles now—where the marginal difficulty of each mile starts to increase exponentially. Each mile after 27 is about 23 times harder than the preceding mile.

So I juggled the options back and forth for a long while, whether to spread the 32 miles out over two days or to try a 32-mile day...the first 30-miler of the trip. Then I wrote in my journal: *"I want to try a 30-mile day tomorrow, but I am not optimistic. We will have to stop several times to tend to my feet, and, even without that, we are looking at least at 14 hours. Will try to get up early."*

Book II: Feel the Selfish Fury (B)(ii)
Dreaming when Dawn's Left Hand was in the Sky.

Iowa City is one of the greatest places to live in the United States. Everyone who has ever lived there agrees: Living in Iowa City makes life seem comfortable and pleasant. It is a liberating and intelligent place. An oasis on the Prairie. The People's Republic of Iowa City. A gorgeous little city with tree-lined streets, and brick-paved streets hidden deep in residential areas. It is bisected by the Iowa River and is a city of bridges, like Chicago or Paris, but small. Downtown and campus have an urban look and feel, so when you first arrive you almost think you are in a quaint part of some rust-belt city, maybe Pittsburgh. The Law School is on the bluff overlooking the Iowa River and the hydropower dam, and from the balcony on the back of the law school you can look out over the river to the Pentacrest that sits atop another hill on the far side of the river. The guy pouring your beer or making your espresso is as likely as you are to have a master's degree. Some of the brightest and most talented writers in the world live in Iowa City and study at the Iowa Writers' Workshop.[10]

And there I was. Right in the middle a little town where anyone can live and be happy! It is the perfect place to just be and to live for a few years while burying your mind into a discipline. The two most important things in Iowa City are fun and academia. It is the college town *qua* college town. And I loved it.

My 1L summer was the happiest of my life. I was a research assistant that summer for Professor Traurig. She was working on a fascinating legal history of slavery and emancipation *in the North* and writing a book about Harriet Scott.[11] I ran every day or night down from the bluff and up onto the Pentacrest, around the Ped Mall, and through tree-lined residential areas. It was really a pleasant summer.

I had a lot of great non-law student friends in town for the summer, and we hung out all the time. We sat on patios outside cafes and drank beers for lunch. They told me about their lives in Croatia and India, and they told me

---

[10] The Iowa Writer's Workshop is arguably the world's preeminent writing program. Among its former faculty and student body are Flannery O'Connor, John Irving, Nelson Algren, John Cheever, Raymond Carver, Philip Roth, and, of course, Kurt Vonnegut, Jr. The list of notables from the workshop could go on at length; it has produced about 20 Pulitzer Prize winning writers

[11] During our first meeting about her research, Traurig told me that in her research she had discovered the story of Free Frank McWorter. McWorter was a slave who bought his own freedom, then the freedom of his entire family. It was my understanding that he walked from North Carolina to Illinois and founded the town of New Philadelphia, about ten miles from where I grew up, although in reality he walked from Kentucky to Illinois. New Philadelphia was the first American community incorporated by a freed slave. The town had long since died by the time I was born. But in the mid-1980s, my history-buff father and I trampled around in a new growth forest and fought our way over overgrown fencerows to find the cemetery where McWorter lay buried. I first heard the McWorter story from my father in the 1980s, and it was perhaps that story that first caused me to think of walking across the continent.

about the chemistry projects they were working on, or their med-school problems, or whatever. I loved it. And I *loved* that for some reason these hyper-intelligent folks, mostly scientists, for some reason treated *me* as the smart one. I was the smart one? Strange, that. *They* were the smart ones, but I let them persist in the perception that I was the "smart law student". We crashed pretentious Workshop parties and drank and danced and made fun of the business school kids. Being in the law program instead of in another graduate program gave me (and the others) a cache that I had never had before and that I loved, even if the cache was largely unfounded.

That was the happiest summer of my life. I loved every second of it until I contracted Lyme disease on a hike near my parents' home in west-central Illinois. But even the Lyme disease symptoms—which are pretty bad—didn't get me down, and couldn't break my stride.

The hiring season starts at the end of the 1L summer—the goal is to get a "summer associate" position. The big firms give summer associate positions based primarily on 1L grades and on a brief 15-minute interview followed by a "callback" interview, usually on-site at the firm. It is very difficult, though not impossible, to get a high paying biglaw job without first having a summer association position with the firm. Biglaw! The largest, most profitable firms that pay the best are given that epithet—biglaw. Essentially, the choicest jobs are won based on 1L grades and little else. The result is that most law students incur *massive* student loan debt to pay for three years of schooling, but at some point during the first year at least the gunners realize that the game is right there in front of them. If you don't kill it 1L year, then you are going to be a "country lawyer" or an "ambulance chaser" or some other, equally stigmatized kind of lawyer. Those stigmas are unfair, but they are real.

"Did you bid on Sidley?" Adam Zimerman asked me. We were sitting together in ill-fitting suits in the lobby of the Tippie School of Business where the OCI interviews took place.

"No," I said.

"Thought you would. I interviewed the other day with [a very large firm] and the recruiter from that firm asked me why I hadn't bid on Sidley. I told them I wasn't interested in Chicago. But everyone says that Sidley is a great place."

"I should have bid on them," I agreed. "But I focused on some place where I knew, without question, I would get a job. I've got loans."

"Me, too," Zimerman said. He had a persistent look of worry on his face, and it always got worse when debt or finals were mentioned.

I interviewed with quite a few firms during OCI week, and got quite a few callbacks. Firms flew me to Chicago and to Minneapolis and put me up in great hotels and took me to great lunches and dinners. I couldn't believe the amount of money that firms spent to recruit *me*, even though the only thing I'd ever accomplished was to do well in my 1L year. The game was over, really, and the only thing left was to get through a three-month summer internship without pissing anyone off and then I would be golden. My head swelled a little. My head *really* swelled when two Sidley recruiters came to Iowa Law during the first week of classes, instead of during the OCI week.

The Iowa career services office emailed me to schedule an interview the night before Sidley came to campus. I had not even bid on Sidley.

I walked into the interview in my crumpled suit, and they were running a little behind. We introduced ourselves to each other, and I told them that I was surprised to have heard from them because I hadn't bid on Sidley.

"We bid on you," the female recruiter said. She was a very successful attorney at Sidley Austin. "We saw your resume and wanted to talk with you."

I knew I was in. Just like that.

These two interviewers were several cuts above the rest I had talked to. They were clearly more intelligent, more at ease and professional, and were both Iowa grads. The interview went very well and I left absolutely knowing I would get a callback interview with the fifth largest law firm in the country.

Book I: The Moments That Turn Us (B)(v)(a)
Gently, Brother, Gently, Pray.

We left North Bend State Park on May 10, determined to push 32 miles through to Parkersburg. We started strong. It was Ohio, Ohio, Ohio. Gateway to the Midwest. We could make up time there. Mabel could do 32 miles on her worst days, and I *believed* that I could do it on my best day. We had plenty of water to go for half the day, at least, so that wouldn't be an issue. The Rails-Trails network was supposed to lead us through some towns along the way, and I had planned to grab drinks and some snacks along the way, even though we were doing well on food.

The path was straight and maintained pretty well along that last section. Along the way we walked through three or four "towns" I had expected, and the largest of them was Cairo, which was little more than a collection of buildings that served as a convenient stop for Rails-Trail hikers. There were a few buildings on one side of what once might have been a square, and a single, central main intersection of two roads. There was a store there called a "bike shop", but there were no bikes there, only convenience store food and drink and a lot of items that a thru-hiker might need or want. I picked up batteries to be sure I would have extra for my flashlight and headlamp, because I knew it would be a long day. The day threatened to be so long, in fact, that I decided to stop for a while at a pleasant gazebo in the middle of Cairo to do some foot maintenance. Holes were beginning to form at the tips of three different toes. I taped the holes up and almost wished that I had the type of skin that was susceptible to blistering—these holes worn through my skin and flesh seemed to be a bigger concern to me than blisters would have been. But I put some antibiotic ointment on them, taped them up, and then gave my feet a good rub to loosen them up. I ate snack foods and drank a soda for energy, and stuffed an extra soda in my pack, just in case. I fed Mabel a second breakfast, too, because she seemed to do better on long days when she ate three times instead of two. It seemed that both of us did better the more often we ate—frequency mattered as much as amount.

The road was long.

We happened upon a woman mowing along the trail outside of Cairo. She didn't own the Rails-Trail, so it seemed odd that she would be mowing it—it seemed like something my grandfather would have done. She stopped the mower and we chatted. She asked and I told her where we were going and what were doing (more or less) and she said she thought I might be the guy she'd heard about. Her cousin or some other relation had seen the story on the news a few days earlier.

"See any snakes?" she asked.

"None," I said. "Just as well, because I hate snakes."

"Oh, me too," she said. "My mom and I walk along here. That's why I mow it. I don't know who is *supposed* to mow it, but I'm the one who does. I just mow this section where Mom and I walk, though."

"Keeps the snakes under control?"

"Not really," she said, and laughed. "But it makes them easier to see. I haven't seen a single snake this year. Not yet. Hope I don't see any."

"Me, too," I agreed. "I hate snakes."

"Well, you'll probably see some. You've got a tunnel up here, and then there will probably be quite a few. It gets wetter up there, and...well...there are snakes there. There will be some snakes. Mom and I don't usually walk up that far. Because of the snakes."

"I hate snakes," I said.

"Oh, I do, too," she agreed. She wished me luck and Mabel and I walked on. I kept a steady rhythm and pace with my new homemade walking stick. My breathing was controlled and in tune with my steps. I was *getting it.*

There are a thousand ways to walk. You can walk with different postures and with different gaits. You can change the way your hips sway, or the part of your foot that makes initial contact with the ground. You can vary the rhythm and the length of your stride, and you can move your shoulders forward or backward to alter the center of gravity. There are a thousand things you can do if you are searching for that *right* way of walking. In the end, there is no right way, and the secret is to keep changing it up. Keep altering and keep inventing and keep experimenting. That's the secret to maintaining pace without causing injuries. I even pulled the walking stick up at about the halfway point and carried it along with me like a spear rather than a cane sometimes.

I was re-learning how to walk.

But I was probably paying a little bit too much attention to *how* I was walking, and not quite enough attention to *where* I was walking and what I was about to step on.

So we were almost right on top of the timber rattler when I saw it and heard its rattle. My heart (and my outstretched right foot) stopped, and I stood there on one leg, about to put my foot down on the thing. The trail in that section is a lot like the C & O Canal—more-or-less a gravel road—and still somehow I hadn't seen the snake in the middle of the road. And Mabel had almost no reaction to it, at all. It was as if she didn't even recognize that it was a living thing. My forehead began to sweat, because the snake rattled and coiled up. It was not very big, though, and as I slowly moved my foot backward and took one step back, I told myself that it was so small that a bite from it would not even hurt, let alone kill me. Of course, I had no reason to believe that was true, but it settled my heart and my nerves. Once we were out of what I figured to be striking distance of the thing, I used my stick to encourage it to get the hell out of my way. We had to make good time, but I didn't want to hurt the snake, so I barely nudged it with the end of my walking stick and it sort of uncoiled and, if snakes were able to have and to show emotions, it would have said something like: "Oh, Sir, I didn't know you wanted by here. I'll be moving right along now." It was so calm and serene. I watched it slither off into the grass.

I felt no fear during that encounter, but I did get a startle, and it certainly changed my level of perception for the rest of the day: I must have seen a hundred or more snakes that afternoon. Mostly they were off to the side, slithering around pools of water or searching out a place to wait to ambush little vermin. There were a few rattlesnakes, but always at a safe distance and no other rattlers made that horrible sound that day. And I *thought* I saw a few copperheads, but even though the copperhead is a pretty distinct looking snake, I couldn't be sure because, thankfully, they were all off on the leaf covered embankments or slithering around in the leaves and detritus gathered along the banks of a trickle of water from a spring.

I don't know a lot about snakes; I can't identify one kind of rattler from another. Who knows what kinds of snakes are poisonous and what kinds aren't? That's a tough business, right there. But here's the thing with snakes: If you encounter a snake in your path and it slithers off in a hurry, it probably isn't a poisonous snake; if you encounter a snake in your path and *it doesn't move*, then it's probably poisonous. They know what they have. Humans are the same way sometimes.

It was very warm that day and I had to stop several times to let Mabel cool down. We stopped about every 30 minutes for little breaks, and Mabel would pant and lay flat on the ground and then look at me with calm eyes and stand when she was ready to go. We went through about three gallons of water that day, which was the most we'd gone through in a single day.

My feet began to hurt pretty badly at about 15 miles, but I felt that we didn't have enough time to stop for me to rub my feet. Rubbing my feet had always greatly reduced the pain and helped me push through the longer mileage days, but on this day we were racing the Sun. At about 20 miles, though, the pain was pretty bad and my shoulders were starting to go, so I decided we should stop at the next suitable location to eat something and to let my feet breathe. We found a picnic table at a trailhead up trail and sat for quite a while, eating and watching my feet swell. Mabel hid from the Sun under the picnic table. And, within about 10 minutes of stopping, a man rode up on a bicycle and stopped. He was a completely average looking man and I would have guessed him to be about 50.

"Hey there, you look like you're goin' somewhere," he said and pulled to a stop. He put his feet on the ground, but stayed straddled over the bike.

"California," I said.

"Well that's quite a ways!" He pulled the front wheel of his bike off the ground and let the tire bounce when he dropped it, like children sometimes do. He was wearing canvas hiking pants and a rain poncho of some sort, although there was no chance of rain that day, and a bizarre hat that cannot be described. He had a fanny pack on, as well, and I wondered if he was a diabetic or if he just liked fanny packs...or if it was a concealed gun.

"How old do you think I am?" he asked.

"Fifty?"

"Hah. Hah! I'm 63 years old. I'm retired. Bet you thought I was 45 didn't you?"

"I thought you might be," I said.

"You got a gun?" This was the second most common question I got on the entire trip, behind the why of the thing.

"No," I said.

"Walking across the whole country? Well, I wouldn't do that without a gun. I don't like guns, but that's your business. I don't like guns. I have guns, quite a few. But I don't like them. I just need to have them. I don't like guns, but what I can't *stand* is insurance companies."

"I'm not a big fan, either," I said. "It's gambling, and I'm not a big gambler."

"House always wins," he said. "House always wins. Guess what I do?"

"You're retired?"

"But what I did? No? Can't guess?" I shook my head. "Doctor. I retired, though. Because I hate insurance companies. I *hate* them."

"They ought to nationalize the whole thing," I said.

"Be a damn sight better than dealing with insurance companies. Except then I'd have to deal with Medicare. But it's different for a doctor. Different in a lot of ways, but I couldn't stand dealing with insurance companies."

The strange thing about this guy was that he did not seem to speak quickly, but he spoke a lot.

"Got out of that. I do a few things now. I have a real estate business that I have been doing for 20 years. I got into that because I couldn't stand insurance companies. But what I really do is I invest in gold. What do you do?"

"I'm an attorney," I said.

"Hah!"

"I am."

"Well, that's something. Where's your office?"

"Don't have one," I said. "I used to work at a big firm in Chicago."

"Which firm?" he asked, and I told him. "Oh, I know that firm," he said. "That's because I read. I read the news, I read everything. People don't read enough. Not anymore if they ever did. I read. That's the firm that handles the Tribune Company."

"Yes," I said. "Sidley handles the Tribune bankruptcy. I was in the bankruptcy group there, but I didn't work on that project much."

"You know, I only know that because I'm a baseball fan. I can't stand to watch it, but I like to read about it. I like to read the stats. And the Chicago Cubs were sold, weren't they?"

"Yes," I said.

"Yes. I read everything. Even the sports section. There's things to be learned all over God's Earth, and even in the sports section. I used to read

117

nothing but medical books, but that wasn't enough for me. So now I read everything. I read the news, and the sports, and I read about the market. Oh, I follow the market closely."

"It's quite something to follow," I said, and put my shoes on while he talked.

"It's something. It's trouble. We *cannot* go on like this. That's the truth. Not with this kind of debt. No nation on Earth in the history of nations on Earth has carried this kind of debt. Not for long. And the whole country will fail."

"I sometimes think so, too," I said.

"It will. I can tell you when. 2030. That's when. This country will fail in 2030. You know why? Because of the Chinese. In 2031, your kids will be learning Mandarin in the schools. That's the truth."

"What if I teach them Mandarin before that?"

"Good thinking," he said. "Best to be prepared." He had sensed that I was about to leave, and he had turned his bike around to face the direction of my travel. "But don't worry if you don't get around to it, because they will. The Chinese will teach your kids to speak Chinese and to eat rice. The whole country will fail and the Chinese will own us all."

"I think the Chinese have some problems of their own," I said.

"Nope. You know they are the single largest creditor to the United States of America? And do you know how much we owe them? You can't even count it. And they can call that debt, call it right up. What if they were to call that debt?"

"Then our economy would collapse," I said, "and China would have no one to sell DVD players to."

"Nope. They can sell to their own people! Like we used to do. Back when we made things and sold things. Now we don't do that. We just buy. And our currency...you think that currency you carry around with you is worth anything? It isn't. It isn't worth paper. And it's just paper. 2030 is when this nation stops."

"Think so?" I asked, and I looked at him, trying to hide a grin. "What's Chinese currency made from?" Then he raised a hand to point at me and said:

"If any man speak in an unknown tongue, let it be by two, or at the most by three, and that by course; and let one interpret. But if there be no interpreter, let him keep silence in the church; and let him speak to himself, and to God. Let the prophets speak two or three, and let the other judge. If any thing be revealed to another that sitteth by, let the first hold his peace. For ye may all prophesy one by one, that all may learn, and all may be comforted. And the spirits of the prophets are subject to the prophets. For God is not the author of confusion, but of peace, as in all churches of the saints."

I did not react immediately.

"You know what that means?"

"No," I said.

"It means take a prophesy to your preacher and ask him if it is a real prophesy. That is how you judge a prophet and his prophesy."

"Oh," I said. "I actually have another, slightly more efficient way to judge prophesies."

I started walking and he rode alongside me. As soon as he started riding, he became uncontrollably flatulent and kept trumpeting farts off the seat of his bike while he talked on an on about things. Red meat: he doesn't eat it. Free market: only true form of government. Ron Paul: next president, if we knew what was good for us and if we weren't already owned by the Chinese. Welfare: turns people into beggars. Black people: would all probably be dead if not for welfare, or maybe they would be employed like the rest of "us".

"You carry a gun?"

"I don't," I said, again. I didn't think this guy was a threat to me.

"You should carry a gun. I hate guns, but I have several. You have to. You *have* to these days. I wouldn't walk across this country without one. I wouldn't walk across Parkersburg without one. I'm not from here, you know, I'm originally from Pennsylvania. But you should have a gun and know how to use it."

"I have a big stick," I said. "And I know how to use *that*. And bear spray. I think I'll be ok."

"You know how to defend yourself with a gun? There are a lot of ways. There are a lot of things you should know. I have a few guys who taught me how to defend myself, but it's pretty much common sense when you think about it. What you need is a holster under your arm. You know why? No, now, most people would think that it's because it's quicker to draw. But it isn't, not always. But it *is* quicker to draw if you are shooting off to your side. And 74% of the time, when someone is attacking you, it's going to be from the side. Think about it! If you were going to attack someone, would you go straight on into them or would you come at them from the side?"

"From the side, I guess," I said. "Most of the time, anyway."

He stopped his bike and motioned for me to watch. He then demonstrated what it looks like when you draw from your hip to shoot off to your side, and then what it looks like when you draw from a shoulder holster to shoot off to your side.

"But that's not even the half of it, really. What you really want to do is...here, hold this bike."

He got off the bike and walked back a few feet and held his hands up like he was about to lecture.

"Now, when you have to defend yourself, and you *will* have to defend yourself. Especially in this world. Right now in this world? Yes, you'll have to defend yourself. What you need to do is just one quick motion where you fall back, sort of onto your buttocks, and in the same motion you have to pull that gun. See? Then you're firing up and the man coming at you is farther away. That's the key, to be as far away as possible. Here, watch this:" He mimed like he was pulling a gun and at the same time took two quick steps backwards. "That's good, sure, it gets you a little ways away from the guy but watch this:" Then, in one quick motion, he mimed like was pulling a gun and fell back onto his ass on the ground and fired his finger pistol at me

119

from between the V his legs made. Mabel barked and lunged at him with her teeth bared.

"Oh, she's ok," he said, as he got himself up. "She's ok. She just knows that that's the best way. That right there. You should work on that move because that could save your life."

"I will," I said. "But first I have to walk to Parkersburg."

"That's a good place to work on it," he said.

He warned me about the segment of trail I was coming upon, a segment that he never travels, especially at night, because there are mean dogs there. But I wasn't too worried, because we had already fought off several dogs on the trip. Then, almost without warning, he stood off the saddle of his bike and peddled fast, shouting: "I have to go, have to beat that Sunset. You have a good trip and be safe!"

Just like that, he was out of my life forever.

But we had miles and miles to go, and those were slow miles. The Sun was setting fast. My feet hurt badly, and my shoulders, too, and by that time my hips were starting to hurt and to cramp in the little muscles of my hip that help to extend the leg during a stride. A cramp in those muscles can end a day quickly, but I slowed when the cramps were coming on and loosened or tightened the hip belt on my pack. It's important to keep shifting the weight a little and to keep shifting, only a little, the places where the pack makes contact with your upper body. And, even though there was pain, I kept walking and could because my mind was empty.

The Sun went down completely and it got cold fast. It was dark by 8:30 p.m. and it was cold, and we had at least another hour to hike—even if we were at our three m.p.h pace, which I highly doubted that we were. I stopped to put on an extra layer on top. I ate another handful of nuts and dried fruit and we set back off on the trail by the light of the headlamp and the flashlight. It was our first true night hike of the trip. Hiking at night is a different experience, because the sounds and shadows at night are unlike the sounds and shadows of the day. With every movement in the trees or every rustle of dry leaves on the ground, I thought for sure a bear would pop out and devour me. I unhooked Mabel from the hip belt, just in case. If a bear did appear and devour me, at least Mabel could get free and run to safety. Or maybe she could run to the next town and bark until someone said: "What is it, Girl? What's-a matter? Tyler's eaten by a bear? Where?" And then she could lead them to me and find my partially eaten carcass laying languid in the pale light of the moon that filtered through the trees into little diamond shaped splashes of light on my colorless skin and the blood stained tatters of my clothes. That would be a decent way to go.

My body began to give out when we walked into a developed area. The trail started to cross roads more frequently, and I could see houses or hear the noises that came from them a little off the trail, and I knew that we were in some sort of a town. I'd studied the map so closely and I knew we had made it to the outskirts of Parkersburg. I pulled the phone from my pocket when I realized I had not secured a place to stay in Parkersburg, and I frantically started calling every motel I could find. There was one that would accept pets; I can't remember what brand, and I told them to hold a room for me. But the motel was another 10 miles away and there was no way I could make it there. So I walked in as far as I could and then cut up through a residential district and walked around until I found a place I thought I could describe well enough to order a cab. It was a grocery store on a dark, empty road. I drank two sodas from the soda machine before the cab driver showed up.

In the cab on the ride to the motel, I told him that I was walking across the country.

"I knew you must have been walking somewhere," he said. "Saw the size of your calves and I figured you were walking somewhere."

"The pack was very heavy," I said. "It's lighter now."

I was starving when we got checked into the motel, but it was no use to try to order food or find food nearby. I collapsed on the bed without taking off any of my clothes except the boots. I fought hard to free the sheets and covers and climbed into bed. I thought "Well, this is my life", and then I was asleep.

BOOK I: THE MOMENTS THAT TURN US (B)(vi)
OH, THE BRAVE MUSIC OF A DISTANT DRUM!

I made "Ohio" a powerful word when I was in West Virginia by repeating it to myself over and over again like a talisman or a mantra. That word kept us going as we came down from the mountains of West Virginia and wound along the West Virginia Rails-Trail. The C & O had almost killed us between the bear, the rain, and the cold. We made horrible time in Maryland, and West Virginia tried us just as hard with mountains, wind and lightning on top of the mountains, and locals who ran us out of town. I came very close to calling off the trip in West Virginia—we had already lost so much time that I knew it would be a race to make it through the Rockies in the July/August window, and I am no racer. After September, the Rockies might swallow us up with snow and we had lost so much time in the rain and storms of Maryland and West Virginia that we maybe had already lost the whole year. We had nothing except for Ohio!

I convinced myself that Ohio would be different. Ohio is the gateway to the Midwest. We would be out of the mountains, and the storms that had killed so many people in North Carolina and Arkansas couldn't go on forever. Ohio! We would make up time in Ohio. Seeing the "Welcome to Ohio" sign would be a morale boost because we would inarguably be crossing into a different region of the country. We would have three states behind us, and we would start seeing open cornfields instead of shuttered coalmines.

Ohio!

I repeated it to myself when my feet felt like they were broken or when I had to twist and contort to put the heavy pack back on my back. I made up little songs about Ohio and sang them to Mabel when we were on breaks. I thought about it when we went to sleep and every morning when we hit the road I thought "Ohio". I said to myself that we only need to make it to Ohio and then it would all be good.

Ohio. Ohio. Ohio.

It was that word, more than food or water or anything else, that fueled me through that first 30-mile hike of the trip that we did into Parkersburg. Mabel didn't need encouragement like that from a word or an idea. She just goes and goes and stops to drink and to eat. It was enough for her to see an occasional deer or turkey, and to every now and again see children running through tall grass. But Mabel didn't understand that we were racing against weather that may or may not hit us in another 2000 miles, months away. And Mabel didn't care if we quit—she didn't understand what quitting means. For Mabel, we quit every night and then started again in the morning, so what's the big deal?

Parkersburg sits at a bend in the Ohio River. Belpre, Ohio, is on the other side. Parkersburg is not a big city, but it is a decent sized town, and it is depressing. It may be the most depressing looking town I have ever seen. It seems to have nothing to offer, nothing to entertain, no animus at all. It seems to have no jobs, no future. It is dirty and disordered and the people there who I talked with all wished they could leave Parkersburg. It is a place where people watch sitcoms and wish for death. We took a day off in Parkersburg to let my feet heal from the 30-miler. Mabel's feet were fine and she was ready to go all through the first day that we zeroed. I knew the importance of taking a day off after long hikes, but that day off was a mistake that would cost me nearly a week and a half.

We headed out toward Ohio on our second morning in Parkersburg. The day began with a clear morning and an easy breeze and we walked along a few miles of a thoroughfare in Parkersburg that is lined with discount grocery stores, auto repair shops, strip malls and houses. We followed that road in to the downtown area and we could see the bridge over the Ohio River. At one of the auto repair shops, a mechanic told me that there was a pedestrian walkway on the bridge and that brightened my day. We climbed onto the bridge and then we were in Ohio!

I took a picture of the sign. It was the lightest and happiest moment of the trip so far. I was so relieved that I started smiling and walking faster and Mabel could tell how happy I was. She started walking with a little hop in her step like she does, and she would look up at me and kind of hop up a little like she wanted to kiss me or to lick my face.

But it was hotter on the other side of the bridge and I began to sweat the moment we stepped into Belpre. Mabel started panting, which she had done only on a few other days of the trip. There were no clouds and none on the horizon so there was nothing to block the Sun. My long beard began to itch. I felt like I had a blanket on my face because of the heat and humidity. Like one of those Mexican blankets you can buy on the beach in Puerta Vallarta. The little hop fell out of Mabel's step and we had to stop a few miles into Belpre. We stopped at a grocery store where there was a little shade and, right in front of me, a hair salon. I parked Mabel in the shade and asked inside the salon whether they "do beards". The ladies in the salon all chuckled, and the lady who cut my hair grimaced a little when she shampooed my hair, probably because it was so awfully dirty. I left feeling leaner, more streamlined, and cooler in the Sun.

Less than a mile later we were stopped in the shade again. I took off Mabel's pack and added it to my own. That helped her, but we were stopped again in another mile, this time in the shade beside a Domino's pizza. And Mabel would go no farther. When I got up to hike, she would look at me, sigh deeply, and force herself to walk. But she was slow and panting heavily and if I slowed my gait in the slightest she would lay down in the cool grass.

We were another 15 miles from our campsite goal for the day and I began to think that we might not make it. Mabel was suffering in the heat, and I was worried it would be too much for her. This was all my fault: I kept the pack on her too long, I didn't focus enough on finding shade, and I set our pace too fast without enough little breaks for her to cool down. I know all this now, but we were still learning about each other at the time. There was no place to stay in Belpre—no park, no campsite, no motel—and I could not be certain how far the Belpre "metro area" stretched before we would enter empty land where we could stealth camp. It could have been another five or ten miles until we would get into a clear area where we might find a place to squat.

We turned around and went back to Parkersburg. Ohio could wait another day. I apologized to Mabel for pushing her too hard in the heat, but she didn't care. She was happy we were headed back. I checked in to the cheapest motel in Parkersburg, bummed to be back in West Virginia and to not be spending my first night in Ohio, but them's the breaks. I thought we would be in Parkersburg one extra night and then start out early with a better game plan. That's not what happened. The weather was not through with us yet.

The clouds gathered above us as we slept on a nasty old bed in the blue flickering light of Game of Thrones, or a Lady Gaga concert, or whatever mindless TV nonsense had bored me to sleep. We woke the next morning to a great rainstorm, not violent like they had been on the C & O and in the mountains, but bringing down buckets and buckets of rain. And I said to myself "we just need to make it to Ohio".

We lost a day.

That meant another day of SpongeBob cartoons and the Weather Channel. Days like that last forever. I left the room and paced back and forth under an awning between my room and the office, and brought Mabel out with me to walk back and forth. I repeated "Ohio Ohio Ohio" in my mind as we paced. I felt as badly for Mabel to be locked up in the motel as I did for myself. So I negotiated with the motel staff for another night at a cheaper rate.

The next day there was rain that cleared early and we hiked out for the three miles to Ohio. We crossed the bridge again as clouds were forming and in Belpre we found that the streets were flooded. We were 20 miles from a campsite with more rain coming and a flash flood closing who knew how many streets. This was our second trip into Ohio, and to be turned back again was infuriating. Mabel was a bit confused, I think. She looked like she remembered having been there the day before, but all the water was new.

We turned back again.

Another night in the motel, Cartoon Network and the Daily Show and what not. I had watched more TV in Parkersburg than I had maybe in the last three months I lived in Chicago. I tried to fill time by scratching in my journal, but I had nothing to write about because nothing had happened. I talked with the lady behind the counter at the motel about the construction workers who stayed at the motel for weeks at a time. When Mabel was asleep in the room I went to the bar next door and had a beer with my dinner. I took another shower. Still, there was rain.

We lost the next day to the rain, too.

It was 23 degrees below normal, and I had sent all of my cold weather gear home after the hot day in Ohio. Time kept slipping by. I sat all day watching the horrible TV and reading on my Kindle. I read the *Rubaiyat* over and over again, trying to commit it to memory like my Grandpa Coulson had done 70 years earlier. I read:

> "Come fill the cup and in the fire of spring,
> the winter garment of repentance fling.
> The bird of time has but a little way to fly;
> and, Lo!, the bird is on the wing."

I had lost track of the hours and the days and was pointlessly repeating to myself "Ohio, Ohio, we just have to make it to Ohio". I got pretty down and frustrated when I realized that I could count the good-weather days on one hand. It had rained on us more or less non-stop since we got on the Canal, almost 400 miles before. And we were so close to Ohio—where I had told myself we could quit and go home without shame.

The next morning there was a little rain in the forecast, but no severe weather was supposed to hit us, so we hiked out on our third attempt to cross into Ohio. Our third trip westward under the Welcome to Ohio sign. No rain fell on us all the way into downtown Parkersburg and no rain fell as we crossed again into Ohio. It was so strange and frustrating to walk the same strip of highway that we had already walked twice before. We stopped at a Speedway gas station that we had stopped at twice before where, to the south and west, there was a clearing in the buildings and hills and we could see for enough miles to see the weather over our destination 20 miles away near Guysville, Ohio.

My heart sank when I saw a sky filled with dark clouds bulging with rain. I dropped the pack at the Speedway and sat on the curb with Mabel; I tried to decide whether to hike into the storm or to turn and walk back to that awful motel. I even sent a tweet to ask for advice—should we hike on or turn around? The consensus was that we should turn around rather than to put Mabel in danger.

Normally Mabel drinks, sits, and then lies down when we stop walking. But when we stopped at the Belpre Safeway for the third time, Mabel didn't sit down. She stayed standing, excited to be on the move and out of that motel. She didn't understand how important it was for us to cross into Ohio because she is a dog. To her, we had crossed a river, nothing more, and that was something, but it didn't mean anything else to her. She probably hasn't ever even looked at a map and I know she doesn't understand how state borders are drawn. Still, she was excited and wanted to move as much as I wanted to move.

We sat facing east so that I could not see the sky where we were headed. I ate a sandwich and drank cold water. After that early lunch, and a few minutes waiting for good measure, I looked at the sky again. It had grown darker to the southwest. I considered for a moment that we might change our course and head northwest instead. So I walked around the Safeway and saw that another, separate front of dark clouds was closing in on us from that direction.

We waited at that Speedway gas station for quite a while. I talked to Mabel and told her we were sitting tight at the Speedway to wait for the weather to clear or to give us a clear sign. She nodded and wagged her tail. But I was lying to her. Were actually stopped there because I didn't have the heart to turn us around...again. I had built up Ohio so much in my mind that I could not deal with having failed three attempts to cross into Ohio. So I bought a cup of coffee and pretended we were only waiting for the sky to clear.

But the sky wasn't going to clear and I wasn't going to risk walking Mabel into another storm like the ones we camped in on the Canal, or the ones on the mountain that nearly carried the tent away with us in it. There had been so many tornados already and so many deaths—and this was even before Joplin—that I was worried about walking Mabel into the weather.

Would we have been ok? Probably. Almost certainly we would have been fine. It was a mistake to not walk into it, as it had been a mistake for me to walk Mabel too fast on the first scorching day of the trip a few days earlier. We should have headed west and gone 20 more miles that day, but I couldn't because I was "managing risk". The thing is, you can't "manage" risk in real life. You can deal with it, and you can adjust your behaviors, but you can't "manage" it. Risk is there. Do with it what you will.

We turned back again for a third, heart breaking walk back into Parkersburg. It was only seven miles, give or take, back to the motel but it took us nearly five hours. I stopped on almost every block to breathe and to try not to cry in public. We stopped under the Welcome to Ohio sign on the bridge, and I breathed and sighed and looked behind us at the gathering clouds. We walked through an area of several blocks lined with big brick warehouse buildings that looked abandoned in downtown Parkersburg and a couple of used car lots a couple of miles from the motel. In front of a particular abandoned building that I will always remember, I dropped the pack and sat on the sidewalk and started crying softly and stupidly like men cry sometimes.

It was so early in the trip and we had lost it already. It was too late. I knew then, really, that we had lost too much time. We couldn't make it to Denver by July. And I knew that we were so far behind that we would hit the hot weather in Illinois and Iowa and Nebraska and that would slow us down even more. We might not even make Denver by August. The Walk, or at least the Walk as I had planned it, had failed already, before we even made it to Ohio. We had lost too much time and spent too much money—there was very little hope of us making it across the whole continent in a single season. We hadn't been able to make enough long days in the east to be in shape for the really long days we needed to make in the big flat middle of the country. For 200 miles I said to myself "if we just make it to Ohio...". But we *hadn't* made it to Ohio.

The world is very powerful. Rain and cold and wind. And hail and sleet. And bears and snakes and thieves. And gravity. Bloodied heads and swollen faces. Broken fingers. Broken hearts. Fear and exhaustion and feet that swell up like footballs. And cold that freezes the tips of your fingers and freezes your breath into frost on your sleeping bag and inside your tent. Water, at 8lbs a gallon, that weighs down your pack and stretches and pulls the muscles off your spine and falls out of the sky and your clothes are never really dry, and your socks are always just a little wet and you have to stop and take off your shoes and socks and build a fire because you are getting trench foot. And fires that you can't build even though you have gasoline and you spend hours feathering out strips of kindling because it has been raining for a month. And wind that blows out the fires and crumples your tent, and drivers who swerve at you to test you and dogs who bound out of the woods and onto the trail and threaten you. And you fail—over and over and over again you fail—but you keep going, keep getting up and failing again and again because you are so afraid of failing and then you fail because you are afraid of failing and then you are scared because *the only* thing you are afraid of is failure. And then you cry softly on the side of the road because even though it is easy you just cannot do it.

I tried to whisper to Mabel. "We can't make it," I tried to say, but I'm sure it was garbled and made no sense. "It is too late. We can't beat the weather to the Rockies, because I am too slow. Because of the weather. Because of too many things."

Mabel had never seen me cry. I don't remember the last time I had cried. But Mabel must have seen someone cry before, wherever she came from. She sat on the other side of the pack from me for a while but wouldn't look at me. Maybe she was embarrassed. And then she walked around the pack and slowly up to me until we were face-to-face. She lowered her head and pressed her head into the space between my chin and my shoulder. She's a good dog.

She walked slowly on my left all the way back to the cheap dirt bag motel we had been staying at in Parkersburg, and she hardly took her eyes off of me. She pressed her nose against my hand, and licked at my wrist to let me know she was still there. Back at the motel we checked back into the same room, still not cleaned from our stay the night before. The room smelled like the smoke and sweat of my gear and the stink of a man and a dog living in a small room during a weeklong rainstorm. The television was still on, and a rerun of Home Movies was playing. I think it was the episode where the kids make a movie called "The Landstander", and I thought of Isra out there somewhere falling in love with someone else and watching Home Movies with him and, in my heart, I wished them luck. I sat down on the bed and Mabel sat in front of me, still looking at me and still periodically touching my hand with her nose.

I can't finish this walk, I told her. In my head, I went through all the million reasons we should pack up and go home, and I considered how easy it would be to pack up and rent a car and be home with running water and heat and good food. And, I supposed, I could go back to work, practicing some other kind of law in some other, new location. But whatever it was that had nagged me would still be there, I knew. Still the indentured servitude of student loan debt. Still the endless works and days. A life plowing out parallel mornings, as flat as tomorrow and as black as yesterday. Every day, over and over, until I just gave in and died.

I had the strangest thought: I was already dead.

"Get some sleep, Mabes. We hike in the morning."

The Walk in Ohio is very little more to me now than faint and retiring half-memories. We walked into Ohio under a dome of blue sky on a breezeless day, but scarce and puffy white clouds skittered across the sky and chased shadows across the highway. The cars were fast and did not give way for us, nor did I give way for them. The heat rose, but we walked on in the hot Sun. I did not wave at drivers, but made eye contact with them when possible so that they would know I had seen them. Mabel had to stop every half hour for water, and it didn't hurt for me to drink that often, either. I zipped off the lower legs of my convertible pants, and suddenly I was hiking in shorts with big hiking boots and thick socks. Every now and again I looked down at my feet and wondered how long they would last. I warned my feet that if they got injured and stopped me, I would cut them off.

We were different when we walked into Ohio. I was different, at any rate, and so Mabel and I as a team were different. Six years of my life had been a failure. I failed to know what to do with my life so I went to law school. I failed to find a place where I belonged and went to biglaw, where I failed to make a place or a career for myself. Through the miracle of compound interest, those were all failures that would nag at me the rest of my life with loan payments, monthly reminders of all my failures. And the only thing in the last six years that had meant anything to me was my relationship with Isra, and I had failed at that. And the Walk? A failure, already. I had been wrong about absolutely everything in my life that had mattered. And time was passing.

We only have so many heartbeats to spend, so many seconds and so many minutes. The Sun and the Earth and the Universe(s) go on for billions and trillions of years. But me? I am small and so temporary. I am nothing. And my life is so inconsequential that I am practically dead, already. Dead at birth, for all intents and purposes. Sometimes knowledge of our own inconsequential impermanence prevents people from really caring about their actions—we are all so temporary that we should not rationally care about the long-term impacts of our actions. We are so temporary that we shouldn't care about the impact of our actions on others. But then, we are so temporary that we shouldn't even care about ourselves. We should care about nothing. Because we are already dead.

So there I was.

Book III: ...And the Moon Says Hallelujah, 01.06.12(2)

Research dinner options; remain at picnic table; note Celio left to procure food for himself. Respond to more questions from Rosie.

R: "What happened with the girl? The one you were in love with in law school?"

T: "I told you: She hates me."

R: "What else did she say?"

T: "I can't tell you. It's personal."

R: "Celio is right. Your book won't be very good if you protect yourself like that."

T: "I'm not protecting myself. I'm protecting her, too."

R: "Sure. That's sweet if it's true. Do you owe it to her?"

T: "No one owes anybody anything."

R: "Do you hate her?"

T: "No. She's a wonderful person, just like everyone else."

R: "But she wasn't nice to you?"

T: "Eh. That wasn't her. C'est la guerre. But she hates me."

R: "You said that. Anyway, I meant, *what happened to her*? She sounded different in law school and then after."

T: "I don't know. I was different after law school, I know that. Maybe she was different, too. I was. Everybody funny; now I'm funny, too."

R: "How were you different? Were you older? Like an old man?"

T: "I'm not that old."

R: "You're *pretty* old."

Breeze flutters the edges of my pages.

See Celio return; answer more questions from Celio, re: "About the walking of the thing". Tell story; Rosie interrupts me to announce that she booked snorkel trip for me for following day. Feel heart race; love the ocean.

BOOK I: THE MOMENTS THAT TURN US (C)
LOOK TO THE ROSE THAT BLOWS ABOUT US.

We were a day from Parkersburg into Coolville, where we camped at the first RV Park of the trip. Then on to Athens, which is a college town and was the first genuine college town of the trip. Real American college towns exist only in the Midwest. Midwestern college towns are unlike any other places, and everyone should live in at least one at least once. Athens was pretty and welcoming and it was pedestrian friendly. We walked through the student housing area, and even though it was almost summer by then and I imagine that most of the students had gone home, we walked by a home with three co-eds hanging out on a second floor balcony. (I have no idea why people still call female college students "co-eds" and I have even less idea why I do it.)

"Look at that dog!" one said.

"OH MY GOD! SHE IS SO CUTE!"

I stopped and they all three leaned over the balcony railing.

"Hi, Sweetness!" one said, waving at Mabel. "Hi sweet baby!"

"Where are you going?"

"My dog and I are walking to California," I said. They laughed and smiled.

"Awesome! Where did you start?" It sounded as though they believed me immediately, which was rare on this trip and even rarer in the Midwest.

"Delaware," I said.

"You walked *here* from *Delaware*?"

"Yup," I answered.

"Oh my God. You must be *parched*. Want to come up for a drink?"

"We can pet your sweet puppy!"

You can bet my mind raced.

"Well, it *is* awful hot," I heard myself say.

"Come on up!" one of them sang out. And I almost did. I wanted very much to take a few days off from walking, and there is nothing better than sitting on the porch in a college town with a cold drink and good conversation. I imagined the girls, all smart and wonderful, showing me in and handing me a drink, and then we would sit and talk through the afternoon until, suddenly, one of them would realize how unbelievably dirty and dingy I was. I could smell myself by that time, and it wasn't an altogether pleasant smell.

"I shouldn't," I said.

"Just for a drink! We're about to order lunch!"

It was probably the only time in my entire life when three young and beautiful women would call to me from a balcony, asking that I join them. "Tempting" is many times over too small a word.

I declined. Those three girls were lovely, and now I wish we had stayed and talked with them for a while and maybe spent a couple of days hanging around real people in Athens. Instead, we headed on and walked along the river on a pedestrian trail. We stopped in the shade up the way a bit so Mabel could cool down and I could pick the ticks off of her and out of her fur. I napped a little and wrote in my journal. Athens was lovely, and those girls were lovely, and that walk beside the river was lovely.

Yes, Ohio was lovely. I think. I remember very little of that time. Each day was like each other day was like each other day. The weather was not awful for most of it, but it was quickly getting too warm. The people were friendly enough, although I found myself stopping to chat with people less and less frequently. I simply didn't care to talk with people, and I went into hiding. And in Ohio, I almost stopped taking notes in my travel journal altogether. Even when I had enough energy to do so, I didn't feel like it. There were nights when I crawled into the tent, with Mabel curled up at the foot of the tent, and I would get the journal out and stare at a blank page for an hour or more. But it was not worth writing—nothing was worth writing down or remembering, really. I camped in or behind dilapidated buildings, and slept underneath bridges. And I didn't feel a stitch of shame or fear.

We had long days walking long hours but not making much distance. Mabel was adjusting to the warmer weather, and she didn't seem to have the same spring in her step that she had had earlier. I discovered a cut on the tip of her ear and watched it, but it didn't seem to heal. I stopped by vet clinics at every chance, but no one would see her without an appointment. I treated her cut with triple antibiotic ointment and she didn't seem to be in any pain. I worried about her and I thought constantly about sending her home or at least leaving her in Illinois when I walked through. The original plan had always been that if Mabel or I had trouble before Indiana, Isra could drive up to help us. That plan had changed.

Somewhere in Ohio, a woman who I'd met briefly in Chicago emailed me. Her name was Heidi and she had gone to high school with an attorney friend of mine at Sidley. Since early April she had been emailing me every now and again, interested in walking across Indiana with me. Once we hit Ohio, she emailed me wanting to know exactly when we would be in Cincinnati. She had family in Cincinnati and would meet us there. So that made me feel a little better, because two make the road shorter.

Now, if this were a movie—and it may be! Hollywood is where good stories go to die—the soft middle of this trip would probably be told in a single, long montage of changing footwear as I walked from Ohio to Colorado.

The midsection of this country is a vast, green factory floor. I grew up in the heart of this thing, in west central Illinois, so I had some idea of what I was in for when we began our trek from Ohio through to the high, arid plains of western Nebraska and eastern Colorado. From Ohio through to western Nebraska, the Earth is cut and cropped to suit humanity's modern industrial needs. There is little "harmony" between the land and the people, whatever that means, and the land bears little resemblance to what it must have looked like to wide-eyed Frenchmen in the 1600s and 1700s. It probably resembles even less what it looked like to the dug-in natives the Frenchmen found there.

At the western edge of West Virginia, I still wore my hiking boots with heavy socks and long pants. In eastern Ohio, I zipped off the pant legs and hiked in shorts. By western Ohio, I'd taken off the thick socks in favor of just the lighter silk sock liners. In Indiana, I got short, lightweight socks. In Illinois, I switched to sandals and heavy socks. In eastern Iowa I wore sandals with lightweight socks. In western Iowa, I wore sandals and the lightest socks possible. In Nebraska, I wore sandals with no socks at all and paid the price for it. By the time we walked into the shadow of the Rocky Mountains, I wore sandals and "hobo socks" that I created out of handkerchiefs.

Yes, that would be the montage: A song plays, and a dotted line scrolls across a map, and the screen is filled intermittently with shots of my feet in evolving footwear. Then, at the song's climax, the hiker and his dog stop on an open and isolated Colorado road; the camera pans up and there you see a changed man, a different man—beardless, trim and strong, staring vacantly into the west—and the camera circles the man and his dog until, almost accidentally, the screen fills with the monstrous Rocky Mountains. They are immense and incalculably old and dangerous, but there is no emotion at all on the man's face except maybe a brief glance away, and the dog looks at the man, and they walk on toward the mountains together. No one knows why they are walking, of course, but everyone knows that they must keep walking.

Yes, that would be a fine montage for a movie, and it would be a true enough telling of the story. But there is more.

This is the strange dichotomy of a cross-country thru-hiker: On the one hand, a thru-hiker could skip Ohio through Colorado and, so long as he or she did the Appalachians, the Rockies, and the deserts, he or she could still claim to have hiked the U.S., and I wouldn't begrudge them their tale because those are the physically challenging bits. On the other hand, though, it is the big, soft middle that makes a thru-hike so challenging. I would never re-hike that portion of this continent—it was simply too vast, too flat, and too boring. It was very easy *hiking*, and it was the most difficult stretch precisely because it was so *easy*.

We crossed Ohio staying almost entirely on the shoulder of Hwy 50. In Ohio, we learned that we were hiking in the deadliest tornado season in memory and, perhaps, the most dangerous in recorded history. A tornado struck the St. Louis airport, and a tornado destroyed the city of Joplin, Missouri. Mabel and I once woke up in a motel near Chillicothe, Ohio, and the news reported multiple tornados on the ground in Missouri and Kansas, all headed toward us. That spring, around 550 people died in tornados in the United States, in Missouri, Arkansas, Alabama, North Carolina, and elsewhere. It was the second deadliest tornado season in America in recorded history. We had a few blowers like that in Ohio, but nothing like we'd had on the Canal or in West Virginia.

Ohio is a blur other than a very few moments—like the three girls and the lovely river in Athens, or like Mary Ann Montgomery. I remember that every time we stopped along the road and Mabel lay down, she stood back up with 10 or more ticks on her. I remember waking up in the tent with dead ticks on the nylon tent floor and suffocated ticks in the sleeping bag. I remember that angry dogs rushed us four or five times and I held them off with the walking stick just as I'd learned to do on the Canal. And I remember the *WKRP in Cincinnati* theme song got stuck in my head and played on repeat over and over again until we actually reached Cincinnati. I remember unexpected hills that tormented me, but that Mabel didn't care at all about the hills.

And I remember that I several times counted my steps in Ohio. The counting just happened, and I didn't do it on purpose. I would discover myself visualizing a machine like an odometer that on the far right counted each of my steps, 1 through 9, and on the 10th step a number 1 would appear to its left, and so on. I counted 5,897 steps once and, as I consciously realized that I had been counting, I lost track and had to stop walking to recapture my thoughts—it was odd, because I knew how many steps I'd walked, 5987, but for some reason I couldn't count higher without stopping and starting over.

Counting steps and replaying the WKRP theme in my head were my mind idling, I think, inventing tasks to keep itself busy with strange, unpredictable business. I let the thoughts happen and tried to acknowledge all the thoughts, even the odd and unsettling thoughts.

The thoughts that hit me most often and powerfully were pictures or visions of myself engaged in domestic activities—washing dishes, folding laundry, paying bills. I saw myself doing all sorts of homebody things, and sitting at a table and talking with a son or a daughter. In my head, I was filing my taxes and standing in hospital waiting rooms. I was hosting dinner parties and complaining about politics to friends and family. That's what happened in my head, and it was a strange experience.

Still, we met interesting people and heard interesting stories.

One day we crested a hill on a fiercely hot, shadeless day. It had been a struggle for us that day because of the heat, and by the time we neared our campground, my face was burned red and I could feel it glowing. A passing motorist stopped and offered us a ride. It was only a mile to the campground, and we accepted the ride. Later in the week she gave us another ride to avoid death in a storm. She was a wonderful lady named Mary Ann who had the cutest and smartest little daughter named Abigail.

"I used to hike all the time," she said and shrugged as she drove us around the storm later that week. "I was never into a whole lot of things, but that was my thing that I loved to do. I like to be out in the woods. When I was in college, I lived in a little shack in the middle of nowhere. It didn't have heat or electricity, and I *loved* it. We used to have the strangest parties there. Once I hiked up this mountain in the Appalachians—about 300 miles south of where you were from the sound of your story about the last storm—and it was supposed to be completely empty and it was pretty much empty. So I started very early—this is kind of like your story about that guy on the bike, that's what made me think of it—I started very early that day so I could hit the top before anybody else, if anybody else was even there. It was a steep hike...it was *beautiful, just beautiful*, and I just loved to go out there and, you know, be alone and see things. So at the top I found this rock that was overlooking the sloping side of the mountain, and it was straight down for like 4000 feet. So I was sitting there, eating some trail mix and sitting there, hanging out. And this...man...just walked *up the mountain* toward me...I mean, not on the trail, but like straight up the mountain right in front of me...and I don't know how, it just looked like he was almost floating, you know. And there were lots of big boulders around, but he came and sat down right beside me. So I was pretty freaked out, really, because there was no one around and this man came out of nowhere and sat right next to me even though there were lots of places he could sit but he sat right next to me. And he said:

'Nice day.'

I, you know, I agreed with him, and he said: 'Just out walking to be with God?'

Well I didn't know how to respond to that because I'm an atheist and I never lie. Or I was an atheist then, but now I sort of lean more toward Buddhism, but anyway. I said, you know, something, like I just liked to hike. And he said:

'Well, be safe.'

And then he left. Just left. Went right back down the mountain the way he'd come up."

Mary Ann gave me a ride through a storm to a motel, but wouldn't let me stay there because she said the town was sketchy and that the motels there were sketchier, and I didn't mind so much because the motel people had been very rude to me on the phone. When she dropped Mabel and me off, she gave us a care package—she gave us a pound of ham (even though she is a vegetarian) and a pound of cheese, a loaf of bread, a bag of apples and a bag of bananas, three different kinds of dog treats for Mabel, a bag of bagels with cream cheese, a bottle of aspirin, and 50 dollars. I didn't find the 50 dollars until after she had gone. She was the nicest person I met on the trip, I think, and one of the nicest people I have ever met in my life. Mary Ann and her precious little daughter popped into my head off and on for the remainder of the trip, right alongside Cary Gillmon and the other people who were so helpful for no reason.

BOOK II: FEEL THE SELFISH FURY (C)
BESIDE ME SINGING IN THE WILDERNESS.

Isra came to Iowa Law as a 1L at the front end of my 2L year. I met her briefly during the first Wednesday of the year during Law Night at a local bar. She was at a table with a few of her new friends, all looking bug-eyed, scared and confused by their new lives as law students.

"My name is Tyler."

"Isra," she said. She had a smooth and calm voice but with an intensity in it like she may have been in on some joke that I wasn't. She had long black hair, and I thought she'd look better with shorter hair, and her skin was caramel colored and smooth.

"Well," I said, "welcome to Iowa. If you want to meet any Indians in town, let me know. I somehow became the token white guy for just about every Indian in Iowa City."

"Who says that?!" she squealed and laughed. Her eyes were big and bright and smiling.

"It's true! I don't know how it happened. But if you want to meet the Indians or the Croatians, I'm your guy."

I spoke with her again a few weeks later after I noticed that she often studied on a bench in the main entryway of the BLB. She and another 1L were on that bench almost every time I walked by. My classes that semester were sort of boring me, and I couldn't get her face or her voice out of my head, so I started inventing little errands that I "had to do" and "could you watch my bag for a second?" I loved the look of amazement she got on her face. "How dare you ask me to watch your bag?!" And then, fake errand completed, I would return and sit to talk with them for a while.

We clicked immediately and powerfully. She was a very odd girl, with a very odd sense of humor that I got a kick out of. That made her feel good because mostly people didn't understand her sense of humor, and mostly people were uncomfortable when she said inappropriate things at inappropriate times. But I loved it! Soon enough the highlight of my day were those extended periods of time I would sit in the entryway of the BLB with her, listening to her bizarre stories about routine things, her self-deprecating comments, and making her laugh with my own stories. After a couple of weeks of this I asked for her phone number, and when I called her later that week she invited herself to my house for a "dance party".

"Took long enough," she said when I called her. I pulled my truck into the parking spot at my apartment.

"What?"

"Took long enough for you to call. Like a day."

"I thought you would be busy."

"I would be," she said. "I do things. IN. LIFE." I could hear the smile in her voice over the phone.

"So what's up?"

"Not too much. Are we having a dance party tonight?"

"What?" I asked.

"Do you wanna have a dance party? It's what I do. I have dance parties."

"Ok," I said.

"Where do you live?" she asked and I told her, and she said she would be over for a dance party at about 8.

She showed up wearing a blue deep-necked shirt and a few necklaces, which was her look at the time, and she had put little lines of makeup out from the corner of each eye. Isra was a stunner. She brought a bottle of liquor and a huge bag of Reese's Peanut Butter Cups.

"Hiiiiii," she said, and walked in. She sat down immediately at my computer and played music from my iTunes folder. When she found a track that she liked, she wiggled her head and shoulders a little, doing a little "chair dance". She loved blues and Led Zeppelin. She drank gin and tonic too quickly and destroyed the bag of peanut butter cups. All the while, we talked about the things we liked and disliked.

"I hate law school," she said.

"Everyone does."

"I fucking hate law students, is the thing."

"Everyone does," I said. "But you are a law student."

"I know. They are all just douches. I hate it."

"*I'm* a law student, too," I said.

"Exactly!"

She had a lot of regret, I think. She had decided on Iowa Law because it was completely free for her to attend. I was smitten because she was so witty and sharp, and I felt like Yale or whatever schools she'd passed on had missed out.

Her favorite show was Home Movies, which I had never seen. So at the end of the night, I said we should get together and watch Home Movies and she thought that was a great idea. She came back the next night with a different bottle of liquor and the complete DVD set of Home Movies. We got drunk together and watched and she slept in my bed with me. Once, after we had laid down, my arm draped across her body almost on accident, and she pulled away just enough for me to know that we would not be touching one another, and that was fine.

She made my heart shine.

Isra and I were almost always together. For most law students, the 2L year is a horribly busy affair. It's the "work you to death" year. But I didn't do a journal. And I didn't take moot court very seriously. A lot of times Isra and I went our separate ways on the weekends, but we spent most weeknights either on the phone together, studying together, or at my apartment having a dance party. I wanted it to become a relationship with her. After all, I wasn't seeing anyone seriously and she wasn't seeing anyone, and so why not! I mentioned it to her casually; I said, in passing and sort of half jokingly that I was her "weeknight" boyfriend and I knew right away that those words had hurt her somehow. The brightness drained from her face, and she looked down at the ground, and after a brief second looked back up.

"Why would you say that?" She had a way of saying "why would you say that?" with a child-like whine that was completely different from her normal tone of voice. Her eyes were beginning to water, but she was not yet crying. I don't know now whether it was my words that hurt her, or whether they triggered some older wound.

"I was just saying, is all. You're always over here, and you know. Maybe we should go on a date."

"No," she said.

"No? Why not?"

"You're outside the box," she said. "You are white, and not Muslim, and...."

"Oh, yeah, like you are a pious Mohammedan?" I joked.

"It's just not right," she said. "It wouldn't be right."

"Fine, whatever."

In the meantime, I went on callback interviews. Law students generally were not eager to talk about their callback interviews because those who got callbacks with good firms were hesitant to find out how different their experiences might have been. When it came out that one person went to place X for lunch and one person went to place Y, they read into it. When one person had been put up at hotel X and another at hotel Y, they stewed about what it could mean. Sometime in September, I did my callback interview with Sidley Austin in Chicago.

I drove my old pick up truck across Interstate 88 to Chicago and checked into a very plush hotel in downtown Chicago. I had to use valet parking—"Be good to her", I said when the valet drove off in my crappy, rusty, dirty old truck. The hotel room was, at that time, probably among the three nicest places I'd ever stayed. A friend of mine was doing an interview at his ideal firm in another midwestern city the very next day and I walked down Michigan Avenue to the river and stood there talking with him on the phone.

"Are you freaking out?"

"No," I said. "Not at all."

"How can you be so calm? I'm freaking out. I'm fighting the urge to drink one bottle of wine on purpose and a second on accident."

"Just relax, Frankie," I said. "It's nothing."

"How can you be so relaxed?"

"Look," I said, "when I was in high school, the odds for me were the military or prison. I just got a free trip to Chicago. This is all gravy for me. I already won, I think."

"Did you, though?" he asked.

I went to Sidley the next morning. The firm is in a brand new (at the time), LEEDS certified, 40-story building in the Loop. It's a beautiful modernist glass and steel building, with a pleasant patio outside with trees and seating, and a marble sign on the corner of the lot that reads "Sidley Austin LLP" in very classy letters. I had interviewed with several big, successful firms, but I had never walked into a building like that, where everything was glass and steel and white marble, and that seemed to be owned by the firm I was interviewing with. The entryway is spacious and clean, and stoic professional security folks guard the doors to the elevators. It all seemed successful and mysterious, like there were very important things going on upstairs but if you didn't know the password, you had no chance of getting in. The security people checked me in and sent me up to the 38th floor to meet my host. The 38th floor was even more impressive than the foyer.

I checked in with the receptionist and waited a few moments, standing like a befuddled fool in front of a panoramic view of Lake Michigan and Millennium Park, before Carolyn, the partner who had interviewed me at Iowa, arrived to welcome me and to take me to my "associate host" for the day. On-site interviews all generally follow the same format—interviews from 9 a.m. until noon with partners and associates, and then a lunch, then afternoon interviews and sometimes, though much less often, there would be a dinner. I interviewed with three or four partners in different groups that morning and with a couple of associates. Then Carolyn and Kyle McDougal (the other Iowa Law alum who had recruited me in Iowa City) took me to lunch with a couple of associates. It was a great time, and I liked everyone I met. The interviews consisted about 50% of the interviewer asking me questions—"What kind of law do you want to practice?", "What is you favorite course so far?", "Where do you see yourself in five years?", that kind of thing—and 50% of telling me how incredibly perfect and wonderful it was to work at Sidley. The only exception to that was a female partner in a specialized litigation group who sort of had a heart-to-heart discussion with me instead of an interview. She was an energetic but tired looking woman who had made partner on track (7.5 years) while still having and raising a family, which meant she worked superhuman hours. She applied lotion to her face and hands about six times during the 15-minute interview. To her, an offer for me seemed like a foregone conclusion, although she didn't seem too happy about that.

"Did you work before?"

I said that I had, and went over a couple of the things on my resume.

"Well that's nothing like this. This is hard. The work's not hard. But it's hard to work here. Or any firm. This is the best of the worst as far as that goes."

"I've heard that," I said, even though I hadn't heard that.

"Lot of smart people here," she said, "and people can get mean. Are you smart or mean?"

"Neither," I answered.

"Then you should do fine," she said, although I don't know if she had heard my answer. "As for Iowa, I don't now. You'd have to talk to someone who went to a school like that to see if there is any stigma about it."

"I imagine there would be," I said.

"We mostly hire Harvard, Northwestern, Chicago. Stanford sometimes, and some Michigan attorneys. I don't think I look down or askew at Iowa or Minnesota. Maybe Illinois."

"Well, everyone *should* look askew at Illinois," I said, even though I meant nothing by it and was only joking; I had gone to Illinois for undergrad.

"Just the law school," she said, and I knew she had been listening after all. "Great university. I mean, it's a public school, but it's a great university. Anyway, I have a meeting."

And that was it.

At lunch, Carolyn or Kyle asked me if I was interested in a dinner that night, but I declined, saying that I had to get back to Iowa City to get back to work. They respect that kind of go-get-'em attitude, I guess. I'd heard that, anyway.

I didn't hear from Sidley for two weeks. In that time, I went to class and flirted with Isra in the main foyer of the law building a little, and sent out thank you notes to the other firms I'd interviewed. The offers for summer associate positions started to come in, and I was feeling pretty good and secure that I would have employment the next summer. That took some pressure off of my shoulders and I could relax a bit. But I had really liked Sidley—I imagine it was because of the prestige of the whole thing. Fifth largest law firm in the country by revenue, around 10th by attorney count. Right in the center of the second city of the country. The people seemed good, and...the money![12]

About two weeks after my interview, Carolyn called me on my cell number. I was about to pull onto Hwy 6 in Iowa City to head to the law building, and a 312 area code number rang my cell phone. I answered it breathlessly and got an offer to be a summer associate at Sidley Austin in Chicago. That was a moment in my life that I will never forget.

"This is great," I said. "Really, this is great. This is a great thing."

"So you're interested?" Carolyn asked, half jokingly, because no one in their right mind would have said no.

"I am. I can't actually answer *right now*," I said. "I have a few other offers, and my second preference firm called yesterday. I promised them I would not make a decision until Monday. So I can't accept your offer right now in good faith. I have to wait until Monday."

"That is the strangest and most honest response I've ever gotten on one of these calls," Carolyn said.

"I am strange and honest," I said.

By the end of that semester, Isra and I began hanging out quite a bit at the law building and after hours. We went to a party together early in

---

[12] When I had applied for interviews through the OCI, a 1st year associate at a biglaw firm would make $115,000/yr, I believe. By the time I interviewed with Sidley, 1st year associate pay had risen to $130,000/yr. There were rumors that it would go higher. Shortly thereafter, the pay scale for biglaw first years rose to $145,000/yr and the whole nation of law students and associates started the rallying cry: "Biglaw to 160!" Think about that— when I applied, I was desperate, hustling, and worried that I would not get a $115,000/yr job, and by the time I started working, I had already received about $30,000/yr in raises. That was more than I'd ever even made in a year. It was certainly more than the $23 I had in the bank when I started law school. Two weeks after I started my summer associate position, the pay scale hit $160K/year.

January or February and had a great time. It was the first time I really went anywhere with her in public—we were "together" at the party even though we arrived separately. But she had to leave at about midnight, and I walked her out. After we agreed that it had been a great night, she turned and ran away down the road and toward her car. She ran all gangly and out of control. It was really a sight to see. And as I watched her run, I wondered why we were not dating. I would keep trying, of course, because I was smitten and because she made my heart shine. We were quite an odd couple of folks together: I'm essentially a redneck, and she was a suburbanite ethnic/religious minority. We studied together, and I tried to help her with her 1L courses, but she rarely wanted or would accept the help. She was sure that she knew what she was doing. She hated law school, but she knew she could beat the system if she could only figure out the game. We studied together at the Java House, and we had her little dance parties at my place, but she rarely stayed over and was a little nervous around me.

"They hide the fucking ball," she said about law school. "I don't even know *what the Hell* it is that I am *supposed* to learn. It's not that I can't learn it, it's that I don't know what I am supposed to learn!" I tried to explain to her what it was she was supposed to learn, but she wouldn't hear me. I think she thought that if she couldn't get it on her own, then she shouldn't get it at all—and that's not what law school should be about. Regardless, I loved spending time with her and I was excited when she told me she had gotten an internship in Chicago for the summer. I couldn't wait to spend time with her in the City in a new and exciting place and, maybe, to show off for her a little by being a highly paid summer associate at a leading law firm. She maintained distance between us still, but I knew that once we were away from Iowa City and the pressures of her 1L year that we could relax and that she would come around. I never wanted to pressure her or to push too much, and tried to treat her with kid gloves because the first year of law school had really torn up so many people I had known.

Book II: Feel the Selfish Fury (C)(i)
In the Fire of Spring.

I packed a duffel bag, grabbed a few reference books I thought might be helpful, and headed out from Iowa City on a clear day in May of 2007. I was about to be a summer associate at Sidley Austin in the halcyon days of summer associates. My truck was still a piece of shit, and I was still listening to the stack of CDs that had been in my truck on the first day I went to law school in 2005—there hadn't been a new song or artist or book or anything in my life since then. No matter, though, because everything I'd dreamt of, worked for, and wanted was happening. Interstate 88 to I 294 and from there northward, and then the big right hand exit onto the Kennedy Expressway, and suddenly you can see the whole city in the distance— monstrous buildings that, from that distance, look like they could be a hundred miles tall. There is so much flat ground for hundreds of miles around that it is hard to gauge how tall those buildings all. The Sears Tower (now Willis Tower), and the Hancock Building, and the Aon building, and then scattered all among them are new glass and steel monsters that glitter in the setting Sun, and out there turning onto the Kennedy you can see the whole skyline broadcast against a blue bowl. It was so much to see for a country boy. They had recently begun construction on the new Trump hotel in Chicago. I thought to myself: "I own that city."

Of course I didn't, and never would—but that is the mindset of a young man. I own this place. Later, I learned that you can never own anything at all, except for the numbered beats of your heart.

I drove into a small, out-of-the-way north side neighborhood called Sauganash. Sauganash is at the extreme northwestern limit of the city limits and, as near as I could tell, is populated almost entirely by retired Irish cops. The Irish-American cultural center is there, which was a surprise to me because you would think it would be in Bridgeport. But they probably have one there, too. And, anyway, all of Chicago is an Irish-American cultural heritage center. Sauganash is relatively difficult to reach by public transportation, and it is several miles farther from the Loop than any other summer associates would live, but I had a good reason to live there: My great friend Carrie and her French boyfriend (now husband) Nic lived there in a beautiful new-build condo over the Whole Foods on Cicero Ave. Nic's French employer had sent him to the U.S. (at Nic's request) with a generous rent stipend, so he and Carrie had taken a very nice and very big place close to the interstate and Carrie asked me to stay with them for the summer on an air mattress in their guest room. Carrie and Nic were out of town when I got there, so I let myself in and started moving in when Isra called.

"Yeah, Sauganash," I said.

"Really? Why Sauganash?" she asked. I told her about Carrie. "My Uncle and Aunt live right there. Like, three blocks from there."

"No kidding?"

"This is *great!*" she squealed. "I can see you all the time! I can just tell my mother that I'm going in to see Tareef-Uncle."

"Or you could tell her you're coming to see me," I offered.

"You don't get it," she snapped. "It's not that easy."

"Ok."

She came over that night and we watched a movie together and ate and made jokes and laughed. Then we went to sleep together on the air mattress and she was careful to keep her distance from me when we lay down. The next day I told Carrie about it, and Carrie was confused about Isra and me, our friendship seemed to be much more than just friendship, but Isra was so often cold and standoffish with me. Isra came over the next night and we repeated, and then again the next night. But on the third night, I woke up at about three in the morning and found her cuddled up against me and sleeping soundly.

In the meantime, I bought two new suits—simple things with light pin striping—and I got several new shirts and several new ties. The dress code at Sidley was "business casual", but I intended to dress like an attorney. So, in total, I had a rotation of four suits. With enough decent ties, an attorney could get by with as few as two suits.

I started work at Sidley Austin as a summer associate on Monday. The bus and train ride into the Loop was long, and it was my first time negotiating more than one transfer on a public transportation system. I made it early before anyone was there, and I took a walk in the Loop. My suit was clean and pressed and my shirt was starched and my tie tied neatly in a half-Windsor. I was completely nervous. But I checked in about 8 a.m., and then my day was filled with Byzantine administrative nonsense one must do when one begins work at a large corporate enterprise. There were 95 or so summer associates in my class, but I started very early with only two other summers. We had our pictures taken for ID badges and filled out paperwork designating life insurance beneficiaries and proving our citizenship so we could get paid, and we read papers explaining what would be withheld from our paychecks and filled out direct deposit paperwork and watched training videos on sexual harassment and all of that. The firm issued to us each a Blackberry, and that was the neatest thing in history until we realized that it was an electronic leash.

In the middle of the day we had a two-hour long lunch with our partner mentor and associate mentor. My mentors, partner Debra Colmes in the Environmental group and associate Daniel Jefferson in the Litigation group, took two of us summers to Le Colonial on the north side. It was probably the happiest lunch of my life.

And I got some very good advice that day; though it didn't strike me how important it was at the time. An attorney in the litigation practice group told me: "Don't believe any of this summer associate stuff; it is not like this in practice. In practice, it's only hours. That's it. There are only two ways to know if you're succeeding—your hours and your telephone. You want your telephone to ring all the time; you want to leave your office with your telephone ringing."

Sidley was and is a tremendous firm with a staggering history. It is an enormous and powerful law firm, with roots in the 1800s. With associated names like Newt Minow, Adlai Stevenson, and, of course, Barack and Michelle Obama, it is no surprise that Sidley is an enormous player in almost every industry in America.

I was assigned to an interior office on the 27th floor that I would have to share with another summer associate in a couple of weeks. It seemed haphazard which summer associates had to share offices and which got single offices. A few even pulled the lucky straw and would be assigned to window offices. (Of course, we then all wondered "what does it *mean*?" that someone got a better office and someone got a worse office.) The whole building was new; the firm had moved there about a year earlier from its old offices in the Chase building across the street. We took a tour of the building, and we met the library staff and were assigned a secretary. Most of that first week was committed to meeting people and touring facilities and having two-hour lunches. We early starters didn't get the Westlaw or Lexis[13]

---

[13] LEXIS and Westlaw are online, subscription-based services in which attorneys (or anyone, really) can, for a fee, search through a tremendous amount of case law and treatise material. In the olden days, lawyers researched legal issues in libraries, fumbling through thick, bound "reporters" that printed published opinions. The vast majority of

training, or any of the training on the computer system, not yet—they saved that for the next two or three weeks when the bulk of the new summer associates began arriving. In practice, that meant that I had very little to do for the first week and the second week was comprised mostly of training. I took one train and two buses to get home to Sauganash and was pretty tired at the end of the day. A few partners asked me if I was interested in dinner that night, but I had plans to hang out with Isra.

Isra came over and met Carrie and we talked and had a good time, but she had to go home that day because Nic was uncomfortable with Isra spending so much time there. He justifiably said "This isn't a hotel", and I agreed and didn't complain or anything. I walked Isra out and asked her on a date beside her car.

"No," she said.

"Why not?"

"Why do you have to ask this? Why do you need to put everything in boxes?"

"I don't," I said. "I just want to take you out."

"No."

"Ok, well can we hang out on Saturday?"

"Yes!" she said with a smile. "Let's go to Devon! We can *FEAST* for like five dollars!" Devon Street on Chicago's north side is a street of immigrants; there is an Indian neighborhood, a Pakistani neighborhood, and a Russian Jewish neighborhood. It is referred to as "Devon" by basically every South Asian in the Midwest, as in: "Oh, haha, yeah! Let's go to Devon!" We went together that Saturday and walked a long, long way to get to the restaurant and then came back to the apartment. I tried to kiss her, and she demurred and then said she had to leave because she had to be some place. I asked her again if we could go out, and she said she didn't know why I had to put things in boxes. When she was gone, I stepped out onto the balcony for some air and I saw her walking down the road to her car. She was in heels, which I'd never seen her wear before, and all that gangly strange walk of hers was gone. And I fell in love with her.

I sat all day at work looking at stuff on the Internet, and then every now and again I would walk around and meet people. There was an electronic bulletin board for summer associate work, but nothing much was posted yet. I stopped by summer associate offices and met my colleagues and then would strike up conversations with partners and associates all over the place. And every day some partner or associate in some group or another would take a few of us to lunch or to dinner or to both. In those days, the budget for lunch was $50 per person, I believe, and $100 per person for dinner. The money spent on us that summer was absolutely insane. The "social events" started the second week after more summers showed up, and then they would kick into a whole new gear once the University of Chicago kids

---

legal research when I practiced was performed on one or another of these online subscription services. Hopefully, free online resources like Google Scholar will replace fee-based models just as the fee-based subscriptions replaced libraries. The "law", such as it is, belongs to each and every citizen and each and every citizen should have equal access to the law.

showed up. (The University of Chicago uses a trimester system, instead of semesters, so the summer associates from the law school show up later in the year.) But *most* of our time in the first week or two was dedicated to talking about "Chicago to $160K".

Our first paycheck was live, rather than direct deposit, and so we had to collect it from the payroll department down on the 10th or 12th floor or wherever. Four of us summer associates happened to be going to pick up our checks at the same time. I had never seen a check made out to me for that much money. My first check was something like $2000 take-home. Beyond belief. Once I saw it in my hands, I realized that I would make more than summer than I had ever made in a year; then I realized I would make more than summer than I ever had in any two-year period. I was going to be rich. As we walked back to the elevators, one summer associate said:

"Jesus Christ! How can they take *that much* from me every week in taxes!"

"I KNOW!" the other said. "It's criminal."

And I bit my lip.

As we rode the elevator I thought about it, and then said:

"I will pay more in taxes this summer than I have ever made in a year."

"That is criminal, isn't it?" the male summer said.

"Yes, it is," I agreed. "It *is* criminal."

About a week later, the pay scale jumped to $160K for first year associates. The raise was retroactive to the beginning of the summer.

BOOK I: THE MOMENTS THAT TURN US (C)(i)
WITH PITFALL AND GIN BESET THE ROAD I WAS TO WANDER IN.

It was hard to keep going in Ohio, so I tried to make "Indiana" a powerful word like I had done with Ohio, but it didn't work. State lines meant very little or nothing to me. So I tried to convince myself that crossing Ohio meant something because we would unequivocally be in the Midwest once we reached Indiana. (To me, Ohio is not really midwestern. It is Ohio.) But I am *from* the Midwest, and so being in the Midwest didn't mean much to me, either. In the end, only two things kept us going: 1) I asked myself every morning if today would be the day to quit, and every time I decided not to quit then I knew that the day belonged to me; and, 2) I knew that we would have a hiking partner once we reached Cincinnati.

Otherwise, Ohio was very green and pretty hot, mostly flat with a few surprise hills. There was no real physical challenge to focus my mind off the boredom of the thing, and I had very little interest in meeting or talking with people. I don't remember having any emotions in Ohio, except for an overwhelming sense of boredom and failure. Ohio was difficult.

We made it into Cincinnati and waited a day for Heidi. She's a very smart, very professional woman, who had spent about 10 years as a consultant in Africa. She spoke a few languages and had an abrasive and cynical demeanor that was, nonetheless, pleasant. We met in a parking lot and I investigated her pack. Her pack was far lighter than mine—I would estimate that her pack, fully loaded with water, weighed 45 pounds or so. Mine, on the other hand, was still at about 70 pounds with water. (Some of that difference was due to Mabel's gear, which I carried.) But she had everything she needed, and I resolved to lighten my load immediately.

I mailed home everything that I thought I could live without. I kept only things that were undeniably necessary. I cut my first aid supplies down, and cut my blister/foot care kit by 75%. If I needed more, I would pick it up on the road rather than hike with it. I re-packaged and re-balanced my food supplies, and re-designed my pack so that my extra water could be stored inside the pack rather than on the outside. I replaced biners and other heavy binding/organization equipment with lightweight straps or string. My big dry sack, for the sleeping bag, went in the mail, too, and I replaced it with a lighter trash compactor bag. I sent my sleeping bag home, and replaced it with a lightweight sheet. I cut ounces and half ounces wherever I could; I cut off most of the handle of my toothbrush.

Heidi brought me a replacement walking stick like the one I'd lost but a few inches shorter. I gave her my homemade walking stick to use, and she said she preferred that one, anyway. It was lighter and it looked much more traditional, rugged.

We decided to hike out in 2 days, and in the meantime, Mabel and I rested and ate and caught up on some correspondence. Mabel, Heidi, and I met for lunch in downtown Cincinnati with a young married couple named John and Kait Seyal. They were planning a cross-country walk with their dogs and wanted to discuss some things with me. I'd received many emails from people who wanted to talk with me because they were "going to do it". Generally, I did not take them seriously because these people seemed usually to be generally happy people going through a little manic phase and would never really walkout. But these two Seyals seemed serious about the decision so I agreed to meet them for lunch. They were a nice couple: She was a beautiful young lady who was quiet during the lunch but had an extremely opinionated and strong tone when she did speak; he was a fit young fellow of mixed European and Pakistani heritage. They had been out of undergrad for about a year or so and were "tired of the 9 to 5 thing". I couldn't begrudge them that. John talked manically, but he didn't seem to be crazy or in a crazy state, so I didn't doubt that they would try the walk.

"My body is an amazing machine," John said during the discussion. "I'm not a good athlete or anything, but I'm just discovering that my body is an *amazing machine*."

I thought they were good kids, basically, but they had some unrealistic goals: full sponsorship for their trip, car support for the *entire* trip. I agreed that car support for the whole trip would be great but that it probably wouldn't be economically possible for them and would not likely be necessary. Full sponsorship was unlikely. But everyone has unrealistic goals sometimes.

I gave them tips on equipment and safety, and gave them some idea of what they had to look forward to. I didn't know how valuable my experience would be to them, but I'd learned a lot, most of it the hard way. John took some pictures of Mabel and me and they paid for lunch—I had a salad and told them that once they got out on the road they'd find that food was always a number one priority but that the food you eat is processed and nasty carbohydrates; I headed straight for a salad or a piece of fresh fruit when I reached a town.

"You can't pack a salad," I said. "Or you could, but it wouldn't last long."

We said our goodbyes and they left for their home in Kentucky. I sent them a sort of conciliatory email that night, because they had come to me for encouragement but I had given them some harder truths than they'd expected. It was important for them to give it a shot, though, I told them, and I wished them luck and would be there for them if they needed anything. I thought that John was a strong and happy looking young man, and I wondered if Isra and I had ever had a child if it would have grown up to look like John. I wondered a lot of things, but then put them out of my mind and got ready to hike out the next day with Mabel and my new hiking partner. That night, Heidi and I stayed in a park on the outskirts of Cincinnati. I think Heidi slept about an hour that night because it was her first night on the trail.

We hiked into Indiana the next day on a 17-mile hike, which was not very hard for Mabel and me, but it was a hell of a thing for Heidi. Her pace was considerably slower than ours. It frustrated me for quite a bit of the day, and then at the end of the day we didn't make it as far as we could have and had to stay in a motel a bit inside Indiana. But I remembered what my own first day had been like, when Mabel and I had gone about 17 miles—and I didn't envy what Heidi must have gone through that day. She soaked in the tub for quite a while, and I watched TV remembering what it felt like to struggle into a hot bath after a long day that left you destroyed. Heidi and I both like whiskey, so I walked to a liquor store and bought some pint bottles—Irish whiskey for me and scotch for her.

Mabel loved Heidi immediately. I considered having Mabel walk with Heidi some, because it might have been a nice change for me to be able to walk on my own, without worrying about Mabel. I decided that it made no sense to put Mabel in the hands of an inexperienced highway hiker; there was too much danger in it. Instead, I kept Mabel leashed to my hip and we walked on as a team.

It was nice to have Heidi with us through gorgeous Indiana. People generally think of Indiana as a flat, boring place (they generally think that of Ohio, Illinois, Iowa, Nebraska, Minnesota, Kansas, and both Dakotas, as well). But southern Indiana was forested with rolling hills and each day was a pleasant hike. Hwy 50 through Ohio, by contrast, had been like walking along an interstate.

But Heidi's body rebelled after that first day. Seventeen miles was too much for her first day and she suffered for many days. I knew it was difficult for her because I watched her do things like take her pack off, sit down on chairs, put on her shoes, and I could see the signs of the same physical pain I'd gone through. Slow movements. Unintentional flinching when a tight leg muscle is stretched to the point of pain. But she rarely complained. Once, when I pushed her to hurry up so we could get out on the road, she laughed and said:

"Fuck you! I'm not going *anywhere* today. I'm taking a day off, but you can go ahead."

I laughed, and stayed there, of course. I pretended I was in no rush anymore, anyway. We took a lot of zero days while Heidi was with us—once or twice she needed a day off, but mostly we took days off because a small heat wave came through. Heidi and I didn't talk much while we were actually hiking, which I think is probably a pretty standard thing among long distance hikers. But we talked a great deal on days off and during breaks, and I learned a lot about her.

She was about my age, but had done much more with her life than I had. She'd worked on AIDS prevention and clean water delivery in Africa, and she'd gone to grad school in New Orleans and again in Michigan. She'd been through a religious period in high school, and she told me some embarrassing stories about that and laughed heartily at herself. And she told strange stories about her lonely 10 years in Africa; she hinted that there were more stories, but she wouldn't share them with me. We were together 24 hours a day for quite a while. Heidi is an absolute gem of a person, or was to me at any rate. I doubt very much if the trip would have gone on as long as it did if not for her.

We hiked through hill country, and we visited beautiful state parks. We climbed roads that opened on top of rolling hills and we looked down into valleys that were green with corn. The shoulders were generally good along the road, but sometimes vanished in the hills and a guardrail ran right alongside the road. Heidi seemed nervous and often sped up when we approached blind corners. Sometimes she hiked too fast during those sections and that put Mabel and me in dangerous positions because oncoming cars could not see us. I had shouted a few times to get her attention, but I was never frustrated or angry with her. But Heidi got more and more frustrated and tired of the experience as the days went on. She wanted to take more breaks and more days off, and wanted to spend more time talking. I was afraid of getting bogged down talking, so I talked with her less and less, and the less I talked with her the more she tried to get me to open up and talk. She only asked me why I went on this trip once. We were in Versailles State Park in Indiana:

"I don't know," I said. "I really don't know."

"You have to *know*. You have to have some *idea* of why," she said.

"I promise you, I do not know."

"That's *bullshit*," she said. "Utter bullshit."

"It's the truth," I lied. It was utter bullshit.

"I'm sure it is," she said. "I'm sure it's the truth. But it's bullshit."

We hiked toward Bloomington, Indiana, and through some really hot days. I had thought we'd had hot days before, but we had seen nothing like this. Heidi had lived in Africa for 10 years, and she was sure that there was nothing she couldn't take and that it wouldn't get "Africa hot". So when I started mentioning that we had to be very careful of the heat, she scoffed and laughed.

"It's *not* hot," she said. "You should try Africa."

"Were you ever *hiking* in Africa?"

"Sometimes," she said.

"Well, it's going to be hot. Maybe not 'Africa hot', but it will be too hot to hike at some point."

We walked along scenic Indiana highways and my back sweat against the padding of the pack. The pack had spaces and air pockets between the padding, which increased the airflow along my back, but it wasn't enough to keep me cool. Sweat soaked my shirt and the pack and dripped down to soak the back of my pants. Beads of sweat gathered and grew heavy on my chin and then dropped toward the ground; sometimes, the drops of sweat splashed coldly against my knee or my forearm. Mabel panted heavily, and I tried always to guide our walk to the shady side of the road (if there was one) and to keep Mabel out of the direct Sun as much as possible.

Heidi, Mabel, and I hiked into Dillsboro at the end of May on the hottest day of the trip so far. We started early and walked quickly; Heidi, especially, was excited for us to get to Bloomington, where she could relax in a decent motel and get a good meal and maybe see a movie. But by afternoon, it was too hot to hike and our pace slowed.

"It's too hot," I said.

"This is *nothing*," she said. "In Africa, this is nothing."

"We're not in Africa," I said. "And, anyway, when it's this hot in Africa, I doubt little African dogs hike around."

"Don't be a sissy," she joked. "I mean, you walked from *Delaware* to *here* and you can't handle a little heat?"

We stopped at a gas station in Dillsboro for a drink, and then we walked on again. We walked by a BP station beyond the edge of Dillsboro at about noon in a little piece of nowhere.

"It's too hot," Heidi said. "We have to stop."

"Agreed," I said.

We stopped at the BP and hid in a small strip of shade along the building. I got a big cup of ice for Mabel and put some of it in a bowl for her; I filled my hand with ice and held it against her where her leg and chest meet, and then on the side of her neck, and lightly pinched pieces of ice against her ears. She protested for a while, then calmed, and then she really protested once her blood had started to cool. The wound on her ear still would not heal.

"How far did we make it?"

"I think about 11 miles," I said. "The forecast says it won't drop below 90 until like 9 tonight."

"What do we do?"

"I think we just sit here," I said, and exhaled loudly. "Damn it."

"It's ok," Heidi said. "We're not in a hurry."

"You're not in a hurry," I said. "Mabel and I are."

"You should relax. It will be fine. It's *too* hot."

"We lost a day already this week," I said. "And a day before that. Whatever. It's too hot for Mabel."

"It's too hot for you," she said. "How are we going to get to the campground?"

There was no chance of us making it to Versailles State Park on foot that day. The Park was another 8 miles or so and then we would have a few miles, anyway, to hike into the park to the campground—a lesson learned back in Greenbelt. It was 96 degrees, and we could not hike safely. Mabel could not hike in heat like that, even though I'd taken off her pack and was carrying it in my own, and it wasn't safe for Heidi or me, either. It is difficult for your body to cool itself with a pack on your back. We sat and talked in the shade of the BP station and moved with the shade as the shade moved from the back of the building to the side, and then moved closer to the building as the shade got smaller and smaller. I refilled Mabel's water a few times and bought a few snacks for Heidi and for me, and talked with a few of the folks who stopped at the BP. One older fellow in a tiny convertible Geo Metro was interested in us and in Mabel, although he never got out of the car. He wished us all the luck in the world before he left. Heidi had an iPod with her, so we took turns listening to songs on her iPod. She and I didn't have the same taste in music, but it was nice to listen to something, and I was tired of reading on the Kindle.

About an hour later, the old man in the Metro pulled up again.

"Where are you going?"

"Camping in the park," Heidi said. "We are *hoping* to make it out there today, but we can't leave until it gets cool enough."

"Not goin' to," the man said. "It's a heat wave. Won't cool down until 10 or 11 tonight. That's what they say."

"I guess..." I started to say, but he interrupted me.

"I can give you a ride out there."

We jumped on the offer. We somehow fit two huge packs and walking sticks into the Metro's trunk, but we couldn't close the trunk. Heidi and Mabel squeezed into the space behind the seats and I sat in the front with the old man and the gear and food that wouldn't fit in the trunk. It was the most people and equipment that has ever been loaded into a Geo Metro in the history of the world.

The old guy never told us his name, so later Heidi and I decided to call him Bill. He was retired from the Army after about 110 jumps with the 101st Airborne, a retired realtor after 30 years in the business, a hobby pilot, and the founder of the Southeast Indiana Humane Society. Mabel poked her head into the front of the car and licked at Bill's face; he petted her and scratched behind her ear and contorted his body as he was driving to pay a little more attention to her.

"I give money," he said, "and I pay for lawsuits against animal abusers. But I don't put my name on the suits, and have never had a title or anything. You tell people you're with the Humane Society and they think you're with PETA and they won't do business with you. But I love animals. I just love all animals, and I can't stand the way some people treat their animals. I've been that way forever, you know, since even I was a kid. Even animals I don't like. There's no sense in not being truthful about it, I just don't much care for cats. But I still love them. We don't have to save as many cats, because cats will take care of themselves better than dogs will. There's nothing tougher than a dog, but they can't make it on their own. Mostly it's dogs and horses."

I told him about a horrible thing that happened to horses near my hometown a few years ago, when their owner had left the country and couldn't find a buyer for his horses so he left them in a barn. When someone found the horses, the horses had been without any food except straw for weeks. The horses could hardly stand up and their ribs were showing and their hipbones, too. Their gums were receding and you could see the roots of their teeth. They had festering sores where their bones pressed too tightly against their skin.

"Those people should be in jail," he said. "You can't save a person like that who would be so mean to animals, or so disrespectful. There's no call for it, and there's always someone, *somewhere* who will take care of an animal. So many lonely people, and still so many animals that are abused. I can't stand it. I can't *stand* it."

He dropped us off near a covered bridge in Versailles State Park, and we hiked in to find the campground. The heat takes it out of you on the trail before you know it. When the trail is hot, you have *nothing* left at the end of the day, even if, like us that day, you walked only 12 miles or so. So it felt good to pitch the tent on a soft, shady spot, drink a quart of powdered milk, and lay down on the firm ground with Mabel sleeping at my feet in the tent. Even though it felt good to relax after such exhaustion, I was feeling a lot of failure in those days.

From Versailles we were on to Columbus, where I had to take a weekend layover. Mabel needed a bit of a "surgery" on her ear, and Heidi had to leave the trail in a rental car to have a girls' weekend with some friends in Wisconsin. Mabel's procedure took a day, and the other two days were so blisteringly hot that we stayed in the motel room and watched TV. During that weekend off, I spent some time with my shirt and shoes off standing around in the parking lot to get some "prophylactic Sun exposure", which is a term I invented. I was worried about Sunburn as Summer came. I wanted to get some controlled exposure to the Sun and build some natural protection, because I generally don't use Sunscreen. It was a hot and miserable weekend, and I was very lonely.

Heidi came back on a Monday, I think, and we headed out westward for Bloomington, the home of the University of Indiana. While marooned in Columbus, I'd changed our route to take us through Bloomington, on to Terre Haute, and thence to Champaign, Illinois. I went to college in Champaign, and I had from time to time been thinking about Champaign ever since Athens, Ohio. I'd only ever really been happy in my life while living in college towns, first Champaign and then Iowa City. Poor Mabel had gone from shelter to Chicago to the road and had never known life in a college town. And Mabel deserved to see college towns, so it seemed right to go through Bloomington and Champaign.

With Heidi with us, Mabel and I camped mostly in state parks and stayed in cheap motels in small towns. Heidi was uncomfortable with the idea of knocking on doors and asking for charity, so we never even attempted yard camping. She didn't need charity, and I guess I didn't really need it, either.

"It's not charity," I explained to her. "It's hospitality."

"We don't *need* hospitality," she said. "I have money. We have money. We can pay our own way."

"I don't have money," I said.

"Oh, come on! What did you make as an attorney, like $200,000 a year?"

"One-seventy," I said. "But I'm insolvent."

"Insolvent," she chortled. "Whatever the *hell* that means."

"My debts exceed my assets. So all my money basically belongs to my creditors—the federal government through Direct Loan Servicing and Sallie Mae. So all of my transactions could be unwound in the event of a future bankruptcy filing because I operate in the 'zone of insolvency'."

"So you have money? In the bank, you have money," she said. "But everything you buy belongs to your creditors? Sort of?"

"Yup."

"Except intangible things? Like...I don't know...memories? Experiences?"

I smiled.

She made fun of me for being insolvent—or for my describing myself as insolvent—as we walked on toward Bloomington. We walked through a wetland area outside of Bloomington with big fields of standing water, and skeletal trees that grew out of the water. The water lapped at the road in some places, and Mabel kept seeing things moving around in the water and kept trying to pull us out into it.

BOOK I: THE MOMENTS THAT TURN US (C)(ii)
EVERY HYACINTH IN THE GARDEN.

We checked into a motel in Bloomington and turned on the TV to get the news. A young woman named Lauren Spierer was missing. She was an Indiana University student and no one had seen her in several days, or maybe it was even a week by that time. We were planning to hike out of Bloomington the next day but we decided to scrap the next day and instead to join in to search the city with volunteers. My stomach churned a little, because I thought there was probably some chance that Spierer's body had been dumped in the sloughs and wetlands that Heidi and I had just walked beside on the way into Bloomington. Heidi and I searched a section of town beside the motel we were staying in, but we didn't find anything. Lauren's story resonated with me: I saw her parents on the TV, and my heart broke for those people because there was such a chance that they would *never know.* Just not know. It must be painful to not know what happened to your child, because *not knowing* is the worst—at least, all the things I didn't know were the worst for me. The day we gave up to search for Lauren was one of many zero days I lost on this trip, but I did not regret it.[14]

---

[14] As of this writing, Lauren Spierer has not been found. Spierer was last seen around 4:30 a.m. near her Smallwood Plaza apartment in Bloomington on June 3, 2011. If you have any information regarding Spierer, please contact Indiana police at 812-339-4477, or email to helpfindlauren@gmail.com.

"This was a good decision," Heidi said as we walked back to the motel.

"What?"

"Taking the day to volunteer here. It was a good decision for you. I know you're in a *hurry*, or whatever." She really didn't seem to understand how far I had to go to get to the Rockies and how dangerous it would be for Mabel and me. While Heidi was with me we had a relatively safe time, and the weather was pretty friendly except for a few very hot days. So I didn't hold it against her that she didn't respect the weather out there quite as much as she should have.

"We are in a hurry," I said.

"I don't know why you're in such a hurry," she said. "You have a *great life* doing this. This is a great life. You can walk where you want to and when you're tired of it you can just go back."

"It's not quite like that," I argued, but she wouldn't listen to me.

"It is, though," she said. She liked to contradict things by saying "it is, though".

"Want to go the rest of the way, then?" I asked her, as a challenge.

"Ha! I have to get back to class," she said.

"Yeah, but *would* you want to?"

"Hell no!" she said. "I said *you* have a great life doing this. I want to go home to my bed and have a nice meal with some friends and a few glasses of wine."

We headed west from Bloomington toward Terre Haute. Terre Haute is a particularly uninviting looking place that I had only driven through before. But I'd heard stories about it being kind of a rough town, and the closer we got the more stories we heard from people about how we had to be careful in Terre Haute.

We made good time out of Bloomington, though, and I was excited to be getting back to Illinois. Our last day into Terre Haute started beautifully. It was a great day, the weather was right, and we were all on the top of our game. But the day turned out poorly. We had about 27 miles to go to get into Terre Haute, and about two miles into the trip, my right ankle turned on some loose gravel and made three loud snaps. It sounded like branches in a tree breaking and hurt like hell. Heidi was about 15 feet in front of me and when she heard the snaps she turned back to see me doing a little hopping dance trying to keep the weight off my right foot. All the color drained out of her face and she looked like she might get sick.

"Oh my GOD!" she said. "Jesus, Tyler. Are you ok? Was that your *leg*!?"

I may have cursed a few times, and said that yes, it had been my ankle, but that everything was going to be fine. We hobbled up about a quarter of a mile until we found a broad clearing on the left side of the road with a big old Oak tree casting a swath of shade. I sat down and took my boot off.

"Does it hurt?"

"It hurts like hell," I said. I winced when I took the boot off.

"What are you doing?" She sat beside me.

"Taking my boot off," I said. "This thing might swell. If it swells, I don't want to cut off the circulation to it."

"Is that the *right* thing to do? Does it hurt? Can you walk on it?"

"YES IT HURTS," I snapped. "Sorry, but yes. You asked, I answered. It hurts."

I took a couple of aspirin from my first aid kit, and we waited for the swelling to start but it swelled only a little. I tried to stand up after I'd given the aspirin a little while to work, but didn't put the boots on immediately. With any pressure on the foot, it felt like that knuckle of bone on the outside of my ankle was going to pressurize and pop. I winced and sat back down.

"Well," Heidi said. "We could call an ambulance. Or we could call a cab, maybe?"

"We can't call a cab," I said. "We're like 25 miles from Terre Haute. And I'm *not* calling an ambulance."

"If you can't walk, then we'll have to call an ambulance. Or at least a cab."

"I'm not paying for either of those," I said. "I'm insolvent."

"Oh, shut up about that."

"It's true. Do you have that flask?"

"Yes," she answered.

"Give it to me, then."

She got the flask out of her bag and handed it to me.

"Are you fucking kidding me?" she said.

"It's, what, 10 bucks worth of whisky? That's a hell of a lot cheaper than a cab or an ambulance." I drank about a quarter of the flask and waited for the whisky to settle in. Heidi looked away with an embarrassed smile.

"Are you *fucking* kidding me?"

"What?"

"What is this, 1850?" she asked. "Who uses whiskey as a painkiller? Is this the Crimean War?"

"Crimean War," I said. "Overrated war, right there."

"Why?"

"I have no idea," I said. "All wars are overrated."

The whisky started to work a little and I put my boots back on. My foot still hurt but I didn't mind so much. I kept the flask with me in the cargo pocket of my shorts. Heidi laughed at me the whole time, but Mabel sat there watching and licking her chops. Mabel had taken the chance to nap a little and when she woke up, Heidi and I were about ready to leave for the road. I got up and had to lean pretty heavily on my walking stick.

"You go first," Heidi said.

"Yes," I agreed. "I'll be slower than you."

Strangely, my pace was not that much slower. I had to walk with a stupid-looking lope, with most of the weight of my body on the walking stick during the right foot stride. And because of the pack, it felt like I was swaying back and forth as I walked, and I have no doubt I looked like I was swaying, too. We walked on and every few miles I stopped to drink a substantial amount of whisky. Heidi admitted that she had another pint of whisky in her bag after I killed that first one, a pint that I had bought for her a few towns back and that we hadn't drunk. She'd forgotten about until a couple nights earlier. I took that, too.

I walked on the whisky for about 20 miles or so, until I was more or less too drunk and/or too hung-over to go on. The alcohol really loosened my legs up and kept the pain down in my ankle, and without it I probably wouldn't have made it that 20 miles or would have hurt myself worse during that time. But, the other side of that coin is that we ended up sitting alongside the road about four or five miles from the motel we were going to stay in. Heidi was in a bad mood, Mabel was tired, and I was drunk. So it was a double-edged sword, I guess. Cut you both ways.

We lost a day in Terre Haute to monitor my ankle. I couldn't sleep that night so I limped around the area around the motel with Mabel. A group of five or six teenagers approached me at about two in the morning and I was a bit worried they were planning to jump us. Mabel growled and barked, though, and I stopped walking and leaned on my walking stick. The kids stopped laughing and talking about me and stared at me as they walked slowly by me. They could have beaten the shit out of me had they tried, and I think they would have if not for Mabel. Teenagers in a pack can be a serious concern for a thru-hiker who looks homeless. There were quite a few times on the trip when teenagers made me feel threatened.

I decided I had to "slack pack" Illinois—that is, have someone carry all my gear and I would walk with Mabel and water. But I doubted I could find someone willing to drive a lag wagon for me. Most people have duties and responsibilities to do during the day that don't include picking up a bag of gear, hanging out all day, then dropping the gear off 25 miles down the road and camping with a guy who smells like an animal.

It was slow hiking out of Terre Haute and Heidi rented a car. She had intended to rent a car in Terre Haute to get back to Michigan, anyway, so she did and she used it to help me get out of Terre Haute and to limp across into Illinois and up to Champaign. Once I got into Illinois and south of Champaign, the trip up to Champaign was almost straight north. The lawyer in me argued that, because it is a northerly detour, and because the cross-country trip is east to west, I was free to accept without regret any north/south rides. It really wasn't a question, anyway, as my ankle hurt like hell. So Heidi drove me north to Champaign where I checked into a motel and laughed to myself about how I didn't have any friends in Champaign anymore. So I showed Mabel the Alma Mater and the campus, and I had lunch in downtown Champaign at one of the cafes I used to walk by all the time when I was an undergraduate student. I sat in the parking lot across from Assembly Hall and played the harmonica and the tin whistle. I'd considered spending a week or so in Champaign to let my ankle heal but, once I was settled into the hotel, I realized that I didn't know anyone in Champaign anymore and it wasn't worth staying. There had been a point in my life where the only people in the world who I knew lived in Champaign—but damn things change.

It is nearly a straight shot across Illinois on Old Hwy 36 (not the interstate) to my home county. We headed out toward Monticello, and walked through a bunch of the small towns—like Bondville and Monticello—

that you *hear* about when you are a student at the University of Illinois, but that you never visit. My ankle hurt badly, and I hadn't been able to find anyone to help me slack pack through Illinois. I worried about that because I did not want to stop because of injury. There were a million reasons why I would have stopped the trip and been fine with it, but injury was not one of them. I don't believe in injuries. I *did*, however, know that the injury made it hard for me to be there for Mabel in case of an emergency. So it was important for me to get my ankle in shape enough that I felt safe with Mabel.

BOOK I: THE MOMENTS THAT TURN US (C)(ii)(a)
HORDE OF FEARS AND SORROWS.

We stayed with Sam Andersen in Decatur. I'd known Sam for a long time, although he is older than I am. We hadn't spoken much in our lives, and not at all for maybe 10 or 20 years. But he had heard about the walk and wanted to help out. The night that I stayed there, we left Mabel at his house and he took me to dinner. On the way, he asked me:
"Do you carry a gun with you?"
"No," I said. "Everyone asks that."
"I don't like guns. I'm not a 'gun guy'," he said. "But if I did this trip, I'd have to carry a gun. Have to."
"More trouble than it's worth," I said.
"I would have to. It's a control thing."
"I can understand that," I said. "I have trouble sleeping and I'm a little edgy. Walking along the highways, mostly. Being out of control like that...I think maybe it's some low-level PTSD or something."
"I had PTSD," he said.
"Yeah? Trouble sleeping?"
"Yes," he said. "And some other things. I'd have to carry a gun because I have to maximize control in every situation. I can't stand to feel out of control. And, man, let me tell you, if you were a victim of a violent crime— I'd want to have that gun there, to be in a little more control. *Because you aren't in control.*"
"I hope not to be the victim of a violent crime," I said.
"I was," he said, a little nervously, but also like he wanted to talk about it. He then told me this story:

I lived in Los Angeles in the 90s, around the riots. I went to school there; worked a few jobs. I loved it, because you know how it is growing up in Illinois. Nothing is better than living in L.A., being near the beach and the beautiful people. And I was still bodybuilding at that time. So it was a great life. But because I didn't have any money, I was renting an apartment in this—it wasn't a bad neighborhood at all, but it wasn't a good neighborhood, either.
My neighbors in this apartment complex were this woman and her son. The woman was hardly ever there. And the kid was named Tony and he was

about 17 years old. He was a good kid, too; he'd dropped out of school, though, and he didn't have a father, and he was—well, he was a troubled kid, I think. He was a good kid, but everyone around him was so troubled that he was troubled, too. You know? And I don't know why, probably because I was a little lonely, or because I just wanted to help out, or for whatever reasons, I got to be friends with this kid and I was trying to help him out. Took him to school with me and gave him a tour, and got him into bodybuilding, and was helping him study for his G.E.D. It's not like I was his father or even his father figure, but I was sort of mentor, I think. I was mentoring this kid. It was hard to watch him suffer so much and have so many years ahead of him that were going to be ruined, so I just felt like I had to help him.

One night Tony called me and it was like midnight, and he says: "Hey, Man, I'm at this party and I need a ride home. Can you come and get me?"

It was pretty late and I wasn't doing anything else. I'd restored this '72 Volkswagen Super Beetle while I lived out there. From the ground up. And the thing about a Super Beetle is that it had no seat belts from the factory. But I installed seat belts as part of the restoration, and I did a good job.

So I left in that Super Beetle and went to this party to pick up Tony, and it was...I don't even remember where it was, but I remember that it wasn't in a great area. But Tony had a lot of shady friends, you know. He was messing around with these people who were into drugs and gangs. I mean, if you were a black kid in the 1990s in Los Angeles, then you were just—I just think they were all around it so much that they couldn't help it. When I picked up Tony he was waiting outside and there was this kid with him, probably about the same age, and Tony says: "Hey, can you give Larry a ride, too?" I was a little leery about it, and looking back I should have said no. I mean, of course I should have said no. But I mean, even at that time, I should have just said no, because I didn't say no and then I just wasn't in control of the situation like I should have been.

This kid, Larry, or whatever his name was, he got in the back seat and Tony got in the front seat and Larry gave me the address to go to drop him off and I didn't really know where it was, but Tony gave me directions. And it was an ok area, I thought, so no big deal.

Well, from the start, there's something strange about Larry. He was pretty obviously on drugs. He was nodding off in the back seat, and just sort of out of it. And, again, looking back, there was tension between Tony and Larry that I didn't notice right away. But we drove to this place that was in, like, Long Beach or something. And we were driving there, and Larry was sort of fading in and out and every now and again he would laugh out of nowhere. It was strange, the whole thing was strange, and when it gets strange like that you need to be in control or to put yourself in control any way you can. I know that now, but I was just stupid. I wasn't stupid, but I guess I was naïve. These were like 18-year-old kids, you know.

We got to the address and Larry wakes up and says "Ah, no, Man, I can't go here. Go here..." and he gives me this different address. Now that is when I should have gotten out of the car and left. But I didn't. I was naïve. Stupid. But we drove on and we had to get out on the freeway. And on the way to the freeway, Larry sort of woke up and he says "Hey, Tony" and lifts his shirt up and he's got a gun. And not a small gun. It's a .44, or something about that size. I saw it in the rearview mirror, and I thought: "What the fuck?"

So I looked over at Tony, and Tony looked like he was afraid. And then I got afraid. Because this is Tony's friend. When Tony was afraid, then I was afraid, because then we weren't in control. And Tony took the gun out and made some joke and kind of pointed it at Tony, and waved it around, then put it back. I was pretty much freaking out at that point. We were on the freeway and there was a kid on drugs in my backseat with a gun and Tony was scared, so I was freaking out. And then Larry says "Hey, Tony" and shot him in the head.

There was blood and brains and bone everywhere. His head exploded, I mean exploded, and I was covered in it. And I couldn't hear, because the gun went off right by my ear. A 72 Super Beetle is so small, anyway, and there were brains and blood everywhere. When I looked over, most of Tony's head was missing, and his throat was gurgling, and he was trying to speak and I just thought "this kid is dead; he is going to die and there is nothing I can do about that." I didn't know what to do. When I saw him and knew there was nothing I could do for this kid, or this corpse, I immediately thought "I've got to get out of here." I have to. You know? I. It was just me then and this kid who was going to kill me.

So I put the Super Beetle into a guardrail. When it hit the guardrail it started to slow down and I jumped out. We were probably going about 60? Maybe 50. I don't know. It didn't matter, because I was getting the fuck out of the car. But when I rolled out of the car my arm got caught in the seat belt and it pulled me under the car and the car ran over me. I rolled a lot, I know, but I don't remember it and I don't remember hitting the ground or anything like that. The next thing I remembered, I was running down the freeway through traffic. I just felt like I wasn't working, like my body wasn't working. A kid's head just exploded all over me in my car—I was in shock. And when that happens, it's like your body takes control of your mind. I remember it was like my legs were telling my head what to do, and my head was thinking: "Something is wrong, because I'm running as fast as I can, but I'm not going fast." Well, that was because I was all fucked up. When the car ran over me, I got pretty badly fucked up. I had a broken leg, and three broken ribs, my shoulder was dislocated, one of my feet was broken, and my hip was crushed. Still, I was running down the fucking freeway, so someone should have stopped. But I looked behind me and the car had stopped and I could see that kid kicking and trying to get out. Because it's not easy to get out of the back of Super Beetle if there's no one there to help you. So that bought me some time.

And thank God that there was an emergency call box up the road. And I called 911 from that thing and said something like "A kid got shot in my car and I'm in trouble and I'm at this call box and my body doesn't work" and I knew, just absolutely knew that that kid was going to kill me. I saw him get out of the car and start running toward me with that gun and I knew he was going to kill me. But I guess because he saw me at the callbox he changed his mind and he ran up this grassy area, like an embankment, and disappeared up there. And it was two and a half hours until the cops showed up. I could have sued them—well, yeah, looking back I could have sued the hell out of them, because this gets worse. I was there waiting two and a half hours on the ground and by that time when the adrenaline started to wear off, I just have never...you can't imagine what kind of pain I was in and I couldn't stand up, even. And for two and a half hours I sat there thinking that this kid was going to come and kill me. He could have, too. He could have gone home, had dinner, come back and blown my head off before they got there. And when they finally got there, they had me in the ambulance and the cops kept me there for two more hours asking me questions.

They thought I did it!

When I woke up the next day I was in the hospital and they'd had me under on morphine or who knows what. I thought it had all been some sort of bizarre dream or something. My first thought was that I'd been in an accident and I'd had a, you know, a messed up dream while I was in a coma. But I didn't know where I was really or what had happened. The TV was on and they were reporting on this murder and traffic jam that had happened on the freeway and there was my Super Beetle! So I was like "OK. Yeah. That happened. That was real."

It was a few weeks before I could sleep alone. The kid was still out there. I didn't know his name, or where he was, or why he'd done it. So none of it made sense, because nothing makes sense if you can't know, and so I just couldn't function. And every time I went out in public, which wasn't often because I couldn't walk or move around very well, every kid I saw on the streets, even white kids and Filipino kids, I would look at them and think "Is that the kid?" Because I didn't know! It was hard. It was hard and I thought I wouldn't ever get over that. But I did. I mean, you never get completely over it, but you do kind of get over it. You have to.

"Jesus, Man," I said. "I heard that something happened to you out there. But I had no idea."

"Yeah, well it's not something you talk about. Not for a long time, anyway. Actually, I haven't really told that whole story to many people. Or maybe not anyone. I don't know."

"Did they ever catch him?" I asked.

"Yes. Well, yes and no. He's dead. He was in prison for something else; they never got him for this. And someone killed him in prison. That's what I heard."

"That must help," I said.

"Yes and no. It helps, but then it doesn't because the crime was never 'solved'. I think the LAPD knows that he did it, but they never pinned it on him. And it's still an open case! It's a cold case, I guess. The LAPD sends someone to visit me every once in a while; 15 years later. It's never over. That's the hard part. It's never over because it informs everything you do. So it never ends. It goes on forever. It's just always there. I can never get it out of my mind. Not completely. There hasn't been a day, and maybe not an hour, since it happened that I haven't thought about it. It's never over."

I talked with Sam about the troubles I'd had sleeping and he gave me a sleeping pill. I'd taken Ambien with Heidi, and it had given me horrible nightmares. But he had Lunesta, so I gave it a shot and I was out like a light; I slept very well that night and the next morning Mabel and I hiked out. But my ankle hurt very badly, so I called a friend of mine from my hometown and had him pick me up. The pain was too much and I wanted to see my parents, so he drove us across the state and I was finally at home with my parents after many months. It was a tough homecoming because my father's condition had deteriorated rapidly in those months from his Parkinson's disease. But it was good to be back home and I spent about a week or so there. I used my Mom's car to drive out and day-hike across Illinois, without the pack, sort of as a way to rebuild the ankle and to do some hiking without the pressure of being "out there in it". It was a nice change but hiking with the added responsibility of a car was burdensome and I couldn't have done it any longer than I did.

For the section between Springfield and New Berlin, Illinois, which is very near my hometown, three of my former colleagues from Chicago drove down to do the 15-mile hike with me. That was a nice day, and it was good to see people who I knew and respected.

Being at my parents always gives me a chance to think about things and reflect, probably a little *too much*, but while I was there I thought a lot about the trip that I was on and what it had already cost me. I hadn't thought about Isra in a long time, but Mom asked me if I'd spoken to her. I didn't call her, but I thought about her and wondered if we would still be together if it weren't for this trip. And I thought about how hard it would be for me to find work after this with a big, strange space on my resume. What would I say about this? Would I call myself a "hiker" or an "adventurer"? I thought *a lot* about quitting and giving up. We were a long ways from the Rockies and we didn't have very much time to get there. The year was slipping away from us—I had intended to be in Iowa City by the middle of May, and here it was the nearing end of June and I wasn't yet to Iowa. But quitting is a strange thing. One night when my Dad was asleep (he slept a lot) and my mom couldn't sleep, I sat with her at her kitchen table.

"I think I might quit," I said.

"If that's what you think is best," she said. Mom's house was very dark; it had gotten darker over the years, as she painted the walls darker and darker colors, and refused to turn on lights at night. In the darkness of the house she looked smaller and smaller each time I visited home. But she was still hard, energetic and strong, with a huge powerful heart that was capable of immense love and immense justice.

"Do you think I should quit?"

"It doesn't matter what I think," Mom said. "What would you do if you quit?"

"I don't know."

"Would you go back to work? Would you try to get back together with Isra? Would you live *here* and practice *here*? What would you do?"

"I don't know," I said again.

"Well, I think you should do what you think is the best thing for you to do. *I* want you to be an attorney. I'm so awful proud of you," she said. "I didn't get the chances you got, to go to college, or to move away, or any of that. So of course I want you to be an attorney. But, to me, it seems like you've made a commitment to do this. You committed to do it, so you should do it."

"I can't," I said. "I mean, I really can't. I don't think that it's possible for me."

"But other people have done it?"

"A few," I said. "It's possible. I just don't think it's possible *for me*. I don't think I can do it."

"Well," she sighed and refilled her coffee cup. "That's—I don't believe that. Of course you *can* do it. If it's not the best thing to do, then that's different. There would be no reason to be ashamed if you quit now. I don't know anyone else who has walked from Delaware to Illinois. That's something."

"It is," I said. "It is. But it's not the whole thing."

"No, it isn't the whole thing. And you said you would do the whole thing," she went on. "Has there ever been anything that you said you would do but didn't?"

"Not really. Maybe some stuff."

"It's just like when we started the business and took out loans," Mom said. She and my father had started a business in 1991. "I made a commitment to pay them back; they had faith in your Dad and I and our work ethic, and they loaned us money and I said I would pay it back. And I did! And just like when you started law school—I think you wanted to quit, didn't you?"

"A little," I agreed.

"I think that about a year and a half into that you were bored and felt like you weren't learning enough. Or not learning what you wanted to learn. But you had made that commitment. And then you finished."

"But there's no point to this, at all, Mom," I said. "I mean there really is *no point* to any of this. It would be embarrassing to quit."

"Don't give me that!" she said, and laughed. "You haven't given a damn what anyone thinks, ever." I smiled and laughed. "You get that from your Dad, not me. We were just lucky that your heart was always in the right place, because I know you don't care a bit for what anyone else thinks about you."

"That's my problem, I think," I said.

"If it's a problem, then it is, I guess. I don't think it's a bad thing. But, look, does there have to be a point? I don't think everything has to *mean* something."

"Sure," I said.

"There you go. Quit or keep going," she said. We paused for quite a while, and Mom looked across the room where Mabel was sleeping. "Mabel sure is a sweet dog. She is the *sweetest* dog and she is so fast and graceful. I can't get over how graceful she is. She's *sleek*."

"Yes, she is," I agreed.

"Well, do what you have to do. But you can't go on with that ankle, that's pretty clear, isn't it? Start there. If you go on, what will you have to change? Start there." She walked off into the darkness with a half empty cup of coffee and a cigarette. "I have to get some sleep, got to be at work early in the morning. Start there, Tyler. Start with the changes."

BOOK II: FEEL THE SELFISH FURY (C)(ii)
OVER THE SHOULDERS OF THE FLAMING FOAL.

Isra and I went on a date that weekend in 2007. She had called me out of nowhere and said: "Ok, then, we'll go on a date." She showed up in a svelte dress and heels and we went to eat tapas together and talked about music and adventure and travel and not at all about law school and then went to Kingston Mines on Halsted, which she said was her favorite bar in the whole world because she loved live blues music. We drank and talked and listened to music, and maybe danced a little bit, and then the night was over and we drove back to Sauganash. I tried to kiss her, but she wouldn't, and I decided that I would not see her anymore. The summer program was really beginning to heat up, and I had a lot of social engagements that I *had* to attend—because if you don't attend, you don't get a job. And I would be late getting home almost every night of the week because I lived so far out in Sauganash, and my priority had to be killing that summer program and leaving with a job offer. I was told that if I *didn't* get a job offer, then I would likely have a difficult time finding work at all. I didn't have time for Isra—certainly didn't have time for a girl I wasn't actually dating! Or, at least, that's how I saw it.

"If you don't get an offer here," a summer associate would say, "then you are fucked. I will be *fucked*. How do you explain that on a resume? 'No-offered summer associate at Sidley.' That looks *so* bad."

"Yeah, and all big firms only hire through their summer program," another would say. "So if you're no-offered here, then it's not like there's a lot of places who would even consider hiring you. A no-offer here and you're in the plaintiff's bar or chasing ambulances." That was the dynamic of the summer—on the one hand, everyone *knew* that in those days no-offers only happened if you made an ass of yourself or got into a fight or sexually harassed someone, or some equally strange and repugnant behavior. Everyone *knew* that. But for some reason, everyone was tense. Everyone seemed scared that *they* would be the one who was no-offered.

I dedicated my summer to "Uncle Sid". The associates called it that when they took us out to dinner: "It's on Uncle Sid!" He was a passionate but distant relative. He gave us everything we asked for and hinted that he'd ask for repayment someday.

I was keen to work with the Environmental group, and I was on their floor. My office was right across the hall from my partner mentor, Debra, who was a partner in the environmental group, but there was very little work in that group. Since the Bush regime had seized power in 2001, there had been no new environmental regulation and no enforcement of existing regulations to speak of. So that was a group that was withering, slowly, waiting for the next round of environmental stewardship fervor to put them back on the gravy train. So I worked with other groups—I did projects for litigation associates, mainly, and spent a "week in the group" with the Banking group. I felt that I meshed best with the personalities in the banking group, although my week in that group was ill-timed and I got to do very little actual work besides some borderline clerical tasks of turning changes and formatting documents. But none of that bothered me too much, because the summer associate program in those days was primarily about social functions and experiencing the City. At that time, partners told me that their view of the summer program was that "All of us there in the program could do the work—there was very little doubt of that—but what we really want you to do is to experience the City and discover if it is someplace you *really* want to live and to work."

People reminded us all summer that we were at Barack and Michelle Obama's old firm. They told us anecdotes about the Obamas and their times at the firm. The most popular anecdotes were: 1) during his summer at Sidley, Barack Obama checked out the Bluebook citation manual on the first day and returned it on his last day, which was not a particularly good anecdote; and 2) Newt Minow loved to tell his story of Barack Obama coming to Minow's office at the end of the summer. "Mr Minow," he said, "I'm leaving Sidley."

"Oh, that's too bad," Minow said.

"And, one other thing, I'm taking Michelle with me."

And then Minow would act like he had gotten angry and say "Why you son of a...well, I can't tell you what I actually said". Then Minow said how he changed his tone when Obama explained that he was taking Michelle away for marriage, not for another firm. That anecdote was actually pretty good, and it was a neat experience to hear Newt Minow tell it. There were about 5 TVs in Minnow's office, but he never seemed to be there. I knew that Obama would win in 2008.

In early June, a managing partner of the firm invited summer associates to a White Sox game in a Skybox. I snapped up a ticket. When I got there, the Skybox was filled with about 10 summer associates—the lucky ones who had gotten the tickets to hang around with John Jacobs, one of the most powerful men in the firm, and a proud supporter of the Harvard tradition. He was a jolly looking and rotund fellow, and when he spoke you could hear in his voice that he was 1) much, much smarter than you, and 2) much, much meaner if he needed to be. I stood in a circle with Jacobs, a few Harvard summer associates, and a few from other schools. They all thought that this was a genuine chance to secure an offer, as if this were the one true, hidden job interview. If you hit it off with Jacobs, your future was secure. I doubted that pretty strongly—I imagined that Jacobs had almost nothing to do with hiring or firing decisions. And, anyway, I have never much been into the ass kissing game. But there I was with some real Harvard gunners, genuine gunner ass kissers.

"Well, I can't tell you how excited I am by the summer program," one said, holding his Amstel Light with a napkin wrapped around it.

"Good," Jacobs said.

"The opportunities here, I think, are a real complement to the education I've gotten at Harvard. And it's a tremendous opportunity to work with such a roster of smart and driven, not to mention successful, attorneys, such as yourself."

"Well, we are pretty proud of what we've put together at Sidley," Jacobs said, or something very near it. Jacobs was all smiles, but he really didn't seem impressed by the affair, and I rather thought he might not have been interested in the ass kissing game, either.

The acolytes went in order, sort of introducing themselves by way of ephemeral praise of Sidley and of Jacobs himself, if they could squeeze it in. They had all heard that Jacobs was loyal to the bone to Harvard, and they were quick to reference Harvard in their discussion. I sort of stood there, drinking a beer, when a lull in the conversation dropped and everyone sort of looked at me as if it were my turn to do some ass kissing.

"And you're not at Harvard," Jacobs said. "Iowa, right?"

"Yes," I said. "From Illinois, but I attend Iowa."

"How has your summer been so far?" he asked.

"Great," I answered.

"Good. Enjoying the opportunities?"

"I have been!" I said. "I've enjoyed quite a few of the opportunities, and I always enjoy the opportunity to watch a Sox game. I think I'll go watch."

I smiled and everyone chuckled as I walked off to the Skybox seats. I sat in the front row beside an older woman who introduced herself as John's wife, and she and I talked all through the game about her children and Chicago and Sidley and baseball and everything in between. She was a very nice lady and I enjoyed talking with her.

When the game ended and we all walked off to get on the red line train back into the Loop, one of the summer associates, though not a Harvard kid, John Gregory, joked with me:

"Kind of blew it with Jacobs today, huh?"

"You think?" I asked.

"Well, it was kind of awkward. I thought it was awkward."

He was trying to psych me out. That's what gunners and assholes do. Even in the summer associate program there are gunners who think that everything in the world *must be* kill or be killed.

"Sam and Brian thought it was awkward. I bet Jacobs thought it was awkward. You didn't think so?" He asked me with this tone of voice like he was genuinely interested in it from a sociology perspective, or as if it were some occurrence that could be valuably analyzed as a piece of anthropological conversation. But really he wanted to get it into my head that I had blown it with the head of the firm.

"I didn't think about it," I said.

"That's right!" he laughed. "You were busy talking with his wife!"

"Yup," I said.

"Well, it was awkward. And I bet he'll remember it—he'll at least remember your name. I wonder if it's a good or a bad thing for the managing partner of the fifth largest law firm in the country to remember your name? It's something to wonder."

"Tough to say," I said. "He probably will. And I'll just have to live with that, I guess. I'll tell you, I bet his wife will remember my name. We had a nice time. I wonder, when he and his wife get home tonight, I wonder if she'll say 'That John Gregory was a nice boy'. I wonder if she'll say that?"

BOOK II: FEEL THE SELFISH FURY (C)(iii)
ONE SPIED THE LITTLE CRESCENT ALL WERE SEEKING.

"Why won't you go on another date with me?" I asked her again on the phone.

"Just stop asking."

"No," I said. "You should tell me. Just tell me you don't want to."

"I DO want to," Isra said.

"That makes no sense. Why would you want to spend all this time with me? Why did we spend, like, every night together in law school and...."

"Well, it wouldn't have been right during the semester because I was seeing someone."

"What?" I asked. She was silent. "What?"

"You knew that."

"No I didn't," I said. "And, for example, when I asked 'Are you seeing someone?' you said 'No'."

"It wasn't anything. It wasn't like a real thing."

"What?"

She told me who she had been seeing, and that she wasn't seeing him anymore because they were in different places for the summer but that she wouldn't be seeing him after the summer, either. It wasn't a real relationship, she said. And I thought of her running down the road the night after the party.

We didn't speak for two weeks. When we did, I had moved into an apartment in Lakeview and she had moved into an apartment a few blocks away from my new Lakeview apartment. She came over and stood in my living room and told me that she missed me like crazy and she started to cry a little. It hurt her that I hadn't called or anything. I said I was over it, and I'd still like to take her out on a date. But she said she couldn't, because she was seeing somebody.

That summer was insane. It was odd and salubrious beyond measure. There were two-hour lunches every day and dinners most nights, all on the firm. And when we went out at night, we would often run into parties of summer associates from other firms, all eating and drinking lavishly on their firm—their "Uncle". There are other firms in Chicago, of course—Kirkland & Ellis, Mayer Brown, Latham & Watkins, etc. The list goes on and on.

There can never be too many attorneys! There were stories in the newspapers that summer about the "summer associate culture", and about how much money was spent to recruit summer associates to big firms. Journalists wrote about the lunches and the dinners, about the opera tickets and baseball tickets.

I spent most of my work time talking with attorneys or researching things in the law that interested me. At that time, I was most interested in environmental issues and the possibility of creating a carbon credit cap and trade system. Back then it seemed like a good idea to me, although I am not so sure now. And that summer was the first time I discovered and read anything about Islamic finance, which is a subject that fascinates me to this day. But mostly I went to lunch at all the trendiest restaurants, and then at night I would go out to a dinner with a partner or a few associates or to a social event with all the summer associates. We did the architectural boat tour of Chicago, we visited the museums, and we had mixers and drinks at places like Shaw's Crabhouse. I generally left the firm early in the afternoons and went back to Lakeview to run along the Lake, which I enjoyed doing and which helped me with the dull sort of pains that I still had from time to time in my joints and in my bones—the lingering symptoms of the Lyme Disease. And if I got any of those pains during the day I would stroll around in the Loop feeling like I had finally made it and done something with my life.

But it wasn't all roses. It became stressful toward the end of the summer. It reminded me of the 1L year when finals approached. We were all safe, or the ones who were safe should have known it. And I probably *did* know that I was safe and would get an offer, but our discussions (when partners and associates weren't around) had shifted and now we talked almost exclusively about whether or not we believed we would get an offer. Rumors of no-offers swirled. Stories that clearly could not have been true circulated like peer-reviewed fact—this person or that person had done this or that and the decision had already been made to no-offer them. And then a rumor went around that *all* the hiring decisions had been made and that there was a *list* that someone had seen. Was I on it? Were you on it? No one could be sure who exactly was on the list, and as the story traveled and grew it became unclear whether the list had been the list of people who would get offers or the list of people who wouldn't get offers. But there was a list out there somewhere, I guess. Or not. I honestly have *no idea* what kind of behavior it would have taken to get on that list. I saw summer associates—not necessarily Sidley summer associates, mind you—be needlessly mean to homeless men and to each other, and I saw them so drunk and vomiting that you would think they were 17-years-old, and I heard stories about them stealing and about them stalking senior associates and partners. The stories were unreal.

Take this story, for example. One night I went to a summer associate dinner with a couple of partners from a group at Sidley, one of their senior associates, and Deepak, a fellow in my summer class who I would later work with. During dinner, the senior associate peppered us with unbelievably inappropriate questions ranging from whether or not we had a consistent sexual partner to whether we were Republicans or Democrats. He drank a lot red wine, because the firm was paying for it. After the dinner, he was very drunk and wanted to play video games at one of the arcades in River North, either ESPN Zone or Dave and Buster's. The three of us went, and the senior associate was so drunk that he had removed his jacket and shirt and was wearing only a t-shirt, through which he had been sweating. His underarms turned purple. We played a few video games, I remember, and shot some baskets, and we played that game where you punch a punching bag and it registers how strong you are. Then, he said:

"Let's play air hockey. I will beat your ass at air hockey!"

"I'm pretty good," I said.

"I have never lost a game of air hockey in my life," he said. "Just like making partner, I will make it happen. You think you can play?"

He was bizarrely aggressive about this, but I agreed to play. And he was *very* good, although I don't know how much it is worth to be *very* good at air hockey. We played two games; I won once out of sheer luck and he was devastated. He was visibly angry, and accused me of cheating. But there were two 10-year-old kids lurking around and waiting to play.

"You kids want to play?" I asked when our second game was over, and the senior associate had thrown up his hands in victory. The kids nodded. "Ok."

"No, no, no," the associate said. "This is *my* table. I've got this table right now. You kids want it, you have to win it from me." The kids were a little uncomfortable. "Come on. Two on two for the table."

I can't remember how much the table cost to play, but I think it was about $1.50. The senior associate demanded that the kids pay for that game, because it is the custom that the challenger pays. The game started and I was trying to "relate" to the kids, which I'm horrible at, and I was letting them win. But the senior associate was *brutal*. He was bigger and better at this game than these kids, because they were 10 years old, but he wouldn't humor them. He hit the puck so hard that the kids were scared. And we "won" that game 7 – 0. The kids put their paddles down on the table and walked slowly away from the table.

"Let's go again!" the senior associate said, but I told him that I had to get home for the night. When I left the table, I walked off and found those kids and gave them a $5 bill. I didn't have any smaller bills and I didn't care about money that much anyway. I told them they should play some more air hockey if they wanted to and to not play like that asshole. They smiled when I said "asshole".

That guy was a successful senior associate at my firm and everyone was pretty sure he would make partner.

The summer came to an end and we had a few get-togethers with all the summer associates. I talked nervously with my mentor, Debra, about whether or not I would get a job, and I told her my preferences for group assignments. My true first preference was environmental, but I knew there would be no jobs available with that group. On my last day at the firm that summer, I sat in the guest chair in Debra's office and discussed my decisions. I fidgeted with the preference form on her desk among her papers. Debra agreed with me that there would likely be no hiring in the environmental group—I don't think any of the big firms were yet prepared to gamble on the 2008 election and, even if Barack Obama or Hilary Clinton were to win, that would not guarantee a substantial uptick in environmental work. If there were to develop a need for a new associate, it might not be until the next hiring cycle or even the next. As we talked, I was aware that I was making an important decision—if I preferenced all litigation groups, for example, and there were only a need for transactional attorneys, then I might be passed over entirely in favor of those associate who preferenced transactional side groups. I asked for Debra's help and advice to maximize my chances of getting an offer and she obliged. Together, we decided I should preference, in some order, general litigation and the biggest, strongest, most stable transactional practice, Banking and Financial Transactions. It was a toss-up to me, really. There was an equal chance I would enjoy either kind of practice, and I was under the mistaken assumption that transactional side work had greater exit opportunities as well as a slightly better chance at having some work-life balance. So I wrote down my preferences: 1) Banking and Financial Transactions, 2) General Litigation, and 3) Insurance Products.

For those among use who were paying attention, it was already a scary time. Many of us knew something strange was coming in the American economy. There were hints of it on the news and among some economic forecasters. There are always the loons—the gold standard and anti-Federal Reserve loons—but even the mainstream media had picked up on the hints. But the lights were always on in the banking group back then, and you could find second year associates billing hours into the early hours of the morning. I had been concerned about the coming upheaval, and had talked to a few banking group partners, but they all said that Sidley had a "well-rounded" practice.

"There is some fear in the securitization market," a partner would say. Securitization was Sidley's bread and butter in those days. "Sure. But there is always some uncertainty. But we have a well-rounded practice and, you know, we are a full-service law firm. We have counter-cyclical groups like bankruptcy that can pick up slack in down times. So even if there were a market disturbance, Sidley is very well-positioned, I think, to weather it."

That was the kind of advice I got while I was trying to decide what groups to preference. And I can still remember the look and smell and feel of Debra's office when I leaned over her desk and filled out those three slots on that piece of paper. I wrote "Banking and Financial Transactions".

That moment turned my life.

I was back at Iowa for my 3L year and looking forward to finishing the whole experience up and moving on. Despite it all, I was looking forward to seeing Isra. I really tried to put her out of my mind that summer—I had a lot of fun, saw a few girls, and did my best. But I couldn't stop thinking about her. I wanted to see her and to know she was doing well. When I did see her, it did not go well.

"Oh, so you're back," she said. We were in the BLB.
"What?"

"You disappeared. Man, it's just like I said it was going to be. Go to the City, and you just disappeared."

"It wasn't like that," I said.

"Whatever, Man," she said and I walked away.

Later that day, Debra called from Sidley and told me that Sidley wanted to offer me a position at the firm after graduation. Sidley would pay for my bar review materials, I would get a bar stipend of $10,000, and would begin employment at Sidley at $160,000/yr. I accepted immediately and my heart felt light for the first time since I'd started law school.

A week later, Isra stopped me in the halls of the BLB and asked what I was doing that weekend. I was gong to a friend's wedding in Southern Illinois, and she asked if she could come along. He was a friend from undergrad who I'd fallen out of contact with but I'd decided to go to his wedding because I had lost contact with almost all of my undergrad and high school friends. Isra and I laughed and had a great time, and were drawn to one another like we had always been. But she was still seeing someone.

I saw her again two weeks later at the bar. A friend of mine and I were standing at the jukebox and she walked up.

"Hello," she said. "Still ignoring me?"

"Michael," I said, "Have you met Isra? She's a fucking bitch."

And I walked away. That was a mean thing to do, or at least immature, and I regret it now. But I did it.

She called me that night at around 1:00 a.m. We were both more sober than we had been at the bar, and she demanded an answer for why I had said that.

"I don't know. Because I like you, Isra. I like you a great deal. We spent like every day together last year."

"I like you, too," she said.

"No, I like you a lot. I want to date you. And you don't want that."

"I do," she said. "I told you, you're outside the box."

"Uh, yeah, but that guy you saw last year is white. And what about this guy you were seeing over the summer?"

"It's not just that you are white."

"Have you ever even dated a guy who isn't white? Why would you lie to me about this? Why would you lie to me about anything?"

"I do like you," she said. "A lot. Like a real lot. Too much."

"Come over here then," I said.

"I'm not going to sleep with you," she said.

"Come over."

She came over and we did not talk. We went to bed together and slept soundly, her on her side of the bed and me on mine. In the morning, we woke up with her cuddled against me and I held her.

"You're outside of the box," she said.

"I don't want to be your friend anymore," I said.

"Ok."

And then we were a couple.

We got a ride across the Mississippi River into Davenport, Iowa, and lay up at a motel for the night. I had heard there was a way to walk across the River at a pedestrian bridge somewhere in the Quad Cities, but I really didn't care to look into it. I grew up by the Mississippi river and I've swum across the thing before, so walking across it didn't mean anything to me. There were, I think, three homeless families living month-to-month in that particular motel—that was a pretty common thing I saw in motels in or near mid-sized cities. Couples with a child or two, and often two incomes, but still not enough income to get out of the cycle of homelessness. Their children walk the hallways of the motel casually, like it's their home, and they have portable grills out back in the grassy areas where they cook each night. I've seen these families sitting together behind motels, sharing bottles of off-brand soda and heating up soup on charcoal grills. Obama came to visit the Quad Cities the next day as we hiked out of town, but he didn't come out to see us.

I made the change to a pushcart in Davenport, Iowa. I knew quite early in the trip that I would have to switch to a cart somewhere, because water is prohibitively heavy in the dry western states. My ankle made it immediately important to switch to the cart. I got a Schwinn baby stroller designed for jogging and I named it "ThePontiac". ThePontiac had 20-inch wheels and a silly suspension system, which I doubt would be necessary even if you had a real live baby in the thing. I had to do quite a bit of packing and unpacking to figure out how best to use ThePontiac and we didn't really have a good system for packing the thing for quite a while. I used the baby compartment primarily for water, and I strapped the backpack on top of the cart—I never got rid of the pack. Jack Planck, in contrast, got rid of his pack entirely once he crossed the Mississippi, but I always wanted to have a way to hike out of a bad situation even if ThePontiac broke down.

The difference was astounding and immediate. First, I was able to carry more dog food, more human food, more water, and generally more supplies at a much lower calorie and pain cost. The cart was easy to push, and I was much lighter and relatively unencumbered once I had transferred the weight from my back to the cart. Mabel noticed the difference, too, because we started walking at a much faster pace. It was clear by the time we'd hiked out of Davenport that, had we *started* with the cart, I would have made it to Iowa and beyond on my original schedule, weather notwithstanding. The wheel must have been the most important invention in the history of Mankind—that, or the Internet. I was better able to protect my gear from wind and water with the tarp, I was more visible to oncoming cars, and I was able to walk much faster. Perhaps the most important difference was in the time it took to water Mabel or to take a break. I needed a break every hour or so when I had the pack on and each of those breaks was 10 minutes or so. But we needed far fewer breaks with the cart and when I needed a break I could simply pull over a little and sit down. It was such a big difference that I had to be careful not to out-walk Mabel, because she would need breaks to rest and to drink, but this cart took so much pressure off of me that I could potentially have forgotten to break for her.

Footwear was another other big change coming out of Davenport. I've heard that each pound on the feet equals five pounds in the pack, and I don't doubt it. I switched to a pair of Teva sandals that I'd picked up in Indiana as camp shoes. They became my everyday hikers and that made a world of difference in terms of speed, foot health, foot strength, and calories. People constantly asked me how I could walk so far in sandals and would never believe me when I told them it was substantially easier and more comfortable than in shoes. I burned far fewer calories without the extra weight of the shoes on each step and was able to cut way back on food.

The third change, and it may have been as important as the other two, was that I picked up my iPod at my parents' house. I would still be alone, true enough, but I would have something to keep my mind distracted. Spending 10 to 14 hours walking with nothing but my own thoughts had gotten a bit freakish.

The changes—cart, sandals, and iPod—made an enormous difference, and our first day out of Davenport we did 30 miles pretty easily on dusty, gravel roads. It was, however, our first day rejected for yard camping. We walked through a tiny village of about 10 houses about 25 miles out from Davenport. There was a farmers' cooperative grain elevator and that was all. We felt strong—although I was thirsty and hungry—but I was a little unsure how my body would react the day after a 30-mile hike, so I decided we should find a place to lay camp in this little unincorporated town. I stopped at a couple of houses, but the homeowners wouldn't let us camp there. We stopped at the co-op and I got a couple of sodas from the machine inside, drank them, and asked a few of the folks milling around there if they knew of anywhere I might camp. They had no suggestions and didn't seem at all interested in the Walk, my welfare, or Mabel's well being. Just down the road from the co-op, a woman was mowing the yard in front of a fairly large old house that looked to be in the middle of a substantial remodeling. The house was clearly uninhabitable. I parked ThePontiac and walked toward the woman as she loaded up the riding mower in the back of a pick up truck. I waved my hand and smiled.

"Hello there," I said with a big wave of my hand, which I had found was the best way to initiate a conversation. "My dog and I are walking across the country." The woman had already looked down at the ground and she looked mean spirited. "We've been about 25 miles today and I was hoping maybe we could camp in the yard here. We'll be out before Sunrise, probably."

She had already started shaking her head.

"No," she said, and gave me a little dismissive wave of her hand. "Not happening."

I was already in a bad mood because of the previous rejections, so I didn't bother talking with her anymore. I said "OK" and turned around to walk back to Mabel and ThePontiac. But as I was walking, she shouted at me: "And you can't have any water, either."

Without turning back to see her, I shouted back "Go fuck yourself".

Not allowing us to camp there was one thing, but telling us we couldn't have any water? That woman essentially said "Your lives are not worth anything, and you don't deserve to go on living, no matter how trivial the cost to me". That's why I shouted at her. I was shocked, because I had lived for three years about 35 more miles up the road in Iowa City and had always found Iowans to be the most pleasant, intelligent, and wonderful people. What kind of person would tell a man and a dog that they could not have water? We hit the road and kept going. I figured there would be a church about two or three miles up the road at a crossroads, and I figured we would wander until dark, camp behind the church and be out before Sunrise—a pretty common practice for a cross-country thru-hiker. Along the way, I met a woman who lived in a huge home and was out tending her beautiful garden. We were in the middle of nowhere. The woman waved at Mabel and me, and I shouted out to her: "Hey there, do you know if there's a church or something up the road?"

"About three miles," she said.

"My dog and I are walking across the country. Looking for a place to camp for the night!" She walked toward me and I walked up and into her yard. "Got shot down back there."

"Yeah, well some people aren't friendly anymore," she agreed. "You need water?"

I filled all of our water containers with water from her garden hose and talked with her for a while. She was a nice lady, and she told me that about five miles to the south there was a family whose yard was *currently* filled with people in tents and that I could surely stay there.

"They are a...well, you know. They're a different kind of family for around here. They deliver their babies at home, and I think she's a midwife of some sort. And every now and again they have a whole lot of people come and camp there. I'm not sure what they do there, but I'm sure they'd let you camp in the yard. One more never hurt!"

I decided that walking five miles off our course was too big a gamble that close to the end of the day. We'd been almost 26 miles already on gravel roads and had done a lot of climbing—Iowa was, for us, a non-stop ribbon of hills. Each hill was about the equivalent of climbing a three-story building, which is not big, but at the crest of each hill I would see five or six more hills rolling off into the distance. So five miles was too big a gamble. Instead, we walked straight ahead until we found the church. But there was a house across from the church and a man about 24 years old was in the yard washing his car. It is always a stroke of bad luck when you find a great place to stealth camp but there's a house right across the street. So I stopped and asked the man if he cared that I might camp at the church.

"I don't care. I don't own it," he said. "You can camp here, too, if you want."

I decided to camp in his yard, and he and I talked for quite a while. He gave me a couple of sodas and a couple of cans of beer. I drank the beers for dinner and saved the sodas for the next day. I left the rain fly off of the tent that night, and we slept beside a young tree where we could see the silhouette of tree branches and where the shadows of leaves danced across the top of the tent, and behind all of that we could see all the stars out twinkling. It was a nice night, and it felt good to be almost back to Iowa City.

BOOK I: THE MOMENTS THAT TURN US (C)(iv)
YOUTH'S SWEET SCENTED MANUSCRIPT.

We hiked into Iowa City the next day. Mabel loved Iowa City. We got settled into my friend Michael's house, where Mabel and I would stay most of the time we were in town. Mike's wife and kids are all great and adorable, and I was glad he was doing so well for himself. He'd been a law student with me, but had decided never to practice. At the time, I thought he was an idiot—why suffer law school and then not practice law? But he'd made his decision to go into academia and it was good to talk with him about how his PhD program differed from law school.

Mabel and I headed down to the Ped Mall in Iowa City to walk around and hang out, but it was too hot, so we sat in the shade outside the Java House where I had practically lived during my first two years of law school. The thermometer on the bank across the street read 103 degrees, and I knew that Mabel and I were in for a long week—hiking in that heat was out of the question. It seemed to be good timing that we would lose a few days in Iowa City visiting old friends and old stamping grounds.

Pamela Ortiz, who had been a classmate of mine at Iowa Law, and who had recently won a case in front of the Iowa Supreme Court, threw a barbeque for us. The first night I got into town, Michael, Mabel, and I hung out at Pamela's house with Pamela and Professor Jerry Bingham, who had come over when he heard I was in town. We talked for a few hours and shared stories about working in biglaw.

"So how was it?" Bingham asked me, and laughed the way he does with a big midrange guffaw.

"Biglaw?" I said. "It, uh...well, it wasn't a perfect fit for me," I said with a smile.

"Yeah! You know, there were some of us in the law school who might have advised you that biglaw wouldn't be a perfect fit for you...had you asked. Ha!"

Jerry hadn't completely loved his experience as a partner in a firm, either, and so he could relate with the idea of walking across the country. Professor Bingham had had an enormous impact on me during law school. We had a great time that night, but I was exhausted and ready to hit the couch at Michael's place with Mabel sleeping soundly on the floor beside me.

Pamela hosted a barbeque for us the next night, and I showed off Mabel to a bunch of folks I'd gone to law school with. It was nice to see them all, but in truth, I hadn't been close in law school with most of the folks who showed up. Our class had dispersed around the country after graduation like most law classes do, so most of the people I'd been close with were too far away and too busy to even think about coming to meet Mabel that night. I was grateful for everyone who did come out to wish us luck. After the barbeque, I went out for drinks with my law school friends Gwen and

Abigail. Gwen had come over from the Quad Cities for the barbeque, and Abigail had driven up from Kansas City to meet Mabel and to hang out with Gwen. We had a great time and I completely fell in love with Abigail, which sucked for me because she is married to a great guy we went to law school with. I met up with a couple of other Iowa City locals who I'd stayed in touch with. One very good friend of mine named Bansari came out to have a drink with me and asked me to go out the next night. So I went out again the next night and Mabel and I went over to Bansari's to stay the night. Her husband was off in Oxford and she had stayed behind to finish up her PhD. She was one of the strangest girls I'd ever met: Because it was hot in her apartment, Mabel and I had to sleep upstairs with the air conditioner and she slept out in the yard on the grass—that, alone, wouldn't be that odd, except for the fact that a couple of times in law school I'd come to her house to find her sleeping in the yard on the grass for no reason whatsoever. Iowa City has some strange people living there. I love it.

The weather was horrible while we were in Iowa City. The temperature didn't drop below 95 degrees and a few days it was so hot that Mabel and I sat in Michael's house in the air conditioning. When the heat finally broke, Mabel and I were eager to get moving. It was a sad thing to say goodbye to Iowa City again, not knowing when or if I would ever go back. But the heat was unbearable and Mabel and I ended up sitting out another two nights in Oxford, about 10 miles outside of Iowa City, with another law school classmate of mine named Clarissa. Clarissa lived in Oxford but worked in Iowa City, and her son was gone for the summer with his father, so Clarissa and I and Clarissa's boyfriend hung out in Oxford and enjoyed the 4th of July parade in Oxford. Ashton Kutcher is apparently from Oxford, more or less, and everyone there spoke highly of him. Kutcher's uncle drove a tractor in the 4th of July Parade there, and the mayor of the town drove a motorcycle while dressed as a pantsless Santa Claus.

We walked through a small town between Oxford and Des Moines, and on the far side of it, as we were almost out of the city limits, a vicious Labrador dog leapt from the bushes and bit at Mabel. Mabel responded, and I was somehow able to get Mabel behind me and to get myself in between the Labrador and Mabel. The dog kept on us, barking and snapping, and trying to gain ground on us, but I held out my arm and would not give up any ground to the dog. The dog circled us, and we circled, so that all of us kept moving in a strange dance. The dog wanted very badly to bite us—it was the most vicious dog encounter we'd had on the trip, and by far the most vicious dog incident since the West Virginia Rails-Trail. I had not managed to get my stick free from ThePontiac but I had the can of bear spray in my left hand. The dog circled, and although Mabel and I did not give up any ground, the angry dog forced us off the sidewalk and into the street, where traffic (albeit a tiny amount of traffic) had to drive around us. The owner of the Labrador was about 70 feet away, smiling and watching the whole affair. I wanted to kill that man. Finally, after maybe six or seven minutes of going round and round with the dog, I shouted to the owner: "Man, this isn't a can of soda I got here. I am going to kill your fucking dog and then I'm going to kill you." The man clapped his hands and the

Labrador was off of us and ran back to his owner. I stared the man down as we walked past him, because I wanted to kill him.

From Oxford on to Des Moines was a long and hot road. The heat we'd had in Iowa City broke, though, and so we were hiking at about 90 degrees—that's way too hot to hike in comfortably, but it was nothing like we'd had in Iowa City. So we hiked slowly and rested for a few hours every hot afternoon and after a few days we walked into the east side of Des Moines through a couple of nasty neighborhoods and settled into a guest condo in the building where my law school friend Simon Henry lived. Simon was a great host while we were there. Mabel and I had dinner at another law school friend's house, and we met her sweet dog. We lost one day to the heat in Des Moines, and two days to a necessary break to deal with a health issue that I had developed. Heidi came to visit from Michigan and we went to a Des Moines Cubs game—it was miserably hot, but we had a good time.

The next heat wave hit us in Stuart, Iowa, 40 miles or so outside of Des Moines. Stuart is a nothing of a town along the interstate with a McDonald's, a Super 8, a gas station, and little else so far as I could see. Mabel and I checked in to the Super 8 motel and the thermometer rose to about 115 degrees. The next eight days were so stifling hot that Mabel and I could hardly even leave the motel room. We were under a "heat dome", which was a term I'd never before heard, but that sounded much more intimidating than a "heat wave".

That eight-day period was mentally and emotionally challenging and I thought about quitting and/or dying every day. Motionlessness felt like death. To be motionless in an awful motel room for eight straight days was torture. I had never felt so lonely or so frustrated. But an anonymous friend of the walk, with whom I'd been emailing for quite some time, sent me his old iPad in the mail so that I could work on a website that I'd started at www.tylercoulson.com. A lot of people had pressured me into blogging so that I could share more about my trip. Working on the blog was the only thing that kept me sane in Stuart. It was so hot that I would get winded if I walked to the McDonald's, a few hundred yards away from the motel. So hiking was simply not possible for me, much less for Mabel.

I was humbled to think that anyone would read the blog. I was such a small and insignificant thing doing something pointless and stupid, so it didn't make sense to me that people would care. I thought about that a lot in Stuart and I realized that there were a lot of people out there who were miserable. Unhappy with their jobs, unhappy with their lives. Most of the folks who emailed me were attorneys. Some of these people told me about their doubts. They doubted law school decisions or their careers in law. They doubt their government. They doubt their relationships or their ability to maintain healthy relationships. They wanted too much, or didn't want enough. They doubted themselves. The people who I met on the Walk were usually in dire straits, poor and living on the verge of bankruptcy whether they recognized it or not (but most did recognize it). Those people were angry—often really angry, and as often angry at the wrong people—but the attorneys who wrote me these emails weren't angry, but sad. Sad and confused. I answered when I could, and tried to help out with some supportive words. I don't know if I helped anyone or not, but I tried.

We finally left Stuart on the 8th day and headed out early and fast to try to beat the heat. It was a lost cause and we had to stop a few miles up the road in Menlo because the heat was too much for either of us. I pitched my tent in the park that day, and a local family invited me into their home for dinner. The hospitality in Menlo was a great change from some of the colder towns I'd visited in the Midwest, and that night Mabel and I slept with full bellies. But we didn't sleep well because we camped about 20 feet (no kidding, 20 feet) from the railroad tracks, and trains came through all night long. I did not sleep and the thermometer I kept in my tent said that it never got below 87 degrees that night, but when I woke the next morning everything was still covered in dew.

The next day we did a long hike and found a park to camp in. We found the park and set up camp quickly at the first campsite we found. We sprawled out inside the tent around 6:30 that night at a park in the middle of nowhere in Iowa. I didn't bother even to eat dinner or critter-proof the campsite. I was exhausted. ThePontiac was about four feet away from the tent. From the tent, I could see the self-pay box about 400 feet away. I looked at the self-pay box, and then at the payment envelope in my hand, and then at the self-pay box, and then at the envelope. Then I put 10 or 15 bucks into the envelope, sealed it, and wrote on the back: "Hi. I can't walk to the self-pay box to drop off my payment. My dog and I walked 25 miles today, and it was about 95 degrees. We are walking across the country. I am very tired and I think my ankle is broken. I'll put this in the box on the way out in the morning. Sorry."

We lay there in the tent. Mabel scooted as far away from me as she could, down near the foot of the tent, and she panted. Water dripped off her tongue onto the tent floor. I was in a t-shirt and underwear on top of a sleeping sheet and I sweated. The Sun went down. A police officer pulled up around 9:30 or 10, just after the Sunset. He left his truck running and came walking toward the tent.

"Is there a problem?" he shouted. I couldn't tell whether he was angry or inquisitive.

"Ah, no!" I shouted back to him, but he was already really near the tent and he probably thought I was shouting at him. "Couldn't walk to the box."

"What? Why didn't you pay?"

I handed the envelope out to him, and I rolled around so that I could sit up. He read the envelope and laughed, and then he shined the flashlight at me and was still laughing.

"Where did you start walking?"

We talked for just a very little bit. He was nice and was interested in the Walk. He wished us luck and said: "I better get goin' so you can get some sleep!"

The night was hot and so humid that all noise disappeared, sound waves muffled in the humidity. I took the rain fly off the tent because it was so humid, but it didn't help much. There was no breeze. Everything was still, and with my sweating and Mabel's breathing, the air in the tent started to get moist and everything in the tent became damp. By midnight, I was desperate to sleep and I stripped off all of my clothes. I would have thought that I would feel vulnerable, naked in a tent without a rain fly. But there was no one around and no motion, and I wasn't scared or bothered by it. I was desperate to cool off.

I thought of walking up to the camp entrance and getting some cold sodas from the machine to hold against the back of my neck, and against Mabel's chest, but I didn't have any money or energy.

A team of raccoons invaded the campground around 2:00 a.m. I did not hear them until they were in our campsite, pawing and nipping at the bag of Mabel's food, about five feet away in the undercarriage pocket of ThePontiac. I rolled my head and shoulders out of the tent and could see the leader of the raccoons trying to wrestle the dog food bag out of the cart. There were three or four shadows behind him that I thought were also raccoons.

"Get out of here!" I shouted. And the raccoon looked at me, but hardly even acknowledged me. "GET OUT OF HERE!" I shouted again, but he didn't even look at me that time. I'd lost a whole bag of dog food to raccoons in Indiana, and wasn't about to let it happen again. I stood up and out of the tent and stepped toward the cart. The raccoons fled about ten or twelve feet, but they came back once I turned back to the tent. I chased them away again, but again they returned.

"Mabel!" I said. "You're worthless!" I leaned in and looked at her. It was dark so I grabbed a flashlight and shined it at her. "You're embarrassing me, Mabel," I said. She yawned.

The raccoons came back. Now two of the raccoons were clawing at the bag, desperate to liberate it from the cart. I took hold of my sandals, one in each hand, and ran toward the raccoons while slapping the soles of the sandals together. Naked and high stepping because I didn't have any shoes on. I shouted "GET OUT OF HERE! GO AWAY! DON'T FORCE ME TO UNLEASH MY ATTACK DOG!" The raccoons ran away. I waited for them to come back, but they didn't come back. Just to be sure, though, I ran around the campsite slapping the sandals together and shouting again. Just to be sure. You can never be too sure.

From there we were on to Grinnell and from Grinnell on to Council Bluffs where we stayed with another law school friend, Omar. Omar had recently been laid off from his job and was in the middle of selling his house and relocating to Washington, D.C., in search of employment. I was sure he would find something and do quite well for himself, but there were just so many of us—so many thousands and thousands of us who took on thousands and thousands of dollars in law school debt, and only later we found out that there were not very many jobs that paid well enough to support those debt payments. And then, even later, we found out that there simply were no jobs to speak of. There weren't too many of us, there was too much debt.

Council Bluffs and Omaha were a good enough place for us to crash a while and work through some supplies problems, too. Most importantly, I bought a large golf umbrella—we needed to be able to make our own shade, for Mabel's sake if not for my own.

From Council Bluffs and Omaha we were on toward Lincoln, Nebraska. A law student in Lincoln named Becca had heard of the Walk from a guy I had attended law school with and wanted to host us. We intended to follow Hwy 6 all the way across Nebraska, so Lincoln was on our way.

We camped once between Omaha and Lincoln, and were up and gone early in the morning. I wanted to speed our way into and through Lincoln, but it was still hot. I stopped for a break on the outskirts of Lincoln, Nebraska, where I could see the train yards, and a fellow walked by us as we were standing there.

"Pretty dog," he said.

"Thanks."

"Where you walking?"

"San Francisco," I said.

"What for?"

"Job interview," I said. I have a dry sense of humor and didn't say it like a joke. "Job interview."

"How many people they hiring?" he asked. He didn't miss a beat. I think his humor was drier than mine. I tweeted that story that day with the hash tag #grapesofwrath. That was our only conversation, but he was my favorite comedian.

Once in Lincoln, we were hurting from the heat pretty badly, so we stopped at the first gas station we found. Mabel and I sat in the shade and drank; I drank a cold orange soda, and Mabel drank iced water. There was a fellow in a Cadillac with a baby in the backseat at the gas pumps, and another black fellow walked menacingly toward the car. I have no idea what started the argument, but the fellow on foot started screaming as the Cadillac drove away:

"Nigger I will fucking kill you!" he shouted. "Do you hear me? I am going to kill your nigger ass. I'm going to shoot you, Nigger!"

But when the Cadillac was gone, the angry black fellow walked up to me and said:

"Hey, Man. You got a smoke?"

"Nope," I said.

"Ah, Man. I want a smoke. Where you walkin'?"

He sat and I told him where we were going and what we were doing. He was polite and seemed very intelligent. We actually had quite a nice talk before Mabel and I got back up and finished the hot walk through the center of Lincoln. Mabel and I stayed with Becca in Lincoln and crashed her party that night. I drank several beers and tried to talk with the young folks there, but I couldn't really. At one point in the night, a couple of the partygoers broke out accordions and played polka versions of pop songs—they were very good, and afterward they asked me to alter my walk the next weekend to attend a Czech festival in Nebraska, but I couldn't. Other than those two accordionists, though, I was out of my element. This party wasn't full of law students, or artists, so I had no one to relate to. None of them seemed to have anything in common with me, and none of them really wanted to talk with me about anything. I felt like they disliked me in that distant, indifferent way that hipsters have about outsiders; I didn't like quite enough stuff ironically, I think. So about 10 o'clock that night, Mabel and I went upstairs and slept on the floor of our hostess's office. Becca came upstairs and kept us company for a while before she went back down to her party. I asked her what she thought about law school, and what she was planning to do after she graduated. I asked her if her classmates were scared, and she said that they were. It was very nice of her to keep me company for a little while that night. I appreciated the hospitality, but it was hard for me to sleep and I wished I were out in a tent somewhere. We took off pretty early the next morning to run some errands in Lincoln. Mabel needed a grooming and I needed to pick up food and supplies. But it got too hot for us that day—far too hot for us—so we ended up getting stranded at *another* motel on the edge of town. We were there for two days.

The Republicans in Congress were threatening to destroy the entire country by not raising the debt limit, and Isra called me because she was taking a bar exam in a new state and needed help and support. I told her she would do what she had to do and I had no doubt she would pass and all of that, and then she told me that she thought we should never talk again because we needed to "move on". We hadn't talked in months, so I figured that meant she was seeing someone, but she said she wasn't. It hurt that she had called me like that and then said we shouldn't speak, but I was numb to almost everything, so I told her that whatever she wanted to do was fine by me. It was August 1, I believe, and my birthday was right around the corner. She told me she would send me a text message on my birthday and I told her not to—if she didn't think we should talk, then we shouldn't talk at all, I said. It's either all or nothing. And that was fair, I thought. We'd been through enough together that it was really up or out for us, and once she had decided that we wouldn't be getting married then what was the use of going backward and becoming some sort of friends? Some sort of friends where I don't hear from her for a bunch of months and then when she needs help she calls me? No, I said, I'm not interested in that.

Lincoln is a lonely place. Or, at least, it felt lonely to me. Nebraska is huge and flat and it was hot and nasty out there, and I had no one around for hundreds of miles who I could count on. The farther I walked now, the further I would walk away from almost everything I had ever known. It was my first time in Nebraska, and I knew no one out there on that prairie, and an overwhelming sense of isolation and desperation took me over. I remember once standing beside a motel beside the interstate as the Sun went down, and Mabel was sitting right beside me watching the trucks that came and went from the truck stop across the field, and I think I have never felt so alone, so tired, or so empty. But not scared. Nothing could scare me.

We hiked in the heat of the day across Nebraska, and in the rain on the few lucky days when we had rain. Mabel and I collapsed alongside dirt roads and huddled underneath a golf umbrella to try to stay cool. I took pictures of roadside markers that commemorated things like the slaughter of Indians and the internment of people who were conscientious objectors from World War I or II. We walked between endless irrigated fields of corn that has no business growing out there on the high arid plains. We saw men on horses in the distance, and were nearly sideswiped by cars. We did epic days of 30 and 40 miles. I learned how much my knees will hurt after back to back days of 35 miles or more, and how I can still walk despite the pain if my head and my heart are empty. Mabel snapped at flies, and the flies bit my calves ceaselessly in the oppressive heat. The dust from gravel roads and from the shoulders kicked up in great plumes despite the high humidity, and it settled all over us leaving a grainy second skin on me, and a film of dust on my teeth. The dust accumulated in the my nose and in my ears, and when I took my socks off and smacked the socks together whole pounds of fine dust fell out in clouds that cut and separated the Sunlight on the side of the road. I patted Mabel and a cloud of dust exploded from her coat. I invented a new way to protect my feet—I tied bandanas around my ankles and under my heel, so that the only part of my foot protected by cloth was the skin that would make contact with the ankle straps of my sandals, and I called them hobo socks. I walked holes into the sandals. My face burnt and peeled, and my chest and shoulders grew dark and red in the Sun. My eyes contracted into a permanent squint as if I were constantly looking past the middle distance to a far off place, my eyes trained on a distant land. The skin on my feet grew thin and broke up along the strap of the sandal, and an infection grew in the cut that oozed out yellow pus.

BOOK I: THE MOMENTS THAT TURN US (C)(iv)(a)
WHERE NAME OF SLAVE AND SULTAN SCARCE IS KNOWN.

We woke before the Sun in motels and in remote campgrounds. We woke before the Sun on the edges of cornfields where we'd hidden away the night before after nightfall. Mostly we walked, and Mabel stayed steady on my left side, periodically touching her wet nose to my left hand to let me know that she was still there, she was still with me. We hid away under the shade of every tree we found in a treeless country, and I held ice to her chest in small towns, even when she was not hot. I checked her paws daily and the pads of her paws stayed healthy and strong. We walked long miles and miles that seemed like we had gotten stuck in some endless loop, like Nebraska was a mobius strip and we could never get free from the one-sided thing.

We woke in a campsite 25 miles from Sutton, Nebraska, and struck out before the Sun on a morning so foggy that we could not see the oncoming cars until they were practically upon us. But we walked fast to keep the heat of the day from catching us in a shadeless roadside hell. I watched clouds form in the southwest as we walked and watched the clouds roll quickly over us before pressing flat against an invisible wall in the northeast. High up there a monster storm formed and began to grow toward us. But we stopped on the side of the road for Mabel to pant and to cool in the shade of the umbrella. A passing motorist stopped and gave us cold drinks and cups of ice for Mabel. We walked on, despite the heat, as the storm gathered in the northeast and grew toward us.

"We have to run," I said to Mabel. "We will have to run."

"No," Mabel thought. "I cannot run. This heat will kill me."

"I can't believe I've got you in this position today," I said. "We have to run. The storm will get us." I watched brilliant flashes of lightning in the far distance crash to the ground as the storm grew steadily and threatened to overtake us. "We have to run." We jogged, and Mabel grudgingly jogged along with me. But it was too painful for me to watch her in that state, so I slowed again and we walked. The storm grew, and I saw little tails or tips of funnel clouds peeking out from the clouds, like the tongues of serpents exploring the air and looking for something to kill.

"We should run," I said. "But I won't do that to you."

Then, in a step, in a scintilla of time, in the smallest unit of time there is in the world, the temperature dropped by 20 degrees like we had walked into the hard wall of air conditioning in a super market. The few trees I could see in the north distance came alive and bent at 40-degree angles in the blowing wind, the wind cutting through us at 65 or 70 degrees Fahrenheit instead of 90.

"We have to run," Mabel thought, and she looked at me. "We have to run now."

And we ran.

We ran for 5 miles, keeping the storm, the torrents of rain, and the wind just behind us. ThePontiac buckled under the added strain, and it laid over to the left until the main support for the body rubbed along the left tire, and I knew the tire wouldn't last long—I doubted whether ThePontiac would make it. The tire went flat shortly, but we kept running until we finally ran around a slow curve into Sutton where I had heard there were two motels. I called the first, but the old woman who owned the place said they would never let a dog stay there. I had called the other motel several times during the day and never gotten an answer. I figured we would camp in the municipal park for $15. Once in Sutton, I was surprised to see the streets rather alive with Mexican families.

"Hola," a man said to me. "Para donde vas?" He was a good-looking man, well dressed, with a wife and three kids with him. They were a family out walking around, getting in some shared time and exercise before the storm that threatened in the northeast.

What?, I thought. Que?

"Como?" I said.

"Para dónde vas?"

"Oh. Voy a California," yo diga. "Mi perro y yo caminamos al través de Los Estados Unidos."

"Qué has dicho?" exclamo, y yo repetí lo que había dicho.

"Que bien! Que magnifico!" dijo el hombre. "Por que caminar?"

"Oh, yo creo que tengo muchas razones," me dijo, y respiro. "Yo tenia mucho miedo que mi vida se le escapaba." El hombre sonrío de oreja a oreja, y yo sabía que el me entendía. "Nadie, ni siquiera a mis acreedores, puede robar esta experiencia. Y por que la ritmo de mi corazón es finito."

"Sí," el dijo. "El pájaro esta en el ala. Cual es tu carrera, amigo?"

"Un abogado," me dijo. Bebí agua.

"Que tan malo por Usted," el dijo. "Mi hermano, también, en México. Pero es diferente. Es el camino exitoso?"

"Estoy capturando el tiempo, yo creo. Pero es demasiado pronto para decirlo," me dijo.

Su hijo pequeño saludo a Mabel, sonrío y río. El y su familia dijo "Buena suerte!" y Mabel y yo fuimos a la tienda en la aldea.

Everyone I saw in the town was Mexican, and seemed to speak no English. At the gas station by the motel that had refused my custom, the lady behind the counter was the first white person I had seen in town, but she spoke Spanish with a perfect Mexican accent and shouted rumors and gossip across the room to a fat Mexican woman who had come in to buy soda and potato chips. I got something for Mabel and something for me to eat, and we walked back toward the park. Halfway to the park I noticed that one of the houses we had walked by had a "no vacancy" neon sign. It was a motel, and it looked to not be a high quality place. I knocked on the door of the house, and a lady came to the door with two kids and two tiny dogs that barked and jumped off the porch to snap at and harass Mabel. The lady said in Spanish that they had a room, that Mabel was fine to stay there, and that it was $20/night. Twenty a night for a shower and a bed is a lot better than $15/night for a campsite in a municipal park while a storm is coming. So I took the deal and we moved into unit number one. It was a shabby place, and it was exactly the same layout as a shabby motel I'd stayed at in West Virginia. My knees and hips were killing me and I felt like my body was covered in mud, and I didn't care how shabby the place was, I was still glad to be in my home for the night. After a shower and feeding Mabel, I collapsed on the bed. As I did, the neighbors turned on that banda or conjunto (oom pah oom pah) Mexican polka music that is so popular and they had turned the stereo up well past the limits of the speakers, but I didn't care. I was asleep.

I woke up about three hours later at around 10:00 or 10:30 p.m. and the party still raged next door. Mabel and I had been a long time out there on the road and I was pretty lonely, and I've never been one to turn down crashing a party. So I got dressed and stepped outside to see what the party looked like. A couple of beers would be nice, and conversation is good when you are alone. But as soon as I stepped outside, one of the neighbors bolted out of his motel door. He was a thin and fidgety looking man with prominent bones in his face and he wore a baseball cap.

"Hay problema?" he asked. Is there a problem?

"No," I said.

"Ah. Quieres un cerveza amigo?" he asked me. Did I want a drink? As he did, I glanced behind him through the open motel door. The "party" next door consisted of two guys, the one talking to me, and the man inside. The man inside looked to weigh about 250 pounds, was completely naked, and was masturbating on the couch.

"Nah," I said. "I need to sleep. I've got a long day tomorrow." My Spanish is not very good to begin with, and it was all broken and chopped with him, but he seemed satisfied with that and went back into his room. I retired into my own room and went back to sleep. You see some strange things sometimes in this life.

I lost the next day in Sutton trying to repair ThePontiac. I fixed the flat, and did my best to bend the frame back into shape. It was pretty well sprung, though, and it wouldn't support the whole pack well. With just the water and a few other things, it was manageable, but it would begin to lean heavily when I put on the whole pack. So I had to lighten the load, re-balance the pack, and carry a few things on my back. I wouldn't have a chance to replace ThePontiac until Denver, but Heidi was planning to fly out to Denver, rent a car, and provide car support in western Nebraska. With any luck, I thought, I'd make it.

When I walked out of Sutton the next day, I walked around another big bend in the highway and over some railroad tracks and suddenly everyone was white. I looked up Sutton on Wikipedia, and it says that only 3.8% of the town is Hispanic. Segregation, forced or otherwise, is a strange business.

One day in Nebraska, a woman in a van mocked like she was spitting on me in front of her children as I walked by her driveway. I assume this was because she thought I was homeless and she was teaching her children the proper way to treat homeless people.

I don't want this to reflect badly on Nebraska, because I met a bunch of great folks there. One day, for example, a lady named Sandy pulled over and offered me a ride because it was hot and she is an animal lover. Sandy also volunteers for an organization that makes and delivers quilts and blankets to homeless people and orphans. So there are good people. Many folks, like Sandy, are good.

But every day on this trip, and even more so in Nebraska, at least once, someone looked at me like I was trash. Worse, even, like I was sub-human. They looked at me this way, or walked all the way around a gas station to avoid me, because I looked homeless. And sometimes they taught their children to spit on homeless people, I guess.

I was not a standard homeless person, I know. I looked and smelled homeless, and I didn't have a house, but it was different for me. I know that. But this lady didn't know that. And, for that matter, it was not possible for her to know that about any homeless person she might have seen. She didn't care if I was a man who had lost his home in the spring's tornados, or who had lost everything due to some medical tragedy. She didn't care if I was an Iraq vet staggered by PTSD. She didn't care if I was a man driven out on the street by schizophrenia. She didn't care, at all, and she was teaching her children not to care, either.

She had an Ichthys, the Jesus fish, on her car.

I don't attend church, but the Ichthys on her car reminded me of the (probably apocryphal) story of the pious John Bradford, an English reformer. While in prison for his devotion to the Church of England (instead of the Catholic Church), he would see criminals taken to the scaffolds to be hanged. Seeing this, he allegedly uttered: "There, but for the grace of God, goes John Bradford." I should think this or something like it, always, when I see someone less fortunate than me. I decided in Nebraska that from then on, whenever I saw a homeless person, or a poor, wayfaring stranger such as myself, I would think about Old John Bradford. And I would think: There, but for the grace of something, goes I.

And there is no end to the amazing people you can meet if you just step out your front door, even in Nebraska. Amazing people do amazing things every day. One day in Nebraska, I met a man named Michael who is actually, on a day-to-day basis, helping to save mankind from extinction.

About 20 miles outside of Hasting, Nebraska, Michael scared me to death. As a rule, you don't see people out there in the middle of nowhere, except for people in cars. And you never hear a human voice, so I almost had a heart attack when I heard a voice from behind me say: "Hey there, what's the story?"

I spun around and saw this fellow on a bicycle, and he was all smiles. We spoke for a while. His name was Michael. He was retired, and he rode his bicycle 36 miles to see his brother almost every day. He gave me a fig Newton and we talked a little while about bees.

Bees are horrible little things that sting and, for those of us allergic to them, threaten our lives on a daily basis. I suppose I had always known that bees were important, despite being nasty things, but Michael had a lot to teach me. Bees are necessary for human survival. We depend on them. No lesser luminary than Old Albert Einstein said "if the bees were to disappear, mankind would only have a few years to live". And bees are disappearing right now.

Bees pollinate the following plants, among others: tomatoes, onions, cashews, strawberries, celery, broccoli, carrots, cauliflower, cabbage, chiles and chili peppers, coffee, cocoa, hazelnuts, squash, zucchini, lemons and oranges and limes, figs, soybeans, cotton, alfalfa and avocados, cherries, almonds, peaches and apples, raspberries, blackberries, cranberries, blueberries, clover, grapes, and on and on. We depend on bees to pollinate many of the plants that we depend on for food. No bees, no food. No food, no people.

Bees are important. As much as I hate getting stung and swelling up and maybe dying, I prefer that to the death of the human race. Bees are important.

But bees are disappearing. In the U.S., the United States Department of Agriculture estimated around a 35% loss of beehives per year between 2007 and 2011. That is pretty alarming. To put it in the language of dollars, something like $15 billion of crops are in danger in the U.S.

This is all the result of "colony collapse disorder". Many theories have been put forward to explain the cause of colony collapse disorder, and Michael and I spoke about them. You probably have heard the whole cell-phones-kill-bees thing. I don't know where Michael stands on that issue, but I tend to think there are a lot of factors influencing colony collapse of honeybees. Where Michael and I definitely agree is that neonicotinoid pesticides, made commercially available due, in part, to lessened regulatory standards under the Clinton and Bush regimes, were then known to kill bees and are currently killing bees. In Europe, specifically Germany and Italy, governments are finally taking steps to ban these pesticides.

Luckily for us, there are folks like Michael. Now, he can't ban harmful pesticides. But what Michael can do, and does, is to take time to educate folks about how they can help the bees. It's pretty easy: Plant some stuff that bees like. The alternative is colony collapse.

The character of the land changed in western Nebraska. I felt that I walked into a different region of the world for the first time since crossing into Ohio from West Virginia. The green corn fields and the irrigation equipment disappeared and gave way to vast open pastures that grew ragged with sick looking grass. It was an endless, treeless landscape of sloping hills and steeply cut ravines where Mabel and I could see for hundreds of miles and see nothing between us and the horizon. Towns were spaced distantly and access to water was sporadic, but Heidi flew out to join us once again. She'd had enough hiking in Indiana, so she rented a car and provided our first taste of "car support" on the trip. There is no way to say how liberated and fleet I felt when I put the majority of my gear into Heidi's rental car and I went skipping down the open highway with only water and emergency equipment in ThePontiac. Mabel, too, seemed to feel relieved, and our already faster pace of about 3.3 miles per hour climbed to almost 4. We jogged some, too, and our average pace topped out at or just over 4 m.p.h.

Out there in western Nebraska and eastern Colorado, it was hard to estimate distances on the sweeping treeless planes. We had already gotten pretty good at estimating the speed of cars, and out there we used that skill to estimate distances. I would pick a point out there in the far distance and measure the time it took for an oncoming car to travel between that point and us. I'd use the car's estimated speed and the travel time to guess how far away that distant point was. Points in the distance are often much farther away than they first appear out there where there are no trees, where there are no mountains, where there are no cities. It's important to keep your eye on the distant points, though, so you know where you are going.

Now, thinking back, I feel tremendous joy when I think of that section of the hike—we were fast, we were trim and fleet, and we had Heidi to talk with and hang around with at night and on breaks. But there was no joy in it at the time. We had become a machine with many moving parts, and little more. For Mabel's part, she had learned to follow the most basic commands that I could give her, and she had learned exactly where to walk, when to slow and when to speed up, and how to negotiate turns and obstacles. For my part, I had gotten stronger and faster, leaner and more focused; I had given up entirely on planning beyond a day or two, and even those plans were nebulous ideas of what we would do or where we would be. I no longer planned for the unknowable. I had given up on comfort and stability, and had no desire for better food or a better place to sleep. This is not to say I was content with eating rice and powdered milk for dinner, but rather to say that I had no room for "content" or "discontent" in my life. These were emotions and feelings that I did not have use for. Mabel and I had become a machine for walking and nothing more—I did not love or hate anything.

I picked an album that was 48 minutes long and put it on repeat every day on my iPod. We walked and jogged for 48 minutes, then took a break for a few minutes, then hit play and did the same thing again. I was so empty that even the ceaseless repetition of albums, over and over, did not frustrate me or bore me. The music, my footsteps, and each of the miles we walked were like hands on a clock ticking away all the minutes of my life, nothing more. My life was flat, changeless and featureless like the soft midsection of this country that Mabel and I had crossed in the violent heat of a furious summer.

We entered Colorado on the high northwestern plateau.

The elevation had started to affect me in Nebraska, and by the time we got into Colorado, it was a real concern. I could not walk but a few minutes before having to stop and catch my breath. We were only at around 4000 feet at that time, but I couldn't seem to get my lungs full and my legs (and even my arms) felt week after only a few steps.

Elevation.

My birthday was only a few days away, and Heidi was leaving for Denver to catch a flight home. It was clear that I had to find a place to camp for a while and hope that I could adjust to the thinner air, or shuttle into Denver to spend my birthday with my brother and to spend time adjusting to the elevation. It was an easy decision—I could hardly breathe and ThePontiac was busted up beyond repair, my sandals had holes in them, and the thought of spending my birthday alone was awful. So we shuttled south near Denver and we walked into the shadows of the Rocky Mountains. I was so strong and light then, and my face was emotionless and hardened. If this were the movie that I mentioned earlier, this is the moment that montage would end— with me standing there, strong and tanned, in hobo socks and a half buttoned shirt, with a kerchief on my head and sunglasses, in the shadow of those mountains. I looked like a different man than the one who had started the Walk several months earlier. I had walked westward for months through an open window of land and grain and weather, with hardly a tree, hill, or rock to block the view. Ohio and Indiana and Illinois and Iowa and Nebraska and now this...this jagged granite wall closing off my whole world from the desert and ocean beyond. I could not breathe at 5000 feet, and I had another 5000 or 6000 feet to climb to get over those mountains; up there where it rained every day and could snow in August on occasion, and we had lost so much time and it was August 14th and we would be at least a week acclimatizing to the thin air. Then we would be a few days' hike before we could get *into* the mountains, and then it is September. We were at least two months behind schedule. It can snow at elevation in September, and at that height, if we could make it up those things at all, Mabel and I would be in dire trouble if a blizzard dropped on us.

I spent the week with my brother and walked around each day to try to get used to the thin air. It was difficult. I stopped by a bike shop downtown to get a new cart to replace ThePontiac and discussed the air with a fellow there who had recently moved up from Florida.

"I'm a strong cyclist," he said. "And when I moved out here, guys that are like not strong cyclists were eating me alive. For like two months. I've only been here three months, but I'm finally getting there."

I replaced ThePontiac with a flat bed trailer designed to be pulled behind a bike but that had an attachable handle so it could be pushed like a stroller. I named it The1976CosworthVega. I spent most of that week either eating with law school friends or former Sidley associates who had left Chicago to live and work in Denver, or poring over maps. The Rockies were the biggest physical challenge I had faced since the Allegheny Escarpment. Unlike the Escarpment, these Rockies went on for miles and miles and miles. And from down there in Denver they looked so tall and steep that I could not imagine them being anything other than a series of long hikes, the first one worse than the Escarpment and each successive climb harder than those that preceded it. I imagined steep, 20-mile climbs at about 10% grades over and over again. I had never been into the Rockies before, and really had no idea what to expect. But the weather had already started to change and it was raining every day in the mountains at elevation. Jack Planck had hiked through the Rockies almost 1.5 months earlier and farther south where elevations are slightly lower, and still it had rained on him every afternoon. We stared in reverence and anger at the mountains.

"We really are screwed," I said to my brother over dinner. He took me out to a steakhouse in downtown Denver for my birthday. I had a very large salad and a very large beer.

"How's that? Too late?"

"Yeah," I said.

"Well, I don't want to bring you down. But if you're going over those mountains, you got to get up there, Man. You got to get movin'."

"You've been saying that since Indiana," I said and chuckled.

"It's been true since Indiana! It can get ugly up there. The mountains will mess you up if you're not careful."

"I know," I said. "I know. But we went as fast as we could."

"You knew in Ohio that you were too late," he said. "But I'll give it to you that you kicked some ass after that. Especially Iowa and Nebraska."

"Mabel and I walk pretty well together when we can get out there."

"You should get a gun," he said.

"I might," I finally conceded. "Just because of mountain lions."

"Yeah, mountain lions," he said and laughed. "And bears. Sure. I'd have one, for another kind of animal. A two-legged animal."

"I know," I said. "I know. Everyone would. Everyone's afraid of people."

"And they should be."

"If you need a gun to walk across the country, then you're weak," I said. "But I already knew that you were weak, so we ain't breakin' new ground."

"You're a funny guy," said Warren: "No wonder they paid you the big bucks. Are you going to go for it, or go home?"

"I don't know," I said. "I'm going to go down to Colorado Springs and hang out with Amrita for a while. I'll decide down there, I guess."

My law school friend Amrita had ended up in Colorado Springs as a public defender, and she wanted to see me on the trip. So she told me I could swing down and stay with her. I had no desire to hike to Colorado Springs, and as far as tackling the Rockies, I had little preference whether to hit them from Denver or from Colorado Springs, except that maybe the route out of Colorado Springs seemed a little easier. And, although at elevation it doesn't matter so much, I thought that the more southern the route the better we would be at avoiding potential winter weather. So I decided to get a ride down to Colorado Springs and to hang out with Amrita for a while to continue acclimatizing.

He picked the last chicken wing off his plate and ate it. "Don't get soft down there. Don't let her take care of you. Gotta be tough to do the Rockies. Gotta be hard."

"Yeah."

"Seriously," he said, "if you get in trouble, give me a call. You're only a few hours away by car, all the way to the other side of the mountains...even on the other side of the mountains. I can come get you."

"Worried about me?" I asked and ribbed him.

"Damn right," he said. "I think you're crazy."

"Think so?"

"Yup," he said. "Doesn't mean I don't worry about you dying up there though. But once you get out of Colorado, I figure you aren't my problem anymore." We laughed.

We walked back to the car and in the night sky the Rockies were big black shadows where no light escaped at the bottom of a deep navy blue bowl of night. Amrita drove up to Denver the next day to get us and we rode down to Colorado Springs. I got a new pair of sandals and more cold weather clothes. A friend of the walk set me up with a guitar to keep me company over the mountains and the desert. While I was there, Amrita got up at about 3:30 every morning, was at work by 4:30, and came home from work about 9:30 or 10:00 at night. She had no furniture in her apartment except for a bed, a single chair, and a single table. On the second day there, I decided to hike out the next morning, but I got an email from a girl named Jenny who had been walking across the country with her dog. She had started about a month after me, but she had started in Maryland instead of Delaware, and she had somehow managed to catch me across Nebraska—she had made it to Denver two days after I made it to Colorado Springs. She said she was unable to cross the Rockies by herself, and she was not at all able to pass the deserts by herself, so she was going to get a ride from her brother to Portland, or something like that.

The thought of that broke my heart. A girl walked by herself all the way from Maryland to Denver, only to have to quit? Heartbreaker. An east/west thru-hike is no joke for a man and a dog, but I wouldn't even consider it as a woman all alone. I would think that a woman alone would face a lot more social resistance to the trip, which would make it more difficult, and would also be much more likely to be perceived as a target for the less law abiding among us. I could be completely wrong about that, but from my perspective it seemed that a cross-country solo hike would have been much more difficult for a woman. So I called Jenny.

"Listen," I said, "I have to get car support for the desert because I can't carry enough water for Mabel and me to safely make it across the long stretches. Since I need to do that anyway, you could come with me so long as we split gas and the cost of food for the driver."

"Absolutely," she said. "That would be great! My only concern is that we, my dog Lucy and me, would slow you down. I've followed you on Twitter, and we've emailed a little, and you do a lot longer days than Lucy and me."

"Well, you caught us!" I said. "You blasted across Nebraska!"

"Yeah, we did," she said. "So long as we won't slow you down, then yes, that would be great."

"Ok," I said. "There it is. Split gas and food, and I'll pay the stipend for the driver, because I need to get him anyway, and you can share the car support. But you'll have to keep up. And you'll have to get to Colorado Springs."

She said that wouldn't be a problem, but it would be a couple of days before she could get down to Colorado Springs. So we waited around for three days or so until Jenny and her dog, Lucy, could get down to Colorado Springs. Mabel and I ate and rested well during those days and took walks during the day to acclimate. During our walks, I kept an eye trained upward to the heights in the Rockies above Colorado Springs to see the weather—it grew cloudy and rained up there every day about 2:00 or 2:30 in the afternoon.

About ten miles to the west of Colorado Springs is Pike's Peak. Pike's is one of Colorado's "fourteeners"—peaks over 14,000 feet. There are only about 550 14ers in the world, and 54 of them are in Colorado. We could see its majestic pink granite peak flash in the clear mountain Sunlight, then hide behind clouds, then flash again in the clear mountain Sunlight. It was the highest peak I had ever seen. We wouldn't have to summit any of the 14ers, but seeing that high peak put our route into perspective. Colorado Springs sits at about 6,000 feet—already the highest town I'd ever spent significant time in—and we would have to climb to 9,000 feet and stay there for an extended period of time. We would have to climb over 11,000 feet to cross the continental divide. The air would be thinner up there. It rained every day up there. It was cold at night up there and during the day the Sun was harsher because of the thin air up there. Bears and mountain lions roam around up there. Hiking over the Rockies is an endeavor to respect—even if you're following highways.

BOOK III: ...AND THE MOON SAYS HALLELUJAH, 01.06.12(3)

See Celio shake his head; lights cigarette.

C: "Friend, refrain with me a moment. Why are you here? Did you make it to California? Because if I made it across a continent on foot, I would not be here on vacation. I would be at home. With the girls I know and with the family who I love."

T: "I needed a break. I had a rough time adjusting."

C: "In what way was it rough?"

T: "Just rough."

C: "What is the rough part?"

T: "Couldn't sleep. Sometimes I start crying uncontrollably for no reason. I had aggression problems."

C: "Aggression?"

T: "Yes."

C: "What kind of aggression problems?"

Don't want to talk about it. Try to change subject, Celio insists, Rosie is gone; oblige.

T: "I don't know. I mean, for example, about two weeks before I got down here, I went out for a walk in the middle of the night. I can't sleep. I walked down this alleyway in Lincoln Park; well, it's really in Lakeview, I think. There was a fellow walking toward me; big guy, taller anyway. Lighter built, and drunk, too, I think. He was dressed really well; probably a fraternity kid when he was in college. And he said something to me. "What's that?" I said, sort of turned to face him, you know. He stopped and kind of turned to face me. "Fuckin' faggots," he said. I *think* he said 'faggots', with an 's' on the end. So I don't even know if he was really even talking to me. Anyway, I don't give a damn if someone calls me gay. I'm not gay, so there's no reason for me to be offended. And if I were gay, I would probably be proud of that and wouldn't be offended. But I stepped at him pretty quickly, and he knew I was coming at him. I punched him in the stomach before he even knew what was going on, then kicked him in the balls, and as he was doubled over I pushed him down on his knees. I straightened out his face and punched him laterally across the nose. He fell and bled into a big maroon pool and moaned and tried to say "You broke my nose" or something like that. I touched him with my foot on his shoulder, to see if he responded. Then I left. I put my hands in my pockets and walked home. I went home and slept for about 7 hours. Was the second night of sleep I'd had since the Walk.

C: "Jesus, Friend. And the other night of sleeping?"

T: "Same thing. Similar story."

C: "Jesus, Friend."

See Rosie return.

R: "What? Did I miss part of the story?"

C: "No."

See Celio shake his head, light cigarette.

C: "That was a different story."

Like the way the Portugese think. Feel shame, embarrassment. Decide to have several beers. Drink a lot at Pedro's; talk with vacationers and ex-pats. Meeting w/more Welsh people. Receive gift of beers from Welsh woman and husband; I tell them: "Never met Welsh people 'till I came to Belize"; she responds: "You have, but didn't know it. Everyone has a Welsh grandmother, didn't you know?" Tell Welsh woman and her husband: "I'm looking to get married to a foreigner for citizenship in another country. Know anyone?" She says: "My sister's friend is beautiful and wants to travel the U.S. Maybe?" I say: "Sounds promising." Find Welsh woman's wallet, later, after they've gone; return wallet to office in morning, after they've gone, note reading that I "was serious, mate". Analyze issue: "Will I ever hear from them Welsh folks?"; conclusion: Likely not.

BOOK II: FEEL THE SELFISH FURY (D)
HOW SWEET IS MORTAL SOVRANTY.

I loved my life with Isra in it, and I think she loved her life for a little while with me, too. I was happy, and I forgot about law school. We were together every day and every night, immediately. From that first night, I think we spent perhaps two or three nights apart. We came back to Iowa City from holiday vacations early to be together, we studied together and went out to eat great food together, and stayed in together all day on Sundays. We laughed constantly. The drudgery and banality of law school didn't matter; catty women and insecure men didn't matter, and the Napoleonic little twerp professors didn't matter. I had a job lined up at the 5th largest law firm in the country, and we were secure in everything about us, if nothing else. We watched movies and played games and had drinks and danced and talked and planned for vacations we would take and places we would see together. I lit up like a flame when she talked about the Upper Peninsula of Michigan, or the Oregon coast, and how she wanted to see it all with me.

After dating a week or so, she was at my apartment in Iowa City one afternoon and we were standing together, embracing, in the kitchen. I said "What do you, uh, want..." about to ask her what she wanted to do for lunch. She, looking away, and absently said "I love you, too. Wait, what?" And she looked at me with terror and fear on her face.

"AH HAH!" I said.

"Shut up!" she shouted, and walked away. "Shut up your stupid face. You don't know my face!"

"You love me," I teased her. I teased her with that, over and over, until we collapsed together on the couch and I told her I loved her, too. We lay together and she confessed some of the little lies she'd told me and some the little reasons she'd been reticent about the idea of "us". She cried a few times and told me that she was embarrassed and ashamed of the way she treated people and herself sometimes.

"I don't know why I did that," she said. "I don't know why I do that."

"Just don't," I said. "If you don't like some behavior, you don't have to do it." That was an easy thing for me to say.

She fell against my chest hard and heavily and she cried against my chest, and she mumbled into my shirt, over and over again, "I love you, I love you, I love you".

And then we danced together in Iowa City until I graduated.

The 3L year drags on and on and on, which is strangely a good thing. Unlike the first two years, there is no pretense about whether the third year matters—if you already have a job, the 3L year is wholly superfluous. If you don't, then it is a chance for you to hide in a college town while you look for a job. But the work is easy and the workload is relatively light and there isn't any of that nonsense about journals and pressures. The cliques that were so tight and stupid during the 1L and 2L years are still there, but those kids have grown up a little bit and have calmed down. Drinking and debauchery are there, but out of habit now. The year seems to last forever. And that is a *good* thing, because you finally get a chance to breathe and to relax. No one has the energy anymore to manufacture stress or, really, to care that much about the little things. By that time, law students are "checked out".

Isra and I spent most of our time either at the Java House or at my apartment. And we talked about marriage—I was for it, in general, and she was against it in general. She said she never wanted to get married and she *never* wanted to have children. Those were her two deal breakers. I wanted to get married and wanted to have children.

"I want to have children before my dad loses his mind completely," I told her one night. It was the most vulnerable I had ever been with another person. "My mother wants him to have grandchildren so badly."

"Maybe you should find someone who will do that for you," she said.

"Yeah, well, I want what I want, too. And you'll probably change your mind," I said.

"No I won't."

"You might change your mind about marriage and children. Someone might convince you."

She laughed and said I was stupid and didn't know her face. But then later that month she started leaving post-it notes around my apartment where she knew I would find them. Or sometimes they would be pasted into my casebooks. And one day I found one in the medicine cabinet in the bathroom taped to the shaving cream can. It read: "I think you are the one to convince me."

We lived at my apartment for most of the first semester but toward the end of the first semester she told me that her roommate was mad that Isra was never home and that maybe I should spend some time over there. I was more comfortable at my place, of course, but I didn't mind and wanted to spend time with Isra wherever she was comfortable.

But I went to her house one day and fell ill—I was *really* ill with the flu. I hadn't had the flu in years, and it was nasty. I slept on the floor of Isra's room and sweated and moaned and fought a very high fever. The whole time I thought that it was a funny way to kill a new relationship, by being sick and weak right at the beginning. But Isra took care of me—she made sure I had water to drink, and she made soup for me to drink, and she checked my temperature. When I was too hot, she brought cold washcloths for my forehead. When I got better, and was finally able to leave to go back my apartment, I didn't want to so much.

"You were really sick, and I'm glad you're better," Isra said to me after I got cleaned up.

"Thank you for taking care of me."

"Maybe you can meet my family?" she said, and I knew that was a big deal. I'd actually talked about meeting her family before—before we were dating, even—but not as a "this is my boyfriend" thing, because I was interested in where she came from. Her stories about her brother left me in stitches, and I wanted to meet him. But as quickly as she said it, she said "No, bad idea. Bad idea. Bad idea!" But I started spending about every day and night at Isra's apartment despite her roommate, Madeleine, who I didn't much care for. From the moment I got there, Madeleine made little jokes about me being a big-time Sidley attorney. I thought she was a pretty bitter girl and she would sometimes rail on and on about all the horrible people in law school and how much she hated them all, and she would drone on about how she supported Sarah Palin and that McCain should pick Palin as his running mate. She wouldn't give me a chance, and I guess I couldn't blame her. No matter; Isra and I stayed in bed late on the weekends and watched Home Movies or some DVD she had rented.

It was a great time.

And my grades fell, of course.

I met Isra's family that spring and loved them immediately, and they *loved* me immediately, especially her mother. Her mother was the sweetest and most wonderful person you could imagine, and whenever I said something that surprised her or that she didn't understand she would say "Oh, Tyler..." with her accent and I got a kick out of that. Her mother cooked enormous amounts of food whenever I showed up and would not let me leave without eating all of it.

But Isra still had another year of law school, and the market had started quivering a little. There was a lot of uncertainty, but Isra and I decided that we would live together that summer in Chicago.

"We already pretty much live together," she said. "I mean, it's stupid not to."

The year slipped by and then I graduated and my parents came to the ceremony. Isra got me a business card holder from Tiffany's with my initials engraved in it.

I moved into an apartment in Lincoln Park, Chicago in May of 2008. Isra had helped me pick out the apartment. She moved in a day or two later. I was nervous about the bar exam and was happy that Isra would be there with me during that time. I noticed that I'd just been trading nerves for nerves—I was either nervous about finals, or nervous about a job offer, or nervous about the bar exam. Being nervous and feeling pressure, whether it was legitimate pressure or manufactured pressure, was just an accepted constant in the legal profession. If you weren't feeling pressure about whatever it was coming next, then you weren't doing it right.

The apartment was truly horrible—it was small, the layout was absolutely useless, the view looked out over a Sunless patio, and the walls and pipes rattled constantly. I was paying about $800/mo for my apartment, but most of my first year colleagues were paying closer to $1600, I think, or even bought places. Isra was working in the Loop, though, and I was spending my days at the bar review course.

Sidley called me while I was unloading Isra's car when she was moving in. They told me I'd been placed in the Banking and Financial Transactions practice group. I had been hoping for litigation, because the market was unsteady and I *knew* that the finance side of the American economy was a shell game. But I was marginally happy that I hadn't been placed in the

Insurance Products group—the other group I'd preferenced—because that industry was disappearing entirely.

I took the bar exam seriously. I studied very hard and took off two days a week to spend with Isra. But it wasn't enough for her. She got angry when I spent an evening studying and she couldn't keep herself busy. She got frustrated. She thought I wasn't paying enough attention to her.

"Listen," I said. "You are not happy here because I am studying. Maybe you could live with your mom during the week and with me during the weekend. That way I won't get on your nerves, we won't fight."

"Fine," she said. "I was thinking that anyway."

So she moved out and I studied. We saw each other on the weekends and some weeknights. Some weeknights she would go out with friends and come to stay at my apartment.

The bar exam was a worthless experience. The bar exam has almost nothing to do with law school, and nothing at all to do with practice. I memorized a vast catalogue of rules, and I learned the little tricks of analysis that they look for in the exam questions—often, the "right" answer is cued off the use of a particular word in the question. Folks seem to think the bar exam is a good idea and I don't have any better idea to offer, so I guess they are right.

We took off for Michigan for my post-bar trip on the day after the bar exam—Isra had "organized" the trip in exchange for me paying for it. We had a good time in the Upper Peninsula kayaking and hiking. Then we drove back to Chicago and she dropped me off in the alley behind my apartment.

"I don't think we should see each other anymore right now," she said.

I was floored by the timing, if by nothing else.

"Are you seeing someone else?" I asked.

"No," she said. "It's not that."

"Did you cheat on me or something?"

"No!" she said. "It's not that. I just need some space to think and I think you do, too. This summer was really hard and you kicked me out."

"I didn't kick you out," I said, but let the issue drop. I didn't want to fight with her. The bar exam had been stupid and overwhelmingly frustrating. Add Isra's reaction to it, and I hadn't had a good summer at all. I wasn't in any mood to fight. I was only a little angry that she'd waited until after the bar trip to tell me—she'd squeezed that trip out of me, I thought. That was how I saw it. We ended the conversation and she drove away. But she was not done with me.

Book I: The Moments That Turn Us (D)
To no such aureate Earth.

We met with Jenny and Lucy at a motel in West Colorado Springs. Jenny and Lucy had stayed with a family friend in Denver. That friend brought her down to Colorado Springs. She called when they arrived, and I went outside to meet her. I had never seen her and I didn't really know what to expect, but she didn't look like I expected her to look, either. She didn't look hardened. Not like I did. When I looked at myself in the mirror, I saw a guy who looked raw and hard, like leather or pig iron. My skin was leathery and I could see vacancy in my eyes that hadn't been there before. But Jenny looked like a 30-year-old woman who had been skipping around and having a decent little time for the last 20 years of her life, carefree. Her carefree look and empty silly smile made me a little hesitant—but, I thought, this is a "hike your own hike" situation, and obviously she had been successful so far in reaching Colorado.

I reviewed her equipment, and was not happy with what I saw. She had no cold weather gear, to begin with. It would be cold in the mountains, and she didn't even have any gloves. I gave her an extra pair of gloves I had with me. She had no warm socks, so I gave her a couple pair of warm socks that I'd received as a gift in Colorado Springs from Amrita's neighbor. She didn't have any layers, either, which are key to maintaining core temperature while hiking in variable weather, but I couldn't afford to give her any of my warm layers except for one base layer that I had that didn't fit me quite comfortably.

"How much water can you carry?" I asked.

"We don't use much," she said. "Lucy's a husky, and huskies are bred not to need much water."

"I didn't know that," I said. "But how much can you carry?"

"Well, I've got a couple of water bottles—one of them is Lucy's and one is mine—and I just stick a gallon of water in that basket at the front of the stroller."

"So...a gallon and a half?"

"About that," she said.

That was not enough water carrying capacity.

"You'll need to be able to carry more than that, don't you think?"

"Well, we'll have car support, right? Can't the car just carry the water?" she asked. She seemed really unconcerned with almost everything in the world.

"Sure, I guess. In Utah. But Colorado is dry, too. I got this cart, though. I can probably carry 10 gallons of water if I have to."

"Well, we don't drink much," she said.

On the first day that Jenny and I hiked together, we climbed directly up into the Rocky Mountains on Hwy 24. It was quickly apparent that Lucy and

Jenny did not hike like we hiked. This is hard to explain, but Jenny pushed her stroller more like someone pushing a shopping cart leisurely through supermarket aisles on a Sunday morning, not like I pushed my stroller: like a person pushing gear that needed to be pushed the hell up the road a long ways. Initially, I wrote the difference off as only a difference in speed and temperament. But it also soon became clear that Lucy and Jenny did not sync like Mabel and I synced—Lucy was constantly pulling ahead or off to the side, and I could hear Jenny behind me loudly correcting Lucy. "Lucy!" she would shout, instead of "no" or "halt" or "heel". It was always "Lucy!" with a sort of surprised tone in her voice, like she couldn't believe that Lucy was pulling at all. This I wrote off as a new change in behavior in Lucy brought on by the introduction of Mabel into Lucy's insulated life. It was possible that Lucy was speeding up and pulling to catch up to Mabel. But right from that first moment, I noticed that Lucy walked *in front* of Jenny's cart, at the end of a rather long leash. That is bad.

"It's just her instinct," Jenny would say. "She's a husky and she came from a sled dog breeder. She wants to be out in front there. It's just her genes telling her to be out there."

Mabel, on the other hand, walked more or less directly to my left. I had to correct her from time to time, but that was usually because Mabel naturally walks quickly and I naturally walk more slowly, so Mabel often got a few feet out in front of me before either of us had noticed. But there was always slack in Mabel's chain. Mabel only ever pulled like Lucy pulled when she caught sight of a deer or another animal.

The road was pretty good that day with comfortable shoulders, but oncoming drivers absolutely could not believe that we were there on the road. With the new cart, I was able to carry a lot more equipment and water. I'd upped our water reserve from the three to four gallons we could carry with ThePontiac to five gallons in The1976CosworthVega, and had re-acquired my cold weather gear and heavier sleeping bag. As an added hindrance, the new cart, although it could hold a lot more equipment, had smaller wheels and a much smaller wheel in the front, so it was harder to push. I would guess that the cart had a laden weight of about 130 or 140 pounds. It only got heavier as we went over the mountains and our water reserve demands went up.

An east/west cross-country thru-hike is unlike the other epic hikes in the U.S., the AT and the Pacific Crest Trail. Unlike those other hikes, crossing the continent from east to west depends much more on interaction with people who are not used to interacting with hikers. The AT and the PCT are established routes, and the people who live on or near them are used to the hikers and, I've heard, appreciate and help out when they can. East/west, on the other hand, you meet a lot of people who have no idea what you are doing and are skeptical of you from the first word. And, unlike those other hikes, the east/west hiker does not enjoy as much stability in terms of equipment needs. Having never attempted the AT or the PCT, I cannot be sure, but my instinct is that the AT and PCT thru-hiker goes through a lot fewer grand re-organizations of his or her equipment. By contrast, I went from cold and rain in the east, to heat in the Midwest, to dry western conditions, then up into the mountains where the weather could be hot during the day and cold at night, rain again, then down into the desert where it is scorching hot during the day and cold at night and where you have to carry ample water or you will die. All tolled, I substantially reorganized my equipment seven times. So when we climbed into the Rockies that first day, I was not very familiar with my new cart or the location of my equipment inside the cart. Unfamiliar equipment in an unfamiliar cart while I hiked into unfamiliar terrain with an unfamiliar person and her unfamiliar dog. I had my reservations.

Jenny and I decided to hike through Woodland Park to a campsite on the far northwestern side of town. It had been a heck of a hike up; we'd climbed about 2000 feet, although it was not so horribly steep as it could have been. About a mile away from the campground, a car pulled over and a woman got out of the car, saying:

"That's Mabel. I know her."

It turned out that the woman had just been reading about Mabel and me about 15 minutes earlier. She was not an attorney, but had found my story from a link online while researching heating pipes. I felt a bit like a celebrity or, more accurately, like a guy who walked a celebrity dog. Jenny gave the woman her business card—she had had business cards printed for the trip. I do not have one of Jenny's cards, but I remember that the cards read "Adventure Awaits!" and listed her blog and contact information. The woman who had stopped to talk with Mabel talked to us quite a while about bears—they were everywhere and this was bear season—and about mountain lions. Bears were, according to her, not "as evolved" as mountain lions, and so you could not reason with mountain lions. Mountain lions were almost certain to kill us if we saw one, she said, and our dogs would attract them. We would be walking on Hwy 24, I explained, and then Hwy 50; mountain lions are shy and secretive, so there would be little chance of seeing one along relatively busy highways.

"No," she said. "That's a false sense of safety. A friend of mine was killed last year while changing a tire. Lion."

In Colorado, people say "lion", not "mountain lion". She was the first person we met who warned us about lions, but wouldn't be the last. Almost everyone we spoke with all the way across the mountains brought up lions. They usually said that we were hopelessly destined to die at a lion's paw. You cannot reason with a lion, they said, and you cannot hear them or see them.

"The ninjas of the animal kingdom," Jenny agreed, and nodded her head.

At the campground, the lady behind the counter took my $12 for the site and warned us that they "had a bear". In camp that night, after we had set up our tents and eaten, Jenny wrote the address of my blog on the back of a bunch of her business cards. I wasn't sure how I felt about that, because I wasn't 100% happy with Jenny as a hiking partner and I didn't want to give anyone the impression that our trips were linked in any way other than convenience.

"I don't get it," she said. "I have like 50 Twitter followers, and most of them are either my family or people I've stayed with on this trip. How many do you have?"

"I don't know," I said. "Maybe a thousand? 1200?"

"I don't understand that," she said. She smiled about it, but I could tell that she was really bitter.

"Yeah, I don't know what to tell you," I said. "I don't understand it, either."

"I mean...you're just an attorney, and I'm a *girl*."

"Yeah," I said, "I don't get it. It is what it is."

I learned the next morning that there had been a bear in our camp that night. The campground manager told Jenny. The bear must not have been a threat because I didn't hear it or wake up and Mabel didn't react at all, so far as I could tell. Jenny said that she had heard something, but hadn't even opened the tent to see what it was that made the noise. Jenny was bothered when the campground manager told her about it, though. She had seen a bear in Maryland, but hadn't had an incident like ours. Even if she had, there is no way of telling how she would have reacted to it. But, at least for me, I was not bothered or scared of bears, at all. When Jenny came bounding out of the campground office and told me that there had been a bear in our camp, I shrugged and put the earphones on.

"Come on, Mabes," I said. "Hup. HUP!"

We hiked on, and I was sad when I realized that we soon would not be able to see the lofty pink granite top of Pike's Peak. We climbed higher, around other peaks, and I scratched Mabel behind the ear every time we stopped beside the road to rest and to drink. "We'll see more stuff," I told her. "We'll see more stuff."

BOOK I: THE MOMENTS THAT TURN US (D)(i)
SUMMER DRESSES IN NEW BLOOM.

We hiked out of Woodland Park toward our first mountain pass, Ute Pass at 9,165 feet. We'd done most of the work getting up that high already. Woodland Park is at about 8400 feet, so we'd done more climbing coming out of Colorado Springs than we did from Woodland Park to Ute Pass. But the air was thinner up there, thinner still than the air had been in Denver. Strangely, the thin air didn't seem to bother me anymore, and it did not bother Mabel at all. Mabel seemed to get stronger the higher we climbed. Lucy and Jenny, on the other hand, had trouble with the elevation. Jenny began having difficulty breathing at about 8800 feet that day. I think she'd spent less time than I had acclimatizing to the thinner air.

"It will get easier," I said. "You'll get used to it."

"I know, I have to!" she said.

"We'll camp around 8500 again tonight," I said. "Maybe higher. That will help."

"I don't want to camp over 9000 feet," she said.

"We will have to at some point."

"Well I'm not going to," she said.

"Ok, but we may have to. We'll watch the weather, of course. And I don't want to camp over 10,5 or 11,000 feet, at all. But we shouldn't have but one pass that high, anyway."

The walking was difficult for Jenny. I was surprised that it was so difficult for her because she'd made supreme time across the midwestern states. But in Colorado she simply could not do the long days that Mabel and I had been doing, and certainly not back to back. But we had a long way to go before the ocean, and I did not intend to get mired down for months in the desert or, worse yet, stuck up in the mountains during the winter. So I pushed her to keep going. She complained about various problems—joint pain mostly. I did not pay much attention to her complaints because, frankly, if you walked from the Atlantic to Denver, then you shouldn't be complaining about joint pain. So rather than get angry or calling her out on it, or arguing about it, I accepted whatever she said and added my own take. Like, for example:

"I have hip problems."

"Yeah, those must be frustrating. But we'll have long days to do, and you'll get in better shape eventually."

"No," she would say. "It's not something I can 'get into shape'."

We had conversations like that very early on. I started to think that she did not intend to keep up with the pace that Mabel and I set. She would rush out to be in the lead, and then set a slow pace. Then, if I got into the lead, she would ask me if she could take the lead because "Lucy doesn't walk well back here; she needs to be in the lead". It went on like this. I let her walk in front most of the way through Colorado because the weaker hiker should always set the pace, anyway, and I absolutely could not stand hiking with her constantly shouting "LUCY!" in that surprised voice behind me.

Her gear set-up had worried me since we met in Colorado Springs, and that concern only grew. In my view, she did not have enough water carrying capacity to safely cross even Colorado, much less Utah. I had no idea how she had made it across western Nebraska on her own with only a max of a couple of gallons of water on a stretch. On the hot days in western Nebraska, Mabel and I could easily drink two or three gallons of water in between places where we could get more water. I started talking with her about the water problem on the first day of hiking. The number one lesson that I had learned was to plan for water, always.

"We'll be fine," she said. "We never use that much. And there's always water."

"Not in Utah," I said.

"But we'll have car support in Utah," she said.

I would leave it at that, usually. Sometimes I would try to explain to her that when you plan for water on a thru-hike, you should not plan for only the day's needs. With water, if nothing else, you need to plan for contingencies. If you are injured, for example, and end up stuck some place for two or three days, then one gallon of water won't cut it. If that happens, and you don't have enough water, you can die from a splinter. With other things—even first aid supplies!—there is not so immense a concern. But you must plan for water, always.

Other than these concerns, Jenny was good to hike with in those first few days and weeks. It was a pleasant change to have someone to talk with, even if we had nothing in common. She talked about video games, which was her true passion, and about comic books and that kind of thing. I had no interest in any of that, and I don't think she had much interest in corporate bankruptcy or what it's like to practice law in a big law firm.

All in all, I was happy to have someone hiking with me, but was soon to feel myself in an extremely awkward position. Jenny and I were bound to spend basically all day together every day for quite a long time. I initially thought I would call it all off and go my own way, but felt that I couldn't, and I felt that way because I had gone to law school! I felt at the time and probably still feel that she could not have made it on her own. She would, I believe, have either given up and gotten a ride, or died of thirst on the western slope of the Rocky Mountains. But she had, I supposed, walked into the mountains only because I had agreed to share car support with her—so I felt there were potential grounds for legal or moral liability in the event that I left her and she were injured or died. So I decided that I would have to gently change her hiking philosophy; after almost six years of being around law students and lawyers, I was not the best at "gently" changing someone's philosophy. But I didn't want to offend her or anger her, because whether I liked it or not, we were bound to spend a lot of time together. So I decided I would try gingerly to impress upon her the importance of water and the need to make good time in order to avoid the snows of the Rockies and the far off Sierra Nevada.

We hiked every day, and by the third day I had already given her at least one gallon of water from my own stash. It was not the last time I would have to give her water from what I carried.

Water and safety concerns notwithstanding, Colorado was a splendid hike. Once we climbed up into the mountains and over Ute Pass, we entered a different world where ancient stones lay about and wildflowers cut the green and stone landscape with flashes of yellow and red. Streams ran aside the roadways that climbed and descended through valleys and ravines. Deer and elk stood proud like statues beside the waters and bounded away powerfully into the trees. Lily pads grew on ponds and around each corner was a new vision or vista of a mountain soaring up to a bald, exposed summit. The air felt clean and the Sun felt clean.

Mabel fell in love with Colorado and with the high mountain air. Each of us suffered for the altitude in one way or another, but not Mabel. Mabel was strong and happy and seemed to get stronger and happier the longer we stayed up there among the wildflowers and the stones. She walked peacefully, only pulled when she saw a deer or other wildlife, and cuddled against me when we stopped for a break or got into the tent at night. She stopped in her tracks atop ridges, with one paw in the air and her tail erect, motionless, staring at tiny, moving specks down deep into ravines and across broad valleys. We humans saw only the proud animals or the stupid animals that ventured near us. But Mabel knew there was a whole other world out there, and I think she was torn a little—she wanted to stay with us and she wanted to run free. But she never tried to get free and she never whimpered. We both fell in love with Colorado a bit.

We camped in small green valley nearly 9000 feet above sea level, where a constant wind whipped across the campsite and made hell of erecting my tent and tarping down #The1976CosworthVega. There was continuous threat of rain, but no rain materialized except in mysterious, brief mists that seemed to come from inside the air itself. The valley was ringed by peaks. Some peaks were deep, pine green and lush with pine trees, and others were rocky outcroppings where, I swear if I looked long enough, I would see a bighorn sheep standing alone in the bracing wind. And the Sun was fierce and clear through the thin air up there, and everything shone in brighter shades than it would down where we came from.

The people in the mountains—and I mean really up in the mountains—all had stories to tell and were all interested in our story. Local folks often stopped us at gas stations and restaurants to listen to our tale and they were amazed and proud that we had walked so far. Jenny was a particular hit among the Colorado folk. That a girl would have walked so far, and alone for nearly 2000 miles, is astounding and makes people happy. And everyone there looked to be only seconds away from a grand adventure, themselves. Coloradans seem to each be minutes way from packing their tents, strapping on their pack, and hitting the trail. But they have no reason to pack up and hike away...because they already live in Colorado. Why would anyone want to leave?

BOOK III: ...AND THE MOON SAYS HALLELUJAH, 01.07.12(1)

Wake up hung-over. Eat breakfast. Need corrective snorkel mask at last minute; have Rosie procure through secret channels. Snorkel w/Kendra and the Canadian girls from Caulker. Research water; determine warm, clear as glass. See fish plentiful on reef. Clear mask over and over; determine Mask doesn't fit. See: sea turtle, octopi, squid, rays, sharks, other. Touch nerf shark. Assist tour guide dropping girls off at pier; travel by boat w/guide, other side of island. Arrive riverside bar and gas station; receive gift of a beer from tour guide. Drink with him in boat. Research tour guide: Nice guy. Return to Pedro's, very tired, very happy. Learn Rosie still could not make a cappuccino.

Canadian skin tans and American teeth rip into grouper tacos at the Waragumu cafe.

BOOK II: FEEL THE SELFISH FURY (D)(i)
THOSE WHO FOR TO-DAY PREPARE.

I cut off my beard and started as an associate at the Chicago office of Sidley Austin LLP in August of 2008, back in the sleek and modern building where I'd been a summer associate a year earlier. Back in the clean and modern office with an installed desk and installed cabinets, but this time with a south facing window out of which I could see the CNA building, Soldier Field, and Lake Michigan. The most senior associates and partners usually sat on the east side, with its views of Lake Michigan and Millennium Park. The north and south sides had comparatively valuable views. Some folks called the west side the "ghetto". I didn't. Each office door has a clear plastic nameplate panel at about shoulder height where you can slide in a piece of paper with an associate's name on it in between the plastic nameplate sheets. On the south side of the 25th floor at One S. Dearborn, there was an office door with a little panel beside it that read "Geo. Tyler Coulson". I walked into *my* office, at *my* new job, at *my* new firm, in *my* new city. I considered taking a picture of the nameplate and sending it to my mother, because I knew she would be proud, but I was embarrassed of how it might look if someone saw me taking a picture of my nameplate. Later, I saw other new associates taking pictures of their nameplates. Fools.

The firm re-issued to me my laptop and a Blackberry that I had when I was a summer associate. There were training refresher courses, and I sat in my office until a computer tech guy came to make sure everything worked properly. I called the building maintenance folks and asked them to install a whiteboard in my office, largely because I had noticed whiteboards in most successful associates' offices. The internal mail folks delivered a stack of reference books—the Uniform Commercial Code, the Federal Rules of Evidence and the like—and I arranged them neatly on the shelves and sat back in my Herman Miller Aeron chair. Then I was an attorney. I had no experience, no job skills, no license to practice yet, and no work. But I was an attorney.

There was nothing that could bring me down. I was a little tired of things after the bar exam, and Isra had left me, and my parents were far away getting older, and all of that. But nothing could bring me down. This was the firm of Newt Minow and Adlai Stevenson. This was the firm of Barack Obama. And, Goddamnit!, this was the firm of Geo. Tyler Coulson.

My incoming class in the banking group was large. Six of us started around the same time, all of us new to practice. As I recall, three of us came from the University of Illinois College of Law, one from the University of Chicago Law School, one from Harvard Law, and me from Iowa. Two other Iowa law grads went to Sidley, too. It was a pretty good group of folks, and we were all happy to be in the Banking and Financial Transactions practice group. None of us really understood the mechanics or the documents of major financial transactions, but we were eager to learn. We wanted to dig in immediately and get our hands into some deal documents. One advantage of working in a big firm, so they tell incoming lawyers, is that the sheer size of the average deal means that baby lawyers get their hands and heads into deal documents sooner. It works like this: Generally, the firm works on these multi- million and billion dollar financing deals, so the little $10 or $20 million deals are often handed down to the new lawyers. So I suppose I was lucky, because I almost immediately got onto a $5 million dollar note purchase agreement.[15] I was working under a new partner in the group, Dorsey Cleary.

Dorsey was a serious person and seemed cold to me the first time I met her. On my second day at the firm, she invited me to a lunch with some summer associates, and afterward we discussed the lunch and the summer associates and, briefly, she smiled and seemed pleasant. But then she went back to being cold and busy busy busy. She was a part of my "pod"—in the banking group, new associates were assigned to a "pod" of partners who are supposed to be the new associates' only sources of work assignments. By doling out work in this way, the idea is that the superstar associates won't dominate all of the potential work assignments, and the new associates will all enjoy a more rational and more equitable distribution of work assignments. When Dorsey called me, I grabbed a notebook and half-jogged over to her west side office.

"You're going to have to take the lead on this," she said, between checking her email and pinching her forehead. "I just don't have time for it."

"Ok," I said, and scribbled 'take the lead on this' in my stupid notebook.

"This is a rounding error here. Five million dollars? That's a rounding error in a firm like this."

"Do we make rounding errors?" I asked, but she did not laugh.

Over that day and the next few days, the lender's counsel sent over deal docs and I pored over them. (Sidley usually represented lenders, but we represented a borrower on this occasion—probably as a favor to this client on other matters.) At any rate, I pored over the docs noted all the questionable language in the representations and warranties that I thought could pose a problem for our client, all the language dealing with default and acceleration, and everything else I thought might be important, and I brought them all to Dorsey's attention. She looked them over and sometimes would say "that's market", meaning it's a market standard to include such a provision. Two other provisions, though, raised her eyebrows, and we made plans to discuss them with the client.

"This default provision doesn't make sense," she said, but didn't even look up at me.

"I know! That's what I thought."

"Is this really what they mean?" she asked, rhetorically. "I can't believe these bastards. One thing you'll see, Tyler, is that on deals like this, the attorneys won't be as *sophisticated* as we are—this bank probably thought they could slide this by."

"Maybe it's a mistake?"

"If it is, then their form is broken."[16]

---

[15] In a note purchase agreement, a bank (or other lender) usually buys notes from the borrower. The borrower issues notes to the bank, and those notes represent the debt that is owed. Any restrictions or requirements you can imagine can be written in to note agreements, but generally notes are transferrable and the lending institution can later sell them—just like they can sell your mortgage and the note on your house.

[16] In a financing arrangement, the whole amount to be paid back generally is not due immediately. The borrowed amount is due back in payments, often monthly but sometimes yearly or semi-yearly. It is just like when you buy a car or a house—you aren't

In the matter at hand, the deal documents included a few provisions that conflicted, and, because of the contradictory provisions, our client would have likely been in breach of the agreement the moment he signed it. In other words, the "form" was broken. Perhaps the bank on the other side of the table wanted our client to be in breach from the first moment, but more likely the conflicting provisions in the documents were an honest mistake. And there are a few ways to handle a situation like that: You could ignore it, and if anything ever happens in the future and the parties have to go to court, then the judge can decide which of the conflicting provisions should govern, but that might be malpractice; or, you could rack up a ton of billable hours explaining to your client why the provisions might not be compatible, and haranguing the lawyers on the other side by accusing them of bad faith and calling them bad names when they aren't around; or, you could call the other side and ask them about the provisions.

On the phone later that day, Dorsey tried to explain the situation to our client.

"No. This is a rabbit hole," the client said. "I feel you're running me down a rabbit hole. I can't afford this, so let's just get the deal done."

"Well this is..." Dorsey started to say.

"No, it isn't," the client said. "I don't understand or care anything about what you are saying. I *have* to get this deal done. That is the end of that. Without this financing, there *is no business.* So it has to get done."

Dorsey was a bit shocked, I think, because she wasn't used to being treated like that. (Retrospectively, I believe she wasn't used to being treated like that because she was a new partner; I imagine clients treat partners like that frequently.)

Off the phone, she said to me: "Well, we can't do this, can we?"

"I think we *could,* but..." I said.

"But, I mean, we *can't,* right? We can't advise a client to sign a broken document that would put him in breach immediately."

"I think we should not," I said.

"He just doesn't get it. You'll see that a lot, Tyler. Our clients are...well, they are risk takers and entrepreneurs, and business school consultants, and...they often just aren't smart enough to understand it."

---

usually liable to pay the whole amount back until the very last payment on the loan. It's the same principle at play on the bigger deals, but with more zeroes. The lender does not generally have the right to demand the whole amount back until the very end of the loan. However, most loans have acceleration provisions built in to them. For example, if a borrower materially breaches the terms of the loan—misses 2 or 3 payments in a row, fails to meet some representation or warranty that it would maintain its current ratio of debt to income, for example—then the lender may "accelerate" the loan, which means to call the whole amount due immediately. Every lender wants its borrower to be in material breach because, if a lender can accelerate the loan, it puts the lender in a great position of power over the borrower. So the lender wants the deal docs written in such a way that the borrower cannot help but be in breach of a material provision of the agreement.

"Well, we are supposed to close Thursday," I said. Dorsey worked with hedge funds and huge banks—I don't think she understood what this tiny rounding error loan meant to a small business. She could not understand that this small business could not afford to care about this issue.

"We can't just *fix* this document. It's in *their* form."

"You could..."

"I've got an idea," she said. Then she called the attorney working for the bank on the other side of the table, and I heard half of the conversation. It went something like:

"Hi, this is Dorsey Mathewson, I'm a partner at Sidley and we are working on this matter with you. Yes. Yes, nice to speak with you, too, I guess. Could you look at provision X and provision Y in the deal documents? Well, I *can* wait a second, I didn't expect they'd be right in front of you...I mean it's only $5 million. Now, tell me, do those two make sense? I didn't think so, either. Could you strike one of them? Great. Thanks, my associate will be in touch with you about Thursday. Best." She hung up.

She turned to me with a little flat smile.

"That lady didn't even understand the implications of the two provisions. She had no idea what I was talking about. You'll run into that a lot, too. A lot of the times, the attorneys on the other side of the small deals we do aren't as sophisticated as they could be. She didn't understand the implications of those two provisions beating against each other. And this was really luck. Our client is lucky that I saw them and understood them."

So there's that, I thought. I went back to my office and added comments in one of the deal documents. Once my comments were in, I ran a redline, which is a document that compares the old and new versions of a given document and marks all the insertions with underlines and the deletions with strike-thrus. This way, it is easy for the attorneys on the other side (and on your team) to see the small changes that are made with every turn of a document.

A senior associate in the banking group called me into his office my second or third week at the firm. He was the senior associate in my "pod", and I'd worked with him during my summer, but we hadn't reconnected yet because he had been on vacation. His office was always neat, with many neatly stacked columns of documents rising nearly to the ceiling. Each practice area attracts different sorts of people and, in my experience, banking practices tend to attract highly organized people who value highly organized office-space. (In the bankruptcy practice, on the other hand, a few offices look as if the FBI or some dark underworld organization had broken in during the night and scattered things everywhere, like in the movies.)

"Scary time," he said. He had gigantic blue eyes, and the strangest smile that was both friendly and not at all inviting.

"I think so," I agreed. "When they called me in the spring and told me I'd be joining this practice, I almost regretted how much I liked you all when I was a summer associate." He laughed. His secretary stopped by the office and shouted in:

"Mike! I need your timesheets when you get a chance."

He nodded and laughed and told her he'd get them right over to her.

"My timesheets were due last week," he said. "It's easy to get behind and not get your timesheets in. The firm is going to start cracking down on that. If you don't get your timesheets in, then how can they bill the client?" He started flipping through a stack of papers he kept beside his computer and transferring information from the sheets to some file on his desktop. Sometimes he would stop and stare blankly at the ceiling.

"What did you do, again, before law school?"

"A lot of different things," I said.

"But weren't you a writer, or a street musician, or something?" There wasn't any judgment in his voice, but maybe a hint of genuine interest.

"Sort of," I said.

"Well...there's *no creativity* in law, at all. You probably know that already from law school."

"I had heard," I agreed.

"But you'll find that timesheets can be a creative endeavor. Keeping time sometimes turns out to be an art."

"How's that?"

"Because you sometimes have to make shit up."

"Really?"

"Not *really*," he said. "Sort of. At the end of your career, you could stack up all your timesheets and have a record of how you spent every minute of your working life. Think about that. Most of our clients are billed in six-minute intervals; so you have to keep track of your time to the tenth of an hour. If you forget and you're filling out timesheets the *next day* or three weeks later, then it's sometimes difficult to describe exactly what you were doing. You have to describe what you are doing in a way that is accurate and in a way that the client will both understand and pay. It's sometimes creative."

Mike gave me some other pointers and told me that there were a couple of deals brewing, and one of them would be an *enormous* securitization—if they happened at all. Like every other banking or corporate attorney at the time, he was unsure every morning whether he would wake up to a North American economy at all, or whether the whole thing might vanish.

We closed the note purchase agreement later that week. I had accordion files in my office on which I kept copies of all the documents that our client had to provide for the deal.[17] This particular deal—which, remember, I was able to do because it was a "rounding error"—produced a "closing book" of about 500 pages. The lender's counsel generally puts together the closing book, which is a collection of all the required documentation and all of the

---

[17] Lenders generally require evidence of good corporate standing, proof that the corporation is a real entity that is empowered to borrow and repay money, proof of security, etc. For example, in this instance, I remember we provided a certificate of good standing from the Secretary of State in the state of incorporation, the corporate charter and bylaws, resolutions from the Board of Directors approving the borrowing, lien searches demonstrating that there were no other lenders with outstanding security interests in all of the borrower's collateral, etc. Additional documentation evidenced that the borrower met the representations and warranties set forth in the loan documentation.

actual deal documents—the loan agreement, the note issuance, the note purchase agreement, etc. This was my first deal, ever, and I was bound and determined to keep all these documents straight; even if we didn't put the deal book together, it had been our burden to produce most of these documents. So I had them all out and ordered on an accordion file or two spread out across the desk in my office.

When we were about to close, Dorsey came walking fiercely into my office.

"What are you doing?"

"Getting ready for the closing," I said.

"Is all this for our deal?"

"Yes," I said.

"Why are you putting these things into a binder?"

"Well, I'm making a sort of deal book..."

"Uh, you know, *we* don't do that," she said. "They are doing that. Why would you do that?"

"Well, I..."

"Well, *I* don't know if someone told you to do this—because I certainly didn't—or if you just thought you'd take some initiative, but this is all wrong."

"It's not *the* deal book," I said. "It's just..."

"Whatever it is, it's a waste of time. The lender's counsel is doing the closing book on this deal. So this has all been a waste of your time, and the client's time. It's a giant waste."

"Ok," I said. She didn't even know what I was doing. This was the peculiar thing, she actually *had* asked me to explain what my system was, but she hadn't let me answer. She knew only that my particular system was not *exactly* what she would have done and so, therefore, I was "wrong"—even though there can be no objectively "wrong" way to do what I was doing.

"I'll just burn all this stuff, then."

"What?" She had been leaning in my doorway and stood up straight. I don't think she'd heard me.

"Joke," I said. "I was joking."

"What are you going to do with all this?"

"I'm going to put it all in that binder I've been using," I said. "Because it helps me keep track of the documents we have to produce. And some of these are originals that I have to send over tomorrow."

"Whatever."

I had been in the office very late every day that week and the week before, but I didn't feel too tired.

The closing went off without a hitch, or almost without a hitch. Most of the closing was done by myself and a woman from another firm who was working for the bank, and there was another attorney in another city who was representing one of the Borrower's officers who was in on the closing call. We stepped through all the documents, and once we were happy that everything was there, I distributed .pdfs of all the signed documents and mailed the originals over to the borrower's counsel and that was pretty much it. The attorney on the other side said it had been great working with me and that she would get a closing book over to me as soon as possible. That was fine with me, and we were done.

That was the first and only deal that I did with any responsibility at all.

The next week, I didn't have that much to do, so I read up on the UCC and milled around and every now and again billed a few hours on some small, one-off project from this or that senior associate or partner. Dorsey, who had been my main source of work so far, was shoulder-deep on a deal that was threatening to explode and that I would have to be involved in at some point. It was a big re-financing of something or another that I completely did not understand, but that involved four or five offshore funds. Dorsey's other minion was a second year associate named Cindy who sat down the hall from me. Cindy, who I was never close with but who I worked with a few times, was a smart and beautiful gal who walked with really, really heavy footsteps from her office to the copier and back. I never saw her in the cafeteria or outside of the building, and she was always in her office from early in the morning to early in the morning.

One Friday, I stayed a little late in my office because I thought there might be work. I stopped by Dorsey's office about eight that night and asked for work, but Dorsey said there was nothing for me to do for her. Then I stopped by Cindy's office, and Cindy looked frazzled.

"I wish!" she said and smiled. "I wish there was some of this that I could give you, but I don't think I can. I mean, maybe I haven't handled this very well, but I can't really delegate any of the work I have. I'm working on getting better at that."

"So I guess I'll just leave," I said.

"Absolutely! Leave now; leave early now while you have the chance. A year from now, it won't be like this for you!"

So I left. It was Friday night, and I had a million things to do at home and wouldn't have minded at all if I could find someone to hit the bars with. I got into a cab and headed back to my apartment in Lincoln Park. My cell phone—a personal cell phone with a personal number—rang when I was about three blocks away from my apartment on Wrightwood.

"This is Tyler."

"What the fuck are you doing?"

"Excuse me, who is this?"

"This is Dorsey Cleary," she said, as if it had somehow been my responsibility to know who she was.

"Hi, Dorsey," I said.

"What the fuck are you doing?"

"I'm in a cab right now."

"Are you heading home?" In retrospect, I think this is where she expected me to lie and say "no, I just stepped out to get something to eat".

"I am," I said.

"How the hell do you think that is ok? How do you think that is ok? I am a *partner*, Tyler, and I am here. Partners are supposed to go home, not associates. And Cindy is down there working her ass off. And you just left?"

"I stopped by your office and...."

"You know Cindy was here until one in the morning *every night this week*. And you think you can just go home?"

"I had nothing to do," I said. I covered the mouthpiece of the phone and told the driver to pull over anywhere and be prepared to turn around.

"Well I think you really need to think about this," she said. "You really need to think about this."

"Do you have something for me to do?" I asked. "I can come back in right now."

"You just think about this."

Click.

I went home and got drunk.

Book III: ...And the Moon Says Hallelujah, 01.08.12(1)

Sit beside pool, a.m.; find Sun grew too hot; move to picnic table by office. See Celio running late for work; analyze issue, re: "Is Celio hungover?; conclude he is not, just misses Portugal and family, will move soon to China where he was most happy. Assess manuscript: is in tatters, much red ink. Add more red ink. Email conversation w/Kendra: "May have dysentery." Respond: "Oh no." Email from Kendra: "It was the Waragumu." Respond: "We had same thing. I am fine." Email from Kendra: "Did I have an iced drink?" Respond: "You had a burger at that burger place with washed lettuce." Email from Kendra: "Culprit identified." Respond: "You may die." Email from Kendra: "Might make it." Respond: "Find locals with healing herbs. Like Zithromax." Email from Kendra: "Have it." Respond: "Let me know if you need anything." See Rosie appear.

R: "I cannot get the milk to froth and it is now ruining my *whole week*. It would make me feel better if you bought one of my candles. My candle company is called Glow Belize."

Note arrival of mysterious Canadian couple, Natalie and Derrick. Research: "Does Derrick think that Glow Belize is best name ever for candle company?; conclusion: yes. See Canadians check in to the hostel, disappear. Calculate chances of running into them later: high.

R: "They are nice. I like working here."

T: "I like being here."

R: "I am moving to Florida. I lived in London for a while, but I am moving to Florida."

T: "Bienvenidos a Miami."

R: "How old *are* you? Geez."

Return to manuscript; find still in tatters. Respond to inquiry from Rosie about the Midwest, i.e., what is it like to walk across it? Tell her, more or less. Sit w/Rosie a long time; determine the story is long. Doubt Rosie finds it interesting; determine I am bored to think of it. See Celio return, listens intently, smokes cigarettes and drinks coffee.

T: "I have to go to dinner tonight with Kendra."

R: "Tell me more tomorrow?"

T: "Sure."

C: "Oh, Tyler, will you tell *me* more tomorrow, too?"

T: "Yes, Celio. I will. I'll probably be back here later tonight, anyway."

Dinner w/Kendra; learn she felt better already, looked healthy.

K: "I have the weakest GI tract in history. It's the physical worst."

T: "I'm glad you're feeling better."

K: "I'm better. But I'm not go-snorkeling-better."

Discuss working at big firm w/Kendra; learn she is happy and unhappy. Determine Kendra to be much better adjusted than 90% attorneys; feel jealousy.

Conclude dinner with Kendra, great time. Determine she is lovely person, happy she is relaxing and reading. Analyze issues: Whether I'm happy, too; conclusion: Yes, I am. Drinks w/Kendra and Canadians. Return to Pedro's. Edit manuscript. Determine manuscript is shit; go down to bar; find Celio is there; find new little German girl is there. Get drunk with the little German girl, good time. Determine hostel small, uncomfortable; relieved to return to hotel. Forget to turn on air conditioner; sleep in hot room; wake up with horrible hangover. Walk into town; breakfast w/Kendra at Estel's Dine by the Sea, phenomenal food. Fall in love w/Belize. Decide am in love with many places. Return to Pedro's to work hard. Learn Kendra still in throes of dysentery.

Book I: The Moments That Turn Us (D)(ii)
Those that after a Tomorrow stare.

We struck camp as early as possible because we had 26 miles ahead of us to get to Hartsel. We were planning to cross Wilkerson Pass at 9,507 feet that day. It was cold that morning. When it drops to 45 degrees at night, it becomes difficult to pry yourself from a warm sleeping bag in the morning. We struck camp slowly, I more slowly than Jenny. My tent was still up when Jenny had her whole cart packed.

We were on the road heading west out of a lovely green valley by 8:15 a.m. The hike was too beautiful for words for several miles—so beautiful that we hardly realized we had begun climbing. We had eaten and slept well the day before, and we were feeling good from the rest and the fuel. Even more, I was pushing hard because several folks had promised that we would have an unparalleled view from the top of Wilkerson Pass, looking down 1000 feet over South Park, a green valley 100 miles by 100 miles, teeming with bison, elk, and antelope. So we trudged onward and upward faster than we should have. We pushed up out of the small valley, around ageless piles of rocks, beside sweeping green pastures, and into Pike National Forest. Each step carried us deeper into more mysterious, more majestic land. Where once there were slices of grasslands there were now hills pinpricked with green pines. And every so often, when the monotony of the green pines was almost too much for me to take, the hills broke open in groves of white birch trees. And up we went, through it all, at about 5.5% grade. Eleven miles uphill, gradually getting steeper and steeper.

With each approaching "summit", Jenny and I assured each other that "this is it, this is the pass". But upon hitting the top of each hill, the road turned and disappeared into a space between two new ridges, and the climb wasn't over. Still, with each approaching hill we assured each other that on the top of this hill there would be a green road sign that read "Wilkerson Pass, Elevation 9,507 feet".

At eight miles in, we were getting tired. We had pushed hard and pushed fast, ever higher into thinner air. Jenny and Lucy began to suffer the altitude and to have difficulty breathing at about 9000 feet—nothing serious, but enough to slow us down. I pushed 130 or 140 pounds and am no great athlete, so it is more accurate to say that at 9000 feet, Jenny and Lucy began to slow down to my speed. Mabel got stronger and stronger the higher we climbed, as if with each hundred feet in elevation a new, previously dormant strand of mountain dog DNA in her came alive and shouted for her to go higher and faster. At 9,200 feet, when Jenny and Lucy were suffering and my lungs were heaving for the weight and the thin air, Mabel began to tug hard on her leash like she was helping me up the mountain.

With two or three miles remaining to the summit, the grade of the road broke sharply up, steep enough to call it *steep*—not steep like the West Virginia passes but out there in the Rockies it goes on and on for miles. But we pushed, because after reaching the summit we still had 17 miles to go to Hartsel, where we had planned to find a camping spot.

We turned a final corner and could see that beyond this last ascent was a clearing where a thick wall of clouds had gathered over South Park. All through the ascent, we had no inclination that there would be weather in South Park. With Mabel pulling hard at my hip, we pushed up until we were there—a green road sign that read "Wilkerson Pass, Elevation 9,507 feet". Now that is not high by mountaineers' standards, nor even by the standards of some casual hikers. In Colorado, recreational hikers routinely hike the summits of Colorado's 14ers. But on a limited diet, with three straight days of hiking behind us—including Ute Pass at about 9,300 feet—and pushing 130 pounds, it was enough to get my lungs screaming and my legs burning. At the top, we pulled into the visitor center for the Pike National Forest.

A husband and wife team, about 60 years old, worked at the visitor center, and had encyclopedic knowledge about Wilkerson Pass and South Park below it. As we gathered our breath and relaxed for a bit, the couple asked us about our trips, how long the road had been and how difficult. They were amused more than anything, and although they wished us luck, I could tell they thought we were all crazy. But they were nice to talk to, and were sweet to us.

And, anyway, we couldn't go down the mountain because Hartsel, in the heart of South Park, was covered in a thick, black rainstorm. We watched the rain fall 20 miles away; we stood at about the same height as the clouds. It was a heartbreaker to have pushed so hard only to be stopped from pushing all the way over by a thunderstorm. But we had no choice but to stay there, up on Wilkerson Pass, where we had cell service, an electrical outlet, and camping—because you can camp anywhere in a National Forest.

Or almost anywhere, as it turned out.

Hartsel's official population is around 650 people, but most of those people live throughout the valley or on top of the mountains. Hartsel proper looks to be more like maybe 50 or 100 people.

We decided, after much hemming and hawing and with great reluctance, to camp on the top of Wilkerson Pass for the afternoon and night rather than to risk death in South Park. So we set about finding a place to pitch our tents. But to pitch a tent, you need some relatively flat ground—some degree of slope under a tent can be good for drainage reasons, and you simply cannot pitch a tent and sleep at a 30% incline. We could find nothing. We looked around from the vantage of the visitor center on top of Wilkerson Pass, but every bit of exposed ground lay on the slope of a mountainside. We could not hike up another 700 feet to the top of nearby summits just to scout for a flat space. In the end, after an hour or so of hiking down and up both sides of the ridge, we found two places: one, about a mile down on the side we came up, but we were not about to hike backward, and the second on a distant hill away from the road and, allegedly, populated by bears. The latter was also not a great choice.

The weather cleared below us, but the day had grown too late to begin the 17-mile hike into Hartsel.

The married couple who ran the visitor center, and who also stay through the summer in an RV on the other side of the visitor center park area, were sympathetic to our situation. They told us that on the other side of the ridge behind the Center, a bit beyond the two RVs up there, there were a couple of picnic tables and some "somewhat" flat ground where, if we stayed out of the way, we could camp for the night. So we pushed our gear up to the top and then back down the other side on a rarely used hiking trail and found two picnic benches. There was a wooden fence about 15 feet from the benches, and beyond that another 60 or 70 feet were two RVs on a "private residence". Now, because we were in a National Forest, and because the visitor center staff lived on the "private residence", I assume that the "private residence" was not a "privately owned residence".

We set our tents on the flattest space we could find that was not rock and then made dinner. I had a Snickers bar and a quart of powdered milk. This was among the worst camping spots I had on the trip. It was exposed to the wind, there were old-ish growth trees above it, the ground was bumpy, and there were animal runs nearby, and elk tracks and droppings. No self-respecting camper would ever choose to camp there unless there were absolutely no other options. But we had no other options.

We ate and drank dinner in relative silence, all four of us were pretty tired and I think Jenny was frustrated that we could not get over the pass that day. I was frustrated by the failure, at any rate.

Soon after we finished eating, a huge truck pulled in across the way beside one of the RVs. We waved at the middle-aged couple who got out of the truck and they timidly half-waved back at us. The woman of the couple did a double take, and I knew she had seen our tents and was not happy. Soon enough, the man of the couple was out milling around outside the RV.

"We are going to have trouble with this guy," I said to Jenny. And, before long, the man walked toward us.

"You all thinkin' of campin' here tonight?" he had a thick Oklahoma accent, like the couple at the visitor center had.

"Yeah," Jenny said. She started to say more, probably that we were thru-hikers come all the way from the east coast. Jenny was good with people. But the old man interrupted her.

"No," he said. "There is no overnight campin' here."

Jenny told him that the folks at the visitor center told us we could stay here, at this spot, but he was having none of it. He marched off down toward the visitor center. While he was gone, Jenny and I talked about what we were going to do. Jenny thought we would be fine, but I was pretty sure this guy was going to be trouble for us. We discussed what our options would be if he threw a fit. It was a minimum of six hours down to Hartsel, which would put us there at 11 o'clock at night, far too late to find legitimate camping on private land, so it would have to be stealth camping. But it would be our only choice.

The old man returned and did not walk near us. He walked silently to his RV and would neither speak to us nor make eye contact. I shouted out "What's the good word from down there?", but he would not respond. Jenny and I sat there. The old man went in and out of his RV, milling and doing nothing, and from time to time saying loudly to his wife that "Well, I guess we will just call the sheriff". Then he pulled out a lawn chair, sat, and stared at us.

I was frustrated, tired, and angry. There were no "no camping" signs on that trail—although there were such signs down both other trails leading from the visitor center, one on the dog trail and one on the bear-populated trail we were first told to camp on. And, even if there were some applicable camping restriction, I cannot understand the value of any law against, or restriction on, any behavior that harms absolutely no one else. Two people, two dogs, on a cross country thru-hike, are trapped on a mountain pass by a thunderstorm, with only one suitable camping spot, all of whom are all going to be in bed asleep by 6:30 or 7, and yet this somehow is offensive? Odd, this. It is a sorry state of affairs when the well being of people trying to accomplish such a harmless goal as ours can be put into danger by mindless restrictions or frightened men.

I did not move, but told Jenny that if we were kicked out that I would be hiking all the way in to Hartsel, 17 miles, in the dark and in the rain, if necessary.

The couple from the visitor center walked up the trail toward us and toward the trail to their RV, and the old man in the RV got out of his chair and walked to meet them.

"Did anyone say anything?" one of the visitor center couple asked. Jenny said that the man had questioned us and, just then, the old man intercepted them. The conversation between the two older couples from Oklahoma was short. And we started packing up.

As I was packing my tent, Jenny asked the couple from the visitor center for a ride in to Hartsel, and they quickly agreed. They would detach their fifth wheel and we could put our things in the back of their truck. But as we were packing, the bitter old man from the RV unloaded the back of his own truck and backed it up toward our campsite. He got out and started to talk with us, and I heard him tell Jenny that they had all decided to go into Hartsel for dinner at the diner, anyway, and we could ride in the back. I was not very happy about the situation, but once Jenny had accepted a ride I could not very well let Jenny and Lucy ride 17 miles away and leave us split up, so I loaded my stuff into the back of the truck and soon enough we were off. Jenny rode in the cab of the truck with the two older couples, and I was in the bed of the truck with The1976CosworthVega, Jenny's stroller, Lucy, and Mabel. The Vega did not have a break, and when Mabel rides in the bed of a truck she must be restrained, so I was stuck with my back to the tailgate, holding Mabel in my lap, and holding tight the Vega with my left foot, which was no easy task. We headed down the mountain, and the old man pushed the truck to about 80 miles an hour. My knuckles were white all the way down the mountain around sharp turns.

And then we were off the mountain and into a great flat swath of pastureland. South Park is a sight to see from above and from below. The wind blew across my face, and whipped the short hair on my head. Suddenly, I was no more than a guy in the back of a pickup truck speeding along beside open fields. I was a 15-year-old kid again. But now I was speeding through a distant, amazing landscape unlike anything I had ever seen before—an expanse of valley sheltered inside a circle of towering mountains.

And I laughed.

In Hartsel, the old man parked directly in front of the diner/bar, which was about the only business in town. We unloaded our stuff, and the old man repeated the things I had heard him say earlier—sorry, but he just couldn't let anyone camp there, because then he would have to let everyone camp there and they would be overrun with campers and, anyway, there was a bear up there. The latter complaint was not worth dignifying, because there are bears in lots of places, and the former was so utterly ludicrous that I could hardly keep from laughing. Yes, yes, you would be overrun by cross country thru-hikers, or day hikers, who climb a 9,500 foot pass in order to camp in the worst camping spot imaginable.

But as he said it, I felt sympathy for the fellow. He is a fellow who has some rules in his life, and he lives by them. Even if they make no sense. And he clearly had come to understand that he was in the wrong in this case, but rather than back down, he decided to give us a ride into town, which he thought would square us all up. He was a silly, petty old codger suffering from a terminal lack of imagination—but that was just from my perspective. From his, we were probably something that he couldn't understand. And once he realized he was wrong, he tried to do right by us. He turned out all right, in the end, in his own way. Or as well as he could, I guess, given his circumstances.

The old man, his wife, and the couple from the visitor center went into the diner and Jenny and I set about finding a place to camp. We wandered around the little town of three or four main buildings, in the middle of the highway, each with one arm outstretched holding cell phones, each trying to get a fine enough signal to call somewhere, anywhere, to find lodging. A

fellow in the beer garden of the bar—the *only* person in the beer garden—
said "Ah! Man's eternal search for a cell phone signal" and Jenny struck up a
conversation with him, telling him our story. He was a trim fellow, about 40,
with a few tattoos that snuck out from beneath the bottom of the sleeves of
his black t-shirt. His name was Ron.

I slid into the Hartsel Mercantile—a sort of antique store/candy seller—
while Jenny spoke with Ron. The proprietor was a lovely older lady with a
puppy on her arm, and she told me the puppy was a mix of a Chihuahua
and a Poodle. She and the pup were both adorable. I bought some Snickers
and a can of soda, and Jenny came in and told me we had a place to stay.

Ron had stuck his head into the bar and shouted "Who do we ask if these
folks can camp behind the community center?". Someone had answered
"Did they ask you?". Ron said they had, and the consensus in the bar was
that Ron was the person to ask. So we were told we could camp there, and if
anyone gave us any grief we were to tell him or her that Ron told us we
could camp there.

With a home for the night secured, we decided to have a real meal at the
restaurant. We sat in the restaurant beside the old man in the RV and the
visitor center folks. The restaurant was a sort of hybrid between a western
cow-town diner and a local Midwestern-style restaurant. While Jenny and I
sat deciding on what to order, the old man turned to our table and talked to
us. He asked us questions about where we had come from and where we
were going, and every now and again tossed in another quasi-apology.

We ordered malts and some dinner. The waitress was a lovely lady in
cowboy boots and a button down shirt worn unbuttoned over a t-shirt and
the malts came in ceramic pint glasses. When we had nearly finished eating,
the old man and his crew paid and readied to leave. Each, in turn, talked to
us more and offered luck and hope for our adventure.

Then another couple at another table, whom we had neither met nor
talked with, readied themselves to leave. And just as the RV man and his
crew were out the door, the waitress came to our table, pointed to the other
couple leaving, and said they had picked up our ticket. I half-hollered thank
you to them, but they were almost out the door themselves. They
acknowledged us with a small wave and a faint smile and were out of my life
forever. That kind of generosity is rare. I have no idea what their names
were, or anything about them, but I thank them. I thanked them all night
long while I lay there full and sleepy and happy in my tent.

When they were gone, the restaurant was empty but for us finishing our
meals and the waitress talked with us. I gathered that the waitress owned the
place, but I could be wrong. She was a lovely person, and she told us she
was thankful there were still great people in the world—great people who do
fool-headed things like walk from coast to coast and great people who pick
up the checks of fool-headed strangers.

I pitched my tent behind an old church that had been repurposed as a
community center. We were bone tired, and I was quickly in my tent with
Mabel. A huge thunderhead at the north end of South Park headed our way.
I tried to sleep, snuggled up in my sleeping bag and afraid that it might drop
into the 30s in the middle of the night. But as darkness fell, I felt a bit

claustrophobic. A vicious wind picked up and made my tent flap and rattle as the thunderclouds neared. Then it passed as quickly as it had come and, because I had been feeling claustrophobic, I opened the tent and the rain fly and stuck my head out into the cool night air.

There was a chorus of angry, vicious howling from a pack of coyotes, and Jenny and I both stuck our heads out of our tents. Neither Mabel nor Lucy moved or acknowledged the angry pack of coyotes, though they were just out of sight in the valley. We listened as the angry pack cornered and then killed a dog—the dog's barking and whining, distinct from the coyotes', grew more and more furious and fearful until it was silenced in a second and everything was quiet again. Mabel sighed.

The sky was as clear and crystal black as any sky has ever been, and the stars were all bright and glimmering. I rolled my head and shoulders out of the tent and lay on my back, looking up. There were planes up there with signal lights blinking and I was sure those planes were full of lawyers and business men taking late night flights to important business meetings in NYC, Chicago, or L.A. In the far north end of the valley, on top of cold, black shadows of mountains, a lightning storm raged with what we called "heat lightning" when I was a child. And Mabel crawled out of the tent a bit, too, and rested her chin on my arm, sighed, and went to sleep.

But the air smelled cool and green, like the breeze in autumn in Illinois, when the weather bursts both with promise and with the threat of winter, and it made me think of all the autumn nights I have ever spent out beneath an open sky, snuggled together with some woman who I loved, or spent beside the lake with a buddy "fishing" one last time for the season but really just telling stories and listening to music, or spent strolling along aimlessly in this or that city or town, always so thankful for the perfect night weather and sky and always nervous that winter would be long and cold.

BOOK II: FEEL THE SELFISH FURY (D)(i)(a)
A MUEZZIN IN THE TOWER OF DARKNESS CRIES.

My last interaction with Dorsey Cleary took place in late September. There was a final push to get a deal done regarding four or five offshore funds. I think that everyone knew something was happening in the economy, and they were all hustling to get this or that deal done before the money dried up. It seemed like this deal was the absolute and only thing in Dorsey's world. I think it was about a $500 million deal. I wasn't ever clear on the details because it was a complicated structure and the deal was done quickly, so I did not have the necessary time to figure out even what the money was for. All I knew is that there was some money moving around and ending up offshore and that it needed to be done post-haste. My role was extremely limited: I collected the deal documents for the closing book, which is a common busy work task for first year transactional associates, despite the fact that it could be done more cheaply by a paralegal, or a college student who is even cheaper, or by a trained monkey who will likely work for bananas and smokes. I also had to turn changes in documents and to manage the "distro list": I collected and distributed documents to those who needed to see them and distributed redlines of changes that originated both in-house and on the other side of the deal.

One day I stopped by Dorsey's office to pick up some comments to one of the deal documents.

"No track change for these comments," she said, and handed me a hard copy. "Computer was down, so these are in ink."

"I'll get to them," I said. "I actually have another project I'm working on."

"Really? What is it?"

"It's a securitization," I said. "A big one. I've never done a securitization, and it is exciting, so hopefully this one happens."

"Well, it's no rush on these. I have a phone meeting with these guys this afternoon, and I wouldn't mind having the document distributed before then, but the conference call is not about these changes."

"Ok, I will get to it by this afternoon. Probably over lunch."

"That securitization won't happen," she said, as I was on the way out of the office. "It won't happen."

I went to my office and sat down at my desk to go over some deal docs on this potential securitization.[18] It was a massive thing, involving hundreds of corporate entities and billions of dollars, and I was excited to organize all this information and to learn how securitization works. About 15 minutes after I sat down, I got an email from Dorsey (with a couple of other attorneys cc'd) that read something like:

"MY GOD! Where the FUCK IS THE DISTRO?"

I started to type a response and got another email from her.

"I was just talking for like 10 minutes about these changes, thinking they had seen them, and they interrupted me because they had no idea what I was talking about. THEY HAVEN'T SEEN THE CHANGES!!!"

Apparently, the phone conference had been moved up by about five hours and I hadn't been told.

I started to write a response, but then decided to set the changes and distribute them. As I was setting the changes (which took about five minutes), I got another email, also cc'd to a few attorneys.

"I mean, how fucking hard is it? I spoon-fed you the changes. You have to make the changes and email them. Is that difficult?"

I had never been in a situation like that. I did not know how to respond. I think now that the proper way to respond would likely have been an email that read:

---

[18] A securitization is a financing structure in which a company that has streams of revenue called "receivables" creates a separate legal entity called a "special purpose vehicle" ("SPV"), sells those receivables to the SPV, and the SPV issues securities to investors. By doing this, the company can sell future income for cash. Some receivables are more stable than others. For example, receivables that will come from an interest in leases is generally more stable than receivables that will come, say, from students paying back their student loans in an economy where no one can get a job. Note that oftentimes, such arrangements would not be allowed under a so-called "Sharia compliant" finance system because, under Islamic "law", people are prohibited from selling debt on a secondary market.

"Please consider your tone when you are writing to me. Despite
the differences in experience, I would appreciate being treated with
the same respect and decency that I extend to you. As for the
changes, you asked that I distribute them sometime before this
afternoon, which I of course will do. As you now need them sooner,
I am setting them now and will distribute them presently."

Instead, I wrote something like:

"Dorsey, I am sorry for any confusion. I am confused about the
timing on this, and now feel that I have somehow dropped the ball.
I have set your changes now and am making the distribution
presently."

She responded with something like: "It's a bit too late to make a
difference. But send them anyway." Or something like that.

Later that afternoon she sent me an email and wanted me to come to her
office. I left her office door open and sat across the desk from her.

"I question your intensity," she said.

"What?"

"I question your intensity, Tyler. The incident last Friday or two weeks
ago or whenever it was, and now this. This kind of thing wouldn't fly in New
York, you know that? It wouldn't."

"So you question my intensity?"

"Yes," she said. "I don't know if you have what it takes to do this job. Not
at this level."

"Well."

"So, I can't believe I'm saying this, but I don't think you and I should
work together anymore."

"Ok, well if you change your mind or if you find yourself in a bind, feel
free to email me."

Her face fell.

"Wow. I didn't think you'd respond that way."

"Ok," I said.

"I thought you would...take this a little harder."

"Well it sucks," I said. "No one likes to be told that someone doesn't
want to work with them. But in this case there's nothing I can do. You're
wrong about everything in this situation that is material."

"What?"

"You're wrong," I said. "You really have no grounds to question my
intensity, whatever that means—I was here until midnight all last week, too.
And I vomited and passed out last week from the flu, and was still locked up
in my office. And last Friday I actually came here to this office before I left—
and to Cindy's—and neither of you could delegate anything to me. And
today, you asked for that distribution to be made in the afternoon. So..."

"Well, I don't have time to listen to this..."

"Ok," I said. "If you change your mind, let me know."

As I was leaving she called out:

"Tyler! I'm really impressed by how you responded to this situation."

"Ok," I said, and left. I decided that I would never work with her again, no matter if she emailed me or not. I felt a constant, subdued, and passive anger for that woman. I am almost certain that Dorsey was a good and decent person, but she did not treat me like a good and decent person would treat someone else. Even if the distribution kerfuffle had been the result of my error, which it wasn't, it would have been no excuse for treating me that way. I have made so many thousands of mistakes in my life, and would as an attorney, too—it felt sick to be blamed and shamed for something that wasn't my fault, and especially for something that didn't really even matter. Later that month, I decided that I hated her in a way I had never hated anyone. I decided I would never speak to her again, let alone work for her.

I didn't see her again for about four months. By that time, I wasn't even in her practice group anymore. I saw her in Lincoln Park—she was a neighbor of mine, as it turns out—and it was about 11 on a Sunday morning. I was returning from the grocery store, walking up an alleyway west of Clark Street and she came by me in a car. Her husband was driving and her baby was playing in a car seat in the back. Dorsey was passed out in the passenger seat; her hair was all mussed up, and she looked like a corpse. It was 11 a.m. on a Sunday.

I felt great sympathy and pity for her and was afraid.

BOOK II: FEEL THE SELFISH FURY (D)(i)(b)
ONE THING IS CERTAIN, AND THE REST IS LIES.

After that last ridiculous deal went down with Dorsey, I had a long weekend and saw my parents and that type of thing. I talked with Isra a little bit on the phone. When I came back to Sidley the next week, I came back to a completely different world.

There was no work.

Lehman Brothers filed for bankruptcy protection on September 15, 2008, and the financial meltdown hit hard in October. Money dried up overnight. No one was lending. And if no one is lending, then there ain't much work to be done in a practice group that works for lenders. Hallways fell dark and silent. Note indentures and security pledges crumpled into tumbleweeds and blew across the hallways as I walked. Partners who billed out at $800 and $900 an hour sat in their offices playing Brick Breaker on their BlackBerries. I sat down at my desk in October with a cup of coffee and wondered how long it would be until I was laid off. Or how long it would be until we realized we were *living* in the post-apocalypse. They could not afford all of us, could they? If we are not billing? If there is no work for us?

Lawyers from the class of 2008 who went to work in biglaw or finance practice in late 2008 lived and "worked" through an unprecedented level of uncertainty that I hope no future class of attorneys will ever live and work through again. The tension of law school was nothing at all compared to the pressure and anxiety of the biglaw hallways in late 2008. At my firm, alone, there were about 65 brand-new attorneys, fresh out of law school with a national average student loan debt of around $85,000 per law school grad, but with no job experience or legal experience at all, and with no work to do to get legal experience. Few, if any, of us were qualified to strike out alone, there were no jobs, and there was no work to do to get legal experience. It was a bad situation.

I have never been good at sitting still, so I wandered around the hallways and dropped into new associates' offices. Almost none of the new associates were genuinely busy. It didn't matter which floor or which group I walked through. Some of the folks in specialized litigation groups were busy, especially the groups that specialized in white-collar defense and securities work. But there were no deals being made on the deal side, and because there was no financing available at all there was no new work coming into the bankruptcy practice[19] (although everyone knew that would change) because companies often need financing in order to seek bankruptcy protection. There was no regulatory work, there was nothing. All the energy in the country, from the media to the legal field, was focused on Washington and on Wall Street. I watched first year associates pretend to be busy, and pretend to have deadlines, but we all knew it was a charade. There was simply no work for anyone.

I stopped by a partner's office once, looking for work, and we sat there and talked for a while.

"What is next?"

"What do you mean?" I asked.

"Bear Stearns. Lehman Brothers. AIG. Just this year, something like $8 TRILLION in investment losses in the U.S. They nationalized the banks;

---

[19] Companies generally cannot file bankruptcy without banks lending to them because the bankrupt company's prepetition secured creditors generally hold liens against the company's cash under prepetition lending facilities. The bankrupt company's cash is their lenders' cash collateral, so the company cannot use it during a bankruptcy unless they can provide "adequate protection" to their secured creditors. It is difficult to provide "adequate protection" for cash. So most bankruptcy companies must get debtor-in-possession ("DIP") financing to use during the course of the bankruptcy proceedings. DIP lenders provide operating cash for use during the bankruptcy that isn't subject to prepetition liens. DIP money is not always necessary in order for a company in bankruptcy to use its cash and, in some circumstances, a company might get relief from the court to use its lender's security for any number of reasons. Another problem facing companies in bankruptcy is that its prepetition credit facilities will likely (or certainly) be in default at some point during bankruptcy and those credit facilities will be accelerated. Once those credit facilities are accelerated, a bankrupt company obviously will not have access to credit after filing for bankruptcy unless it can get a new lender and new credit facility—so companies will often need a loan to get out of bankruptcy, called "exit financing". There are, of course, several caveats to each of these general observations. But, for these reasons, it is difficult for financially distressed company to even seek bankruptcy protection if there are no banks willing or able to lend.

say they didn't, but they did. And nothing is better. What do we do next?" my partner asked.

"Buy canned food," I joked.

"Is that really where we are?" my partner asked again, and was serious. There was no pretense that my partner was "better" than a lowly first year attorney like me, nor of having any better understanding the world of finance, the current situation. *No one knew anything.* My partner had no idea how the world was going to change in the next few weeks or months. "You might be right."

"I hope not."

"We did this," the partner said. "Not you and me. Not Sidley. But people just like us. Doing the same work. Securitization was Sidley's bread and butter for 10 years, or 20. There was so much work and so much money. What Sidley did was *good*; we are the good guys. But not everyone is a good guy. Some firms put out bad products. And the mortgage market! Sub-primes for people who *couldn't* afford it! They..."

"I know some of those people. I know people who tried to buy $120K houses and the bank said 'No, we'll loan you $200K but not 120K'."

"Whoever is to blame, the products were shit."

"But if the products were shit..."

"Of course the products were shit! Everyone knew that, or everyone that should know. It was sophisticated parties selling to sophisticated parties! The whole decade was a shell game."

"The whole country is a shell game," I said.

"Of course it is. We *know* that. What scares me is that it *looks* like no one knew it. It's like we weren't ready. But *everyone knew*!"

"How *could* we have been ready for what is happening right now?" I asked. "How could the country have been ready for it except by not letting it happen in the first place?"

"I don't know," my partner said. "We should have bought more canned food."

BOOK I: THE MOMENTS THAT TURN US (D)(iii)(a)
IN INFINITE PURSUIT OF THIS AND THAT ENDEAVOUR AND DISPUTE.

Monarch Pass intimidated me. Jenny might have been afraid of Monarch Pass, because she did act like she was, but I cannot be sure. Mabel didn't give a damn about that or any other pass. She'd cross them all.

Monarch Pass crosses the continental divide, so any blood, sweat, or tears we shed on the ascent would make their way through a vast network of waterways to the Atlantic Ocean. But on the other side! On the other side, any blood, sweat, or tears we shed would follow a different set of waterways, to the Pacific Ocean.

Monarch Pass would be the highest we would get on this trip, at about 11,300 feet. For miles and miles, and days and days, locals had been warning us about Monarch Pass—it is about a 10 mile climb, they said, at a 6.2% grade. That is steep enough to call it steep. When I was staying with a law school friend in Colorado Springs, a hundred miles back or so, I had a drink and a bite to eat on the porch with a couple of my host's neighbors—in between telling me how beautiful my host was, even though they had never worked up the gumption to talk to her, they warned me over and over about Monarch.

"You're going down Hwy 50?"

"Yes," I said.

"So you're going over Monarch?"

"Yes."

They shook their heads and took sips of beer or drags off their cigarettes. "Gonna be tough. Over Monarch."

And they'd given me that warning all the way back in Colorado Springs! The closer we got to Monarch, the more bewildered folks became when we said we were going over. People smiled at us and chuckled, because they did not believe we'd make it. And pushing my 130 lb cart up and over that kind of grade for that kind of mileage worried me. It had become late in the year—the word came down to us that several mountains in Colorado had been dusted by snow above the tree line already. Jenny wouldn't have her winter weather clothing until we hit Grand Junction. We had cold nights even back before Wilkerson Pass, and the thought of camping at such an altitude worried us.

"You're doing better," I said to Jenny on our ascent up Poncha Pass on the way to Monarch.

"It's getting easier," she agreed. "But 11 is too high. We can't camp up there."

"I don't want to, either," I said.

"Mabel is fine," Jenny said, and smiled. "She'd be fine. But I don't want to make Lucy sleep that high."

"I agree," I said. "And *I* don't want to sleep that high, either. So we have to make it up and over in a single day."

"We do," she agreed. "I just don't know how I'll do at 11 thousand feet. But...there's a campground at the top, I guess, in case of emergency?"

"Emergency," I agreed. "But we'll have to get over."

"Yes," she said. "And I can do it."

"Yes, you can," I said.

So we split the ascent up into three pieces—a first, tiny bit up to a campground about 15 miles from the summit, then on to the "town" of Monarch, about six miles from the summit, then over the summit and on another 10 or 12 miles to Sargents where we had heard there was a campground. It was still a dicey plan, because if there turned out to be no campground in Sargents, then we would have to stealth camp and would quickly deplete our water reserves. But it was the best plan we could put together, given the circumstances.

On the first night, we slept in a yurt at a campground in the middle of nowhere. It was bitter cold that night, the yurt had no heating system, and the yurt was far too big for our body heat to warm it. I slept poorly, and had nightmares about the night I nearly killed myself of smoke inhalation in a tipi in West Virginia. The next morning, I killed about an hour talking with a sheriff's deputy from Texas, and we heard rumors that there had been bears and a mountain lion in camp that night. That gave us some motivation to hit the road.

We struck out and continued the ascent. It was a clear and beautiful day and there was a lot of shade along the road from the forest around us. We were hardly scared of mountain lions. About halfway up that day, I stepped in the wrong spot and a honeybee stung my foot. It was the first time I'd been stung in maybe 20 years. I was a little worried, because I'd been allergic to bees as a child. I was pretty alarmed that I might end up dying there, and then there would be Jenny with a dead guy and his dog. Two bikers came down the mountain, and I asked them if either might have an EpiPen or some Benadryl, but they didn't have any. We stopped in the shade, and we waited to see if I would start having any trouble breathing.

"Are you, like, really allergic?" Jenny asked.

"I was when I was younger. I don't know now. I *have* Benadryl. I just can't find it." I fumbled through The1976CosworthVega.

"What happens?"

"I swell up," I said. "We just have to wait a minute and see if I start having trouble breathing."

"Are you going to, like, die?"

"No," I said. "I think I'll be ok." I found some Benadryl and took it, just to be safe. We waited for a while, and I did have some difficulty breathing at one point, but I tried to downplay that—I think it was mostly just nerves. My foot swelled a little, and my leg stung for a quite a while, but I don't think I was in any danger from that one sting. We continued up the mountain.

After several hours, we neared the town of Monarch, which, as near as I can tell, consists solely of the Monarch Lodge motel and a few houses behind the Lodge. A young and extremely pregnant lady behind the counter at the Lodge checked us in and, for reasons we could not identify, kept lowering the price for us. Right when we started checking in, we asked for a deal and she told us that she had already given us the lowest rate—then a bit later she took 10 dollars off, and then a bit later took off 10 more, and then a bit later waived the pet fee. It was the strangest and most successful negotiation of my life. The less I say, the better I do, I guess.

We stayed the night there, and I got a chance to eat a decent dinner and Jenny watched Mabel so I was able to spend some time in a hot tub. That was a nice treat, and exceedingly rare on a trip like this.

The next morning we struck out for the top of Monarch Pass. We did the six miles to the top in about 2.5 hours, which is just under a normal, prairie pace. Jenny had some difficulty breathing near the top, but otherwise it was smooth sailing. It was almost too easy. Wilkerson Pass had been a nightmare by comparison. We chalked it up to acclimatization making us stronger and being in better shape, then we stopped at the gift and food stop at the top and ate lunch. The food at the top was bad and pretty expensive. But we took pictures looking out from the continental divide over the Atlantic side of the continent, and we took pictures beside the continental divide sign. On one side of the sign, you are in Atlantic America, but on the other you are in Pacific America. At one point, Mabel and I stood on different halves of the continent. While we stood there beside the sign, an enormous RV pulled into the parking lot and, confused by two people with strollers and dogs and camp gear, sat there for a long time. I think the driver was unsure whether he was allowed to drive past us. People stopped and took our picture when we weren't looking, and a few people asked us to take their picture as they stood beside the sign. We obliged, and talked with a lot of folks.

We met a man on a bike on the top of the pass whose name was Mike. He worked for the EPA in D.C., but had come to Denver for a conference and training so he was using the chance to take some vacation days and bike around Colorado. He had biked across the U.S. a few years earlier, but his trip in Colorado was harder, he said. Locals had convinced him to change his route and his new, improved, and local-approved route had taken him over the continental divide four times in the last four days.

"Everyone in Colorado is just so intense," he said. "I mean, this is 'better' than my route, but it is killing me."

He looked very happy and physically tired.

We headed west down the mountain after about an hour on the top, and down into the pacific side of the continent. The road down the mountain was about 6 to 6.5% decline for about a 10-mile stretch, followed by a mile or so of flat leading into Sargents.

I was almost killed on the descent. Twice.

There are several inescapable truths that one will encounter while walking across the United States. You can't walk from Delaware all the way to Colorado without learning a lot of things that you maybe would rather not know. Chief among these inescapable truths is that American drivers are, by and large, morons who suffer from an overwhelming sense of entitlement. There was no better example of this on this trip than on the Monarch Pass descent.

The Monarch descent on Hwy 50 is a large road that has a large shoulder area in most places. Hwy 50 is at least three lanes all the way down (or up, for the oncoming traffic). There is a lane for drivers heading down the mountain, and two lanes for drivers heading up the mountain. Anyone who has ever driven up a mountain will know that there is a lane for slow moving vehicles and a lane for faster vehicles. So we walked against two lanes on a shoulder that was usually ample.

Walking down a mountain is more dangerous than walking up a mountain for a few reasons. First, if your cart has no breaks, like mine, you must constantly apply backward pressure to the thing to make sure it doesn't escape your grip. Gravity is a constant enemy on a descent. On top of that, downhill walking is painful. You put tremendous pressure on your feet, knees, and hips when you walk downhill. But the most dangerous thing out there on a descent is the parade of drivers who think they own the entire mountain to the exclusion of all others, and who are determined to ascend the mountain at 70 miles per hour, no matter if they are towing a boat or an RV.

And they will not scoot over. At all. Even though there is another empty lane right beside them.

The mind boggles.

When we ascended mountains against cars descending, the cars were generally under control and generally moving at a respectable speed. Drivers often stared, took their hands completely off the wheel, and screamed "what the fuck!" or "are you fucking kidding me?!". (Seriously, I can see through windshields, so I could see what they are saying.) But hands-free driving and insults notwithstanding, the descending driver can be trusted. The ascending driver, on the other hand, is a relentless and greedy beast that delights in nearly killing pedestrians and, if given the chance, would likely kill you and go on about his business.

And I want to be dead serious here for a minute: Even if you have the right of way, and even if someone is walking where they shouldn't be walking (neither of which was the case during my descent from Monarch Pass), *you are not entitled to endanger the life of another person.*

My first brush with death during the descent came when we were about a quarter of the way down the mountain. We were on a portion of the road with an ample shoulder, bounded by a guard rail beyond which was a drop of about 900 feet. We were at a light spot in the traffic, and were breathing easy for a minute but still descending. A red pick up truck, I believe a Ford, pulling a white pop-up camper came zooming up the mountain in front of us in the furthest right lane, the slow lane. There were no cars or trucks or anything in the fast lane. The truck was close to the white line, so Mabel and I pushed over as close to the guardrail as possible.

The red pick up truck, whose driver was looking right at me, right in the eyes, then veered on to the shoulder. I estimate the speed of the truck at about 68 or 70 miles per hour. (Estimating vehicle speed is a skill you pick up on a trip like this.)

The driver maintained eye contact with me and moved farther onto the shoulder.

We have all heard it said that when you are about to die, your whole life flashes before your eyes. That didn't happen. What did flash in front of my eyes was a white pop up camper. It flashed about three inches in front of my eyes. A rope or a strap of some kind on the camper smacked against my cart.

I shouted some unkind words during this episode. And, I swear, although I am not proud of it, I wanted the driver to pull over because I was going to kill him. And I don't mean that in a flamboyant, "I was *soooo* mad!" kind of way. I mean in a very cold, and very rational way, I thought "if that man pulls over, then I am going to kill him". I would have. It was the second, and final, time on the trip that I would have killed a man.

The second time I almost died on the descent was a bit scarier and I am not actually comfortable enough with it to think about it or write about it. Sorry.

That's a big surprise to me about this trip. There are quite a few things that happened that I can't think about. Odd, this.

Work at picnic table; buy beer and drink it in warm breeze. Scrap all Book III. Review November/December timesheets; determine too difficult to write, everyone seems awful in Nov/Dec. Regret many things. See Rosie appear, late afternoon; talk; watch Rosie disappear into office. Greet new Canadian couple, Derrick and Natalie. Sit w/Canadians and talk. Respond to inquiries about Walk; tell them some of story. Observe that Canadians smile a lot; want to do similar trip, were travelers by nature.

R: "Tyler, will you drink a cappuccino if I make you one?"

T: "Just coffee is fine."

R: "TYLER! I want to *practice*."

T: "Ok."

Natalie: "Do you not know how?"

R: "No. I'm *learning*. By *doing*."

Natalie: "I can show you."

R: "You know how?"

T: "All Canadians know about coffee."

Natalie: (laughs) "Yeah. I graduated from coffee college, Second Cup. I'll show you."

See Rosie and Natalie disappear into office; observe Derrick smile, say: "She's a certified barista." Analyze question: Does Derrick love Natalie very much? Conclusion: Likely, yes. Note Canadians all appear calm, well mannered, love a laid back laugh. Hear Natalie talking about coffee; resolve to document lesson w/camera phone. Research issue, Natalie: Natalie was ESL teacher, lived in Korea 5 years, met Derrick there, fell in love, back to Canada, now on vacation. Travel to office to watch and learn. Observe Celio appear, stick head into office, laughed and shook his head, walked away. Attend lecture, Natalie on use of espresso machine: milk container and milk should be cold, hold milk at angle, move container thusly, bang out extra air, swirl, cup should be warm, look for bronze layer atop espresso; learn cappuccino is .3 espresso, .3 steam milk, .3 foam; learn latte is .3 espresso, .7 steam milk; see tops of cappuccinos dusted w/cinnamon.

A Russian man checks into Pedro's Inn, and locals argue loudly in the street. A street dog noses through garbage beside a street vendor.

Drink first cup of Rosie's cappuccino. Research issue: "Is Rosie's cappuccino good?"; conclude: Very promising, room for improvement.

R: "Is it the best cappuccino?"

T: "Close."

R: "There is too much cinnamon."

T: "Impossible. Cinnamon is best."

See night fall. Sip coffees and cappuccinos on patio w/Canadians & Rosie. Ask them for their stories. Research Canadians: determined are wonderful people. Research Rosie: determined is wonderful girl, very funny. Note Canadians get kick out of Rosie. Respond to more inquiries about Walk. Note that I was happy I met the Canadians, Rosie; Miss Celio. See

Celio return later, still in uniform; hear Celio order cappuccino; watch Rosie prepare.

Feel night cool; feel sand flies biting feet, calves. Hear Pedro ring bell in the bar, bought round of Jager shots. Resolve to be inside for next round free shots. Say goodbye when Rosie leaves to make candles and Canadians and I laugh and drink and talk North American politics. Sand flies bite and street dogs roam and the palm fronds crackle in the wind that carries the smell of grilled fish and pork across San Pedro's cobbled streets. Wish the little German girl hadn't left for Guatemala or Honduras.

Bottles clink together and docked boats rise and fall gently on their moorings.

Book I: The Moments That Turn Us (D)(iii)(b)
Sans Wine, sans Song, sans Singer, and—sans End.

The descent from Monarch Pass seemed to take a disproportionately long time. It was only 9 or 10 miles and with gravity in your favor; you would think it would take no time at all. But there are a lot of stops on any descent—stops to rest your joints, stops to negotiate blind corners. The blind corners are the funniest of all the stops. The blind corners ended up being among the safest dangers to negotiate, because we were uber-careful. Beneath Monarch Pass, the shoulder on our side of the road often disappeared before a blind corner, so we had to move to the right hand side of the road. It is neither fun nor safe walking *with* traffic, but sometimes it must be done. So we approached most of the blind corners on the right hand side.

As a single person walking alone, a blind corner can be dangerous. But with two people, it should be as safe as pie. We approached the blind corner on the right and stopped before the turn. One person stays put and watches behind for traffic coming down the mountain. If there is such traffic, that person shouts something like "hey, friend-o, here comes a vehicle that might kill you if you stay in the road" or "car!". The other person ventures out into the down bound lane far enough to see around the corner and determine whether the two should cross the road and re-take the shoulder on the opposite side of the road or to hustle around the blind corner and stay on the right hand side shoulder. This way, it is possible to know whether there are cars coming from either direction and whether or not crossing the road will get you back to a safe shoulder.

The process, which is hard to explain but easy to execute, is nonetheless disastrously comedic in action. There is a lot of inching forward and then running back to the safety of the shoulder. There are a lot of nerves and a lot of funny frustration. But with two people, it can be done safely so long as cars stay on the road.

Still, all the blind corners slowed us down quite a bit. Jenny seemed constitutionally opposed to any and all cooperation; she consistently argued that we should round blind corners on the left side, even where there were no shoulders at all, and more often than not, she would not actually warn me

225

of descending cars. This was because she had never-ending faith in mankind. It was around this time that I first began to notice that Jenny usually did not pull her cart *off* the road when we stopped for breaks—even if she was digging around in her cart for lunch or water, she'd leave her cart and *herself* several inches into the road. We ended up taking a lot of breaks along the road, and it drove me crazy when cars sped by her and she was still in the road. While we were stopped that day, we saw several fresh signs of mountain lions—fresh tracks, fresh scat. Several. That actually sped us up a great deal, and probably even cancelled out all the time lost blind corners.

Just before the final descent, we stopped in a roadside pullover and took in a great view of the valley below us.

When we reached the bottom of the mountain in Gunnison National Forest, the road flattened out immediately and we could see the town of Sargents a few miles up the road. It was a relief to be off the mountain, on flat ground, back in a land of green grass and cattle. Sargents is in another of Colorado's valleys, so splendid and gorgeous in the late afternoon Sun. On one side of us, we could see over a rolling plateau to rocky outcrops high on top of mountains 10 and 20 miles away. On the other side of us, the Sun chased shadows across bulbous green hills, and sometimes we could see little black dots walking and grazing on the grassy hills.

We tented in at the campgrounds behind the Trading Post at Sargents. All four of us were tired, but we talked at some length with a couple of cyclists who rode into camp in the night. They were Andrew and Scott and they were both as dirty as I was—they were cycling the Continental Divide Trail from Banff in Canada all the way down to the Mexican border. Scott had recently set the world record for a solo bicycle ride from Prudhoe Bay, Alaska, down to the southern tip of Argentina in 125 days, beating the old record by almost 20 days. He was a Scottish fellow and his hair and skin were burned and dried from the exposure. Those two were up and out of camp before I was awake and they left me with a stash of electrolyte tabs.

We lost the next day to the rain, and Jenny couldn't bear the idea of sleeping in a tent again, so she rented a cabin at the campgrounds. It was close quarters and I would rather have stayed in my tent. I got coffee at the Trading Post and listened to an old man rant about the Post Office— apparently Congress was now threatening to close the Post Office. He thought it was a good idea because private actors in the free market would do the job. UPS could do it, he said, and Fed Ex. One old friend of his asked: "Do you think UPS or Fed Ex is going to come all the way out here just to deliver one or two social security checks? Not going to happen." The second old man was right.

We spent the day reading and watching the rain and not stretching. Jenny said she was very sore, and I was sore, too, but we didn't do any stretching or walking. It was cold and rainy that night, and I was worried that we'd lost too much time and that winter was coming. We were still pretty high in the mountains where snow comes early. We woke and hiked out early the next morning in cold weather and with rain threatening.

"We have to just hit it," I said.

"It's a long ways," Jenny said. "I don't mind the rain so long as I'm prepared."

"You have very little cold weather clothing," I said. "And cold weather is coming. We have to make it to Gunnison today."

"That's 32 miles," she said.

"We're doing that," I said. "We're going to Gunnison today."

"I don't know if I can do that. But the thing about walking somewhere is that you won't get there unless you walk there."

"You'll have to," I said. "Because I'm not staying up here any longer."

We hiked hard that day, stopping only to drink and once to rest and eat. The dogs were fine, and Jenny never complained *verbally*, but I could tell she was not happy. I could have complained, too, because it was a long hike and I hadn't eaten enough the past several days. I had it in my mind that I wasn't hungry, so when we stopped to eat, I had a Snickers bar and that was all. I found an iPhone on the road into Gunnison, and called people in the phone's address book until I could locate the owner. I thought for a moment about keeping the phone to use as a camera, but it made no sense to keep the phone when I could find the true owner. We hobbled into Gunnison early that evening and got a motel room on the edge of town.

We were later getting started the next morning because Jenny and I had errands to run in Gunnison and we didn't think we'd make it far that day, anyway. I was weak when I woke up, but was not sore at all. Jenny went off to do things in Gunnison and I stopped by the post office where I mailed off the iPhone to its owner and picked up a package sent to me by a Friend of the Walk—an attorney in Delaware sent me a new camera because, she said, the pictures I posted on Twitter were not good enough. It was a nice camera, and I imagine it cost her about $500 with all the accessories. I resolved to take more pictures.

I felt ill after that, like I was dying. I was not in pain, but it felt like I was dying on a cellular level. I was worried when Mabel and I left the Post Office, because I thought I was going to die. I latched Mabel to the cart outside the Firebrand Café and went in to order something to eat. Their sign advertised a six oz cup of tomato soup for about $1.75. I didn't even bother to straighten my clothes or adjust my hat before I went in—all that pride was long behind me. I placed my order with the lady behind the counter.

"Hiking?" she asked.

"Yup, me and the dog. Came from Delaware and headed for California. We did about 60 miles in the last three or four days. Were about 20 miles up and over Monarch."

"You came over Monarch?" she asked, and nodded.

"Yeah. Lost the day before yesterday, but we were 32 miles into Gunnison yesterday. Today I feel like I might be dying."

"That bad?" she asked, smiling.

"Yeah. I'm not in any pain, but I feel like I might be dying. I'm not sure I'm thinking straight. I might not have eaten enough yesterday."

"How much did you eat?"

"I had a Snickers," I said.

I sat down at a table by the window so I could watch Mabel and I tried to read the instructions to my new camera, but my brain wouldn't focus on the words. Then the lady brought out about 64 ounces of soup and six toasted and buttered bagels.

"The guy cooking heard you," she said. "He's a long distance cyclist. He said that you have either altitude sickness or altitude exhaustion and that if you don't eat this you might die."

"Ok," I said. And I ate it all. I ate it all and it felt like I had eaten nothing, but I was a bit stronger. I thanked them and spoke with the cook a little bit. He was a serious man who had ridden cross-country a few times. He wasn't a leisurely, touring cyclist. He did tough routes and tried to do them quickly, and he did it for no reason whatsoever. He and I related pretty well.

Jenny showed up complaining about the same symptoms I'd had, and I told her we needed to eat. So we checked into a motel on the other side of town near a grocery store and bought a bunch of food. I ate a chicken and drank seven Sprites. I can't remember what Jenny ate, but it was quite a bit and she started feeling better immediately.

That night I could hardly sleep because I was so excited. That day had been *brilliant.* I had pushed myself literally to the brink of death and had lived to tell about it. It meant something to me that I had pushed so hard and so fast that I might not have *reached* my physical limit, but I had gotten close enough to have an idea where it is. I resolved to eat more for the remainder of the trip.

Jenny hated me. In her mind, I'd pushed her too hard and too fast and caused her pain and nearly death. For some reason, she didn't see the experience as a brilliant test of the will and endurance of mankind. Our relationship, or our *espirit d'corps*, had been strained since the first day, but the Monarch debacle increased the tension between us. Some people do not revel in pushing themselves so hard. Some people do not want to hike like that; some people do not want to bill 3200 hours a year at a large law firm. People want different things, and I should have been a little more sensitive to that.

Still, I do not regret my decision to push us that fast. Gunnison is at 7700 feet and it is one of the coldest places in the United States due to its location at the bottom of valleys. The season was late already and we *needed* to be out of the mountains and down to a safer elevation. If we had to hike hard and fast to do it, then we would. Jenny would not be getting cold weather clothes until Grand Junction where my law school friend Don Wessell had taken delivery of a package from Jenny's mother. We had to get to Grand Junction, and we had to get down off the western slope of the Rockies before the weather came.

BOOK II: FEEL THE SELFISH FURY (D)(ii)
WHAT, WITHOUT ASKING, HITHER HURRIED WHENCE?

About a month into Isra's 3L year, she called me and gchatted me. It had been about six weeks since she'd broken it off with me. We danced around some issues for a while, but eventually, after a day or so, she came out with it. She wanted back with me.

"Did he break it off with you?" I asked, because I figured she'd been seeing someone else.

"No," she said. "I just think I needed to know if I *really* wanted to be with you, or something. After a while, I was just like, 'this is stupid. I want to be with Tyler all the time'."

I was flattered and my heart was all filled up when she said it. But I was angry and hurt, so it took us a long time on the phone to talk through what was going on. The bar exam had been a silly time, and combined with the economic collapse, I was feeling pretty confused. If I had failed the bar, I would have been out of job and could *never* have hoped to pay off my student loans. And Isra had not handled that stress well, at all. Then she had been offended and put out that I asked for space to study, and she left me right before I started work at the new firm. That was all a lot to take in. And she was leaving the country in January, anyway, for a four-month study abroad program in New Zealand.

"This is tough," I said. "I don't think we...or at least 'I'...I don't know. If we get back together now for, what, two months? And then you're off to New Zealand? I don't think that will work."

"What do you mean?"

"We aren't in a place where we can survive that. Not this relationship," I said. "You hurt me and it will take time for me to trust you again. And if you run off to New Zealand, I don't think we can make it through that as a couple. So what's the point?"

I'd thought about it all and analyzed it all, and I was right: Our relationship wouldn't have worked out like that. I knew that I would not have waited around for her, not after she had bailed on me. And so I wanted to give her a chance to say no and get out, for good. Of course she loved me, I thought, but I didn't think we would work together. It didn't matter that I loved her and that I wanted to marry her—what mattered was that she needed to figure out what she wanted from me and from her life.

"You can't force me to not go," she said. "I've already bought the tickets!"

"I know!" I said. "I'm not asking you not to go. I'm just saying that this relationship isn't strong enough right now to make it through this as a long distance thing. So why should we start up again and waste another two months?" I should have had the guts right there to end the whole thing.

This went back and forth for a long time until she finally, crying, told me that she wanted to cancel her trip to New Zealand to be with me. Four hours later, on a Thursday night, she walked into my Lincoln Park apartment that she had helped pick out. She was nervous and coy, and then fell against my chest and hugged me.

We were back together and it was great again. We were on the phone all the time, and every weekend (and some weekdays) she was in Chicago with me or I would go to Iowa City to see her. We did fun things like see Prairie Home Companion live, and see shows. And she was always smiling and happy and we were in love. But she, too, had conditions on our getting back together. She wanted three things: 1) to get married, 2) to get a puppy, and 3) a post-bar trip to Oregon.

"You want to get married?" I asked.

"Yes."

"I will get the ring this week," I said.

"I want shiny things. I can't help it, but I do."

"I will get the ring this week."

"We can't get engaged right now," she said. "Er, we could, but we can't tell anyone in my family. Not until my sister is engaged. Or until she's too old to be offended."

"When will that be?"

"I don't know."

"When?"

"I don't know."

"Ok," I said, "How about I get you an engagement ring this week that's just between you and me. It won't be extravagant, but it will be nice. And then when we set the date, we'll get the real thing?"

I got her a ring in Chicago's Jewelers' Row. The ring that caught my eye was a pretty thing with diamonds and emeralds. From time to time I have pretty good taste, and that was one of the times. I bonded pretty well with the guy who owned the shop.

"Listen," I said. "Weird request. Can I borrow this thing for about an hour and bring it right back and either buy it or find something else?"

"Why?"

"I need to check something."

"Ok," he said. "I trust you. But leave your ID."

"No worries."

I took the ring back to Sidley and went to the office of a first-year associate in the banking group who I worked with. He was a great guy, and had almost the same skin tone as Isra.

"Hey, Man, weird question," I said. "Can you put this ring on so I can see what this looks like against your skin?"

"Is it for Isra?" he asked.

"It is. If it looks good."

He slid it onto his pinky.

"Oh my God!" he said. "This thing is beautiful! It will look great on her."

I bought it that day and gave it to her shortly thereafter.

She was delighted.

BOOK II: FEEL THE SELFISH FURY (D)(iii)
WHAT BOOTS IT TO REPEAT HOW TIME IS SLIPPING UNDERNEATH OUR FEET.

The work never came back in November or December. A senior associate started me on a couple of projects, only to tell me "pencils down" after a few hours. There were banks and companies out there who wanted to do deals, but no one could get their heads around the risk, I think. No one knew, for example, what the fall out from the AIG situation would be, or what the fall out of all the credit default swaps would be. No one knew which assets, if any, were good. So a few deals got started, but stopped in the first few steps. And here's the real deal: Everyone in finance had known all of this for a while, but by November, it was affecting *everyone*—you know, the "little people", who, I don't know, work, and who do things and build things. People were out of work, people were scared, and the economy all but stopped.

I went to work every day and wondered if it would be the day they would lay us all off. If you mentioned the fear to a senior associate or a partner, they did their best to put you at ease. The rallying cry was "Sidley has *never* done layoffs" and followed up with "and even if they did, they wouldn't lay off *first year associates*". The prospect of being a laid off first year associate in that economy was so frightening that it made people sick. I saw people get sick in the bathroom from the stress. But I convinced myself that everything would be fine, and the work would come back. I saw Isra on the weekends, and sometime during the weeks, and she and I shopped for an apartment to move into in March. I believed that things would work out. And first years wouldn't be laid off! No firm ever lays off first years!

Well, first years were laid off at biglaw firms.

The day it happened sent a shock through first year associates across the country. It was Latham and Watkins[20] who did it first, and they suffered a public relations backlash. The news of the layoffs hit Above the Law quickly, and we first years started making phone calls to each other. I knew about the layoffs slightly ahead of the curve because a law school friend of mine had gone to Latham in Chicago and had been one of the first to get the axe. She changed her gchat status update to "Got laid (off)". We chatted a second. She was crying, and she told me that her mentor had come to tell her the news and that her mentor had cried, too. The first years at Latham got something like six months' salary and they could use their offices to look for work. Six months' salary at $160,000/yr is nothing to sneeze at, but it couldn't keep a person going in the city for that long with big monthly student loan payments.

True to their word, Sidley didn't lay off first year associates. Instead, a few first years were offered something like $80,000 if they could find a public interest job to hide in for a year, and they called it a fellowship program. Their jobs would still be there at Sidley at the end of the year when it was time to come back. (To the best of my knowledge, Sidley would have hired back any of those who took the year deferral, but I don't remember any of those folks actually coming back.) Other firms adopted the "fund public interest jobs" policy to avoid doing layoffs. The impact of that policy was that public interest jobs became even harder to get that year because the

---

[20] Latham & Watkins is one of the largest, most prominent law firms in the world. Originally based in Los Angeles, it now employs 2000 attorneys in 31 offices across the globe. Lathan & Watkins has regularly posted enormous profits and was the first U.S. law firm to eclipse $2 billion in yearly gross revenue in 2007. However, only a year later, in the face of falling profits and a bad economy, Latham laid off 190 associate attorneys and deferred the starting dates of incoming associates. No partners in any of its offices were de-equitized or similarly laid off.

market was flooded with highly talented young attorneys who were working *at no cost to the public interest agency.* Big firms like Sidley were footing the bill! Isra was looking for a public interest job in Chicago, and she would be affected by the influx of these attorneys who worked at no cost to cash-strapped public interest places. Isra, for example, had her heart set on working for a particular public interest agency in Chicago, and I knew of at least a few attorneys from big firms who had left for the year to work at that agency. It would be hard for Isra to find a job, and she knew it. But I told her not to worry, because I would take care of her until she found something.

I was bored out of my mind by the end of December and was frustrated by spending each day in fear of being laid off. So I became proactive. I went to the head of my group and asked if I could start looking for work in other groups. That was a risky move, I think, because within each law firm there is competition among and between groups, and the groups value loyalty. But the head of the Banking and Financial Transactions group was an absolutely great guy, so far as I could tell, and we got along quite well. He was a tall and jovial guy who wore a backpack instead of carrying a briefcase, and everyone loved him. We'd talked about hiking and camping, which we both loved. He said that I could look for work in other groups, but that he doubted I would find anything.

"Then could I actually transfer to the Environmental group?" I asked. That was probably even riskier. Environmental had been my first choice of groups, anyway. He said he would look into it for me, and I don't doubt that he did. But I never heard another word about that. Instead, he stopped by my office during the last week of December.

"There are going to be some changes," he began. I thought for sure that this was it, this was the moment I would be laid off, and, frankly, I wouldn't have cared so much so long as there was a separation package of a $100K or so. But I didn't get laid off. "We've never done anything like this. But times are very unstable right now, and the market is always moving. The firm wants to migrate a few attorneys into the Bankruptcy group—just for a year!—because they are overrun with work up there right now. There are first years there on track to bill 3000 hours, and that's not what we want for first years—those are second year hours. They have too much work and not enough people. So the firm is prepared to ask for volunteers to transfer to the Bankruptcy group."

"Have you asked anyone yet?" I asked.

"You're the first. But don't...I mean, don't read into that. I asked you first because you've got the closest office to mine. From here I'm headed to everyone else's offices."

"Look," I said, and he appreciated my straightforward tone, I think, "I'm hearing this as basically 'Volunteer to move to bankruptcy, or there will be layoffs'."

"I'm not saying that," he said. "I'm not saying that."

"But it's there?"

"Of course it is there," he said. "And I don't know *who* would be laid off. I mean, none of you have done anything. The only one of you whose job would be safe, for sure, is Colin. And that's because he got some actual experience before the collapse."

"The rest of us, who knows?" I asked.

"I don't know how that would happen if it ever came to it. And I'm not saying it would come to it."

"But it would. I'm saying that," I said. "I don't have any desire to work in the Bankruptcy group. I have not worked with them, and I don't like the work that they do, and I'm not sure about the people there."

"You did that assignment for Pat Baker in the bankruptcy group," he said.

"Yes, that one. I did that, but I got that fed to me from a partner in this group. I don't have *any* desire to go to that group, but I *do* have a desire to pay my rent. I'm not in charge here."

"I know," he said, and nodded.

"So do whatever you have to do with me. I'll go wherever, but I'm not going to volunteer. Not unless it means someone's job. If you need to move me, you can. But I'm not going to volunteer unless it gets down to either 1) I volunteer or 2) one of us loses our job."

"Understood," he said. "Anyone?"

"Yes. Before anyone loses their job, I would volunteer."

"Understood."

He left, and I knew my days in the group were over.

I heard later that day that a few of the banking first years had volunteered and a few had vehemently opposed it. Two, in particular, had said they would quit rather than go. And those two folks kept their jobs in the Banking group. The rest of us, three in all, were moved to the bankruptcy practice in January of 2009. For me, it meant moving up one floor and into a windowless interior office.

"Are you happy about this?" Isra asked me.

"No," I said. "I'm not happy or unhappy about it. I mean, I would rather go to Environmental or some other group. But I'm happy and grateful that I'm keeping a job."

"Are you happy?"

"Yes," I said. "I think so."

"I think you should quit," she said. "I think you should just quit."

"Who would pay our rent?"

"Fuck you. You know I'm trying to find a job."

"I know," I said. "I'm just being realistic. When we move into the South Loop in March, someone will have to pay the rent. I can pay it by myself so long as I am employed. But without a job?"

"I'll find something," she said.

She didn't find anything, really. She looked all over the country and couldn't find a job. Isra finally found a way to work at the agency she'd been desperate to land a job at through some program to encourage volunteerism. She got paid something like $15,000/yr and got a rent stipend of something like $400 a month. If she had had substantial student loans (like I did, for example), she could never have meaningfully paid down her loans with that income. We were excited about moving in together, because we hadn't really lived together since our 3L year when we essentially lived together. She had already started getting nervous about money and about the bar exam, but the thought of getting a puppy dog kept her going and she sent me links from dailypuppy.com every day and sent me links to various puppies available on petfinder.com.

But that was all a few months away.

Midway through January, I moved officially to my windowless office in the bankruptcy practice and was immediately staffed on a bankruptcy that was to file shortly. We were going to file Cairo Company[21] in bankruptcy court in a little over a month. Cairo was a mid-market company. A senior associate in the bankruptcy group would more-or-less lead the bankruptcy. I could hardly contain how excited I was to *finally* be getting some work. After my first meeting with the Cairo team, I could hardly sleep that night. My life and my career were finally starting!

I did not see the Sun that February. I had a windowless office, and the Sun rises late and sets early in a Chicago February. There was more work than I could ever imagine, and at first I felt like I was feasting after an exile in the desert. My job and my career would be safe here. It wouldn't be the kind of work that I wanted, but it was work. Isra and I were safe. We could have a few years to live together and save, and maybe we could finally get married. I could afford to get her a nice ring like she wanted. We could get a car eventually, if we wanted to, and buy a house. We were going to be safe and happy. That made me happy.

But I did not see the Sun that month.

A massive amount of preparation work goes into filing a Chapter 11 bankruptcy.[22] I worked on the schedules, and the first day motions, and the

---

[21] I've changed the name of this and every other company mentioned in this story.

[22] When a company has debt that it cannot pay, that company will sometimes seek the protection of the federal bankruptcy court. As soon as a bankruptcy is filed, the debtor's creditors are subject to an "automatic stay", which means that creditors cannot take action against the company or its bankruptcy estate. In short, its creditors can no longer pursue collection of the debts the company may owe to them, and creditors cannot cancel or amend contracts without the company's consent. On the other hand, the company in bankruptcy cannot do anything of any significance that would affect or impact the value of the company without court approval and generally cannot access its cash accounts, which constitute its secured lender's "cash collateral", or pay pre-petition creditors without court approval. In effect, the court and the attorneys are in control of the company. Before filing, the debtor and its attorneys must prepare a ton of materials. Chief among them are the "schedules", which are schedules of all the company's assets and liabilities. (The schedules are generally not filed on the first day, at least not when massive companies file, but work on the schedules begins pre-petition. In practice, there are often assets and liabilities that are missed, but the schedules can later be amended.) In addition to the schedules, the company and its attorneys must draft and file a barrage of "first day motions", which are filed on the first day of the bankruptcy, or shortly thereafter, and seek approval to pay certain pre-petition liabilities. Because the court is in charge of the bankruptcy estate from the moment the bankruptcy is filed, it is necessary for a company to get pre-approval to do all manner of things that it must do to keep in business. For example, the company must continue to pay its employees—therefore, the company must file a first day motion asking for permission to continue paying its employees. Likewise, the

234

motions to retain professionals, and it was never-ending. It was the first time I'd ever done anything as a true "professional" in a "profession". The work I was doing was hardly exciting or challenging. There are forms for almost everything and you only have to change names and numbers and dates. Every now and again you might run into something in a form that doesn't make sense anymore and that should be changed; sometimes the law has changed and the forms need to be updated. But, on the whole, drafting administrative and first-day motions is an exercise in plagiarism—or, at least, an exercise in "creative comparison". The work was never-ending, and that felt good to me after all those months of treading water. But the work wasn't really "legal work" like you'd imagine it to be; it was data wrangling, as much as anything.

Isra hated how busy I was, of course, because she was still stuck in Iowa City and I was stuck at the office until late at night and had less and less time to talk with her. We spoke every day. She came to visit me a few times that month. For Valentine's Day that year, we went to eat at Boka in Lincoln Park. She was so incredibly beautiful that night that Boka became my favorite restaurant.

My eyeballs strained more than they ever had in law school. In law school, they teach you that you will have to strain your eyes and your mind when you are an attorney engaged in close reading of cases and laws. But they are wrong. At a big firm, during your first couple of years, you have to strain your eyes close reading the placement of commas. You have to strain your eyes reading the chicken-scratched comments of some overworked associate or some over-worked partner who barely has time to call his husband or wife, let alone to give you comments on some motion that doesn't matter. And, of course, all of the motions *matter*, but they are so ordinary course that they hardly *actually* matter. No one will read them closely. No one will object to them. They will simply be filed and approved. The judge won't have enough time to actually read the motion to approve payment for utilities or to pay the critical vendors who provide the raw materials for the business. It's precisely because of that that first years get

---

company must continue to pay the power bill and the phone bill and other utilities, so there is a utilities motion. Most companies have critical vendors—vendors from whom they buy materials without which the company could not continue operating, so there is a critical vendors motion. There are others, as well. The most important, from the standpoint of the attorneys, is probably the motion to retain the firm—the company files a motion to retain the law firm handling their bankruptcy.

Every bankruptcy needs a whole crew of professionals, from attorneys and consultants to accountants, and every professional firm that is retained specifically for the bankruptcy must be approved by motion to the court. Sometimes the board of directors will need its own firm of attorneys because they have interests that are not 100% aligned with the interests of the company. For each of these firms, there must be a motion to retain, and that requires statements from the firm about their fees and about their conflicts. Then there are ordinary course professionals, which are professionals that the company was already using or would probably have had to retain even if there had been no bankruptcy filing, and that takes a motion to retain all of them.

(stuck with) the chance to hone their skills on these vitally important filings. And they *are* vitally important filings.

And the fact is that I was *lucky* to have had the chance. The great majority of first year associates at biglaw spend their first year or two doing discovery and due diligence projects. They get hired at these white shoe firms, and then they are shipped off to a warehouse somewhere where they spend all day and all night sifting through endless bankers' boxes of documents. Mindless nonsense and wheel spinning. And that is how you fit in and succeed: You monopolize as much of the mindless nonsense as you can; you identify lines of work from partners, and you grab hold of those lines of work to the exclusion of all other associates in your group, because *only hours matter*. It is a *business* more than a profession. In corporate law, you eat what you kill, and if you ain't billing, you ain't killing.

It doesn't have to be this way.

Book I: The Moments That Turn Us (D)(iv)
In that old Potter's Shop I stood alone.

We hiked into and through a different world outside of Gunnison. The western slope of the Rockies is a different universe of topography, climate, flora, and fauna than the eastern slope. We followed the Gunnison River toward the Blue Mesa Reservoir. This was canyon country. This was a country of dry earth and sagebrush. It was desert country, the American Southwest. We saw open country and sparse sad scrub brush poking out of the desiccated earth, dry stony outcroppings. We entered new country, and I thought back: the Eastern Seaboard, the Appalachians, the rolling hills of Ohio and Indiana, the Illinois prairie, the Tall Grass Prairie of Iowa and Nebraska, high and arid western Nebraska and eastern Colorado, the Rocky Mountains, and now the American Southwest. We had come a long way, through many distinct regions. We were only two or three days hike from Montrose, Colorado, when we could say without reservation that we had hiked over the Rocky Mountains. It was a good feeling.

There was not much traffic that day and that was a nice change. The weather played hell with us, though—it was a hot day with bright Sunlight, but the wind was cold, so it was difficult to maintain a comfortable temperature.

The ridges and peaks around the Blue Mesa Reservoir are rocky and rugged. The air and land are dry, but the reservoir is deep and blue with water that will be sent off to Arizona and California. We camped that night in the Curecanti National Recreation Area, which runs along the river and the reservoir. A Curecanti officer stopped to talk with us, and told us he loved what we were doing because he was a minimalist in his life, too. Mabel stared at him and then jumped up with her paws on the driver's side door of the truck. I recognized that I had become a minimalist, if I hadn't been before. There are campgrounds there, with an office and pay showers but neither Jenny nor I were interested in paying for a shower. The officers at the welcome center were kind and informative. That night I slept under a southwestern sky for the first time in many years, and I was a bit worried because Jenny had no idea what the southwest was like. She still didn't seem to understand that there is no water.

We were not in dire need of supplies when we left the Curecanti National Recreation Area. We had plenty of water and plenty of food to get us all the way to Montrose and, if not, at least to Cimarron. But nothing beats the frustration of the road like a hot sandwich and an ice cold Mexican Coca Cola. Our only hope for that was Sapinero, a little speck of a town on the map.

People told us for miles and miles around that there was simply nothing in Sapinero. There had been a gas station "of sorts" there, but it had closed down years before. No, we had no hope for anything in Sapinero.

We hiked along the Gunnison River and Blue Mesa Reservoir. The Earth was dusty and dry and grass didn't grow. The only color out here, besides the burnt yellow ground, came from the scrub brush that looks like twisted bark skeletons, and occasional evergreen things that sprouted dull yellow flowers. In some low places there were errant trees, their seeds having been dropped accidentally near this river, this man made reservoir. In this land, there are rock formations—mesas, cliffs worn scraggly from a million years of erosion. There are mysterious standing stones, and sheer cliff faces, all the colors of rock and shadow.

No, we had no hope for Sapinero.

It was either burn in the Sun or freeze in the wind. Our pace was strong, despite it all. We rounded the last corner into Sapinero and, over the green ridge in front of us, there was a faded, ageless sign that read "Gas" and a fluttering American flag beside it.

"Good sign," I said. "Could be open. They got a flag up there."

"I've been fooled by flags before," Jenny said.

"Me, too. But it is a good sign."

Around the corner, and up a steep cliffside, there was a squat old building with a brilliant new coat of yellow paint and it read "Sapinero Village Store" in red paint. So we climbed the hill and ate like fools. I had a microwave sandwich, one of those boxed gas-station pies, two Mexican Cokes, a Snickers, and some fig Newtons. One big surprise about a cross-country hike is how poorly a person eats. Jenny, so far as I could tell, ate only peanut butter and chocolate covered pretzels unless we stopped by a gas station. I lived mostly on gas station food and powdered milk by then. We ate on the front porch of the store while the storeowner paced around and spoke on her cell phone about important matters that I tried not to eavesdrop on.

Sapinero is a collection of houses and buildings that are built on a cliff side around a giant curve in the Blue Mesa Reservoir. Although we were technically in a canyon, it does not feel like a canyon. Instead, because the water in the reservoir is so blue, and because the cliff sides are so steep, it feels like a town built on an ocean inlet in a dry, Mediterranean country except with more 4x4 trucks and ATVs.

The old city of Sapinero now sits under 200 feet of reservoir water. The reservoir went up in the 1960s. The locals—or the old locals who are still locals—are torn on the value of the reservoir. It brings some recreational tourism in, sure. But hundreds of acres of farmland were lost to the reservoir—and the water in the reservoir is for agricultural irrigation in far-off places like California and Arizona. It is difficult to see the big picture when the little picture is your home and livelihood. At any rate, the reservoir went up, and life goes on. And, anyway, not everything in Old Sapinero was lost. Someone moved some of the shacks, buildings, and the old schoolhouse—picked them up and moved them higher up the canyon wall to where they now sit at the Sapinero Campgrounds, Village Store, and Murph's Place. Jim Murphy and Jeri Tharp bought the place a time back and had been cleaning it up for the last year. The previous owners had given up on it in 2004.

Jim told us about the substantial work he had done to the place, moving cubic yard after cubic yard of debris off the property, painting, replacing fixtures in the shacks at the top of the property, plumbing, etc. I was pretty beat and was having a hard time following along as Jim spoke because Jim is an energetic man who speaks very quickly. But a few things leapt out me from Jim's speech: 1) it was 8 miles to the next campground, 2) that the next 8 miles were pretty much straight up hill, and 3) there were shacks at the top of the hill. I inquired about the shacks. They had water and electric, and down the hill was a "bathhouse" with shower and toilet, and the shacks were 25 or 30 bucks a night. Hell, any campground is going to be at least 12 or 15 bucks a night.

"Well", he said, "hop in my truck and I'll take you up there! See if it suits ya!"

It was a steep, steep, steep climb up to the shacks, and Jim talked the whole way. He was an absolute encyclopedia of advice about the upcoming 50 or so miles of our trip. He told me where we would expect hills, how big the hills were, where we could camp and how much it would cost, where we could camp for free, and on and on.

The shacks are not on the top of the canyon wall, but pretty close. They look like they may have been old quarters for miners or farmhands.

These shacks were amazing. Rustic? Yes. And I couldn't pass up the chance to stay in these cabins, especially with the next campground eight miles away, uphill. Jim had three shacks up and running: the standard, two beds, stove, and a sink; the bunkhouse, four beds, stove, and a sink; and "The Luvshack", which had one bed, stove and sink, and an old fashioned curtained changing area. The Luvshack also had wallpaper depicting nude Roman women. I chose the standard shack. Jim gave us (and all our gear) a ride up the canyon to the shack and we settled in.

Jenny let Lucy out just before Sundown and there was a doe deer about two feet from the door. Lucy bolted after it and disappeared up the canyon wall. By the time Jenny told me what had happened and I had gone outside, Lucy was nearly to the top of the ridge. I snapped a picture of Lucy silhouetted on the top of the ridge and assumed it would be the last I saw of her. Inside, I leashed Mabel up and took her out to search for Lucy. Jenny had gone loping up the canyon without a flashlight, so I took a flashlight, too. Mabel was on the trail and pulling hard to try to get us to catch up with Lucy, but Jenny was confident that Lucy would come back. She did, in her own time, and it was pitch black out when we all walked back to the shack.

We hiked out of Sapinero into and out of two steep canyons. One, the Black Canyon of the Gunnison, is as beautiful and mysterious as its name implies. From Sapinero to Montrose, we crossed through southwestern terrain, then descended into forested canyons, and climbed the steep roads up canyon walls. Drivers were angry that we were there, but some smiled and honked at us. We saw big buck deer and heard the rustling of a million forest critters. The weather was perfect. But Jenny had started having tire problems on her stroller. We lost a lot of time in Colorado, stopping to fix or inflate tires.

Everyone we spoke with warned us that we were in mountain lion country. There were warning signs posted at the gas station in Sapinero—the signs told us we were in mountain lion country and told us how to behave if we saw one. I could not use the iPod there in lion country, because they are sneaky and you must have your wits and your senses about you. It was a pleasant place to be without music, though, and as I walked I thought about how difficult it would have been to cross Iowa and Nebraska in silence.

We camped again near Cimarron at a campground and restaurant. The restaurant had fresh pie made daily on-site and there were hummingbirds flitting about the front porch of the place. Jenny and I each set up a camp near the quiet brook behind the restaurant.

"Bears?" she asked.

"Probably," I said. "But we're camped right beside a couple of trash cans...so hanging the bear vaults is probably overkill."

"Eh," she said. And she got into her tent.

"Listen...when we get into Montrose, we have to go to Wal-Mart or somewhere like it and you need to get foam inner tubes for that thing."

"Think they'd have them in my size?" she asked. "How much are they?"

"They're probably a bit more expensive than regular inner tubes. I'm getting some. We can't have flats in Utah."

"I'll get some slime," she said. "Just a can of slime."

"That stuff hasn't really been working for you so far. Anyway, we should do that. Can't have a flat in Utah—and I imagine there are any number of thorns and cacti in Utah."

We ate pie and malts and sandwiches at the restaurant and talked with the owner and a German lady who worked there, and then Jenny went to sleep. Mabel and I climbed into our tent and I lay awake wondering how to convince Jenny that she needed to get foam inner tubes. Or how to convince her to carry more water instead of using mine. Staying mobile is key in the desert, otherwise you can't make it through the big dry stretches. We had two separate 100-mile stretches without access to water coming up. I could carry enough for *me* and for *Mabel*, but not for Jenny and Lucy. And if that weren't unsettling enough, she also now was refusing in her passive way to get her stroller "up to code". I was certain that agreeing to help her across the mountains and the desert had been an enormous mistake on my part: She would make it, but the question was how much it was going to cost me.

That night, I put Mabel on a long leash and walked about 500 feet away to use the campground showers. Mabel followed me to the end of her leash, and then whined a few times when I kept going. I showered and Mabel was still sitting there, in the exact same spot, when I finished showering and walked back to the camp. I don't think she'd taken her eyes off of that place where I'd disappeared the whole while I was gone.

We hiked one pass the next day (although the two canyons were like hiking passes) and once we'd climbed the final pass of the Rockies we were on a high ridge looking down over Montrose, Colorado.

"That's it down there," I said. "That's the other side of the Rockies."

"I can't believe I just walked across the Rocky Mountains," Jenny said. She was excited. "This is awesome."

"It's pretty great," I said.

"I don't think you have the same...I mean...I just don't think you can appreciate nature as well as I can," she said. We stopped atop the pass to breathe. "I mean, can you even believe that view?"

"I can," I said. "I can see it. It's nice."

"I think some people like you just can't appreciate nature the same way. I'm in awe."

"Yup," I said. "It's quite a thing to cross the Rockies."

It was a slow, steady descent into Montrose that never seemed to end. Jenny got a few flats on the way down.

We headed into Montrose on Hwy 50, and about a mile outside of town the lady who ran the fresh pie restaurant drove by. She stopped and her employee, a beautiful and strong German lady, shouted "Those are our campers!" out the window. Jenny smiled.

"Yes we are!" Jenny said.

"You guys need a ride?" the woman asked.

"We're walking," I said. "But...."

"We have to get to Wal-Mart," Jenny said. "Do you know how far it is?"

"It's a ways," the woman said, "and we're heading there anyway!"

It took a long time to break down The1976CosworthVega into small enough pieces to get it into that van, or any van for that matter. The handle had to come off and the front wheel. I had to remove the ironwood staff and the pack from where I'd fastened them on top of the cart. To get into smaller cars—like the support car we'd end up with in Utah—I had to completely unpack the Vega and collapse it down as far as it would go. It was a long process. It was not very far to the Wal-Mart.

We unloaded at Wal-Mart and I got several cold sodas and drank them in quick succession. I got foam inner tubes that would never go flat once installed, but Jenny got a couple of replacement tubes and a couple of cans of slime. We checked into a motel near a veterinarian so we could take Mabel and Lucy in for check ups, and I used some free time to connect with Don Wessell, a fellow Iowa Law alum living and practicing up in Grand Junction. He was looking forward to seeing us.

We hiked out of Montrose and were a day to Delta under skies that threatened to rain all day but only rained when we were quite near to Delta. Jenny and I had flat tires all day from thorns alongside the road, and I went through all my remaining tubes before we were even to Delta. I had the new foam tubes, though, and was excited to get them installed and would do so in Grand Junction—if my tubes lasted that long. We would have beat the rain by several hours had we not had the flat tires to contend with. Mabel got a thorn in her paw on the outskirts of Montrose and limped, but never whined, until Jenny noticed and called up to me. I stopped her and pulled the thorn from her pad. Then Mabel sighed heavily and licked my face and was ready to get back on the trail.

Book III: ...And the Moon Says Hallelujah, 01.08.12(3)

Return to room late, alone, little drunk. Write essay on November/December; destroy essay, like previous. Think about Mabel. Miss her; wish she were here; count days until I would see her again. Go back outside to get WiFi; email Gloria about Mabel; receive email that Mabel was fine and very happy; review pic attached as proof. Determine Mabel is happy up there, I should relax.

Email roommates Sirinder and Tommy; update on progress with book and with relaxing; include account of little German woman and Canadian woman; describe Belize. Walk to seaside; attract attention from locals, no issues arose. Drop feet into Caribbean; count stars up to 890; give up counting stars. Decide I was not a horrible person, room for improvement. Renew previous resolution to justify decision to be decent person. Consider authoritative comments on morality, e.g., "do no harm", "do unto others", and "love thy neighbor". Resolve nothing; dry feet; return to hotel. Feel very tired. Receive inquiry from a man in street: "Looking for something?" Respond I wasn't. "Want a party?" Respond I was too old. "Cali bud? Got sweet Cali bud?" Respond did not. "Want sweet Cali bud?" Respond did not. "You look like Taliban, anyway; fuck you."

Sit beside pool at Pedro's. Remember what it felt like to be called "Muhammed", "Taliban Tyler", "Terrorist Tyler", and "Hajji". Remember what it felt like to be called "Ahmed". Decide was not happy living like a dorm-room crasher with Sirinder and Tommy, no other option. Decide Sirinder and Tommy are good people, should stay. Consider what to be when I grow up; decide not to grow up.

Waves break ceaselessly over the reef on a soft, Belizean night.

Book II: Feel the Selfish Fury (D)(iv)
With the clay Population round in Rows.

I had lunch most days at Sidley with a group of first year associates from a few different groups—we had all been friends as summer associates and, as attorneys, meeting for lunch was about the most we could do to keep our acquaintanceship going. We met at 11:37 every day, which is an early lunch, and thus we called ourselves the "Farmers' Lunch". We were: Ellis (bankruptcy), Hastings (Real Estate, but who would transfer to Bankruptcy), Dr. Cravath (Health Care), Wendy (Commercial Competition, who would later transfer to Bankruptcy and who attended Farmers' Lunch infrequently), Cromwell (fourth or fifth year in Insurance Products who would leave Sidley at end of my first year), and a few others who showed up from time to time. It was the closest thing to real human interaction that happened while I was at Sidley, and even these lunches weren't free from posturing.

Conversations usually devolved into arguments about something, legal or otherwise. These were not arguments like you see on Jerry Springer, mind you; these were legal arguments. We discussed music and places to have lunch and how best to get a close shave and the economy and everything you can imagine—and we always discussed them in a neatly articulated way, all rational and presented as a legal argument would be presented. We could test each other's logical reasoning skills that way and keep our own sharp. Cravath and I, in particular, often used logical reasoning to push conversations to the most ridiculous propositions imaginable. For example, if someone began a discussion about whether it was or was not a good time to buy Chicago real estate, we might, through logical reasoning and argument, conclude that the best way to achieve market stability in Chicago real estate prices would be to amend the Constitution to remove the Third Amendment—utterly nonsensical, but fun to argue about. And we complained about workload (when there was workload) or having no workload (when we had no workload). We complained about partners who were awful to work for. As we progressed in our respective practices, our lunches became more and more infrequent, but I don't think a week went by without at least two more-or-less fully attended lunches.

Ellis was a bright and proud young man. He grew up in a lower socio-economic stratum (not quite as low as I did, I don't think, but close enough) and so we bonded. Hastings, too, was from a working class family. (He would often point out that he had brothers and cousins with Sarah Palin posters in their yards.) Cromwell and Cravath were first generation Americans. I doubt any of us noted it at the time, but our lunches tended to be populated with relative misfits. Once, early on, I mentioned that I'd done a paper in law school about *parkour*, and trespassory art in general, that discussed the aesthetics of fleeing and pursuit as a legitimately expressive art form. And Ellis asked:

"That's fucking fascinating. Do you see that in your life?"

"What do you mean?"

"I mean, are you fleeing or pursuing? Did you go to law school and do well and then go to biglaw because you were pursuing the brass ring, or because you were fleeing from your backward childhood?"

"It wasn't *that* backward."

"You know what I mean."

And *that* kind of question never went over well with the Farmers' Lunch, because Ellis and I were the only people who liked to discuss things like the aesthetics of art or the potential for recognizing transcendent truth through art, through philosophy, through religion, or through comparative legal studies. Hastings, Cravath, Cromwell, the others: They didn't *do* that. If they didn't have something concrete to rest an argument on, then they couldn't argue their positions—it wasn't that they weren't smart or hadn't read widely, but they were not comfortable arguing about things that don't fit inside the constraints of legal reasoning. (And aesthetics do *not* fit within the constraints of legal reasoning.) They could have, but they were not practiced at it. Ellis brought that question up at Farmers' Lunch maybe once every two or three months, and I was the only attorney who would engage with him on the question.

And, on the topic of aesthetics, I generally wear a beard and have for many years. But as a new attorney I bought into the idea that beards were improper in a business environment. At biglaw, the feeling is that one must *earn* the right to wear a beard, either by becoming a successful partner or by subscribing to a religious view that encourages or requires the wearing of a beard. I was neither a partner nor a religious person, so I had shaved my beard when I went to Sidley. However, upon overhearing a partner at Sidley say to another partner, regarding Isra, "Yeah, I saw [her at the holiday party with Tyler]! She's a hell of a lot hotter than I would have guessed, but, then, she's a Muslim so maybe they go for his type" I decided that I would let my beard grow back in because screw them, that's why.

In March, I moved into a South Loop apartment that Isra and I had picked out. She would move in completely in May, and she wanted a lot of say in our apartment. She picked it out, really. It was a great one-bedroom place with a huge den on the 17th floor of a high rise in the South Loop. There was a view of the Lake and Soldier Field, and it was a block from a grocery store and the Red Line train. It was only a mile to my work, and a hair under a mile to her work in the Loop. I took her down to Pike County, Illinois, and we adopted a dog from the local shelter. Her name was Radio, a beautiful black and white hound dog. Isra was basically a dog whisperer, although she'd never had a dog before and had almost no first-hand experience with dogs. It was something to watch her "train" Radio—it wasn't even like "training", it was more just like a conversation they had. Radio always knew exactly what Isra was thinking, and was quickly the most well-behaved dog in the neighborhood. Radio helped Isra through the difficult time of studying for the bar, and I did what I could to make the bar an easier experience for her than it had been for me. It worked.

We were happy and less stressed once Isra's bar exam was over. We took a trip to the Oregon coast and it was lovely. Isra wanted to elope while we were there, but I said that it was not fair to her mother. Isra should have a grand ceremony and her mother should get to see it. Or maybe I was scared of making a decision. But we came back refreshed and renewed. And we were happy there, all the way until February of the next year.

The Cairo bankruptcy was ongoing that year, and I continued doing grunt-work on it. As the year went on, though, some of the grunt-work dried up and the proceedings started to focus on higher-level issues that were discussed and decided among lawyers with much more experience than I had. During the summer, I looked for work from other senior associates and partners. Once, I think in May, I stopped by a senior associate's office and asked for work on an upcoming bankruptcy filing.

"You got any work available on the Versailles Inc. filing?" I asked. "I could use more work."

"But aren't you on Cairo?" he asked.

"Yes, but I've got time to fill."

"Well, Sam said you belonged to the Cairo team."

"I've got time."

"I'll see," he said, but I knew I'd get no work on that particular filing. Sam, I surmised, needed me to be free to pick up slack on the Cairo proceedings, and had told everyone that I was working solely on the Cairo project. I didn't *fight* to get work on that upcoming filing, and I suppose I should have, because having lines of work is the name of the game in biglaw. In biglaw, only your hours matter, and you can't get the hours if you don't have the lines on work. Sam had shut one line of work off for me; I don't know whether that was intentional or not, but I doubt it, and I did not and do not blame Sam for it. It's the goal and the job of any smart senior associate to keep first year associates available for when they need help—to protect themselves against overwork. I think Sam billed something like 3500 hours that year.

In other instances, though, young associates will cut off other associates' lines on work. It's math: If you have work you have hours; if *they* don't have work, they don't have hours; the more hours you have, the safer your job is and the greater your chance at making partner. Few associates admit to it, but when a partner asks "Hey, do you know if Frank has time?", the smart young associate says something like "No, I think Frank is pretty much slammed with other matters, but *I* could help you". The smart young associate gets as much work as he or she can from as many partners as he or she can; he or she focuses on making those partners and senior associates with *too much* work comfortable with the idea that the other associates are too busy. It's the business of building relationships, because partners don't want to *start* building relationships with a second, third, or fourth year associate who already has ways of doing things and systems they're comfortable with—they want to start working with first year associates who have not yet settled into a particular work-flow style. It makes sense.

I didn't play that game well, so rather than having constant lines of *too much* work, I was staffed on a single on-going bankruptcy and picked up one-off jobs from all (or most) of the other proceedings that we had. (I tried to stay away from a couple of our projects, for various reasons.) In my free time, I tried to do things that I thought would help my professional development (because Sidley wasn't doing that for me, at all). I had become interested in Islamic finance the previous summer, and Isra was Muslim, after all, so one of the things I started to do was to attempt to learn Arabic. (I failed at that, miserably.) I had a couple of Arabic books in my office and a Qur'an (which is a pretty standard text for learning Arabic because, unlike most modern Arabic, the Qur'an contains all the vowel markings, called diacritics, which makes it much easier to use as a learning tool.) So there I was: I was researching bankruptcy issues and fielding many of the work-a-day questions that arose in a mid-market bankruptcy, and I was researching my pet interest and trying, failingly, to learn a bit about my girlfriend's culture and heritage. Keep in mind that I was wearing a beard again by then.

The summer wore on and I worked with more associates and partners. Some were better to work with than others, and I learned a lot of important lessons. There are different work management styles, or rather "work management" styles. Lawyers are, on the whole, horrible managers. As a junior associate, you must do a lot of "managing up"—this will often go beyond simply managing expectations. In many cases, I found that associates under whom I worked were unprepared or incapable of managing workload or delegating tasks effectively. Some could hyper- or micro-manage, but few could effectively delegate and manage work. The ones who could were the more successful. The greatest difficulty that comes with working for bad managers is the tendency of bad managers to take all the credit for your good work and to throw you under the bus for everything bad that happens. Although I was never thrown under a bus (to the best of my knowledge), I did *see* it happen routinely (and I'm not talking about Sidley, but at other large law firms, as well).

Other bankruptcies were filed and other associates got involved in them. The Cairo case began to slow down after all those other bankruptcies had been staffed up, which left me with more time than the other associates. When Cairo went away all together, I had to hit the streets sending emails and visiting offices to ask for work and one-off projects from the other teams. There was still work to get if you hustled for it, but it was slowing. That worried me, because I knew the signs that work was slowing down drastically. I didn't want to be staffed on the one enormously huge bankruptcy proceeding that we had, and didn't much care to go on hustling for research projects—the bread and butter is in getting the recurring projects, like claims administration and that kind of thing. That's where the hours can happen. But you have to be staffed on a case to get those projects.

So I hustled around at work and came home to Isra at night.

That's probably about the time that everything started to fall apart.

At work, people began talking about "pipeline", and by that they meant a discussion about incoming work. What that really meant was that I wasn't the only associate who had become uneasy about the amount of work available. Our class in bankruptcy was stacked pretty heavily—the group usually took one or two per class year, but because we'd all been transferred over to bankruptcy there were eight of us. It wasn't a "happy time" at work, because a few of us were not getting enough work and a few of us were billing 3000 hours. There was tension.

When I came home at night, I listened to Isra complain about this or that thing that happened at work. I tried to be sensitive and understanding, but I was in my own world. The cold weather came and that depressed us both a little, so Isra pushed me to take a Caribbean vacation. I thought that was a great plan, but I didn't have time to plan one. I think she was uncomfortable with the idea of planning a trip that I would pay for—or maybe she just didn't want to plan it—so we ended up taking a last-minute trip to Cozumel, and I loved it. I think she did, too. But who knows.

I thought "we" were happy, even though I wasn't.

But I came home at night and watched TV and ate dinner, and that was about it. Sometimes I'd play the guitar for five or six hours. And Isra and I talked about what hobby she should take up, because she was desperate to have a hobby.

In February of 2010, after I re-signed our lease on the South Loop apartment, I came home and found Isra sitting quietly in the living room. She told me that she thought we should stop seeing each other. She was moving out. She thought she would move out in about a week. I told her there was no use in waiting, it was either up or out for us at that point, so she should just go. Either/or. Black or white. I gave her a high five and took a room at a nearby motel so she and her mother could move her stuff out without me in the way.

That weekend I came back to the apartment as a single father to a beautiful dog. And I went about my life for about a month. Without Isra in my life, Sidley was about the only thing going that could give my life any meaning. And that was a lost cause—biglaw can't give meaning to a guy like me. Every experience is unique and every *person*, I suppose, is unique, so I do not doubt that there were and are attorneys at firms like Sidley who take unbridled joy from their jobs. But that wasn't me.

In March, I went to the annual bankruptcy associates' retreat, held that year in Los Angeles. Everyone got very drunk the first night at the hotel bar and at a few other bars in L.A. There are at least two distinct cities in L.A., one for the super-rich and one for everyone else. This was my first experience in L.A. living high on the hog with a corporate sponsor. We drank an enormous amount of wonderfully overpriced liquor at the trendy Standard Hotel. The next day we sat in a boardroom and listened to associates and partners give talks about the state of the practice group and the state of the bankruptcy industry. It was a "pipeline" talk.

The second night, we all went to dinner at a trendy gastronomy restaurant in Beverly Hills where you can't recognize the food but it all tastes great. Somewhere in the lab in the back, a guy had liquefied olives and reduced them and sealed the reduced olive essence into little gelatin skins; they broke open in your mouth and tasted like eating 10,000 olives at once. Life changing olives, really. Rumor was that it cost about $1000 per person—but Sidley was paying, so we didn't know for sure and didn't care. Then we headed out to the bar for bottle service, which we heard cost something like $500 per person, and everyone got really drunk. At about 11 p.m. that night, a senior associate in my group—for whom I did work and who was a *great* manager, but who I did not much care for already—came rambling up to me as drunk as he could be.

"Fucking nice look," he said.

"What?"

He was with an up and coming partner in the group who everyone loved and respected. It's a boys' club, of course. I never really fit into that. Maybe I respected women too much to fit in, or maybe I'm just not manly enough. I don't know.

"Taliban," he said. "Taliban Tyler."

"What?" I asked, hoping that I had mis-heard.

"You look like a fucking terrorist, dude. With the Koran and the girlfriend. Fucking *Taliban Tyler*."

I do not know whether that up and coming partner (who was also drunk) decided to defuse the situation out of professionalism or because he was more familiar with my type of person, but he took the senior associate by the shoulder, laughing, and lead him away. I decided right at that moment that I would leave Sidley. I believe that was March 11, 2010. That night I wrote the first draft of my farewell e-mail.

I had no choice, really. This associate was protected and loved at Sidley, and I had no one to complain to, anyway. Even if I did "talk to someone" about this incident—or any of the many others that I haven't written about here—then what?

Ellis and I rented a car the next day and drove down to San Diego for the weekend. Ellis spent most of the time in his hotel room doing work on a major bankruptcy that Sidley handled. I didn't spend my time that way. We had dinner together that night and he went back to his room to do work, but I stayed out drinking and carousing. Around midnight on March 12, 2010, I sat down on the beach in Ocean Beach, San Diego. It was a nice enough night, breezy and cool, and the air smelled the way it always does in San Diego. And I thought to myself: "If I were homeless, I'd want to live in San Diego, even if I had to walk from Chicago...even if I had to walk from New York!" And then I thought: "If I were homeless, walking from New York to San Diego, I would probably be happier than I currently am."

I decided that I would walk across the country

When I returned to work after the associates' retreat, I imagine my demeanor was different. I was completely done with roaming the halls asking for work, and I was completely done working for almost anyone in the group. My main partner-source for work was tied up on a project that I wouldn't work on, and my main associate-source for work...well, we'd had a falling out when he'd called me a terrorist. So I quit hustling. I didn't quit *working*, but I quit hustling for work. There wasn't enough work for too many associates, and I was done hustling. Those other associates wanted it more than I did and, frankly, they needed it more than I did. I had no kids, no wife. And I was so depressed that I had no desire, either.

Because I'm an attorney, I tempered the decision I'd made. I told myself that I had a year—if, in that year, I found some equally high-paying legal job, I would take that and not go on the Walk. But if I didn't, then in March of 2011, I would start walking. I didn't try very hard to find work. I talked to a couple of legal recruiters, but I think I only ever sent my resume to one of them. And I applied to a few jobs on-line—but only for crazy, bizarre-o jobs, like working on oil and gas leases in Mongolia. From March of 2010 on, I mainly read about equipment and routes for the Walk and read literature about walking and journeys. I billed very few hours.

I rarely turned down work that came to me, though. If a partner or associate came to me looking for help on something, then I would do it (unless it was one of the associates who I had determined I would not work with). But I didn't hit the streets looking for work, and as a consequence I had a whole lot of free time. And it was glorious.

For the Walk, I determined that I needed to focus on three things: 1) physical training, 2) equipment, and 3) routing/scheduling. The rest, I told myself, would fall into place. I began eating immediately...and I mean *eating*. I ate massive amounts of everything I could. I started walking, too. I walked about five miles a day on a treadmill. It wasn't much, but it was the most I had time for. I did push-ups in my office and I took the stairs up to my 26th floor office a couple of times a week. I took the stairs *down* every day.

I wondered if I would have the guts to do it.

BOOK III: ...AND THE MOON SAYS HALLELUJAH, 01.09.12(1)

Wake in early hours; turn on TV; watch Spanish language show. Decide I should make sense of things. Review some of the interviews I had done with lawyers/law students; analyze similarities and differences in experience. Note that no one has answers. Re-read interview one, highlighted quote: "Going to law school and being a lawyer has made everything about life harder than it should be. We look for adversity in everything." Consider times when I'd been blamed for things that weren't my fault, and when I had blamed people for things that were my fault. Fall asleep.

BOOK I: THE MOMENTS THAT TURN US (D)(v)
MY CLAY WITH LONG OBLIVION.

We were another day into Grand Junction, where we checked into a motel. Jenny complained that the motel was expensive and so I ended up paying for the whole room. We stayed two nights in Grand Junction so we could meet two law school classmates of mine, Don and Julie Camp, who lived and worked in Grand Junction. We moved to a cheaper motel near a college in Grand Junction the second night and Don brought over the care package he'd taken delivery of for Jenny. She finally had warm clothes.

I went to dinner with Don and Clarissa that night and we shared gossip about people we'd gone to law school with and we talked about our professional development or, in my case, "professional development". Don went to Colorado after law school and practiced as a public defender. He loved his job. We talked about Amrita, who I'd stayed with in Colorado Springs, and Don told me that she had been nominated for Colorado's Public Defender Attorney of the Year. Julie clerked for a year in New York City after law school, then moved to Colorado to work for a private firm specializing in immigration matters (and to be with Don). She left that job for a teaching position in an immigration clinic at a law school in Wyoming— she commuted 10 hours each Sunday and 10 hours back to Colorado each Friday. She was no fan of the traveling, but she was happy to be in a teaching position that she enjoyed. It was funny, I told them, that they seemed so happy—all the people who "won" law school and went on to the lucrative biglaw positions seemed so unhappy.

"Well there's nothing in it," Don said. "I'd like to make a billion dollars, but what do they do? What did you do?"

"I helped rich people get richer."

"Exactly. I don't want to do that. Some people do, though."

We stood beside Don's car after dinner, looking at maps and discussing our options. Don spread topographic maps out on the hood of the car.

"Have you been to Utah?"

"I've driven through," I said. "Are you worried about me?"

"Yes," he said.

"Me, too."

"How much water do you guys carry?"

"I can carry 10 gallons for sure, and I think up to 14 if I really pushed. But that will slow me down."

He thought about this for a while and Julie smiled.

"Jenny?"

"I think she can carry almost two gallons now."

"Two?"

"Two."

"Two?"

"Two," I said.

"You can't make it," Don said.

"I know," I agreed. I showed him our route on the map.

"There's no water from here to Crescent Junction," he said. "And I don't know for sure whether there is a gas station in Crescent; there *was*, but I don't know now. And you're not going through Dewey? Down from Crescent to Hanksville? There is nothing in between there. That's two long legs without water."

"I know," I said. "Jenny kept telling me she had some friend in Moab who was going to do car support. But that friend never contacted us. I was hoping you could help us out."

"How long will it take you to get to Hanksville?"

I told him that I thought it would be six days' hike. He could not take that kind of time off of work. He had three days.

"I can get you to Crescent, I guess. I can't *hike* that with you, though, because Julie is leaving tomorrow afternoon. So I'd have no way back. *And* that's a really boring hike."

"Could you drive ahead and cache water?"

His eyes lit up.

"And then draw you a treasure map? Yes. I'm going to do that."

"That's not really fair for you," I said. "You wanted to hike."

"I wanted to *camp* and hike," he said. "Tell you what...we'll drive to Arches. I know a great camping spot over there. You'll lose...30 miles, maybe 40? Then you two can hike out next day"—his finger traced along the route—"and I'll cache water all between Crescent and Hanksville."

"We might not need..."

"I *am going* to bury water in the desert," he said, and laughed. "I don't care if you need it. I am going to bury water, and draw a treasure map."

"Ok," I agreed. "I'm pretty sure Jenny will like the idea. I know she hitched a little earlier, so she'll be fine with it."

"Well, let me put it this way...I *will not* help you at all otherwise. I can see that you have enough water through to Hanksville. But I won't help or be involved with someone who hikes into Utah with two gallons of water. You could ditch her here in Grand Junction."

"I could," I said. "I'd be glad to be rid of her."

"She could hitch a ride out of here. She'll get expensive in Utah—where is your car support meeting you?"

"Not sure. St. George? Maybe sooner. It's Mika's little brother, Jon." Mika was a classmate of ours and she'd volunteered her little brother, Jon, as a support car driver. Heidi pledged her car to the cause, so Jon was to drive out to Utah in a borrowed car at some point and to meet us somewhere. Scheduling is difficult when you are on foot.

"She agreed to pay half."

"She won't pay a dime," Don said. I knew he was right, I think.

"She agreed."

"She won't pay," he said again. "She doesn't have any money to pay, I don't think."

"I know," I said. "But she's come a long way. She has to make it." He nodded and folded the map.

"Well," he said, as if it had all been decided.

BOOK I: THE MOMENTS THAT TURN US (D)(v)(a)
AND MUCH AS WINE HAS PLAY'D THE INFIDEL.

The next day we hiked out to the edge of Grand Junction and met with Don and Julie. Don's car was packed with his camping equipment and his enormous Bernese mountain dog. We loaded my equipment and Jenny's equipment into a Land Rover that Don had borrowed from some attorney he knew, and bought about 20 gallons of water. Then we were off into Utah and onto the dirt roads cut into the BLM land. I rode with Julie, and she cursed Don the whole time for leading her out onto such awful roads in a borrowed car, but it was all friendly ribbing.

"Donald Wessell!" she said. "I just cannot believe him."

We camped beside a rock formation on the Bureau of Land Management land, the "BLM". The BLM land is the closest thing to a state of nature you can get in the United States. There seem to be no laws, no regulations. You can camp anywhere; you can take any dogs or pets. You can fire guns. You can do pretty much whatever the hell you want to do. I was in Abbey Country. Finally.

We took the next day off to hike around the border between the BLM land and Arches National Park. There are a few natural stone arches there that were accidentally not included in the Park. We paid no entrance fees, and we didn't enjoy easy access, but we saw La Boca Arch. We hiked through a canyon and up rocky inclines. We climbed to the top of *our* rock formation where we camped, and from up there we could see pretty far to the south where the Earth disappeared into deep canyons. Canyonlands National Park, to our south, was the last bit of North America to be surveyed. The wilds of Alaska and northern Canada where there is only ice and rock were surveyed before these canyons of stone and shadow.

My heart was light when Mabel was off-leash, running and exploring. She strayed, but never too far, and she investigated everything. She was the first in our party to race up to the pocket of La Boca Arch and looked down at us, and her hazel eyes glimmered. Her red coat was almost the same deep red/brown as the color of the stone in the shadow of the arch, but the bright swath of white from her chest and her little chrome paws flashed in the shadow. She was the happiest dog in the world.

We drank cold beers that night and cooked Indian food on Don's portable grill. We lay on our backs on top of the rocks and looked up into an infinite sky. Distance has no meaning under a sky that big. We argued about which star was the North Star and, although I knew the Latin name for the star and the history of its use as a navigational point, I chose the wrong star from the night sky. Don and Jenny laughed at me because I had been so adamant and so wrong. Mabel climbed the rock and descended and climbed and descended. She curled and slept atop the rock while we played and sang little songs on the guitar.

We hiked out and west along an old highway that parallels Interstate 70. The highway is sometimes labeled 6, sometimes 50, sometimes 128. I was never sure. Grass grew up through the asphalt in long and jagged green lines but wouldn't grow off the side of the road. We were in a gray, shadeless desert, and the Sun was hot. Shade would determine and guide our breaks from that point on. In the desert, even if it is not particularly hot, the Sun is deceptively fierce and dehydration becomes a serious concern for people and for puppies. Don raced ahead of us to cache gallons of water on the barren stretch to Hanksville.

The stretch was ugly and dusty. We walked by signs that warned of waste facilities run by the United States Department of Energy. The signs said something like "DO NOT ENTER—U.S. Department of Energy Waste Management Facility". I pointed them out to Jenny and she laughed.

I began hiking several hundred feet in front of her, when possible, because I was tired of not being able to take any pictures without her or her dog in them. (I was also kind of sick of hearing her say video game things like 'Achievement unlocked!' whenever she climbed a hill, or 'Level up' or 'Health restored!' whenever she drank water.) Jenny had never, to the best of my knowledge, let Lucy off the leash while hiking before that day, but she did let Lucy off leash somewhere in that barren stretch and Lucy raced up to us and scared the hell out of me. She jumped into a puddle of water in a ditch beside the road, and I shouted at her:

"Lucy, get out of there. Get up here."

Lucy came back up to the road, and Jenny was hurrying up from behind.

"Did he yell at you?" she said, in her talking-to-a-puppy voice. "You can go for a swim. Go swim!" Then she said to me: "She knows the command 'swim'."

"She shouldn't be in that water," I said. "Didn't you read that sign back there?"

"Yeah."

"I'm guessing that's a waste management facility for spent nuclear fuel. I'm guessing it's in that mountain right over there." I pointed at the mountain.

"Well, I'm sure this water is safe. It wouldn't be standing here if it wasn't," she said.

"You have to keep her on the leash," I said.

"She was pulling," Lucy said. "She just can't handle not being in the lead. It's in her DNA."

"Well, if I'm in front, please keep her on the leash," I said. "How you deal with the pulling is your business. But she won't pull if she understands she's not supposed to."

"She's not like that, not like Mabel," Lucy said. "She's a leader."

"You go ahead," I said. I sighed.

We made it to Crescent Junction and found that there was still a gas station open there. We camped in an open lot behind the gas station. Part of the lot doubled as a junkyard, and we found a makeshift home near a grove of trees where drifters had built a hovel in the shade of the trees using junk they'd found lying around. We drank cold sodas from the gas station and waited for Don.

Don found us around dusk and was smiling ear-to-ear. He gave me four hand-drawn treasure maps he'd drawn in wonderful detail. The first map showed the entire route from Green River to Hanksville. The other three maps broke out sections of the larger map and showed exactly where he'd buried the water drops. They had directions like "Dirt road and fence to right; locate large mound; south side, north mound, find three bushes; 45 degree angle from bushes, an arrow made of rocks on ground points to two small unnatural mounds, ringed with rocks; dig". He'd buried four caches, but wasn't sure we'd need the fourth, which was close to Hanksville. He'd buried the largest cache of water near Hanksville in case we ran into trouble.

"You'll be ok," he said. "Look me up when you come back through and we'll do some more camping."

"Will do," I said.

"Are you taking 50 across Nevada?"

"No," I said. "We were planning to. That's the big reason we're getting car support. There's nothing out there."

"It's too late," Don said.

"I know."

"It'll snow in the Sierra Nevada soon. It's really too late for you to do it. You could...but not with Mabel, I don't think. And definitely not with Jenny and Lucy."

"I know," I said again. "We're breaking south."

"L.A.?"

"Not keen on crossing Death Valley," I said. "And less keen on walking in Los Angeles. It's hard to walk across pedestrian friendly cities. L.A. would

252

be a nightmare. Probably San Juan Capistrano. Depending on easy routing, we might end up in San Diego. Heartbreaker. Goal was San Francisco."

"Yeah," Don said. "You've really screwed it all up. Should probably be ashamed."

He smiled broadly, and for a moment I almost let myself think that he was right and that *this* had been something. It was a pretty grand feat.

"You need to worry about Utah," he said as he got into the car. "It's dry out there."

I thanked him for all his help. We went back to the camp where Jenny was already climbing into her tent. When Mabel and I were settled in for the night, I thought about how happy Don seemed and was happy for him. He's a good sort. I was nervous about the next few weeks of the trip. I didn't want anyone to die.

We were another day to Green River on an empty highway. We didn't see a car that day except for the Interstate traffic a couple of miles to our left. The highway was straight and dusty and we could see a big plume of green many miles ahead of us where folks lived along the Green River.

On the road into Green River, but still many miles away, a coyote bounded up alongside the highway beside us. The coyote was interested in us, probably in Mabel and Lucy more than me or Jenny, and it did not seem afraid at all. It came up very close to us and lay down, and it looked at us through the scrub brush and licked its chops. We stopped and took pictures; it moved closer, then farther away, then closer again. It did not seem rabid or sick, just interested and maybe a little lonely. Mabel and Lucy barked at it and were aggressive, but the coyote was calm and reserved. I thought for a second that it might have been kicked out of its little pack of coyotes and was out looking for a new home and that maybe it wanted to join us. But then I remembered that I'd heard that coyotes are tricksters—sometimes, when coyotes see domesticated dogs, they send out an emissary to greet the dog to lure the dog into the pack. The dog, always torn between the domestic life and the wild life, still sometimes follow, its little heart racing because it has finally broken free to join the sick mad joy of life in the wild. Then the coyotes kill and eat the dog. We walked on, and Mabel barked angrily at the coyote.

Jenny found a couchsurfer to stay with in Green River and Mabel and I stayed in a motel. It was strange to at once feel so lonely and alone but at the same time to want some time to myself.

We hiked out the next morning. Green River is not a very big town, but it took a bit for me to walk through it. We met Jenny at a grocery store near where we would hike out of town on an old county road. We went over the water maps again and each took pictures of the maps on our phones, just in case we lost the paper copies.

"When is the driver getting here?" she asked.

"I don't know. I'm working that out. It's not going to be cheap, so I don't want him here until we need him. Maybe St. George?"

"St. George!?"

"Yes," I said. The hike into Hanksville was bound to be the longest, driest section until Nevada, but we had water cached. And I saw no reason why we should need car support before Nevada, so long as we made good time and got down to the lower elevations around St. George. "We have to make good time from here on out."

"Well, we have to make good time to Hanksville," Jenny agreed. "We have to get there by Friday. I'm getting a package in the mail there."

"Oh?"

"Dog booties," she said. "The ground is too hot for Lucy."

"Has she been having troubles?"

"A little. She's limped a little," Jenny said. It was the first I'd heard of that. I twisted an ear bud into my ear and hurried ahead of her. "Keep Lucy on the leash today. I want to do some running."

We each drank a great deal of water that day. I had quite a lot of water in The1976CosworthVega, but it was important to pick up each cache to guarantee we'd have enough. When possible in the desert, you should always replace your water.

Jenny and I argued about the route when we reached a bend in the road. She thought we should take a left down a dirt road, and I conceded that Don's map *looked* like we should take that left, but when I compared Don's map to the real map I was almost certain that we should not take that left. She conceded and we followed the road. A couple of miles later I began to doubt my decision.

"Keep an eye out for the oil barrels," I said.

"What?"

"The sign we're looking for, for this first water drop."

"Oh, yeah."

According to Don's map, we were looking for a point where a gravel road and a paved road intersected, and near that intersection would be three or four rusted old oil drums. The water was hidden under a pile of rocks near the oil drums.

Several miles later, the road changed from gravel to pavement, and pavement is much hotter than gravel. We walked on into the late morning and the heat rose in waves off the road. We needed to stop, but I wanted to find a shady space.

"Look at that," Jenny said. "It's so neat. It's a mirage. It looks like water."

"It looks like heat rising," I said. "To me. I've never thought that looked like water. Just heat rising. It's neat, though."

We stopped near a depression that might, in wetter times, be a brook or a creek. There was no hope of finding natural shade, so we each sat beneath golf umbrellas.

"I must have been wrong about that road," I said. "You must have been right. We should have gone to the left. Because I didn't see an intersection of gravel and pavement. And I didn't see oil drums."

"Oh, there were some oil drums back there," she said.

"What?"

"Yeah, back where this road changed from gravel into pavement, maybe a mile? Like three or four of them."

"Why didn't you mention that?" I asked.

"I didn't figure that we needed water. I've got a gallon left. And you have, what, six gallons in there? Plus, there's this next two gallon drop up the road, what, 20 miles?"

"It's like 60 miles to Hanksville, Jenny," I said. "Make sure Mabel doesn't run away." It did not make sense to me. I was carrying the reserve, so picking up extra water wasn't even a cost to her.

I leashed Mabel to the cart and ran back a few miles. I found the oil drums and from there I found a mound of rocks with a couple of gallons of water buried underneath them. I don't know why I hadn't seen the drums from the road, and I felt bad about that. I carried the water back to where we had stopped and gave Jenny half of the water but did not speak. We waited another half an hour or hour for the day to cool, and when the day did not cool fast enough, we headed back out on the road under a fierce Sun. The highway was completely empty and weeds and scrub had grown so far into the road that about a lane's width of pavement was clear on the two-lane road. The rest was covered in growth.

"I'm going ahead again," I said, and I hurried a few hundred feet ahead. Lucy joined me shortly, and I turned to see Jenny not even looking or paying attention. She'd let Lucy off leash to run in the desert. Soon after Lucy caught up with me, a pronghorn antelope appeared on a near ridge to the west and Lucy took off into the desert after the animal. I shouted a couple of times, but Lucy wouldn't listen to anyone by that time. We stopped and waited for Jenny to catch up.

"Don't worry about it," Jenny said. "She'll come back. She just likes to chase animals. When we hike, I pretty much always let her off leash and she runs off to hunt and sometimes she comes back with a rabbit or something. And she always comes back."

"It's 100 fucking degrees, Jenny," I said. "And your husky just ran off into the desert at a sprint."

"She'll come back!" Jenny said.

"That's not the point," I said.

We hiked on and Lucy came back in her own time, and then we had to take another break because Lucy was exhausted and overheated. Lucy drank a lot of water—for her, anyway, as she never drank much water—and rested under the umbrella for a long time and then we headed off again. We met up with the highway that runs down into Hanksville and were back among traffic. But out there in the west, the traffic isn't the same—there is far, far less of it. Don had marked a potential camping spot on the map and we were eager to get there. But the camping spot was along the banks of a river that ran in a low spot and we ran into a cloud of mosquitoes as we climbed the rise that overlooked the river.

We ducked quickly off the road to the left and found an outcropping of rocks that formed a flat ledge over the small valley of the river. The mosquitoes were thick. I grew up between two big rivers in the Midwest and still had never been in a swarm of mosquitoes like this. In the desert, where so few living things roam around, mosquitoes seem to flock from miles around. They can smell your blood and your carbon and they come screaming. They attacked my face and ears relentlessly and exploded in little clouds when I slapped at my forearms and shins. Neither Jenny nor I did any camp-prep that night—neither of us cared about bears or mountain lions or rain or anything. We set up tents as fast as we could and retreated into the tents atop the slick rock pinnacle of the ridge. I took a quart of water and a packet of powdered milk into the tent and had powdered milk and pop tarts for dinner in the tent while mosquitoes swarmed so thick on the tent that I could not see out through the clear netting of the tent roof.

"We're up and out early tomorrow," I shouted over to her tent. "Before the mosquitoes." It was a funny demand, because Jenny was always up and ready shortly before me, or at least had been for most of the trip.

We woke early the next morning, before Jenny and Lucy, and were packed up and ready to go a little ahead of them for the first time since we'd joined up. We hit the highway pretty quickly and made good time. We found two more caches of water and drank most of it as we walked. It was brutally hot that day, too, and the road had a much wider shoulder, which meant that more heat reflected up from the pavement. Lucy began favoring a paw, then began limping.

"We have to get to Hanksville for the dog booties," Jenny said.

"Won't help now," I said. I was gloomy on the subject.

"I checked her pads. She's got a blister thing on her right paw."

"She'll have them on other paws, too," I said. Jenny didn't like my negative outlook, I don't think.

"She's had no problems this whole trip," Jenny said. "None at all. I don't know why they would start now. I guess because the pavement is hot."

"Yeah, that, and because she ran for 20 miles chasing an antelope."

"Well, I'm picking up dog booties in Hanksville."

We pulled off the road near Goblin Valley State Park and camped near a grove of trees that night, about 22 miles from Hanksville. The sky was empty and black and clear. The nights in Utah were almost all like that: so empty and clear that I felt like I could reach out to the end of the Universe.

BOOK III: ...AND THE MOON SAYS HALLELUJAH, 01.09.12(2)

Arrive at picnic table early; begin second read of Book I. Learn Rosie arrived early, too.

R: "You look tired. Or nervous. Or both."

T: "I am. I am not getting enough exercise."

R: "You look fit."

T: "I mean since I've been in Belize. In Chicago, I go to the gym a lot."

R: "Are you one of those guys?"

T: " No."

Consider how to explain it, couldn't think of how. Tell Rosie that I was just accustomed to physical pain; tell her I liked the climbing wall because I am deathly afraid of heights; tell her that I've had no fear response or much of any emotion at all for some time. Determine she didn't understand; note issue for future research: "Did Rosie not understand because she couldn't, or because I didn't explain myself?"; note follow-up research: "Did I not explain myself well because I *can't*, or because I don't want to?"

R: "Do you have any children?"

T: "No."

Laugh. See Rosie smile, look embarrassed.

R: "Why is that funny?"

T: "It's just funny."

R: "Why?"

T: "Because my Dad is really old."

R: "I don't get it."

T: "He's always wanted grandkids. Mom told me he wanted grandkids and she wanted him to have grandkids."

R: "I was joking the other day. You aren't *that* old."

T: "My dad is ill. He's got a degenerative disease. He won't be with us mentally very much longer."

R: "None of that is funny."

T: "It's funny. Because my ex-girlfriend told me that if I hadn't gone on the Walk then we'd be married and she'd be pregnant by now and that "Because of my stupid fucking selfish walk my Dad will never know if he has grandchildren"."

R: "That's not funny!"

T: "Try it from a different perspective."

Watch Rosie leave abruptly. Determine she'd been offended.

BOOK I: THE MOMENTS THAT TURN US (D)(vi)
NOW THE NEW YEAR REVIVING OLD DESIRES.

We struck camp early. It was our second night out from Green River, through a dry and rugged patch of the desert. Between my water reserve in the cart and Don's water caches, we were in no danger of dying of thirst. I was awake by 4:30 or so, because it is hard to sleep in Utah—right outside the tent is the clearest, cleanest, biggest sky you can imagine. There are a billion articulated stars, crisp and bright, and the sky itself is so clear that it isn't even "black", it is just nothing. You can see emptiness. And the Milky Way is a bridge painted across the sky, and if you follow it from one horizon, all along the bowl of night, you see deep black shadows all along both horizons and you know they are mountains but you swear they are million year old ruins of a larger, fairer society that lived in this desert before it was desert and before anyone walked on two feet. So it is hard to shut your tent and shut your eyes and go to sleep when you have that to look at. It makes a man wonder why television was ever invented.

Lucy and Jenny were up by 5:00 a.m. We were all on the road by 6:00 a.m., still in a darker part of the night. But there is no traffic even during the day out there, much less at night, so there was nothing to worry about. Mabel was ready to go, and seemed even to be excited to hit the road so early, and so was Jenny, but Lucy was not in good shape from the very beginning of the day. She had blown out her paws during the two days previous. We had to reach Hanksville that day before four, because Jenny had dog booties and a camera waiting at the post office—if she didn't make it to the post office, we would be stuck in Hanksville until the Post Office re-opened on Monday.

A few miles into the hike, a vibrating blue replaced the darkness. The Sun was not yet up, but in the light of the false dawn all of the desert felt blue. I cannot explain it. But I was smiling all the same, and struggling to walk southbound while craning my neck to the east to watch the Sunrise. I have never seen or imagined a Sunrise that could in any way equal the Utah Sunrise I saw on the road to Hanksville. I stopped to snap some pictures, and I remembered hearing my grandfather, who was a lover of poetry and a farmer, say:

> "Awake! For morning in the bowl of night has flung the stone that put the stars to flight!"

And, Lo!, I thought, the Hunter of the East *had* caught the sultan's turret in a noose of light, after all.

We made good time in the cool morning, but it was clear by three or four miles in that Lucy was in sore shape. We stopped by a tractor-trailer parked beside the road, totally unattended, and I sat on the long flatbed trailer and ate a snack. It was hard to not be angry with Lucy, but she is just a dog and she had done admirably over a couple thousand miles. It wasn't her fault.

We decided that Lucy and Jenny would try to flag down a ride and that I would head on toward Hanksville and send someone back for them. I had little hope that they would actually flag down someone—there was little traffic, and none of it seemed inclined to stop. I put about a half a mile between us, always looking back over my shoulder to make sure they were still moving, albeit slowly. After about a half or 3/4 of a mile, I looked and they were gone, and at the same time a van slowed to a stop alongside me. The driver pointed at the back and said: "We got your better half and her stuff and her dog. Dropping her off in Hanksville."

"She's not my better half," I said. "See you in Hanksville!"

I nodded and they were off. And then I was off. I was determined to make it to Hanksville by noon. If I couldn't, then the heat would catch me and we would have to find shade to wait out the afternoon. So it was either race in by noon—which meant a total of 22 miles in six hours, minus the 1/2 hour stop we had at the trailer and whatever breaks we would need during the rest of the hike—or else not reach Hanksville until six or seven at night. There was no reason for me to rush to Hanksville, but after so many months on a trip like this, you start setting ridiculous, pointless goals and treating them like the most important goals in the whole world. And, anyway, in Hanksville there would be a hot shower, hot food, and cold drinks, all of which are motivations after three days in the desert.

We walked fast. The Sun rose higher and hotter, but we kept going. We stopped once in the shade of a butte for about 30 minutes with seven or eight miles left to go. Our last water cache lay behind that butte, but I decided to leave it in favor of making good time. But it looked like Mabel was favoring one of her paws when we started again. She was not limping, but it looked a bit like she was favoring a paw. I wasn't sure, but I am a worrier when it comes to Mabel, so I tossed her up on top of the cart. When the cart started moving with her on top of it she looked at me with the exact same expression I imagine was on Einstein's face when he formulated his equation for general relativity. Take a kid raised in some dark jungle in some "uncivilized" tribe, let him grow up to be about 18 years old, eating only manioc and squash and what not, and give him an ice cream cone. That's the same look. Of course she had known all along that she "could" ride up there, but My God!, it was so much better and more elegant in real life than she could ever imagine!

So my 120-pound cart became a 165-pound cart. But I was determined to be in a cold shower before the heat of the day, so I started running. Running is not my thing, really. And running while pushing a heavy cart, in the heat, with a guitar on my back, is really not my thing. So I ran a quarter of a mile and walked a quarter of a mile, ran a half a mile and then walked a half a mile, over and over again, and I made it to Hanksville by 12:30. I don't think that is too shabby. Not quite marathon time, but I was getting better. The first thing I did when I got to Hanksville was drink about a quart of ice cold orange Fanta, which had become my second favorite thing to drink an ice cold quart of after a long hike, right behind grape Fanta.

Jenny had taken a room for all of us in a cheap motel in Hanksville.

"Nice place," I said when I opened the unlocked door.

"Isn't it? I got the booties."

"Great. I have to run up to the store for some food, I think."

"Lucy's paws are pretty bad," she said.

"I know."

"She'll need a day off."

"I know," I said. "Probably more than a day. I don't mind a day for Mabel, either. Phone works here, so I'll talk with car support." I arranged for our driver, Jon, to meet us in Utah. He would have to get from Chicago to Michigan to pick up the car from Heidi, then drive out to Utah. I had had almost no real contact with Jon except through email. I'd not even talked to him on the phone—but he came highly recommended by a wonderful woman I'd gone to law school with, his older sister.

And there we sat for three days. Each morning I woke and asked and each morning Jenny said that Lucy couldn't walk. She took Lucy for little walks in the parking lot, and I watched, and Lucy simply couldn't walk. Blisters had formed and broken on at least two of her pads, and they looked angry. I felt bad for the poor puppy, because she shouldn't have been allowed to run around like she had. Jenny tried the dog booties, but Lucy would hardly walk in them at all. She would high step and whimper and fight until the booties would slip off.

"Not today?" I asked.

"I don't think so," Jenny answered with a big smile.

The next day was the same and the next. I began to worry about Lucy being able to hike at all, so we asked around in Hanksville to find out where our next stop could be. We'd be hiking through some pretty open country, and I was sure we could find plenty of places to camp, but I was worried about having access to enough water and communication. Jon would be headed our way shortly, and I wanted to be in contact with him. There was a motel some miles up the road, I think about 20.

When we finally hiked out, we had lost a lot of time. Lucy could hardly walk. She struggled for the first mile or so, and then she gave up entirely.

"She can't walk," Jenny said.

"I know. Give her to me."

I pulled her up by the scruff of her neck and the skin of her hips and put her on my cart. Lucy was offended by the indignity of it. We pushed on, and I had to keep a hand on Lucy's neck to calm her for a long time because she was nervous at first on top of the cart. She never completely stopped fidgeting and sometimes decided to jump off the cart but then she would be unable to walk and I would pick her back up and put her back on the cart. Mabel was jealous for a second, but then she calmed and seemed to understand what was happening.

We came across a store-like-restaurant-thing in the middle of nowhere and that saved us, I think. It was called Luna Mesa. It was two buildings—one a store and one a building of three rooms for rent—and they sat on a flat valley between ageless, crumbing mesas. The owner and her daughter, both stout blonde women, were there running the restaurant—which really wasn't much of a restaurant, but it did serve beer—and we took one of the rooms. There was WiFi, although it hardly worked. I went out to the room and found that it was full of someone's stuff, so I went back to ask about it.

"Oh, yeah, don't take any of that stuff," the owner said. "That guy's going to come back after he raises some money. He was crossing the U.S., too. On a horse."

"Ah," I said.

Then she told me that the bed in the room had been John Wayne's. I'm not a John Wayne fan, but I decided that it would be a neat story to sleep in John Wayne's bed, so I went back to the room to claim the bed before Jenny did. When I got there, though, Jenny had already claimed the bed.

"Did you know this was John Wayne's?" she asked and laughed. "Can you believe that?"

I unrolled my bedding on the floor.

We were there another three days. Each day I checked, and each day Lucy was unable to walk. The WiFi there was spotty, but every now and again I got service and got email updates from Heidi in Michigan. They read: "Jon's getting here tonight." Then the next read: "It's all fucked up w/Jon. He doesn't understand how time works, so he won't get here until midnight." Then: "UHM...Did you know he is NINETEEN YEARS OLD? Who the Hell did you loan my car to?" Then: "Jon can't leave this morning, because the car is in the shop. He'll leave tomorrow morning." I replied to her and we had a conversation. Heidi had no faith at all that Jon could find us. Heidi confessed that she was not sure she could even find us on the map.

"We are near Koosharem," I typed.

"Where the Hell is Koosharem, Utah?" she asked. I did not answer, but she must have found it. "You have to get to Koosharem," she typed to me. "I've gone over the route with him and I know he can find Koosharem. You have to get to Koosharem."

"We can't just get there. It's at least one, probably two days' hike and Lucy can't walk."

"Ok, but he won't find you unless you make it to Koosharem. He left already."

"He's got a phone."

"Yeah, so do you, Dumbass! And how is your service?"

I returned to the room. Jenny was reading something.

"We have to get to Koosharem," I said. "I'm going to ask the girl here for a ride. We can get everything into that Subaru she has if we have to."

"Ok," Jenny said, and went back to her reading.

The girl—probably 20 or 22 years old—agreed quickly to take us into Koosharem the next day. Later that night, though, she told us that she couldn't because she had decided to go to Salt Lake to hear the "Prophet" speak and to see her boyfriend. I guess that's a thing for Mormons. Her mother could take us, though. But her mother only had the big pickup truck, so we'd have to fill the gas tank back up when we got there. I agreed.

We loaded the truck the next morning and settled up our bill. Jenny paid her half and, to the best of my knowledge, that was the last time she paid for half of anything on the trip. From that moment on, she paid for no gas, no food for Jon the driver, and didn't split any of the motel rooms. She did, from time to time, take her own motel room—a practice that I thought made sense and that I rather preferred.

The Mormon mother shuttled us to Koosharem. She made small talk and asked us where we were from. Jenny said Maine and I said Illinois.

"Illinois," she said. "Lincoln was from there."

"Yup," I said.

"Did you know he was a vampire hunter?"

Jenny and I chuckled. I think we'd both heard of that book that had come out called "Abraham Lincoln: Vampire Hunter". It was a comedic historical fiction piece premised on the idea that Lincoln fought vampires and that the Civil War was actually a struggle between vampires and regular people. I'd never read it, but the premise is pretty easy to figure out from the title. The Mormon mother went into great detail telling us about the plot. And, maybe five minutes into her re-telling of the story, it dawned on Jenny and me that she might have been *serious*—I still don't know.

"Well, I don't know," she said. "I always thought vampires weren't a real thing. But I guess I was wrong about that. They're all in China now, though. And we've got Lincoln to thank for that."

Conference w/Self on issue: Omission of November/December from Book III. Review Nov/Dec time sheets. Decide to include two timesheets, i.e.:

12.25.11
Woke early; determine Mabel and I must return Chicago. Note Chicago apartment empty; determine "alone" better than current situation, people & cars, etc. Packed; meeting w/parents all morning, some afternoon. Discuss traveling plans, etc.; note that my Mom smiles re: traveling.
T: "Where would you go if you could go anywhere?"
Mom: "I'm happy living here."
T: "I just mean to visit."
Mom: "Oh, everywhere. I guess Paris and Africa are the two things I'd most like to see."
Resolve to see Paris & Africa for Mom.
Finish packing; prepared to leave. Hug Mom.
Mom: "Ah, it looks like your Dad wants to say something to you."
Go to Dad, on couch; help him stand; hold his hand as he stood, balance. Note Dad had been thinking about this moment a long time. Note it is hard for Dad to speak, gather thoughts; research his eyes: Almost empty, now.
Dad: "I don't have any fatherly advice for you."
Note frustration, Dad is still "in there". Determine Dad didn't know what I was 'going through', but knew it was something.
T: "Sometimes no advice is the best advice."
Smile.
Dad: "You won't get off that easy!"
Laugh. Note that Dad still speaks quickly when joking; conclude disease has not affected humor/wit portion of brain; consider irony.
Wait for Dad to speak, minutes pass.
Dad: "One time....Sometime....you'll come here..."
Try to interrupt Dad; know what he will say, he won't let me, he's put thought into it.
Dad: "I won't be here."
Hug father.
T: "I'll be home again this month."
Regret sentence; resolve to edit later. Analyze better response option, i.e., "You'll always be there Dad, no matter where or when". Try not to cry; determine does not matter, Dad cannot see tears. Hug Dad again; note he felt small.
Leave for Chicago.

We camped in another RV park in the center of Koosharem. It is not much of a town, but there is an RV Park and a grocery and a cafe that opened every now and again. The nights got cold. We had lost over a week of time/distance due to Lucy's injury, but we had made it to Koosharem. It had been a difficult process to work out the car support logistics. If Jon made it at all, it would be none too soon because Lucy could not walk without being carried on my cart, and carrying enough water for all four of us taxed the limits of my cart and my body. So we would wait in Koosharem for Jon to show up. But I had no cell reception there, either—to contact Jon, I had to ask Jenny to text him. I would ask her to text for updates, and sometimes she would and sometimes she wouldn't. Add to that the fact that Jon's service was spotty and he wasn't so good at keeping up with texts either, and we were all living in bubbles of ignorance.

There was a single RV in the park when we arrived, and two deer carcasses hung from the trees beside the RV. Deer carcasses hanging from trees are an almost everyday sight in my hometown, and I think probably in Jenny's hometown, too, so we weren't taken aback. The dogs, on the other hand, were keen. I took some pictures of the deer and chatted with the hunters, Gene and his son.

Gene and his son drive down several times a year from Ogden to hunt in Koosharem. They are Navajo, originally from New Mexico, but have lived in Utah for years and years. This day, they had taken two deer during the muzzleloader season and were done for the season. Gene gave me a beer and he talked with Jenny and me for quite a while about our trip and about Utah and about all sorts of things. Gene has run 58 marathons, and is a soft spoken but direct kind of fellow, and is the sort of fellow that really makes a hike like mine sing. I could have talked with him all night but Mabel and I were tired and Gene and his son were beat out from climbing a mountain and dragging deer carcasses down the mountain. He gave us four turkey dogs for dinner, and gave each of us a zip lock bag of oatmeal cookies. (Aside from my late grandmother's oatmeal, raisin, walnut cookies, they may have been the best oatmeal cookies on record.)

Gene told us about his family. He talked about his son playing high school football, and about his wife's career and the cookies she made. He told us how much he enjoys and treasures these weekends he gets out with his son to hike around hunting, and the time they get together. About how he took an early retirement, but was too young and healthy and had to go back to work to fill his days. Gene is the kind of content man that makes those around him feel more at ease.

Then I pitched my tent on a patch of grass in the park, far enough away from the deer that Mabel wouldn't be tempted to bolt out of the tent for a midnight snack. It was already dark out, but that made no difference—pitching the tent was second nature to me by then. I could do it in the dark, in the rain, in the wind. I could put my home up on gravel, on sand, on slick rock and in mud if I had to. I could guy out the sides on stakes or trees or large rocks. And in a pitch black night, I could put my hand in my cart and know by feel alone which four bags I needed with me in the tent at night— the sleeping bag, the tent supplies bag, the clothes stuff sack, and the emergency sack. So even though it was dark, I had the tent up and ready in a few minutes. A few minutes more and I was in the tent on my back on the cold familiar earth.

There is nothing in the world so comfortable as the ground to sleep on, once you are used to it. Soft beds make soft people. When I sleep on a soft bed, I wake up with any number of kinks and sore joints. But when I sleep on the ground, I wake up feeling strong and limber.

And there is no better place than on the ground to think about the mistakes you have made and the course your life is on. That is life on the ground.

While in Koosharem, I wrote this in my journal:

I don't smell good, and I can't seem to wash it off. It is not a bad smell, to me, because I am used to it, but I know I don't smell good. I know I smell like a hybrid bum/cowboy/marathoner/camper. The smell is in my clothes and my hair and my skin.

You don't think about things like this before you walk across the country.

Or, you do think of them, but you really have no frame of reference.

I had a pretty grueling time crossing the mountains in West Virginia, and when I got to Wolf Summit, on the western side of the mountains, a nice lady in town let me stay on her sofa. She had to go to a basketball game or something that night, but told me to make myself at home and to use the shower, laundry, or whatever I felt like using. So when she had gone, I left my pack in the living room and took a shower. When I was done, I felt fresh and clean. Then I walked out of the bathroom and through her kitchen and her house stunk—I mean really badly. It smelled like a sweaty horse had been locked in a smokehouse accidentally and had to fight his way out. I thought it was odd that such a nice lady with such a well-kept house would let such an odor linger about. I also thought it was odd that I hadn't noticed the smell until after my shower. Then I realized it was actually the clothes in my pack. In the living room.

It was hot, humid, and dusty in Iowa and Nebraska. That is a horrible combination. Your whole body gets muddy. After 20 or 30 miles in the heat, you get...grimy. I stayed at a lot of people's houses and in a lot of motels across those heat wave states just for access to a shower. The water that collected in the shower would look like mud. When I rinsed my mouth, I could feel whole layers of dust rinse away.

In the east, when I was still hiking in boots, a cloud of dead skin would puff off from my feet when I pulled my socks off.

Your arms and legs feel dirty. Your hands. Your eyelids feel dirty. There is grime under your fingernails that appears just seconds after you clean them. In the east, your hair gets dirty and mats together, and in the arid west it dries out like straw until the individual hairs crack and break if you try to run your fingers through your hair.

And I have two pairs of pants. One is for hiking and the other pair is for more formal occasions, like walking from a campsite to a gas station in the middle of the night when you realize you have no food. They are both dirty. I do my laundry mostly in motel sinks. If you walk 200 or 300 miles in the same shirt and pants through a hot, dusty land, and then wash them in a motel sink, you get perspective on life. My clothes are usually so dirty that they are noticeably lighter weight after I wash them.

It is one of those bizarre tricks of nature that Mabel, who, despite a whole lot of people's attempts to anthropomorphize her, is a dog, manages somehow to stay cleaner than I do. When I stop at gas stations or grocery stores after long hikes, folks will run right up to Mabel and hug her and let her jump on them, but they keep a healthy distance from me. I guess that is because I look and smell like a homeless guy, but a dog can never really be homeless. If we end up busted up and out of luck on the side of the road, someone will say "oh, look at that sweet stray! Let's take her home!". But no one will say "oh, look at that sweet homeless man and his fragile male ego! Let's take him home!". No. I am out of luck there.

I got rare updates of Jon's progress filtered through Jenny and through spotty cell service; it was like playing the telephone game as a kid. He'd stopped a night in Chicago, a few hours away from where he'd picked up the car. And Jenny and I waited. Then he'd stopped in Iowa to stay with a friend rather than pay for a motel, which made complete sense. And Jenny and I waited. Then communication dropped off. I found out later that he'd lost a day to a flat tire—a flat tire that the service station had not charged him to repair, thankfully. Then lost another day when he grew tired in the afternoon in Nebraska. He was not used to waking up early, and I could relate to that because I had been a 19-year-old kid once. Then he lost two days in the mountains of Colorado because the weather turned against him. But at the time I didn't know *any of this*. So I sat in the campground growing angrier and angrier. We were still at quite a high elevation and we couldn't *move* because Lucy was crippled. And I really couldn't leave Jenny behind in a town of 20 people. I walked around the town to pirate WiFi signals on my phone, and to keep in contact with Heidi. Together, we decided that, when Jon got there, if I didn't trust him or like the look of him, I would have him shuttle us to Salt Lake or a similarly developed city and send him directly back with Heidi's car.

I cannot remember how many days we lost in Koosharem, but it was many.

Jon finally pulled into town in the middle of the day, and he was easy enough to spot. He was the only black dude for about a thousand miles. He's a lighter skinned black fellow, and his facial structure is sort of half-African, half-European, and half-Hopi, and he's got an explosion of curly hair on top of his head like Sideshow Bob. He's not an especially tall fellow and he's not a very big fellow, and he hardly talks *at all*, but he's got a rather big personality that shines through all of that. He's a quiet, artistic type.

"Sorry it took so long, Man," he said. "It's a long drive."

"No worries," I said.

And I was immediately put at ease. It would work out. I found WiFi and immediately emailed Heidi: "Jon's here. Car's fine. Jon's fine. This will work."

"Jon, come around back and I'll introduce you to Jenny."

Around back of the RV Park, Jon and Jenny shook hands. Jon is the most laid-back person I've ever met, I think, and it's almost impossible to gauge what he is thinking about anything. And he'd not had the easiest life growing up, first as a white kid in a black neighborhood and then as a black kid in a white neighborhood. So he was no stranger to tense situations. Jenny left shortly to see if the grocery store was open.

"Alright," Jon said. "Good to be here. This is going to be pretty cool, I think. Is she your, uh, girlfriend or something?"

"Nope," I said. "Just a hiker." Jon nodded and looked around.

"Not really what I expected so far."

"It gets better," I said. "There will be some good skies and some good weather."

"Nice. I haven't spent much time in the desert. This is a pretty cool thing, Man. Pretty cool." He had a satchel full of books with him and he dug into them right away.

Jon settled in, and Jenny returned.

"I'm *really* low on food," she said. "At the store they said there's a town about 50 miles up the road with a grocery store and a Wal-Mart. I need more tire stuff, too. So I'm going to go up there, if you need anything."

"Jon'll have to drive," I said.

"I can," she said.

"No. Only Jon and I are insured to drive it. Heidi didn't want everyone driving it. Just Jon and, in emergencies, me." Jenny looked confused and a bit angry.

"I don't mind," Jon said. "I don't mind."

"It's cool," I said. "Jon's here to drive. He should drive."

They took off together and I stayed behind to watch Lucy and Mabel.

Book II: Feel the Selfish Fury (E)
Ah, take the Cash in Hand and wave the Rest.

Isra called about a month after she broke up with me. We talked, and she wanted to get back together.

"Yes, I want to come back," she said. "Can you forgive me? We could go on a trip together."

"I'm going to Europe in August," I said. "For Carrie's wedding. I already bought the tickets."

"Am I still invited?"

"No," I said.

"I couldn't go, anyway."

"You're not invited. I already RSVP'd."

"I don't know why I do the things I do," she said. "But I'm done with it."

"You want to come over?"

"Yes. No, but yes. I mean I want to, but I don't *want* to *want* to."

I don't know why we got back together the last time. If I did know, I would probably better understand why I went to law school, why I went to biglaw, and why I went to walk across the country.

"Can we be ok together?" she asked me. "Will it be ok, or is it tainted?"

"It can be ok," I said.

"I'm moving to [a different state]," she said. "I think. I interviewed the other day, and I think I'll get the job. Can we be ok together if we're apart?"

"Yes," I said. "I'm leaving Sidley to walk across the country."

"You are? Finally?"

"Yes," I said. "In March."

"Jesus that will be awesome."

"I know," I agreed.

"But can *we* be ok?"

"Yes," I said. "Just don't ever fuck me over again."

"I won't," she said.

Somewhere around March, I started working on a project with a partner in the bankruptcy group. It was the most awful experience of my life. The project should probably have taken me about eight hours and, indeed, my first turn on the project took about eight hours. But the partner I was working for turned the project into a circus. He and I met for two hours every day...*every day*...at the end of each day, and for two hours he would assail me with questions to which there were no answers. That's fine, if you're engaged in some Socratic dialogue to reach a deeper philosophical truth. But when the question is "what does this term mean?" and the answer is "it's not clear from the documents what the term means" then two hours of adversarial discussion about the question seemed to me to serve no purpose other than to fill billable hours. The whole process was adversarial...*but we were not supposed to be adversaries.* I drafted an eight-page memo on an issue and, after turning comment after comment after comment from the partner over *several* months, the memo turned into something like 75 pages. It was a freaking treatise. After each turn of comments, I would discuss the comments with the counsel who worked with me on the project. I said, over and over again, that the project was being blown way out of proportion. I knew the client would not be happy with it, because the "answers" to the legal questions presented—in so far as there were answers to be had—were as clear as a bell on the very first day and set forward clearly in the very first eight page memo. (Incidentally, they had been set forward pretty clearly in a similar memo on the same issues for the same client but prepared in a different practice group.) But this partner could not accept the answers as I presented them. Once, after a particularly stupid turn of comments, I remember thinking: "Is this lawyering? If this is lawyering, I don't think I want to be an attorney." And, the thing is, the partner was generally respected and considered to be a great attorney. So he was no doubt "right" that *this was, in fact,* good lawyering.

After about three or four weeks of working with this partner, I came to the only rational conclusion I could: This assignment was a career-killer. I had been tasked with this assignment (with this partner) because there was no room for me in the bankruptcy group. I could not get work through regular channels because I'd come into the group at a bad time, and I was no longer willing to hustle to get work from a bunch of frat-boys and racists. Therefore, I had to go. I was pretty sure they wanted me out and that's why I was forced to put up with this nonsense day after day after day after day.

BOOK III: ...AND THE MOON SAYS HALLELUJAH, 01.09.12(4)

Meet pretty American stranger on street, Annelise; have drinks in Old Town San Pedro. Chuckle at her southern accent; remember I have southern accent when drunk/tired.

A: "What do you do?"

T: "Very American question."

A: "Just because I'm ahn vacation doesn't mean I'm not Amurrricun."

T: "I walk around. I just walked across the US with my dog."

A: "The whole way? That is amazing! Where is your dog?"

T: "Back in Chicago. I miss her. I love her. She's with a friend and I get an email update every day telling me that she's ok."

A: "That is so sweet. That is so strange, you know, I heard about a guy doing that last year. He was a lawyer. Know him?"

T: "Yeah. I've heard that story."

A: "Do you know him?"

T: "It's a small community, cross-country thru-hikers. We all end up knowing each other a little bit. Email and what have you."

A: "This is so cool!"

T: "It's cool enough. It's not really cool."

A: "When I read about that guy, I thought it was something that like *nobody* did, you know?"

T: "Not many people do. Maybe 10 people attempt it every year? Maybe three might make it? Maybe not that many. Who knows?"

A: "Still, it's an *amazing* accomplishment. And when I read about that guy and his dog, it really hit me, you know, like really hard, because I'm an attorney and I'm not really happy with my job."

T: "I really have to get back to the hotel."

Return to Pedro's; edit manuscript. Speak at length with Australian travelers, not impressed by their demeanor; wish I were younger again. Re-write substantial section of manuscript; note improved consistency in tone and voice. Drink two beers. Note that Rosie was busy checking guests in; wait until no one was looking, sneak into office and made pot coffee; drink cup coffee. See Celio arrive; shout: "CELIOOOOOO".

C: "So tell me more of this story."

T: "Ok."

See Rosie appear, smiling, sits at table.

R: "More?"

T: "I guess there's more."
R: "Tell us about the hardest part of the trip."
T: "It was all difficult in different ways."
C: "Ah, such is life, Friend."
T: "Yup. C'est la guerre."
C: "Yup. Such is the war, Friend."

BOOK II: FEEL THE SELFISH FURY (E)(i)
THE WORLDLY HOPE MEN SET THEIR HEARTS UPON.

Isra lived with me that summer, more or less, and until she moved away at the end of August. She was supportive of the Walk, loved the idea, and gave me pointers about dog packs. We talked a lot about the routes. She asked a lot of questions. I was happy for her when she moved away—I wasn't happy that we'd be so far apart, but I was happy that she'd finally gotten a job. And I was happy, too, because I had always wanted to live in the state she was heading to.

Mostly we talked about two things: 1) What kind of dog I would get for the Walk, and 2) What we would do after the Walk was over. I was on the fence about even taking a dog with me. I love dogs, and didn't want to go on the Walk alone, but I didn't know if I could handle the added responsibility of a dog. Isra was certain that I should take a dog with me, and she sent me listing after listing of puppies available for adoption. I researched what kind of dog would do best on such a long trip, and settled on a blue heeler. I have always loved blue heelers, anyway, and everything I read indicated that the blue heeler (or red heeler) would be the best breed of dog for such a long trip over such varied terrain.

I flew out to visit her and Radio several times, and those were great weekends. Isra was nervous about the next summer, because she'd have to take another bar exam while working, but when I was there we relaxed and hung out together like we used to. We went to bookstores and got books about long distance hiking. We went to outfitters and looked at different kinds of boots and sleeping bags. She had a lot of good input, but she mostly pushed me to get a dog.

"I don't believe you'll *get* a dog," she often said.

"I will, it just takes time to find the right one!"

"Yeah, yeah. You never do what you say you're going to do."

"I do," I said. "Don't I?"

We talked about how long the Walk would take, and when I would be able to move in with her. We discussed what months we could get married in, and whether we should have a destination wedding. She loved to talk about destination weddings, but we knew we would have to get married in Chicago because her family was there.

In the meantime, I ate and I "trained". The training was nowhere near as serious as it should have been, but I did still have some work to do and I spent a lot of time with Isra. And I spent a lot of time trying to convince people to come with me on the Walk. Isra could not come with me, but I asked her. When she said no, I asked two high school friends who I'd not spent a lot of time with over the last few years—Scott and Everett. Both initially said they would come along, but I knew they wouldn't. And, sure enough, they dropped out over time. I asked a few associates at Sidley, too, but I *really* knew that none of them would go. One girl in the bankruptcy group *almost* went, and she wanted to. She was the biggest supporter of the Walk in those days. Her name was Wendy, and I would stop by her office and talk to her about the Walk. I'd answer her questions and tell her that she should come along. Wendy left Sidley before I did.

And one day in the hallway at Sidley, I ran into a partner in the group who was primarily responsible for making sure associates have enough work.

"What are you working on lately?" she asked.

"Nothing," I said.

"You have nothing on your plate?" she asked.

"I *have no plate*," I answered. She promised me that someone would contact me by the end of the day to staff me on a project, but no one did. And I didn't care.

BOOK I: THE MOMENTS THAT TURN US (E)(i)
ERE THE BETTER MOON AROSE.

From Koosharem, we were a day south to the campground at Otter Creek Reservoir. Lucy rode in the car that day, and would ride for most of the rest of the trip. Jon drove ahead five or six miles and waited for us, then we'd meet with him and he'd drive ahead another five or six miles and wait. Jenny and I were still hiking more or less together at that time. The road out of Koosharem was in a high, green valley between mountains and it was quite pretty. It was not hot and rain threatened. The nights would be cold until we got down off the mountains. A driver pulled over to us late in the day and gave us chicken dinners his wife had made and stuffed into recycled cottage cheese tubs. I thought of Isra's mom, who saved every plastic container that came into her house. The meal was delicious and we ate alongside the road.

It was late in the day when we made it to the reservoir and night started to fall, so Jenny, Lucy, and Mabel rode w/Jon the mile or so east to the campground. I hiked on alone in the desert and sang songs to myself until Jon returned to get me and we rode to the campground. The campground was right beside the reservoir and there were mosquitoes, but not like before. The wind started to pick up and big thunderheads formed around the edges of the valley all around us. The wind was cold and strong.

"It's $15 for the night," Jenny said.

"A piece or for the plot?"

"The plot," she said. "I didn't pay yet, but I'll pay it later or pay it in the morning."

"Ok," I said. I'd paid for our entire stay in Koosharem, and was happy to let her pay the whole $15 for the night. We pitched our tents and helped Jon pitch his enormous 8- or 10-person family tent. It was the only tent he had and, because he was driving rather than hiking, the weight of it didn't matter that much. Jon's family had urged him to bring far, far too much stuff with him and the little car was pretty well packed with just his stuff. That would be a problem, but there was nothing I could do.

"Yeah, man," he said as we stared into the cramped trunk. "They just kept giving me stuff and making me take stuff. I have like four jackets in there."

"They couldn't have known," I said. "And it's better to be safe than sorry—to have it and not need it, rather than to need it and not have it. Can we mail some of it home?"

"I don't care," he said. "Sure."

We all camped and the wind blew hard. It pulled the stakes out from Jon's tent and his tent half fell over in the night because the large walls of it caught the wind like a sail.

In the morning, we decided to ride ahead to the next town to scout the terrain and search for a cell signal so that Jon could call his family. He had been out of touch since leaving 170 days earlier. There was allegedly cell service in Circleville, and I hadn't been in contact with my mother for many days, either.

"We'll be back," I said, and Jenny nodded.

Just outside of the campsite, on a hill driving toward Circleville, about five cops pulled us over. We hadn't seen five cars that close together in weeks, and here we were being pulled over. I was 33 years old, an attorney, and had been pulled over several times in my life. I knew we were fine, but I still had that little twinge you get when you get pulled over. But Jon said "Well, looks like we're being pulled over" as calm as a cow in Calcutta. It struck me that he and I had led very different lives.

The officers asked why we'd stayed at the campground without paying, and I explained that I thought Jenny had paid and, at any rate, we hadn't actually left the campground yet. All our stuff was still there. There was an officer on the right hand side of the car who looked to be in a bad mood, but the one dealing with us was pretty cool once he heard that it had been a mistake.

"Well, I can't just let you go," he said.

"Can I just pay it here?" I asked.

"Sure."

I paid and he gave me a receipt.

"That's not how it would work in Chicago," I joked.

"No?"

"Yeah, no. I'd give you $15, but I doubt I'd get a receipt."

He laughed and we laughed and then we went on to Circleville to check my voice mail.

We were a couple more days through the desert down to Panguitch. The nights were generally cold by that time, and I was starting to worry about our safety, especially Jon's safety. Jon is a bright young man, but he had little camping experience and, most importantly, his tent was *gigantic*. It would take several bodies sleeping in a tent that size to raise the temperature considerably. A properly sized tent can help keep you warm, but his was so big that he may as well have been in the open. And that could be dangerous on cold ground because a stray foot or limb on the ground all night could get very cold, and maybe frostbit.

Jon and Jenny rode ahead and over the mountains in the Dixie National Forest to scope out Cedar City (where we'd initially planned to meet Jon) and came back with pretty rough news. It was cold up there, and snowing. We altered our route and were a day and a bit of a shuttle to Cedar City. We hiked again southbound, but it was cold and weather was on its way. We stopped into a motel to re-evaluate and watch the news and the weather forecast called for a snowstorm. I called several friends to "seek advice". What I really wanted was someone to tell me that the decision I'd already made was the right decision and the only decision we could make. First I called my friend Tuk, a biologist and outdoorsmen I'd known for 10 years.

"How cold is it?"

"Cold," I said.

"Snowing?"

"There are flurries right now."

"Elevation?"

"About 5500? Something like that. Maybe 5200?"

"And you're three people, two dogs. Has that girl got warm clothes yet?" he asked.

"She does, but not a lot, really. And I don't have any real *winter* gear. I can sleep warm and hike warm, but if there's snow then I'll have trouble keeping my feet dry."

"And the kid?"

"He's got a ton of clothes and a car. But his tent is *huge.*"

"Get off the mountain," Tuk said.

I called attorney friends and spoke with them.

"Is it a dangerous situation?" they asked.

"I think so. My friend Tuk thinks so."

"And Jon is 19?"

"Yes."

"Do you two have any legal relationship?" they asked.

"What?"

"Is he your employee?"

"I wouldn't say he's an employee," I answered.

"Are you paying him?"

"Well, I mean, I'm paying for his room and board while he's out here. And I'll give him a stipend, I think."

"Get off the mountain."

I went back to the room. Jenny and Jon were watching TV.

"It's about 48 miles to the edge of St. George," I said. "We're riding there tomorrow."

"Ok," Jenny said.

It snowed all through the night.

We took a room north of St. George, Utah. We could see the winter storm up at elevation and were glad to be safe and low. I was pretty depressed that we'd been too late and gotten stuck in winter weather at elevation. I blamed myself for taking on too much responsibility with Jenny and Lucy and Jon. Jenny had slowed Mabel and me down considerably in Colorado and then Lucy's paws had stopped us in our tracks in Utah. I suddenly wanted the trip to be over, quickly. I hadn't run very much since Nebraska, and I decided that I should try hard to speed up our pace. I could tell that Jenny was getting pretty road-worn, too, and was sure she'd adjust and keep a faster pace.

We had a short day out to a campsite along a waterway outside and to the west of St. George. I was happy that Jon finally got to do some decent desert camping, and the sky was nice that night, although not as clear or clean as we'd seen at elevation.

The hike through and out of St. George took us, descending most of the way, into a lowland that ran along a waterway. We walked through the Shivwets Band of the Paiute Indian Tribe Reservation. It was a beautiful hike on a perfect day. We spent quite a bit of the time following a dry riverbed; there were 1950s era cars discarded in the riverbed, and I wondered if they'd been abandoned there after crashing or whether powerful floods had washed them there. The right hand side of the walk was forested all through the Paiute reservation, and then we broke out of that into a hot and dry desert with steep climbs. Jon found us a little past mid-day, and I put Mabel in the car with Lucy because I didn't want her to overheat.

Near the end of the afternoon, we climbed a long and slow rise and the landscape gave way to low desert scrub brush and Joshua trees. It was getting late and I decided that we should make it into Littlefield, Arizona, to a campground there. We crested the final rise at about 23 miles for the day and looked down into a broad, high valley and could see the Interstate and Littlefield spread out before us. We could see Jon parked about a mile ahead, and I figured Jenny would give it up for the day when we reached the car.

We took a break beside the car with Jon and discussed the plan for the night. I thought we should push to Littlefield, and Jenny agreed that we should camp in Littlefield that night, but she'd had enough walking for the day and would shuttle the last couple of miles. In reality, the Littlefield campground was probably four or five miles away, but we were at the top of an enormous valley ringed with mountains and were looking down into it. Interstate 15 snaked long and white across the brown and red of the desert and it threw off our perception of distance. Jenny loaded her equipment in the car and they headed off into the campground with Lucy. I decided to keep walking, but asked that Jon return to get me before dark—I'm not a huge fan of being out in the desert alone at night. We watched the car disappear into a dot in the distance, and I jogged along into the valley.

Littlefield never seemed to get any closer. We kept jogging, pushing the cart in front of me, and the Sun dipped lower in the west almost beginning to kiss the tips of the mountains. We'd done probably 23 miles that day before I'd started jogging. I usually started to feel some effects of the "runner's high" at right around 25 miles. Just as I saw and neared the Welcome to Arizona sign, at about 25 miles for the day, the whole of the western side of the valley seemed to catch fire and burn cool orange as the Sun set. Joshua Trees were silhouetted pure black against the flaming orange backdrop of the western sky. No cars passed, no animals stirred, and the world was silent. Even my own footsteps made no sound. I jogged on watching the valley glow in that cool orange as if the whole world were on fire over there. The mountains were black, and their ridges and peaks were neatly rendered against the orange. To my left, the night rose clear and black over the eastern mountains, and a bashful moon peaked out from behind them. Those eastern mountains, though, were not washed in black like the western mountains because the light of the moon lit them up in gray shadows.

I stopped to take pictures and slowly realized that we were not alone— there was a pickup truck parked on a gravel road about a quarter mile away and a man stirred near the truck. The man looked beyond old, looked to weigh maybe 100 pounds, and carried a walking stick; the door to his truck was open and he was eating dinner. His name was Eli, and he was born in that corner of Arizona. He'd moved to California to be a horse jockey. He'd enlisted in the military, but they cut him for being too skinny and too small. Now, he lives back there where he was born, deep into the desert on an old gravel road and he tends to some cattle for a man who lives in northern Utah. For dinner, he drives into Littlefield and drives home with the warm dinner on his passenger seat, and always has to stop there to eat because it is not safe to drive into such a blinding Sunset. He told me about the Joshua Trees, and about the abandoned school that used to be out there before a flood washed it away. He told me about the rattlers that live all around, that the population of rattlers in that area was higher than anywhere else. Sometimes mountain lions ranged down for the cattle in his care, he said, but not too often. It's the snakes that I'd have to worry about, he said. But it shouldn't be too bad after nightfall. They'd be off hunting other things and not hanging around waiting to be stepped on my hikers. He wished me well on the rest of my trip.

In the middle of the sky above me, the rich blackness of the night met softly with the orange of the dying day and slowly overtook it.

We were a night in the Littlefield campground and then we rose in the morning and exploded into Nevada. It was a short 10 miles into Mesquite and we began the day thinking that we would overshoot Mesquite by many miles. But it was hot. For Mabel and me, anyway, it was the hottest day we'd had since Nebraska or maybe even Iowa and the heat dome. We were in low desert now, where the days are hot and the Sun is cutting. My head began to hurt in the burning Sun.

Halfway into Mesquite, Jenny's cart broke down again and she gave up.

"I could fix it," she said. "I called Jon and he's on his way back with my tire stuff."

"You don't carry your tire kit with you?"

"Jon has it," she said. "That's what car support is for, right? But it's so hot and Lucy's gotta get in with him, anyway. I'll probably ride into town."

"That sounds good," I said. "It's really too hot. When Jon passes me, I'll put Mabel in with him. But, the good news is that we got a place to stay in Vegas."

"Where?" she asked.

"THEhotel at Mandalay Bay. A Friend of the Walk emailed me and he's putting us up there."

I told her the dates and the details. I hate Vegas and had never been to Mandalay Bay, but the Friend of the Walk told me it was quite a nice place. The Friend of the Walk—who had sent me an iPad in Iowa—had emailed with me quite a bit. He worried about me and about the trip and somewhere along the way the trip began to mean something *to him*. He's an attorney, a successful partner at a biglaw firm. The Walk meant something to him, and he said that Mabel and I deserved a break in a real hotel and a massage and a good meal. He made me swear to keep his name confidential, and I intend to.

Brutal heat stopped us in Mesquite, Nevada. We were unaccustomed to it and it stopped us with headaches and exhaustion, so we laid up in Mesquite for the night. We were forced into another motel in Mesquite, but it was cheap, and Jon and I hung out around the pool and the hot tub all night long. But we were all awake and out early the next morning. It was another scorching day. We, along with Jenny and Lucy, made about 10 or 12 miles before the heat stopped us that day. The land all around was privately owned, so we could not camp there. Instead, Jenny and Lucy went back to Mesquite with Jon and checked back into the motel.

"Are you coming?" Jon asked.

"No," I said. "Take Mabel and take most of my stuff. I'm keeping a bunch of water and I'm going to keep going."

"All alone?" Jenny asked.

"Yeah, but Jon can come and pick me up in a bit."

"Well, ok," Jenny said. "It's just as well because Lucy can't keep going today."

"I'm going to run, though."

"Run?"

"Yeah. Jon...make sure you have your cell phone with you and make sure you're in a coverage area, just in case I get into trouble. If you don't hear from me at all before 3:00 or 3:30, then come to find me. I'll be on this road."

They left and I ran. Or I jogged, at least. I had the hiking boots on that day for some reason, and my feet baked inside them. I ran until I got too hot, and then I stopped to drink and to slide into the shade beside the rocks. I saw a turtle on the road and stopped to take pictures of it, and a local fellow with his son stopped to inspect the turtle. He and his son kept turtles together and he was thinking about taking this one home with him. But the turtle had already made it safely across the road, and the man was unsure whether it would be fair to take that victory away from the turtle. I ran on and I don't know whether the man gave the turtle a home or left him in his habitat.

The Sun and the heat felt like a blanket around me, but I kept going and kept stopping to drink. I went through a massive amount of water. I climbed a few hills, and when I was probably at the 18 or 20-mile mark I reached another hill and it was tough going up the thing. I stopped about halfway up and rested and wished I hadn't forgotten my umbrella. I saw a man jogging up the road from the bottom of the hill and decided to wait for him.

"What are you doing out here?" he asked. I told him.

"I'm parked at the bottom," he said. "I normally come out here and run about 5 miles out and 5 miles back. But not today! I'm just going to finish this hill and turn back."

"Are you ok?"

"It's just so damned hot!" he said.

"I agree. Need some water?"

He drank all the water in his water bottle then filled it up from my gallon jug and then he did it again.

"Do you need a ride?"

"No," I said. "I've got car support. He's off in town."

"Mesquite?"

"Yeah. He'll be out this way shortly."

The man ran off and I trudged up the hill after him, but I was pretty beat by that time. He met me again on his way down and he waved and then I crested the hill and the road turned. It was too damned hot, and I decided to sit and wait. I got out my phone to call and Jon called as I was dialing.

"Ok?"

"Yeah," I said. "Head on out."

The next morning we shuttled to where he'd picked me up as early as we could to beat the heat of the day. Jon dropped me off first and then returned for Jenny. I took Mabel with me because it was early and not so hot and we started running. When Jenny and Jon caught up to us that morning, they were shocked. We'd made quite a few miles and I felt sort of proud of myself for the first time in quite a long while, I think.

I put Mabel in with Jon and he went ahead of us. Jenny and I hiked; I was in the front and she fell a bit behind. But then I got tired and she caught up and then we were into tiny Overton. We stopped to break at lunchtime because it was terribly hot. We found a gas station with some picnic table seating under an awning and we sat there and ate and drank.

I felt like I had become a team leader and it was a team of a bunch of really bad tourists come from afar to visit American gas stations. But that was ok, because we were making good time.

We headed out in a bit and hiked out of town to the north end of Valley of Fire State Park. Jon had driven ahead to find the campground and told us it was another 20 miles or so into the park campground, so we decided to shuttle over to the campground. On the way, we saw a hilltop where people in RVs were squatting in the desert—we could have walked there to camp, but Jon had thought it was a town, because he'd not been on the road as long as we had. The Valley of Fire State Park is a shining, beautiful thing in a dry and barren desert in southern Nevada. There are standing rock formations and petrogylphs and all the rocks are a fiery red.

We camped at Arch Rock campground and quickly set about arguing. First we argued about whether or not to hike out the next day or to take the day off to enjoy the Park. I cannot remember *why* we were arguing—as I recall, Jenny said that we should stay the next day in the Park to look around and I started arguing just because I could. I could be remembering that wrongly, I guess. But we decided to spend the next day in the Park and I drove back in town to buy sodas and food, but really it was to get away from Jenny. The next day we hiked around and looked at petroglyphs and standing stone formations, and we talked with park rangers who told us that they were having trouble with killer bees in that area and all the way to Mojave. The rangers told us what to do if you encounter an angry bee, which is "not much"; be very calm, walk away, and don't operate any mechanical devices. If you're getting swarmed, run like hell. Then again, in Africa they tell people to fall down and kick up a cloud of dust. So there's that.

We set about arguing again that night. We planned the hike for the next day. We were fairly close to Vegas, but our reservations were not for several days. There were two ways out of the Park, a western and a southern route—the southern route was longer but followed paved roads. The western route, by contrast, relied heavily on BLM roads and other roads that hardly showed up on the maps. Further, there were two ways of hitting the western route—we could either head out the way we had come, or we could follow the gravel road on which the campsite sat up and over a hill to the other side. The latter route was not on the map, and we knew of it only because we were looking right at it.

"Well that way's closer," Jenny said.

"True, but I'm not sure the road is good." I went on talking, but I don't know if she was listening. "Look, the road's probably bad. And if it is shorter along the western route, that just puts us into Vegas on the 16th or 17th. If we go the southern route, we're in to Vegas on the 19th...and that's *ideal*, because it's only one day early. We should get there one day early, anyway, because this arrangement sucks for Jon—so he should get an extra day to see a blues show or something. But our reservations aren't until the 20th...so the western route, even if it were shorter and the roads were good, would still be three more nights in a hotel."

"I'm staying with a family friend," she said.

"I'm not," I said. "I'm paying for Jon and myself. And for gas."

"It's *shorter*," she said.

"I'm not even sure it is shorter," I said. "I'll go up there and check the road in a bit, anyway."

"It's *shorter*," Jenny said. "We need to go the shorter route, don't you think?"

"The road doesn't look good," I said. "And, just like I told you before, we can't take Heidi's car on these awful roads. I'll check it in a bit."

I took Heidi's car and drove it up the road a ways, and the road was no good, so I went back to the campsite.

"Can't do it," I said.

"Well, it's *shorter*," Jenny said. "So I think we should."

"The road is bad," I said. "We can't take Heidi's car..."

"What do you even think could happen? It's *shorter* and..."

"We're NOT. TAKING. HER. CAR. ON. THAT. ROAD." I said, and my tone was harsh. I could see right away that I'd offended Jenny. She left the campsite and walked around with Lucy. Jon shook his head a little and strummed on his guitar.

"I won't go that way," he said. "We'll go out the way we came."

"I don't want to damage Heidi's car," I said.

"We'll go out the way we came," he said again, and I wondered whether I was in charge or if he was. He's a sneaky fellow.

"This could get ugly with Jenny," I warned him. "At some point, we might have to have a horrible argument. Just warning you ahead of time. Either Jenny or I will probably say some really awful things about you. Just because that happens. But you're doing a great job, no matter what gets said."

"No worries," Jon said. "Doesn't bother me."

We struck camp early to get out of Arch Rock campground in the Valley of Fire. Nevada had tough on us so far, and we were not yet far into Nevada. Out there, our bodies *knew* how hot it was, and pulled toward shade like the dowsing rods of those old men who claim they can locate water underground. And it had been dusty—my whole body was covered in fine layers of dust by the time we reached Valley of Fire. It was in my hair and in my beard and between my teeth and my toes. My hiking shirt felt as though it had been starched from all the sweat and dust that had dried on it, leaving behind a tie-dye pattern of salt and dirt in the material.

I think Jenny was desperate to be near a freeway because she had not had good cell service for a long time. So Jenny got up earlier than I did that morning, got ready and hit the road about 40 minutes ahead of me on the western route. I was still packing up when she told me she was taking the western route and she took off. Again, I couldn't leave Jenny and Lucy stranded in the desert, so when I hiked out I *had* to follow the same path. On top of that, we got a slow start because Mabel or I had ripped the Big Agnes during the night—there was a snake sized hole at the foot of the thing, big enough for snakes and varmints to come through in the night. I could not patch it.

I caught up with them about an hour and a half later, and about 15 miles after that we reached I 15. The "frontage road", such as it was, was in bad shape. Jon and I tried to drive up it a little ways, but had to turn around.

We all sat in the blazing Sun for a long time, trying to decide what to do. Our options were to shuttle back to Valley of Fire and take the other route, which would now put us into Vegas either on time or a day late, or to shuttle 10 miles down the interstate to the point where the frontage road once again became paved, which would put us into Vegas four days early. After much hemming and a bit of hawing, we decided to camp that night about a mile down a side road, and then shuttle over to the paved frontage road the next morning. Jon would drop me and Mabel off at a Love's truck stop and then go back for Jenny and Lucy, and we would hike into Vegas from there.

Now we had another problem—we had been making such good time, that a shuttled 10 miles on top of that put us into Vegas four days early. Candidly, the idea of an extra four days in Vegas sounded pretty appealing to me. I was desperate to do laundry and to get a shower because I was temporarily sharing Jon's tent after the Big Agnes ripped. It was a big tent, plenty of room for Jon and Mabel and me, but I felt bad about making Jon share a tent with someone who smelled as bad as I did. At the same time, though, I did not want to spend money on four nights in a motel.

The next morning at the Love's truck stop, we sat in the shade of the building and discussed our options. Jenny spoke with the manager inside and learned that we could sit in the shade that day, park our car there that night, and camp on the BLM land across the street. So we decided to spend the day reading and eating and then to hike into Vegas the next day.

We each had breakfast and several bottles of soda or juice. And then lunchtime came around and we each bought a big lunch with some drinks, and I got Mabel some beef jerky. We met and talked with some interesting people and made phone calls we'd been meaning to make for days or weeks.

When the Sun moved over us, the shade began to disappear and we had to move to the other side of the building. The dogs were fine in the shade, but in the Sun it was simply too hot for them. So we walked to the other side of the building and then around to the far back where there is no entrance and the only reason to be back there is to either be in the shade or to walk to the dumpster. I had an afternoon snack and we waited in the shade for it to cool down enough to go across the road and set up our tents.

But then, as Jon was on the phone and Jenny was reading, a red shirted manager came outside—not the manager Jenny had spoken with but a new fellow there to take over for an evening shift.

"Do you have a problem or something?"

That's what he said. How do you even begin to answer that question?

Jon pulled phone away from his face and said: "Well, no, we don't have a problem...."

And before Jon or I could say anything else, Captain Manager said: "Then get out of here or I will call the police. You have been here an hour." And he stormed off.

It was still far too hot and sunny to sit in the desert without shade, and the building was the only shade for miles and miles. But Jenny was quick to walk over to the BLM to look for a place to set up her tent. I was wary about even parking the car there overnight, however, because Captain Manager seemed pretty inclined to ruin the days or nights of anyone he possibly could. So I went inside and asked for him.

"Hi," I said to him. "We were going to camp on the BLM land and park our car here overnight, which a lady told us earlier we could do. But she also told us we could use your shade so we and the dogs wouldn't die, and since you want us to leave the shade, I thought I would check about the car."

"Are we going to have a problem?" he asked, trying very hard to intimidate me, which was rather pointless.

"What?"

"There is no loitering here, Pal, and signs everywhere saying so". (I checked, and there were no signs, actually, but that is completely beside the point.)

"Ok, sure, what I am asking about is parking the car in your parking lot, overnight."

"If you can't loiter in the day why could you loiter at night?"

"No, see, we will be on the BLM land."

"The what?" he asked.

"Bureau of Land Management land. Right over there and all around us."

"Well that's not my property."

"Yes, I know that," I said. The problem was that he was not even entertaining the idea of listening to anything I had to say. He stared at me, trying to look "hard" and waiting for his next chance to use the words "loiter" and "police". I went on: "I am asking about the car. Parking the car here."

"Were you here last night?"

"No," I said.

"You weren't the homeless who parked here last night?"

Well, that question basically sums him all up, I think.

"No," I said. And by this time I had already decided we were not going to park the car there, nor were we going to sleep anywhere near this belligerent idiot.

"One night," he said. "A car can be parked here one night."

"Ok, whatever, we are leaving," I said, and started to leave, but he had to use the word "loiter" again.

"And there won't be any loitering."

"Great," I said. "Just for the record, though, we weren't loitering". I was going to enjoy discussing with him the fact that I had actually read the Nevada loitering laws.

He came out from behind the counter with his chest all puffed out and stood right in front of me. It was really like dealing with a 17-year-old punk boy except that this guy was at least 40. Too many people are like this, all defensive and belligerent for no reason at all.

"Well why don't we get the police out here and see what they think?" I was pretty sad just then. This fellow really seemed to be enjoying this, like this is what he lives for. He had sort of a look like this was an important moment in his life.

"Call the police if you want to," I said. "I might call them."

We took our time loading up and planning what to do. I don't know if he called the police or not, and I don't care.

We looked up and down the nearby county road for a place to camp. Jon dropped me off at the first spot that looked good, but bees overran the site while he was gone to get Jenny and I was pitching his enormous tent. Mabel and I hung out in the road about 400 yards away until they came back and then we all waited until it got dark because bees don't like to fly around at night. Then we quickly gathered the tent and the other stuff and moved a few hundred yards down the road. We camped on BLM land about three miles away from the Love's truck stop and, against my better judgment, I decided to buy my breakfast there the next morning.

Book III: ...And the Moon Says Hallelujah, 01.09.12(5)

R: "They should make a movie about this."

T: "No, they shouldn't."

R: "I would watch it."

T: "It's not a very good story."

R: "Not to you, maybe, because you did it."

T: "It's so long. I find it boring."

R: "You could cut the whole middle out."

T: "Yeah, well, that would have to happen. It would be a montage, you know. The whole Midwest."

R: "The Midwest?"

T: "Yeah. The whole middle. That was an important part, but it would get cut out. Would have to cut out Mary Ann, and Heidi, and my parents, and all the people in Iowa City. The three gals in Ohio, and Sam. It would just be a bunch of shots of my feet in different footwear."

R: "Shoes."

T: "Yes. And sandals."

R: "And they would change as you went on?"

T: "Yes."

R: "And a song would play?"

T: "Yes."

R: "And then..."

T: "And then we'd walk into Nebraska and across it and into Colorado and then we'd be standing there, just me and Mabel, in front of the Rocky Mountains."

R: "What did they look like?"

T: "They were big. The mountains were big."

R: "And what did you look like?"

T: "Different. I think I looked different."

R: "What about on the other side?"

Book I: The Moments That Turn Us (E)(ii)
Make Game of that which makes as much of Thee.

We approached Las Vegas from the northeast, through desiccated and rocky ground. Aside from the furious orange beauty of the Valley of Fire state park, it is a landscape of gray, dry death. The desert supports scrub brush and chaparral, but there are no Joshua trees or stately Saguaro cactus out there. It is dirt and dust and rock, and there is always trash in the low-lying places beside the road. Discarded couches and tires and washing machines. Along I 15 there is a Paiute truck stop that sells gas and sandwiches, has a casino, and is otherwise a large fireworks store—the open multi-acre lot beside the store is littered filthy with fireworks packaging and beer bottles, and as we came upon the field it looked to me like the floor underneath the bleachers after a basketball game at my high school; you could light a fire that would burn forever. When we found places to pull over and camp, and where Jon could park the car for the night, we had to be careful not to pitch our tents on shards of broken beer bottles or the rusty spent rifle casings that litter the desert.

You know you are getting closer to a town or city by the amount of roadside trash there is. Cigarette packages are everywhere, for example, and beer bottles, but McDonald's bags and Starbucks cups mean you are getting close to a town. I imagined chubby fingers quickly and greedily stuffing sandwiches into puffed faces, and pouring fries into open mouths before tossing their garbage out the window. But out there in the Nevada desert, on the seldom-used roads, the trash is spectacular. I imagined long, heartfelt discussions in a poorly decorated apartment when two young lovers discuss whether or not to get rid of this couch, their first couch, and when the woman of the couple finally accepts that the couch must go and asks what they will do with it, I see a sly smile on the Man's face and he says something like "now, don't you worry your pretty little head, Sugar, me and Tommy'll take care of it". It is a hard life for a couch that no one wants around anymore.

Out there in the 40 or 50 miles before Las Vegas, there are surreal Sunsets that take your mind off of all the trash, and from as far away as 50 miles or more there is a Sunset that never ends but burns all night long. When the Sun drops behind a far away ridge, or behind a mountain, its last sigh in the dying day is a halo of light that it spits up and over silhouetted mountains. Those last minutes of daylight shining behind southwestern mountains saved otherwise awful days in the desert—from the edge of Colorado all the way through Utah and Arizona, those Sunsets alone would have made the Walk worthwhile.

But out there, on the road to Vegas, the Sun never fully disappeared behind the mountains. Instead, the orange and yellow lips of light over the mountains only changed color to a translucent blue, almost green, lip of light that never disappeared through the night. It is the light from the Las Vegas Strip, but it is difficult to believe that any man-made city could glow so brightly. And it *is* comforting out there to think that somehow the Sun has gotten stuck and will never set completely on you. You might never be alone in the desert at night so long as the Sun is always setting in Las Vegas.

But every morning, the Sun comes up in the east as it should, and soon enough you are walking through fields of trash in a barbaric heat. C'est la guerre.

We walked in to Vegas on Hwy 604. About 20 miles out, the road crests a ridge and the valley opens up below you and there is Las Vegas. From that distance it looks almost like any other city, except with a replica of Seattle's Space Needle. From that distance, the Strip looks like any other metropolitan downtown. You cannot see from that distance that it is a city of gambling and tourism, or that it is a city of facades. You cannot see the people huddling up shoulder to shoulder to watch the fountain at Bellagio. You cannot see or smell the banquet of ribs and shrimp and sushi and any other food that you have ever imagined in such bounty. You cannot see the giggling girls taking turns having their picture taken with this-or-that B or C list movie star they ran into on the Strip. You cannot see the arguing families, or the hookers, or the thousands of men handing out calling cards for "straight to your room" dancers. You cannot see the vomiting frat boys or the crack heads who walk the streets. But you can see all of that if you keep walking!

We walked beneath the flight path of planes taking off from Nellis Air Force base. The stream of jet fighters was endless, hundreds of fighter jets one after another all through the day, running exercises or whatever it is they do. Sometimes flying straight up until they disappeared into dots in the sky, sometimes flying in tight formations, and sometimes circling the city like the mosquitoes that buzzed around my tent at night. And then we walked by the Vegas Speedway, where cars thundered round and round in endless circles.

And a friend of Jenny's family picked up Jenny and Lucy out there on the edge of North Las Vegas so she wouldn't have to walk through areas we'd been warned to avoid. Jon brought me a sandwich from town and we sat there together on the edge of Vegas, eating lunch in the heat. He was not looking forward to an afternoon of driving around Vegas looking for shade, and I was trying to summon up the strength of will to walk through a city on such a hot day. Neither Jenny nor I were scared of North Las Vegas; we'd both walked through several rough neighborhoods on this trip—I did in D.C., and Cincinnati, and Decatur, and Springfield, and Des Moines, and in other smaller towns. But I was desperate for a shower, and walking urban areas takes forever. So I deferred another dream, and instead of finishing a marathon to Mandalay Bay, we rode a mile into the historic Travelodge motel beside the Circus Circus. Then we had to go to an outfitter to replace my tent with another Big Agnes tent, and I needed a new, smaller pair of pants.

We were checked in to the Travelodge beside the Circus Circus. It was the cheapest pet friendly motel on or near the Strip, and I emphasize "cheap", and Jon was none too keen to stay in that awful little room. He went out to see things and to hear things and to do things. I was a bit tired and didn't want to leave Mabel alone, so I stayed in the first night we were at the Travelodge. But I told myself that I would go out and live it up once we checked in to THEhotel at Mandalay Bay. So I checked to make sure that all the parts were included in the new tent that I had purchased, and I did my laundry at the KOA Campground behind the Travelodge, and I answered emails and returned phone calls. And I told myself that I was staying in because I wanted to do all those things. But the thing is, I stayed in because I was uncomfortable on the Las Vegas Strip with all the people. When Jon and I walked to dinner, I was nervous about all the people out walking around.

And the second night, around 11, I walked the length of the Strip and back. I had no patience for the tourists and was overcome with anxiety. There were so many people, all shoulder-to-shoulder and all walking at weird, leisurely paces. Hundreds of people were queued up outside Bellagio to see the fountain, and my heart raced and skipped beats as I walked beside and among the tourists. After every few steps, I looked first slightly in front of my left foot and back to slightly behind in a sweep that I constantly do to check on Mabel, to make sure she is there and not limping and not asking for food. But she was back at the motel. And every time I left her alone, even to get a soda pop, when I came back she went crazy and I knew she was thinking I would never come back. She was like that when I was packed for the day, too, whether in a motel or in a campsite. Each time she thought "Well, this is it! This is the time he forgets me!" I told her that I wouldn't ever forget her, but she doesn't speak English. And I tried to tell her that she will have to get used to being alone sometimes, and that she will have to learn to trust that I will come back every day and feed her and walk her and all that. But she doesn't understand and was always afraid that the next time I walked out the door I would never come back.

The Strip is unreal, and it ain't my thing. It's a few miles long and is as bright as noon at midnight, glittering and flashing and strobing. It's gaudy and disgusting and so over-the-top that it almost circles back around to being in good taste. The sidewalks are clutch after clutch of people from all over the world. I heard English and Spanish, and Urdu and Hindi, and French and German, and Russian and everywhere Chinese—probably both Mandarin and Cantonese, but I can't tell them apart. There were Sikh men in turbans and German men in socks and sandals, and even a group of four young Muslim women in hijabs. If you are a Muslim woman who wears the hijab, I would think you would not be inclined to vacation in Las Vegas: Everything in Vegas is a bit haram I would think. But to each their own.

There are homeless men in Las Vegas who sit with signs asking for money, and there are street performers playing the guitar and bagpipes and everything in between. Thousands of men and women hand out calling cards for strippers and prostitutes, and preachers on corners tell everyone in earshot that they are going to Hell. Everyone is selling or gambling or buying or a little of it all. And there I was. I didn't buy or sell or gamble. There is no place for a guy like me in Las Vegas.

But we stayed THEhotel at Mandalay Bay. Jenny stayed there two nights, as well, in her own room, before she went off back to her family friend. I got a massage and ate good food and had a few drinks. My mom mailed some clean clothes to me, and it was strange to wear regular clothes after so long on the road. My niece was in town by coincidence, and we met up at a casino so I could hang out with her and her husband. I was glad to leave Vegas when our time was up, but wasn't too glad to leave behind the beautiful hotel and hot food and clean sheets.

We left the Mandalay Bay with the car loaded to bursting with Jenny's gear and my gear, and we were out of water. It would have taken two hours, at least, to fill our many empty gallon jugs of water on the 20th floor of the hotel and then to carry them down to the car. So Jon and I didn't fill the water bottles. Anyway, we had all of Jenny's stuff, all of my stuff, Jon and Mabel and me in the car, so the car was packed tight. I texted Jenny and asked her to pick up water on her way out of town. Jenny and her host had decided to meet us outside Las Vegas that day and we would camp out there in the desert on the outskirts of the city that night. On our way out of town, though, Jenny texted me back asking why she should have to get water and didn't we have a bunch of water bottles in the car?

That pissed me off like you cannot imagine.

Since Koosharem, she had not put in a dollar for gasoline, which had been the agreement back in Colorado. She had not put in a dollar for Jon's food, which had been the agreement back in Colorado. I felt good about helping her achieve a dream—especially a dream so similar to my own goal. But she had been disagreeable, petty, and argumentative about everything since the car had arrived. She had constantly questioned my decisions about routing and about what roads the car could and could not traverse. She had argued about every thing she could argue about, and had slowed Mabel and I down by weeks: Lucy could not even walk, but Jenny never said thanks for the car support. And now this—she had her friend driving her around in Las Vegas, and we had all of her equipment, but she couldn't take a half an hour out of her day to get water? In the end, Jon and I stopped and bought water. I texted her to stop and get her own water if she wanted to have any, and of course she did.

I would provide no more water for her, and I would no longer slow our pace at all to accommodate her. She could keep up, be left behind, or could shuttle every day. We had never really been "sharing" car support to begin with...she had been using my car support. And I decided to start using it as I wanted.

We camped that night on a big, open patch in the desert where gun enthusiasts come to shoot their long-range rifles. A few showed up while we were there and we could hear their weapons crack the silence of the desert. We had a long and hot trek ahead of us.

We more or less followed along Interstate 15 southwest out of Las Vegas, toward Primm, Nevada. It was desolate hike, but there were plenty of places to camp. We hiked toward Primm on a stretch of empty gravel roads, far off from the paved roads. The roads were gravel, but they were not so bad that I felt that Jon could not drive on them. In the desert outside of Primm, there is an old town called Roach, which was not much of a town at all, so far as we could tell. The gravel road that goes through Roach and into Primm comes down off a hill on a pretty steep decline and empties into a dry lakebed at the bottom. Jenny and Lucy had trailed pretty far behind me for most of the day, but I slowed down for her to catch me at the bottom of the hill where the road entered the dried lakebed.

"How is Lucy?"

"Not good," Jenny said. "She can't go any farther. We need to get Jon to pick her up."

I told her that I had already called Jon to come to us because I had known she would want Lucy to ride the rest of the day. We walked along the road in the lakebed, but the road was upturned a few hundred yards into the lakebed. The road was so seriously deformed that the car would clearly be unable to drive on it. The lakebed, on the other hand, was fine for cars to drive on, but I did not know whether the lakebed would rejoin the road up near Roach or not. So it was not clear whether Jon could drive into Primm by this route or if he would have to turn around before Primm and go back the way he had come.

"Let's wait here," I said.

"What? Why?"

I explained to her about the road.

"That's stupid," she said. "What's the point of even having a car if it can't go on the road?"

"What?"

"I mean, what's even the point?"

"To carry your dog around?" I said. I was smiling, but I don't think it sounded like a joke. "Look, he's almost here."

We could see a plume of gravel dust up on the hill, and Jon pulled up moments later. I drank some water and had a snack and Jon and I leaned against the car while Jenny packed and repacked her equipment in the car, I guess making room for Lucy to sit in the back seat. Suddenly, she freaked out, screamed, and slammed the car door four or five times before running away screaming. There was a bee, and she had tried to kill it with the car door. She violated basically every rule that everyone had told us about how to behave when encountering a bee in that area. Jon and I walked away, too, but calmly, and from about 15 feet away, we watched as the extremely angry bee and two of his friends settled down on the handle of my cart. Who knows if these were killer bees or regular European honeybees?[23] Who knows how far from the hive we were? Who knows how close their buddies were? None of us knew the answers to any of that.

This is what we did know: I had a relatively untested juvenile allergy to bee stings, which Jenny had seen in action on Monarch Pass, and we had a 20 year-old kid with very little experience in high pressure situations, let alone dealing with a man dying of bee sting allergies, and we had three bees that may or may not have been killer bees. If they were killer bees, the one thing we absolutely could not do was start the car. We basically had to either wait for them to get bored and leave, or gamble on them being relatively non-aggressive European bees. Gambling is a hell of a lot easier to do when it is not your life you are gambling.

"Well this is stupid," Jenny announced. "Lucy and I have to get walking." And she left.

Not only did she leave, she left at a faster pace than I had ever seen her walk.

I was livid.

Jon was as close to angry as I ever saw him.

Jon and I waited until two of the bees had gone, and then we sort of crouched, ready to pounce at the first chance.

---

[23] At the time, I Tweeted that there had been Africanized honeybees on my car because the bees looked just like a picture of killer bees I had seen and not like the bees I had known growing up in Illinois. Later, I learned that Africanized honeybees and some European honeybees are nearly identical, and only a careful analysis and measurements can distinguish the two. So these bees may not, and probably were not, the dreaded Killer Bee. But the point was, at the time, we did not know that.

"As soon as that bee leaves the cart, I'll grab it," I said. "When I do, get in the car and shut the door. Give me five minutes or so, then start it and drive like hell in the other direction. I'll meet you in Primm."

That's what we did. The second the last bee flew away, we took off like bats out of hell. Mabel and I hiked fast, running off and on. We made great time despite the heat, and still we did not see Jenny and Lucy for hours. I first caught site of her as she was rounding the last turn into Primm. She had made better time in that section than she had on any other section of the hike. I was so pissed that I could hardly think straight. She had literally abandoned a 20-year-old kid with a man with a bee allergy after she'd angered potentially Africanized honeybees. There was and is no excuse for that, and no excuse for putting Jon in that position. When we finally met at a gas station in Primm, she was casually chatting with a couple of tourists talking about her grand adventure. I did not say a word to her and wondered if I would say another word to her for the rest of the trip. Jon knew how angry I was, and that made him uncomfortable. I felt like he was always a little bit on edge—despite how intensely laid back he was—that he might have to run away from an ugly scene and argument. I walked beside him near the car at the gas station, and he said:

"You said it yourself, Man, gotta hike your own hike."

"That's not what I meant," I said.

"I know."

I didn't want to argue with Jenny, even though I knew an argument was overdue. So, instead of dealing with her, I spent two or three hours on the phone with my student loan servicer. I hate them even worse than I hated Jenny just then.

We stayed that night in a motel in Primm. Primm is a bizarre little town made up of a gas station, an outlet mall, and a few casinos and hotels. Until recently, the town had been called State Line. We stayed that night in a casino/hotel. I considered waking up Jon early and hiking out without her. I didn't.

We hiked into California the next day, and all of the sudden we were in the last state of the trip. I began to think that Mabel and I might make it coast-to-coast after all. Mabel and I ran some of the day and walked most of it. It was a hot day and I was sick to death of my feet being hot in the hiking boots. We found a place to lay up for the night north of the Mojave, and while I was milling around and doing nothing much important, my right ankle—the one that was already more or less sprained—rolled over on itself. My hiking boot ripped and sort of blew out on the side when my ankle rolled. I decided to drive back to Primm to get a new pair of shoes. I was tired of my feet being hot, my sandals were blown out, the hiking boots were making my ankle weak, and now the right boot was ripped out anyway.

The new shoes turned out to be mixed blessing. I bought tennis shoes partly for the reasons I listed, but also partly because I really wanted to run quite a bit of the remainder of the trip. I like to finish strong when I can, and since coming down out of elevation I was pretty sure I could run a marathon. But the very first day in the shoes almost ended the trip and probably should have at least delayed the trip. The new right shoe dug a hole into my right Achilles tendon. I noticed a pinching sensation in my right foot all during the first day in the shoes, but paid it little mind. When I took my shoes and socks off at the end of the day, the socks were spotted with blood and there was some flesh exposed on the tendon. I did not tell anyone in the party about it, though, because I wanted the damn trip to be over.

The Mojave Desert Preserve spread out in front of us, perhaps the last challenge of the trip—and hardly a challenge compared to the Rockies and the deserts of Utah and Nevada. I knew for a second that we would make it and my mind began to wander. I had not been much of a person from D.C. to Denver. I had been completely fearless and almost free from desires, too. My only desire had been nothing. Mabel had carried a zombie across the country, or maybe a hypnotized man. I doubt that I would have walked on if I hadn't had Mabel with me to take care of. I certainly wouldn't have finished the Walk. But from Denver on, it was like I was waking up slowly from a dream. And I woke up on an almost deserted highway in Arizona to find that I was a different person than the guy who had started the trip.

And I wanted to share that with Isra. I emailed her and told her that I didn't know why she'd stayed with me that whole time if I had been so bad for her. It was a mistake, I think. But that didn't matter—talking with her felt good to me. And I think it felt good to her, as well.

"You do sound different," she said.

"I feel different."

"Are you happy?"

"Yes," I said. "I think so."

"I didn't think you could ever be happy."

I laughed and agreed.

"Yeah, it must have seemed like that. How are you?"

She told me that she wasn't doing that well and that it had been a rough several months. She wasn't happy with a lot of things and wanted to leave the guy she was seeing.

"Well, maybe we should try again," I said.

"I don't think so," she said. "I still maintain we should have gotten married when we were in Oregon."

After we talked, I called her back and asked her to marry me. I told her she could meet me in San Diego and we could get married.

"Just think about it."

The next morning she texted me, and asked whether that had actually happened or whether she had dreamed it. I told her it was real, and we talked again that night. She wanted to know whether I had really changed. There were things about me that she couldn't stand before, she said, and we talked about them. But none of them were a big surprise to me. We talked about all the things that had ruined our relationship before: I came home from work in a bad mood; I wasn't there for her. I hadn't been a partner, or really been a part of her life, she said, and then I thought I could fix it all by paying for vacations and paying the rent and all of that. She hadn't wanted to spend my money; she had wanted to spend her time with me. More than that, she had wanted me to spend my time *for* her.

"This trip was all about you," she said. "That was too hard for me to take. I *needed* someone. But I've been all alone these eight months and I shouldn't have been. I've been all alone, and I don't know if I can get over that." I felt like she wanted to fight about this. I don't even know why we were fighting—but when you're trained to fight over every little detail and every little point, then that's what you do. It's not just attorneys.

"This trip wasn't just about me," I told her. "It wasn't just for me."

"Oh, you're so full of shit," she said. She was probably right.

It's not just attorneys who fight over every little point like this, I don't think. Sometimes I think relationships train people to interact with each other this way. But Isra and I—we treated each other like a law school class. I'm pretty sure that we tried to be good to each and good for each other, but we weren't and I don't think we knew how to be.

"It was about you," she said. "Maybe it wasn't for you in your mind, but it was about you."

"And, I mean, you haven't really been *alone*," I said. "I mean, you left me for a guy. Whom you're still with."

"I have to think about it," she said. "I want to say yes, but I don't *want* to *want* to say yes. I still maintain that we should have just gotten married when we were in Oregon."

When we got off the phone, I went back to the motel room and Jon was playing his guitar on the bed.

"What the Hell, Man?" he asked. "You ok?"

"Yeah," I said.

"You look drained. Somethin' wrong?"

"No," I said. "I just asked a girl who I used to be in love with to get married. I told her to meet me in San Diego."

"Wow."

"Yeah," I said. I shook my head. "Wow. She's going to say no."

"But she hasn't said no?"

"No," I said. "She said she wants to. But I know she won't. She's not like that. I can't believe I asked her like that. This might get ugly."

"Do you want to get married to her?"

"I don't know," I said. "This could get ugly."

"It's gonna be ugly if you keep walkin' around on that foot," Jon said.

"What?" I asked. I hadn't yet mentioned my foot to either Jon or Jenny, and I thought I'd hidden it.

"Saw the limping," he said. "Saw that...wound... last night."

My right foot *was* killing me. The shoes I'd gotten in Primm had destroyed my Achilles tendon in only two days' hiking. The shoe had worn a hole into the flesh and down to the tendon. The wound was inflamed and hurt so badly that I could not walk without limping. The wound was odd, though, or at least the way the new shoes fit was odd, because I could run with relatively little pain—I suppose it was due to the angle of impact, and that when I run I land primarily on the front sides of the balls of my feet rather than on my heel. When I walk, though, my heels strike first. I tried the ruined sandals and the hiking boots, but both rubbed exactly in the same spot.

"It's getting worse," I said. "I think it is sprained. I think I sprained it in Nevada."

"Just outside Vegas?" he asked. I was shocked that he'd obviously been paying such close attention.

"Yup. It's hurt more or less since Indiana, but it got really bad in Nevada that day."

I didn't tell him how badly it hurt. It hurt like hell, even before the wound, and since the wound had started developing the pain was getting dangerously close to debilitating. The pain around the wound was so bad, and was growing quickly, that I was worried it would get infected if it had not already.

"I'll be running tomorrow," I said.

"What?"

"You'll take Mabel," I said to him. "Keep her in the car all day with Lucy. I'm going to run. As far as I possibly can. We need to make time." I was worried that the wound would get bad and I would have to stop. We had a deadline, so I wanted to get as close to San Diego as possible before the injury could slow me down too much.

"Running, huh? Ok."

"You don't mind watching Mabel all day?" He shook his head. Of course he didn't mind! Jon Gamble was about the most laid back, well adjusted, and chilled out young man I had ever met. He was absolutely ideal for the job I asked him to do, despite the few silly things he'd done (and some he continued to do) that made the experience a little less efficient for me. It didn't matter: He was awesome. I resolved to give him some sort of gift in addition to the stipend, and had decided to give him an acoustic/electric nylon string guitar that I had.

The next day I ran off like an idiot into the Mojave Desert Preserve. Over the next two days, I ran off and on through entire days, averaging about five m.p.h. by alternating between running and stopping entirely. Sometimes I walked, but slowly and leaning heavily on my hiking stick. I met with Jon about every hour for water. And doing this, I left Jenny pretty far behind. At the end of the day, Jon could pick her up and shuttle her to wherever I had made it. On the first day into the Mojave Preserve, I made about 25 or 30 miles, and Jenny was somewhere back there. But I didn't care where she was—Jon could take care of her if she needed anything. I put the iPod on, cradled the stick in my right hand, and ran.

No matter how long I live, and no matter how many things I do in my life, I know there will never be a stretch in my life where I am stronger, more focused, or more driven than I was during that stretch of highway. I ran through exquisite pain, through intense heat, thirst, anger and joy. It frustrates me now to know that no matter how many hours or how many words I spend, I will never be able to explain the transcendent joy that I knew during that last week of the trip while I ran through the desert toward the ocean. At first, I ran because the pain of walking was annoying and I thought, wrongly, that I could avoid further injury by running. But then it started to hurt while I was running and I ran to spite the pain. And then, I don't know, it was just habit.

That first night in the Preserve, Jon circled back to pick up Jenny and I ran on. When they passed me on the highway, they told me that the campground they'd checked out was unreachable by car. I was sure that Jon had made that decision, not Jenny.

"Go on ahead then and look for the next camping spot," I said. I got my tent out of the back of the car and tucked it inside the cart, and I took Mabel back from the car. "I'll camp somewhere out here, and won't be more than a couple hundred feet off the highway. Find me in the morning."

"Ok!"

They were gone, and Mabel and I ran on. But we did not make it too far before the Sun began to drop behind a line of mountains in the west. We turned off the road, over a mound of dirt, and I started to scout for a place to camp. We'd taken only a few steps when I heard the first rattle. We stopped in our tracks, and Mabel and I both looked immediately to our left. There was a coiled, pissed off rattlesnake. It was a diamondback of some sort, and I imagined it was one of the Mojave greens we'd been warned about—the needlessly and surprisingly aggressive species. It was about 20 feet away, I'd say, or maybe a little more, so I was not worried that it would strike. But, just as I'd calmed myself from that start, we heard another rattle, this one coming from in front of us. That rattler, also pissed off, was somewhere in front of us, but I could not see it. It must have been as far away from us as the other one, I hoped, but I could not see it for all of the scrub brush. Mabel and I turned to our right to make for an opening that I could see in the scrub brush and desert bushes. There was a clearing large enough for us to pitch the tent and probably sleep soundly.

Then, another rattle.

This rattle was dangerously close, and it was a snake coiled in front of us in the bushes where we were walking. I used the walking stick to move the snake, and Mabel stayed calm and almost motionless. I used the stick to shake and disturb the scrub as far in front of me as possible, hoping that any snakes would leave.

Then we saw more. In total, I saw around 15 rattlesnakes before we made it to the clearing. Once there, but before I'd started to pitch the tent, we heard more rattles. They were all around us. I wanted us in that tent as soon as possible. For some reason, I thought that the tent would protect us. That was probably a silly notion. And as I started unpacking the tent to pitch it, I had to shoo away another rattlesnake. I felt like we were surrounded by these things, and the Sun was dropping rapidly. I wasn't sure whether that was a *good* or a *bad* thing—sure, the snakes would have to be less active during the night, because it would be cold and snakes are cold-blooded, but, then again, that might make the snakes more interested in investigating my body heat.

I opened and *drank* a can of baked beans while trying to unpack the tent, and then my phone rang. It was Jenny and Jon. They'd been up about 40 miles in search of a campsite but couldn't find one. They were headed back my way, and the night was so clear and the road so empty that I could see their headlights about 30 miles away. They were coming back toward us and were going to head into a little town that was about 30 miles *behind* me, and then they would come back out in the morning. I lost an important 5 minutes talking to them, and it was pretty dark. I decided that I would pack up, too, and go with them in to whatever town there was. None of this would work out well, of course.

They pulled up about 20 minutes later, and I had packed up everything and was trying to figure out how the hell Mabel and I would make it back to the road. Jon pulled over, and Jenny jumped out.

"DON'T COME OUT HERE!" I shouted.

"What? Why not?" she asked, and kept moving. "Snakes?"

"DON'T COME OUT HERE!" I shouted again. "There are snakes."

"Snakes?" she asked.

"Yes," I said. "A lot of snakes. Hundreds probably. I've seen and heard maybe 30. There must be more."

"What do we do?" she shouted at me.

"What is it, snakes?" Jon asked.

"Yeah, snakes. Stay there, Jon. Jenny, Jon is *not* coming out here. Just stay there."

"Can you get out of there?" she asked.

"Yeah, I don't know."

It was dark by then, and I was not keen on walking the couple hundred feet back to the road. There were almost certainly snakes out there between me and the road, and I didn't want to step on one and then die.

"Don't come out here without a stick and a flashlight," I said. Jenny had already pulled out her golf umbrella and a flashlight. She walked 10 or 20 feet off the road, maybe a little more, and stood there.

"Nothing here," she said. "If you can get *here* then you're golden!"

It was no easy thing to push that big cart through all the scrub brush. But I did, slowly, stopping often to shine the light around and to prod the scrub ahead of me to scare off any snakes. Once I made it out to the road, I said:

"Ok. Well, that was awesome. I guess you guys go ahead and find a place. I'll be here on this road. Come back for me, I guess."

They left, and I ran off after them, chasing them into the black night. There were no cars out there at night, and I could not see anything except by the little droplets of starlight and the fuzzy haze of a small town somewhere up in the distance. Jenny and Jon found a cheap room in a cheap...motel? ... bed and breakfast? It's tough to say what it was. But Jon came back and found me after I'd retraced maybe two or three miles, and all five of us slept in a tiny room. That was pretty miserable.

We shuttled out in the morning to where I'd been picked up the night before and Jenny took the day off. She was pretty ill from the heat, I think, and she'd had a couple of snake scares of her own.

"Are you seriously running again?" she asked.

I nodded that I was. And I took off. I think she and Jon were still talking about my stupid decision when I took off.

My goal was to clear the whole Mojave in two days, and I probably would have had it not been for my slow start that morning. But I ran through the day and drank a lot of water and made it pretty far through the Preserve. I met Jon and Jenny sitting in the car with the two dogs at a little junction of three roads at Kelso in the middle of the Preserve. There was a grocery store there, but it was only open seasonally and it was the wrong season. They decided they'd look for a place to camp and I ran on. I made it nearly through the Preserve that day, but not quite. I missed my goal of making it through the Preserve in two days by about four hours, I think.

My ankle bled pretty severely in those days. The wound wouldn't heal because I was up and running on it. At the end of the day, it hurt to take off my short socks because they'd fused in blood and skin to the wound. They tore at my ankle when I removed them. I started bandaging the ankle and even used an ACE bandage—which I never would do in normal circumstances.

South of the Preserve, we ran into a 45-mile stretch of road that ran alongside a Marine Corps Base and some sort of salt mining activity. We stopped for drinks at a roadside gas station on Old Route 66 and to plan our attack into San Diego, and were advised very strongly not to walk along the military base. We were advised *very* strongly not to camp alongside the base. So, again, we shuttled directly south around the base and then hiked into Twenty-Nine Palms. This was truly the home stretch of a long trip, and my ankle was killing me. I could not walk without limping and I'd begun limping while running, too.

We were two days from Twenty-Nine Palms around Joshua Tree to Palm Springs. Friends and Twitter followers sent me emails telling me that we were about to walk through the Banning Pass, which, for some reason, has an incredibly high rate of gang activity. So a lot of my friends and Twitter followers warned me and were afraid for me. I have never been particularly afraid of ganglands because it seems unlikely that I'd be mistaken for a gang member. So I thanked them for their concerns, but didn't give it too much thought. I was, however, giving a lot of thought to my ankle.

I took a picture of the wound and sent it to my doctor friend. His response was not good. He agreed with me that from the looks of it and my description of it, it had likely been infected, although it didn't look infected now. However, it also didn't look like living tissue. He thought I would probably need to have it debrided soon to prevent serious injury and possible sepsis. I put a Lincoln penny up by the wound—like you do to measure the depth of tread left on a tire—and the wound was deeper than the top of Lincoln's head. It reached almost to his brow. Good for tires, not so good for wounds.

"You *have* to go to a doctor," Jon said.

"I'll be ok, I think."

"No, Man," Jon said. "Like, you *have* to. As in, I'm going to make you go to a doctor."

"I'll slap some triple antibiotic ointment on it," I said. "It's getting better."

"Ok. But as soon as we see a doctor or, like, an urgent care, then you're going. You have to."

Jon had a little trouble saying what he meant. But I could tell from his tone that I really, truly didn't have any choice. He was right, of course.

Jon shuttled me over the freeway the next morning from Palm Springs back to the route outside of White Water. I ran west along the route while Jon returned to pick up Jenny and her things. I reached a crossroads where we'd agreed to meet, and I stood there waiting. There wasn't too much traffic out there, but I'll be damned if some gang members didn't drive by. So I guess all those warnings had been right. The two guys who, at any rate, looked like some rough gang-types, drove around the corner and slowed *way* down when they saw me standing there all broke and homeless on the side of the road but with a nice, big cart full of who knows what. They drove on, but came back about five minutes later. This second time, they drove very slowly and stared at me. They didn't hide the fact that they were sizing me up. I looked at them, but didn't really stare, and had almost no reaction at all. They drove off and Jon and Jenny showed up.

The next several miles of the trip were confusing and frustrating. The directions were wrong several times. We had to shuttle back and forth over the freeway several times. There were roads on the map that didn't exist in real life, and there were thru-roads on the map that were dead-ends in real life. I had difficulty making decisions. That was a strange day in that we walked probably 20 miles, and we ended up about 20 miles away from where we started, but with all the shuttled backtracking and shuttles over freeways, we *traveled* probably closer to 40 miles. It was a frustrating day, and I knew that Southern California would be a challenge simply from a pedestrian standpoint.

We were close.

And the closer we got, the more disconnected Jenny got from the "team", to the extent that it was a team. (Which it wasn't, and hadn't ever been.) Jenny took separate rooms at her own expense in the last couple of motels, despite not having any money for gas. I was glad to have some space away from her—although I suspected that she was planning a quick getaway so that she could avoid having a discussion with me about the costs of the trip.

On my last day with Jenny attached to the car, we started out heading south for San Diego. We were all on the side of the road, discussing plans for the day. By that time, they both knew about my ankle and about how badly it hurt.

"I don't think you should run on it," Jon said.

"Neither do I," Jenny agreed.

"I'm going to," I said, and tied my shoes. It was a long, flat road that day through a pretty, fertile valley. We were coming down into Temecula, and I hoped to make it to Escondido that day. "I'll see a doctor in Escondido."

They were still talking when I took off running. I ran, off and on, all day and all the way through Temecula. Jon brought me water about every hour and I would drink it down quickly and reach my hand in through the back window to pet Mabel. Then I'd run off again.

Jon caught me the last time north of Escondido. I'd done about 30 miles that day, and Jon told me that Jenny was almost 20 miles behind me, in Temecula. Jon and I stood by the car and talked for a long time. I played with Mabel a bit and favored my foot. My sock was stained with blood. Jon's phone rang and he answered it. Then, he got off the phone and turned to me.

"Well, I have to go back and take Jenny's stuff to her."

"What?" I asked.

"She's getting some other car support," he said. "She's back in Temecula, and her cousin or something is going to do car support for her for the rest of the trip. So she needs me to bring her stuff."

"Uh...no," I said.

"What?" Jon asked.

"Absolutely not," I said. "She's got a car? She can come and get her own stuff."

"Ok. That makes *sense*, Dude," Jon said.

"Yeah, text her that. Tell her I said to get her own stuff. She's safe, she's on her own. I wish I'd not gotten into that arrangement."

Jenny and her new car support met us at an Urgent Care in town. They arrived as I was inside seeing the doctor. The physicians' assistant, didn't want to do anything for me. He said that it was probably just a really bad blister that had broken and that I needed to stay off of it.

"Listen," I said. "I get where you're coming from. I do. But here's the deal—I'm going to walk 20 miles a day for the next three days in socks that haven't been washed since Las Vegas, Nevada."

He called in a regular doctor and the doctor prescribed me some antibiotics to protect against blood infection and some sort of antibiotic, topical steroid cream. The doctor said he didn't think debridement would be necessary, but that I should have it looked at when I was done with the trip for another opinion.

I left the office and found Jenny and her cousin, or whomever she was, in the parking lot talking to Jon. I felt bad that I was so glad to see her go. She said good luck and I wished her luck finishing out the trip. Once I'd started running, we'd made up many, many days and we were pretty far ahead of schedule for a change. Jenny said she'd probably take a week off and then finish in a rush on the 11th. I told her that I was still going to finish alone on the 10th and then have the public finish on the 11th. She left and I never saw her or her dog again.[24]

The rest of the trip into San Diego was easy enough. The weather was gorgeous once we got close to the sea, and there are few places on Earth quite so pleasant as those hills around San Diego. It's desert, but it feels like a lush desert where people could live and be happy and have families and little communities. On the last day into San Diego, I crested a hill on the road and could smell the ocean. I stopped and breathed it in a few times, then got out my phone to check the map. I was about 10 miles away from the ocean, as the crow flies. It struck me that I could, if I had the notion,

---

[24] Just to address the question that invariably gets asked about Jenny: No, Jenny and I were never involved in any romantic way. In fact, I believe we shook hands when we first met, but otherwise I don't remember us even being within a few feet of each other except when in a car or a shared motel room.

turn to my right and run flat out for an hour or so and be in the water. I'd made it.

BOOK II: FEEL THE SELFISH FURY (E)(ii)
ANOTHER AND ANOTHER CUP TO DROWN THE MEMORY OF THIS IMPERTINENCE!

I stood in my apartment in front of the tall sliding glass balcony doors to look at my reflection because I did not have a full-length mirror. The custom suits that I had fit well, but I still looked fat and tired. Even in the dark reflection of the door I could see that my eyes were hollow and my skin was sallow. I was fat and tired and ugly and miserable. But I was all dressed up for the group holiday party. In December of 2010, the Bankruptcy group had a holiday dinner party at a steakhouse in the Loop, as it did each year. We needed to bond in a non-working environment, I guess. The firm always had a firm-wide holiday party, and some years they had a formal ball, but in 2010 the ball had been cancelled due to the economic downturn.

I called Isra.

"I might burn some bridges tonight," I said.

"You always say that," she answered "Just go and schmooze or whatever you people do and then forget about it." She didn't get it that I was really done. She didn't believe that I was leaving, and she didn't believe that I going to do the Walk. She didn't believe anything about me. I can't blame her.

"I am a little nervous."

"Yeah, I don't really have time for this," she said. "Going out for another free dinner is not really a crisis, you know."

"Yeah," I said. "I know. I'm just..."

"It'll be fine. I'll be here for you, even if no one else is." I believed it when she said things like that, against all evidence; I think because we both wanted it to be true.

I arrived at the steakhouse earlier than almost anyone. A couple of other associates and I took over the reserved ballroom and I started drinking. The other associates started drinking, too, but not quite as quickly as I was. It was cold out, so we stood by the bar and watched our colleagues come in from the cold and check their coats and then come toward the bar, rubbing their hands together and smiling that big plastic smile that we all do.

"Coulson," a senior associate said and put his hand on my shoulder—the same associate who had called me "Taliban Tyler" at the associates' retreat.) "So cold out I wish I had that beard!" I shrugged a little and dove back into my glass of wine. I had already had a couple of beers and a shot of whiskey.

Everyone showed up, one by one, all "dressed" for the occasion. The heads of the group, and a few of the partners were suit-types and some of the associates were in suits. Most of the partners were sport jacket types, including Clifford Linklater, who had run me through the ringer all summer. Even that senior associate who had called me Taliban Tyler and Muhammad traded in his tweed and pastel for a night in a regular sport jacket.

296

"You guys see this guy," he said to whoever was listening, which, at that time, was a young partner in the group and me. "Think I should grow a beard like this to keep me warm?"

"There are two types of people who walk around without beards," I said. "Women and little boys. And I am neither."

"That's clever," he said and drank from his beer. "Didn't Socrates say that?" (One problem with drinking with attorneys is that they likely are just as familiar as you are with all of your obscure quotes.) "You're a philosopher, Coulson. Maybe I should join your Philosophers' Club." He smiled his goofy smile and rubbed at his cheeks and chin.

"You could try," I said. "But I wouldn't advise it."

"Why's that?"

"Failure might impact your self-image."

That was the end of that conversation, and he turned to talk to a young partner in the group. The partner smiled.

Everyone spaced out at tables for dinner to be served and I sat at a table with, among others, Clifford and Pat, who was sort of a sub-commander in the group. A fresh faced first year associate sat to my left, and a couple of other partners and associates were at my table, too. The first course came and I drank another glass or two of wine. I was getting drunk, which was about the only way that I could handle listening to the nonsense that I was about to hear and to say. Group dinners were always forced, banal things, with everyone keeping themselves in check to not offend anyone or share any real opinions. Only partners whose jobs were secure ever offered anything remotely close to a worthwhile opinion.

Pat was about the most charming person you could ever meet, with a huge, infectious smile and an Oklahoma accent. When she was working in her office, she would never look at you, but at parties or socially when she spoke with you, she looked you right in the eyes and you felt at once a bit threatened by her presence and a bit calmed that she was so intensely listening to you. Unlike a lot of partners, she really seemed to enjoy talking about politics at the table and she would guide the conversation towards some touchy subjects; her personality was so big that she could guide an entire table. That night, she for some reason started us on the idea of an inheritance tax. Pat was on the fence, she said, but Clifford was, of course, adamantly opposed to the idea of an inheritance tax.

"I can't see a meaningful distinction between an inheritance tax and theft," Clifford said.

"Well, that's where we differ," Pat said. "You're a conservative, I'm a liberal, and we come at it from these different perspectives."

"It's Un-American," Clifford said. "And it's already *been* taxed. How many times should one person be taxed on a dollar they make?"

For some reason, this is where I broke into the conversation. I think it's because I don't like that argument that dollars have "already been taxed". Dollars are never taxed, the *transactions* are taxed.

"Some people would say that the lack of an inheritance tax is un-American. Some families came to the United States in part to avoid systems that centralized wealth by encouraging intergenerational transfers of wealth."

The table sort of looked at me and didn't speak. The thing is, I kind of have one of those personalities like Pat has—but just a little, and not in a good way.

"But..." someone started to say.

"If I ever have children, I won't leave them much of an estate," I said. "But even if I could, I wouldn't. Inheritance is a wholly non-productive transfer of wealth to individuals who have done nothing to earn it."

"Intergenerational...?" Clifford started.

"Well, that's where you and I differ," I interrupted him.

Pat moved the conversation on to another topic, but it was unfortunately another political discussion. The waiter refilled my wine glass with each trip by the table and I was getting drunker and "opening up" in my way. Pat, or Clifford, one of the two, moved the conversation from the inheritance tax to the Bush Tax Cuts. Clifford shared his opinion, which of course was that taxes were far too high on those folks who made a shit-ton of money and that the tax cuts stimulated the economy.

"And, anyway, can we afford to let the tax cuts sunset? As a country, I think we have some serious, structural and financial problems. Can we afford the damage it would do to the economy if Congress let those cuts sunset? Of course, I am coming at this as a bankruptcy attorney."

"What are these financial problems?" I asked. Before Clifford, or anyone, could answer, I said "It's my understanding that the country's primary financial problems stem from entitlement programs whose funding has been looted by Congress, and by overextension of defense spending. Shouldn't the government increase revenue in order to meet the shortfalls? Isn't increasing revenue the only rational solution to these financial problems?"

"Cutting spending," someone said.

"Of course," I said. "Obviously we could cut spending—but that's a difficult nut to crack. Right now, the problem is soon to be meeting previously incurred obligations. Short of a massive spending cut, which won't happen, the options are increasing revenue or printing money. Or more borrowing. Should we borrow more money?"

I looked at Pat and Clifford.

"Lower taxes increase investment and stabilize the economy."

"Yeah, done a bang up job so far," I said. "Clearly the Bush Tax Cuts didn't stop us from falling into this depression."

"Recession," Pat said.

"A recession is a depression that doesn't affect the wealthy," I said. "Thirty years of this supply side bullshit and it's done nothing but cause economic inequality and send jobs overseas."

At some point, Pat changed the conversation again, but Clifford pulled it back to politics and the healthcare debate. The healthcare debate was on everyone's mind, anyway.

"That's another thing we cannot afford," he said. "We just *cannot afford* it. Now, we all here come at this from the perspective of a bankruptcy attorney, of course. But on the front-end, it's clear that we can't afford..."

"No it isn't," I said. "It's not clear. What is clear is that healthcare costs are *currently* spiraling out of control. What else is clear is that there are three parties in any health care transaction, the patient, the doctor, and the insurance company. Two of those parties are necessary, and one of those parties is a huge profit-motivated party that is unnecessary. It is clear as day that the first way to lower aggregate health care costs is to remove the profit-driven..."

"And replace it with what? A nationalized health care system like in Canada?" Clifford asked.

"Where infant mortality is lower, where average expected life span is longer and not dropping. Where per capita health care spending is lower."

"The free market..."

"There is no free market in health care," I said. "When was the last time you were at an emergency room and you heard a guy having a heart attack say 'Well, that all sounds reasonable, but let me go check around for another quote'? There is no free market in the provision of health care. There's never been a free market. Economics is a cult, and the free market is Santa Claus."

"That argument is not really...it's oversimplified," Clifford said. "And it proves too much. And I don't believe emergency care is a significant portion of overall health care costs in the U.S. But even if that were accurate, it can't change the economic realities. We *cannot* afford it."

I held my hands up like I was weighing a cup of grain against a nugget of gold.

"Yeah," I said, "Trillions of dollars on never-ending occupations of foreign lands that gain us nothing but $4 gas, or an expensive health care system here at home that might keep your kids or your parents off the streets, out of bankruptcy, and healthier longer...tough call."

That was pretty much the end of the table conversation. Shortly after that, Pat said something uncharacteristically awkward, like, "I think we should maybe get up and mingle around before the night gets away from us."

Later in the night, Clifford pulled me aside to talk with me. Me in my fat, drunken suit, and he in his sport jacket, pulled aside into a darker corner of the bar.

"Tyler, should we talk?"

"What's that?" I asked.

"I sort of felt that there was some hostility from you at the table tonight."

"Ok," I said.

"Was there?"

"Yes," I said.

"Why? Was it directed at me?"

"It was directed outward," I said. "Toward the world."

"Well, it seemed to me that you have some hostility toward me."

"Yeah," I said, "probably some of it. Because you're a fucking asshole."

"Wow," he said. "Just....wow."

So there was that. I spent the rest of the night mingling around and probably making an ass of myself. It was a rough evening.

The group heads always leave these things early because they have work to do. The head of our group, a fellow Iowa alumnus, stopped by me at the bar as he was leaving.

"Be safe tonight and have a happy holiday season," I said.

"You, too. We have a couple of stressful weeks coming up," he answered. "The Monticello Inc. case is blowing up next week. Will you be available?"

"I would say that is likely," I said with a smile, and he smiled back. We shook hands and he headed out. He and I had never had much of a working relationship, but had always treated each other with respect.

The partners disappeared one by one and we associates ended up at a nearby bar drinking until about midnight, expensing all of it on the firm. I drank a great deal and did a little dancing, and talked with all the associates. They were all intelligent, driven people; I hope they were and are happy. I kept drinking because the firm was paying for it and I wanted to suck as much out of the experience as possible.

I was angry and I was depressed, I think. I was bitter and I was not long for the world of Sidley Austin. The thought of spending time with any of those people—even the good ones, of which there were plenty—knotted my stomach and made my head spin. I must not have been the only person who felt that way, because there was always a lot of drinking at those events. There was always a lot of drinking among attorneys, period.

I don't remember much of what happened after the partners started to leave, and I don't remember the cab ride home. Alcohol poisoning was a concern. My memory starts to return later that night at my apartment, when I was on the floor of my bathroom vomiting all over myself and everything else. The world spun and my heart slowed and the smell of vomit and rancid wine was thick in the bathroom, and there were pools of purple vomit near the toilet and on my crumpled suit on the ground and splatters of it on the wall and on the rim of the toilet and, probably, in my beard. My face dripped sweat and my hands were cold and slippery and I could not grab hold of anything to get to my feet, which was just as well, because I would have fallen over if I could have gotten to my feet. And I was fat and bulging out of my white t-shirt and my boxer shorts, and sweating under my arms and trying desperately to stand up because laying there like I was, with my head against the wall, I could see the bulge of my pale gut coming out from under the white t-shirt and I was disgusted so I tried to stand up to get away from that sight and from that smell of vomit. I spun around and nearly vomited again, and then with my right hand on the side of the bathtub I tried to stand, but slipped and fell onto the floor among the pools of my vomit and with a slowing heart rate and rapid, shallow breaths, and everything faded away in a second and the world was all black and I was asleep.

BOOK III: ...AND THE MOON SAYS HALLELUJAH, 01.09.12(6)

Edit Book II in some detail. Begin work on Book III. Decide to use Rosie and Celio as template/composite characters. Ask permission, they agreed. Respond to requests, i.e., Celio requested to be taller; decide he would be 6'4" in the book instead of 5'8". Brunch w/Kendra at Estel's Dine by the Sea; learn she is healthy again; inform her that I was less than healthy myself. Note that she looks very good, rested; determine vacation has done wonders for her. Decide to see Mayan ruins at Lamanai day after tomorrow. Return to Pedro's. Request Rosie to book trip for us; ask Rosie if she had seen Lamanai; learn she had.

R: "Your book sounds very good. Now that I'm a character in it, it's better."

T: "You can read it when I'm done."

R: "What happens to my character?"

T: "I think you and Celio fall in love and run away together."

R: "Celio? But he's not really my type."

T: "It's a book. Books need to have happy endings."

R: "In all my favorite books, some people have happy endings and some people don't have happy endings!"

T: "Right. That's life."

R: "C'est la guerre".

Question whether a Belizean can say 'C'est la guerre'; determine they can, but meaning might be different. See Celio arrive.

C: "What's that?"

Pour coffee for Celio.

T: "Telling Rosie about the happy ending for the book. You and she fall in love and run away together."

C: "Pfft."

Hear Celio laugh; watch Celio leave.

R: "I guess I'm not his type, either."

Begin work on new project, called Project 777.

BOOK II: FEEL THE SELFISH FURY (E)(iii)
THE IDOLS I HAVE LOVED SO LONG HAVE DONE MY CREDIT IN MEN'S EYE MUCH WRONG.

My year-end review was scheduled for two days after the holiday party, and I went to work ready to let them have it. I had rehearsed and practiced what I would say, how I would tell them, and what I would expect from them. It was likely that they would see it coming, I knew, and there was a good possibility that they were out there rehearsing the same thing from their end—especially after the holiday party fiasco. I absolutely did not care. Getting out of there was the most important thing in my life right then, and all I wanted was to get as much from that place as I could before I left. I would have the Walk, and then I would have a happy life with Isra wherever we ended up together. I couldn't wait to see her and to have her and Radio back in my arms. And I talked to Isra about it on the phone and she gave me support and told me it was the right thing to do.

"They're probably going to fire me," I said.

"Not if you quit first," she would say. "And who fucking cares! The sooner you are out of there, the sooner you can start walking and the sooner you can get down here and we can be together again."

I paced around my office that morning, dreading what was about to happen and thinking without ceasing about my student loans. And at about 10 in the morning, Pat and a partner from the Los Angeles office showed up for my review. They were all smiles and they came in to sit down. I was almost ready to let them have it, when:

"Tyler, this is going to be a hard conversation for me," Pat said.

"Ah!" I said. "Well who should go first?"

"We think you maybe would be better off in a different group here at Sidley, or a different firm if you aren't happy here."

I couldn't tell if they were actually firing me, which would have been wholly unwarranted, or if they were *actually* saying that they recognized that I would be a better fit in a different group. You can never tell because, at least in biglaw, there is a premium put on being a fence-sitter and being mysterious and never actually saying anything directly.

"This may be a shock to you," I said, "but I have identified another option that might be a better fit for me right now."

"Oh, you have?" the Los Angeles partner asked. And they were actually *shocked*.

"Yes," I said. "There are very few jobs out there in this market. But I've been looking at another option and am leaving in March."

"Oh! March?" Pat said. "This works out well, then."

So there you have that. After I'd left Sidley and during the Walk, quite a few media outlets picked up my story. Almost none of them actually contacted me, by the way. Most of them spun my story as an epic "fuck you" email where I resigned at the spur of the moment, or something. But that wasn't the case. The case was that I quit working, more or less, in March of 2010 and the Sidley bankruptcy group and I parted ways at the beginning of 2011, neither of us happy with the other. I wished nothing but luck and well-being to all the people at Sidley. But I also want to leave them with no illusions: some of the attorneys there created a hostile and meaningless working environment for me. When I realized that everyone in biglaw works in a hostile environment that *need not* be hostile, I could no longer stay at that moment in my life. I still wish them all the best. It's a tough environment to work in, and it's tough to be a good person—or even a person at all—in an environment like that. I hope that those people who I worked with did not take their frustration and intensity home with them to their families and loved ones; I did, and I regret it deeply.

We ended the meeting joking with each other about all sorts of things. I had no hard feelings whatsoever for Pat—I liked and respected Pat, and I thought she was a decent person. I had no hard feelings for that Los Angeles partner, either—I did not *like* him, but I'd worked with him on a couple of projects and thought he was quite a decent partner to work for. I could tell by their reaction that they had been prepared for more fireworks, or waterworks, or whatever normally happens when a biglaw associate is rejected by his colleagues like a wolf that has been cut out of its pack.

Lawyers often think of themselves as wolves. But they're not. They're coyotes.

Book I: The Moments That Turn Us (E)(iii)(a)
The Nightingale That in the Branches Sang.

We checked into the Motel 6 in downtown San Diego on November 6, 2011. We were 6.3 miles from the ocean, but I had scheduled my final day as November 11, 2011, so we had several days to wait. We unloaded *all* of my gear and wheeled it into the room. Jon and I discussed his route home. He had a few stops to make on the way back to the Midwest, and I doubted that he would get the car back to Heidi by the 13th, when she would leave for Buenos Aires. Jon had done a hell of a good job being patient and being helpful. He had been out there with us for a long time—carrying Lucy around and, later, carting Mabel through half of the hot desert days—and had never once complained. I didn't think I would miss him, but I was sad to see him go. He was a great guy.

And then we were all alone again.

Mabel and I hadn't been truly alone like that since before Colorado Springs, although we'd been lonely. I talked with Isra for a while on the phone, and she said that she wanted to come to San Diego but that she couldn't because it wasn't right. "It wasn't right" and she wasn't a spontaneous person. I agreed with her, but I didn't tell her that. We argued instead. She hated me a lot, I think. And I didn't blame her, really. We'd been awfully bad for one another for a long time, but I guess we kept at it because we couldn't stand the idea of failure. She had, at least, been brave enough to walk away from a bad relationship. Then I went back inside the motel and got ready to sleep. I wouldn't sleep well for several months. I ordered a sandwich and fed Mabel and we were asleep pretty early in the night, but I woke up about two in the morning and couldn't get back to sleep. I watched television while Mabel slept on through the night, and I thought about the beach that was only six miles away.

Six miles.

Nothing. Two hours? Not even. We could walk it in an hour and a half. We could jog it in an hour. We could run it in 40 minutes, maybe less. Six miles? Nothing.

Mabel was sleeping soundly, and I could not sleep, so I went outside to walk around the block a few times or to stand in the open air. Six miles. I probably smiled a little to myself because I had been sure I *could not* possibly make that last six miles into Denton, Delaware, so many months earlier. It struck me that I could run six miles to the beach and six miles back before Mabel had even noticed I was gone. I looked down at my feet. There is something magical about the way feet touch the ground, about the way two feet keep a whole mind upright. Watch a person walk sometime, and watch their feet. Watch the way feet connect with the ground, lift up into the air, and then reconnect with the ground. Watch how intricately the toes, the ankle, the knee and the hip all work together. And the shoulders, and the many articulations of the spine. Watch how the whole body works—watch how it takes a whole body to move a single foot. And do it yourself. Take off your shoes and see what it feels like when all those thousands of nerves in your foot contact the warm Earth, the cold Earth, the only Earth we have.

Just six miles.

It would be hard to wait, I thought. Hard to come this far and then wait for five days to finish because I'd said that I'd finish on the 11th. Five days and six miles. Five days alone with nothing to do but walk Mabel and watch TV. I decided that I would probably head down to Ocean Beach the next day, or maybe the next, and stay with someone there who had offered a place for me. I wouldn't step on the beach until March 11, and that would be a good compromise, I figured.

It was silly to be out walking around for no reason and I was tired of being hassled by homeless guys and shady-types, so I went back to the motel to watch TV. Mabel woke up when I got back, and she repositioned herself on the bed so she could sleep with her back touching me, I guess so she would know that I was there. I might have slept for an hour or so, but I can't be sure. Everything was a little like a dream and a little like reality at that point, so maybe I was awake and maybe I was sleeping. That was about the same feeling I'd had on the beach in Delaware, and it's unsettling.

The next morning I took Mabel out and we walked around and I talked to my mother on the phone. She was awfully proud of me, and she asked me what it felt like to be so close to being finished. And I talked with my brother, and he asked me the same thing. I got some emails and some text messages, all from people telling me they were proud of what I'd done and asking me what it felt like to be so close to being done. It didn't feel like anything, really.

The thing is, you think that there will be some moment where you have a realization about something. Like the "meaning of life" is going to smack you in the face. You think that you'll walk and walk and then you'll sit down under a tree somewhere and all of the sudden you'll be enlightened. All of the sudden you'll know the answers. You think that somehow life is a riddle that can be solved. There has to be a solution! There has to be an answer…a *right* answer. But that doesn't happen. There is no answer. There isn't even a question. Some guy sometime in the distant past *made that up.* Just about everything is all made up, fabricated with pieces of philosophy and junk and science and wonder, all cobbled together into someone's "new" vision of the world to create answers to questions that some other guy made up. The questions are imagined. It doesn't matter how far you walk, or how high you climb, or how beautifully you sing, the only "answer" you'll ever find is going to be something that you make up. You invent it. That's it.

And there is no single Moment that can define your life. It's silly to think so. There is no "*Moment*". Sure, there may be a Moment or two that you remember forever in crystal clear detail, but that's not "you". If there is something permanent in a person, then it takes a whole legion of moments to see it. You cannot walk far enough to put straight the things you have made crooked. You just walk. That's all.

And you walk through Moment after Moment after Moment. The Sun sets so powerfully in Arizona that it seems to set the whole valley on fire. Cool wind dries and burns your face as you ride in the back of a truck at 90 mph through South Park, Colorado. A turtle slips from a log into the muddy water of the C & O Canal. Three beautiful women yell down from their balcony at a passing pedestrian. A bear shuffles back into the woods after being humbled. A man gets angry at his ex-girlfriend and, over the phone, he calls her a horrible name that he should know has special meaning and will hurt her. You write your name on a piece of paper. Somewhere, sometime, a man loses his faculties and puts the barrel of a gun to his forehead. Birds chirp in budding trees.

A couple's hands clasp together as they walk through a department store.

A man measures his newborn's fingers against his own.

Somewhere and sometime out there in the world, it all happens in Moments.

The driver takes his eyes off the road to send a text message. A lawyer puts his head to his desk and wonders why he's done this to himself. She says to him "and now your father will never know if he has grandchildren". A bill drops softly into a cup full of dimes and nickels, and a man who knows how to fish can eat for a day. And waves break ceaselessly over the reef a mile off the Belizean coast.

"What did you learn on this trip?" my friend from Sidley, Jorge Cromwell, asked me over the phone.

"About what?"

"The world. You."

"Which?" I asked.

"Both," he said.

"I learned that I am no longer afraid of anything or anyone."

"Good," he said. "That's good."

"It's not, is it?" I answer, quickly.

"And about the world? What's the meaning of life?"

"In every word, decision, or action that you take, you should do everything in your power to limit, or to eradicate entirely, any unjustifiable harm you would otherwise cause to another person, another living thing, or to the planet."

"That's deep," he said. "That's like the Golden Rule except for lawyers."

It was nice to talk to all those folks on the 7th of November, but by noon I was restless again and I was uncomfortable being inside. So I left Mabel inside and went back out to walk around downtown San Diego. I was listening to some tunes on the Old iPod, but I can't remember what I was listening to. I sort of wish I could remember, but then I kind of am glad I can't. Because I saw something. I don't know what it was that I saw out of the corner of my eye, or maybe even straight in front of me. It was a car, or a cat, or a person, or maybe a piece of paper blowing past me. I have no idea what it was. But it scared me to death.

And then, I guess, there was a Moment.

I was suddenly scared. Not scared like "ooh, that was a close call". But scared like I was actually about to be killed. The first thing I was afraid of was the cars, even though mostly they were *parked* cars, I was afraid of them. And the cars driving by on the road gave me little heart attacks. And then I was afraid of bears. Bears. In San Diego. I cannot explain it, but I was afraid of bears. And the weather. And of running out of water. And of Mabel getting hit by a car or bitten by a snake. I was afraid of absolutely everything, and was afraid with every part of my body. My skin was afraid, and my toes were afraid. I tried to control my breathing—kind of like I had learned to do back on the Canal—because I could tell that I was losing control of my body and my mind. My heart began to pump fast, and I counted it at about 160 beats per minute. I thought it was a heart attack at first. There were a few seconds where I wasn't sure if I could walk back to the motel room; I ducked for a second into the space behind the motel where no one could see me because I was afraid and because I was embarrassed because I could *feel* that I was about to start crying. I had no idea why.

When I made it back into the motel room, I was pretty much a mess. I was bawling pretty heavily, and couldn't think straight at all. No matter how much effort I mustered, I couldn't get my thoughts straight. Look, I tried to say to myself, there are *no bears* here. There are no cars here. There is a tap with water. Look at Mabel! She's fine and happy and she's staring at you because you're acting like a fool. But that was all rather pointless, because I could not stop crying and I could not keep my thoughts straight. All curled up almost in the fetal position on the floor, and I remember thinking: "Jesus, Dude, this is so fucking cliché. Get up!" But I couldn't get up—not because my body was tired, but because I couldn't *focus* enough to move my arms and legs and body to stand up.

My brain did not work right.

I must have been there for about two hours or so. Maybe longer. Not sure.

But Heidi called. And I answered.

"Congratulations, Man!" she said, and I couldn't answer. I started crying harder. It was so kind and considerate of her to have called to tell me congratulations.

"Are you ok?" she asked me, over and over again. And she said "Just breathe for a second, just breathe for a second. Are you ok? Do I need to call a doctor?"

And I pulled the phone away from my mouth farther so she couldn't hear me crying.

"Do I need to call a doctor? Tyler, tell me if you are alright."

"No," I said. "I don't need a doctor."

"What is wrong? What do you need?" she asked me. Over and over, patiently, waiting for me to answer.

"I don't know," I whispered to her. "I don't know."

"What do you want?" she asked me.

"I want to go home," I said. "I want to go *home.*"

"Then go home," she said. "Go home right now if you want to. You don't even have to go to the beach."

"I told everyone," I said.

"Yeah, yeah, I know," she said. "They'll understand. And if they don't, forget them. Who cares? How far are you from the beach?"

"Six miles," I said.

"Jesus Christ, Tyler. You *have* to finish. Right?"

"Yes," I said.

"Ok, then no problem. Get up in the morning, walk to the beach, then come home. No one will care. They will all understand. Even if they have to eat the cost of nonrefundable tickets. They will understand. And if they don't, it doesn't matter. Can you reserve a car?"

"I don't know," I said.

"I'll do it," Heidi said. And she set about reserving a rental car for me while she stayed on the phone. "There. Did you get a confirmation email?"

"I got something," I said.

"Just finish it up tomorrow and then go home."

"I don't really have a home to go to," I said.

"Ok. Well, think about that later. Right now, just finish the walk and then go to your parents' house. That's home. Or *like* home, right?"

"Yes," I said.

It took me a while to get enough composure together to call the friends who had planned to meet me in San Diego. I held my breath when I talked to them, trying my hardest not to cry. And I said to each of them something like: "Here's the deal, Man, I'm having kind of a rough time and I think I need to get this Walk finished and go home. So I'll probably finish tomorrow and not on the 11th." And each one of them completely understood. My friend Dean, who I hadn't seen in 10 years, said:

"Oh, come on! I just followed you for 8 months online, Man. You don't owe me anything. You do what you need to do, Buddy. If anything, I owe you!"

And, of course, I started crying when he said that. I basically cried all day.

I called Jack Planck, and held myself together really well when I talked with him.

"Hey, Buddy!"

"Hey," I said.

"Finish?"

"Not yet," I said. "Hey, when you called a couple weeks ago...when you finished did you sort of have crying fits?"

"Absolutely," he said. "Still do. It gets better."

I started crying again, but pulled the phone away so he couldn't hear me.

"Mine started the last week of the trip," he said. "And I had *family* with me! So I took a lot of showers. When I felt it about to happen, I'd just say 'Oh, I better take a shower'. And I'd go hide in the shower until it passed."

"So this keeps going?"

"For me it has," he said. "But it's getting better."

I did not bill an hour in 2011, to the best of my knowledge. Instead, I focused solely on planning the Walk and finishing gearing up for it. I'd had a pack for a while, but there was a lot that I needed. The battery and solar panel, the warm weather gear and sleeping bag and the boots and the socks and on and on. And I spent a lot of time studying and researching different ways to save weight and to save money on hiking equipment. And I continued walking every day on the treadmill, but added a 50-pound weight vest to make it a bit more realistic.

In January, Isra called me out of the blue.

"I did it," she said.

"Did what?"

"I got you a dog."

"Oh my God," I said.

"Wait 'till you *see* her! She is soooo cute and wonderful."

I flew out to see her that weekend. Isra's apartment was crowded with her, Radio, and the new puppy. The new dog was quiet and didn't seem healthy. She had gastrointestinal problems, and she wasn't very social. She was a red thing, and she mostly hid in the corner. But she would come to me when I sat on the couch, and I took her out every couple of hours, and she seemed to like me well enough. Through all the lethargy and sickness, she was a regal looking dog.

"I think we need to call her Shannon Murphy," Isra said.

"Shannon Murphy?"

"Because she's red! And that's the reddest name!"

"But I work with an attorney named Shannon Murphy," I said.

"She won't care. And I don't care if she does care. Who is she to think she's so important. She doesn't know this puppy's face!"

"I'll ask her."

"Or we could name her Matilda, or some other southern name. She needs a southern name."

"I don't like Matilda."

"How about Mavis?"

"Can't do that," I said.

"We could name her Laal."

"What's that?"

"It's 'red' in Urdu, but it's like red for red food."

"Eh... How about Mabel?"

"Mabel? Mabel. Mabel. Mabel. I don't know," she said, but I had decided.

We had the problem of how to get her back to Chicago, but Isra said she would drive her out to me the next weekend, which she did. We spent the weekend together and then she left to go home, and left Mabel there with me. I walked her out to her car when she left, and then Isra disappeared. Mabel looked up at me and, just like that, we were in this thing together.

I spent all of February walking with Mabel, and teaching her to walk on my left side at about my heel. I experimented with different food for her, and took her to the vet to get checked up—she had an infection in one of her mammary glands that I had to give her antibiotics to clear up. She learned her name and she made all the other dog owners at 5 E. 14th Place jealous because she was such a fine looking animal.

And I put the finishing touches on my farewell email.

I sent my farewell e-mail at around 2:30 p.m. on March 4, 2011. Farewell emails at biglaw firms almost always—and I mean 99.9% of the time—follow the same template:

> "Today is my last day at [FIRM]. You may reach me at [NEW AWESOME JOB] where I will [DO AWESOME THINGS]. It has been an honor and a privilege to work with such intelligent and driven people here at [FIRM], and I will always cherish and value the memories and training I've received here."

But that's not what my farewell email said. I'd written and re-written my farewell email about 100 times over the last year, and I'd run it by several of my attorney friends to get their comments. I wanted the email to have an actual impact; we all agreed that the farewell email is an undervalued thing. People don't recognize how much impact they can have, but I wanted mine to mean something. We toyed around with the idea of a very *long* farewell email, and with the idea of a one-word farewell email. We discussed and drafted farewell emails filled with profanity, and we discussed and drafted a long farewell email written in "legalese". Ultimately, guided in part by some powerful input from a particular associate at Sidley who would rather not be named, I settled on this:

> "Today is my last day at Sidley. You may keep in touch with me at --------@gmail.com, through Facebook at ---------------, or via Twitter, @ibuildnosystem. Beginning next week, I am walking from Delaware to California with a tent and my dog, Mabel. I will have limited access to email, but will check messages frequently."

That email was, to date, the best thing I've ever written. I wanted a response, and I got one.

My phone started to ring immediately. Within seconds. And my Outlook inbox on my computer screen started scrolling with emails coming in. Most of the people who called were partners in other groups—highly successful men and women, many of whom I had never met, let alone worked for. And the conversations were *all* the same: They all wanted me to know that I was doing the right thing. One of those conversations that I remember clearly, went like this:

Partner: "Is this real?"

Me: "Yup."

Partner: "Listen, I love my children. Don't think that I don't. I do. But they are expensive. And I've made promises to them. I've promised them cars and braces and good schools. *I cannot leave here.*"

My phone rang off the hook and emails flooded in. I didn't even try to read the emails, really, because I was too busy on the phone. But I did see an email pop up from the partner I'd worked for the previous year—the one who had turned my 8-page memo into an 80 page thing, all the while telling me I needed to value brevity and concision above all else. Yeah. I'll remember his email verbatim for probably my whole life: "Good luck, Tyler, on your transcontinental trek across this land."

Brevity, Good Sir. Brevity. And concision. And brevity.

I sat in my office fielding phone calls for about an hour and a half, I think, before I finally gave up and walked away. The phone was still ringing when I left my office at Sidley for the last time.

By the time I got home, my personal email account was flooded, too, and people from around the country had begun to follow me on Twitter. The next morning, the legal tabloid www.abovethelaw.com ran a story about my farewell email, and the emails flooded in again. On Thursday of that week I had two Twitter followers: my brother, and my friend Sirindir. By Monday, I had something like 500. People told me that lawyers had started office pools betting on when or how I would die.

Mabel and I drove from Chicago to Delaware in a rented car. We drove all night long. By the time I reached Philadelphia, the guy behind the counter at the rental car agency recognized us—he was an aspiring law student. I got emails and Facebook messages from attorneys and from animal lovers.

Mabel and I took a room in a motel near the beach in Rehoboth Beach. We hung around Rehoboth for a couple of days, waiting for a couple of last minute supplies to arrive in the mail. I read emails and thought about things. I was scared. I was intimidated. I was unsure of myself.

She and I woke up early on the 11th and walked down to the beach before the Sun was up. We sat down on the cold sand and listened to the waves. I didn't even know this dog, really. And she didn't know me. But I felt like she trusted me and maybe loved me a little bit. I told her that I was going to be happy one day and that I wasn't always going to be so miserable. A lot of lawyers are miserable, I told her. And a lot are not. But they all love a good story.

It was such a nice feeling to be outside and to listen to the sound of the ocean that I fell asleep.

BOOK I: THE MOMENTS THAT TURN US (E)(iii)(b)
WHEN THYSELF WITH SHINING FOOT SHALL PASS.

I didn't sleep at all that night. I packed and unpacked and repacked all my equipment and clothes over and over again. I did a load of laundry in the actual washing machine in the laundry room because I thought I would like to have clean clothes for the big finish. Not that it mattered at all to anyone, not even to me. But I couldn't sleep and I needed to kill time. I talked to a law school colleague named David Lichtenstein who was living and working in his native San Diego. He told me that he would be there the following day when I finished, and I was happy that someone would be there. A lady from San Diego would be there, too, because she is a filmmaker and wanted to film the big ending and to ask me some questions. I kept trying to kindly suggest somehow that maybe she should not bring a camera, but she wouldn't hear me. I probably should have been a bit more direct with her, because I did not want anyone to be there.

The next morning I put a couple of bottles of water in a small backpack that I had with me, grabbed the walking stick, and Mabel and I headed for the beach. I called all the people who I loved while I walked and said that I was thankful that they'd followed along with me and had helped in the ways that they had. And Isra and I had a horrible argument and we both said a bunch of things we would probably regret for a long time, or at least I would. I lashed out at her, partly because I wasn't getting my way, I guess, but mostly because I never really communicated with her. I never actually told her all the ways she let me down or all the ways I knew I let her down; I was tired of the point-by-point discussions and nuanced arguments. And I felt like I'd finally, maybe, accomplished something I could and should be proud of, and here she was trying to ruin it—even though I *invited* her to ruin it. I just got frustrated. So when she said mean things to me, I shouted mean things at her. C'est la guerre.

It was a beautiful day. But every day in San Diego is more or less beautiful, I think. The Sun was hot but not so powerful like it was in Utah and the Mojave, and every now and again a salty sea breeze swept over us and cut blonde waves into Mabel's bright auburn coat. I don't think Mabel knew we were about to finish a walk across a continent, but she knew there was an ocean up there, and she knew that I was excited. And that was enough for her.

I walked and limped because I did not want to run anymore and because the wound on my right Achilles was still there. The shoe rubbed hard against it when I stepped forward.

We climbed a couple of big hills, and then a final, huge hill and from the top we could see the ocean a few miles away. A sliver of blue and green bordered all the treetops and roofs of houses and businesses in San Diego. There wasn't much traffic at all, and were no pedestrians. For most of that last six miles it was just us, just Mabel and me. And I liked that; I liked that no one would ever see us walk that last few miles. No one would ever know we'd even been there and then we could vanish. We will vanish, she and I. Someday. Someday she will die or I will die and then there will be no more "we", just Mabel. Just Tyler. And then the other will go, and there will be nothing of us left at all. And a thousand years from now, no one will ever remember that we were here. No one will remember that Mabel and I walked six miles to the sea on November 8, 2011.

At the bottom of the last hill, the salted air filled my nostrils and I could smell water and salt and fish and sand. And we limped on.

A few blocks from the ocean, we met David and a partner from his law firm. They were neatly dressed in blue suits and perfectly tied ties. Strangely, both of them seemed happy. Content and happy. That was a change from the last attorneys I'd known, all with dour and cold faces. Maybe attorneys in San Diego are happy. Who knows? I knew it was great to see David, and he gave me a hug and smiled so big because he was amazed that we'd made it. He was proud of me, too, in that way you can be proud of people you've known in your life who do something that no one would ever have guessed. He and the other attorney went on to the beach to wait for us, and Mabel and I limped onward. I must have looked a wreck.

At the Ocean Beach Dog Beach we climbed up a sandy embankment to a bike trail and the Ocean stretched vast and blue in front of us. It went on for thousands of miles, many more thousands of miles than we had walked. We are all very small.

The filmmaker was there with a man who was working her camera. I saw her at the end of the path and beyond her were David and his partner in blue suits. I stopped at the end of the path and took off my shoes and let Mabel off leash to run around in the sand with the other dogs. While I was sitting there, the filmmaker asked me questions and I gave stupid, blank answers, because I am a stupid, blank person. She asked me about mileage, and food, and where we had slept, and how Mabel's paws had held up. And then she asked me if I was a spiritual person, and I said "No, I'm atheist" and that basically ended her questions.

Mabel and I walked together toward the water, and the closer we got the more she leapt at me and sprinted ahead, then turned around and begged for me to hurry up. Then "GO ON!" I said, and she bolted for the water and splashed and jumped and I walked into the ocean up to my knees. Mabel ran out onto the sand to get better traction, then ran fast into the ocean and jumped into me to body check me against my hip. And she jumped up to nip at my nose and she ran around with another puppy in the water, taking turns chasing each other and begging to be chased. Back up on the beach I saw David and his friend wave at me and I could hear him shout: "You made it!"

I knelt in the surf and Mabel sat in front of me. She pressed her forehead to mine and licked at my beard. I dribbled a palm full of saltwater over Mabel's neck, and she shook to dry her waterlogged coat. I cupped a handful of saltwater over my head and then splashed a handful of saltwater on my face.

Then we turned and walked back inland.

I was sure that the world was ending behind us and the Earth was a bridge that crumbled beneath our feet as we walked.

Book III: ...And the Moon Says Hallelujah, 01.11.12

Meeting w/Rosie, re: Continued disapproval of book ending.
R: "The ending sucks."
T: "I know. I agree."

R: "What's that?"
T: "Notes. Different project."
R: "What kind of project?"
Share details, Rosie approved.
R: "That's a better ending for your story!"
T: "It's not for the story. The story's over."
R: "Eh!"
T: "Would be too long!"
R: "Eh!"

Acknowledge Rosie's continued disapproval, says I did not see whole picture, says I lost perspective when I became an old man. Leave Pedro's for Lamanai trip.

Meet Kendra at pier. Water taxi one hour across Caribbean, into a brackish mainland river. Deboard. Talk with locals; see local crafts, bowls carved of hardwood by Indians of the jungle; learn they are Mayans and not Indians. Board bus; hour on bus into Belizean mainland. Hear guide say many funny things; say many funny things, Kendra laughed many times; laugh many times. Deboard for second boat trip. Travel hour up the New River; see house of famous computer programmer. Meet monkey who lives in jungle; look into monkey's eyes; consider how similar our eyes were; wonder if monkey wanted something from me; watch monkey return to jungle; travel. Enter New River reservoir, largest body fresh water in Belize. Deboard, historic ruins at Mayan city of Lamanai. Consider weather: spectacular; trees and grass were lush green. Eat lunch with tourists under palapa at the park; talk with older Indian man (pronounced Gujarati accent) and his young African-American wife; decide they were nice people; determine they were only Indian/black mixed race couple I had ever seen. Finish lunch and walked to ancient-lost-rediscovered-ruins at Lamanai, first Temple is quite near. Note for reference in Book III:

[The Mayans built this rise in the Earth with dirt and debris in order to raise the land high enough not to worry about flooding. Thousands and thousands of hours they must have spent, moving all that earth! Planning, shaping, carrying. Thousands of Mayans whose names I will never know completed this monumental earthworks project just so they could get started on more monumental projects: the construction of stone temples.]

Say to Kendra:
T: "I love interracial couples."
K: "They're *ok*. But, I mean, they're *couples*."
T: "Yes, but they're interracial."
K: "But they're couples first. Isn't that the important part?"
T: "Sure. That's the important part. But I love interracial couples and I'm just on the fence about other couples. I can't explain that."
K: "It's probably better that you don't try to explain it."
T: "Probably."

Hike to top of the rise; see first temple (The Temple of the Jaguar). See....Thousands of perfectly cut and perfectly shaped stones in about six levels with steps along the face of it to the top. Thousands of perfectly cut and perfectly shaped stones that had been cut and placed by thousands of perfectly shaped hands. Imagine it.

We walked along from the Temple of the Jaguar to another, smaller temple. Our guide, Eddie, translated hieroglyphics from a mock up of a standing stone in front of the temple. The stone dedicated the Temple to some ancient priest. Some ancient politician. Some ancient person. The man in hieroglyph on the standing stone wore royal bracelets, and one of the tourists asked jokingly if the bracelets had read "Eddie" on them, like Eddie's own bracelet. Eddie did not laugh.

"I do have the blood of kings in me," he said, dryly. "Mayan culture collapsed, but Mayans are not extinct. There are 20,000 Mayans in Belize today."

Everyone was silent.

"What happened to the Mayan culture?" someone asked.

"There are three main theories," Eddie said. "Four, now, because I have my own. The first: disease, perhaps introduced by foreign invaders—not only Europeans, but other Central Americans. Second: economic collapse; it is possible the Mayan culture spent too much money on building these temples and on subjugating foreign tribes, and not enough on the welfare of its own citizens. Third, ecological collapse brought on by climate change and drought or the overuse of the land."

We waited and Eddie looked at each of us individually, in turn.

"I have a fourth theory," he said. "You saw the rubber trees? They were labeled 'rubber tree' for those of you who do not know what a rubber tree looks like. Mayan culture had rubber. And we Mayans have been making beer and wine for thousands of years, because we know how to have fun. While Europeans drank beer and wine, they had only the intestines of animals to use as condoms. We had the real thing."

Everyone chuckled and we walked on the High Temple. The High Temple is the third largest structure in all of Belize, and the first two are also Mayan temples, farther to the south. It is about 120 feet to the top of the High Temple and I had to climb it. It was not difficult for me to climb it, and I passed quite a few huffing Americans on the way up. Kendra said: "Will you be able to get down off of this thing with your fear of heights?"

"I hope so," I said, and trudged ahead. I thought it was funny that Kendra, who had always been in such great shape, was having such a hard time climbing the temple steps compared to me. Walking across a continent might not be good for much, but it prepared me to climb the Temple.

From the top of the High Temple, I could see for 40 or 50 miles in all directions. I could see the lowlands of Belize, and a great swath of the New River basin and the New River Lagoon, the largest body of fresh water in Belize. If there had been less humidity, maybe I could have seen further, to South America or to Antarctica.

"Is this awesome or is this awesome?" Kendra asked. I nodded that it was, indeed, awesome.

"You can end your book right here," she said.

"I could," I said.

"Stayed with me in D.C. at the beginning of the trip, and now *here you are* at the end of it. We're on top of a temple in Central America. And you *walked* up the Temple. That's nice. You can give your readers some closure and resolution." She swung her arms around in one of the flailing, sweeping gestures that she liked so much to do.

"I'd be lying. There's no resolution," I said.

"No?"

"Nope. And Mabel's not here," I went on. "Can hardly end the story without Mabel. The story has to end in San Diego, on the beach."

"Well, maybe just end the *book* here, then. The *story* can end earlier. Or it can keep going on and on," she said.

"Maybe."

There had been a few tourists at the top with us, but one by one they went down and then Kendra went down, too, because she was nervous about descending the steep steps. And I was all alone there for a little while on the top of the High Temple. It was the second time in my life I had been alone on the top of a tall structure; the first was the Empire State Building when I was up there alone on a cloudy day and could see nothing. The High Temple was different, though. On the High Temple I could see a very long way.

I could see the top of the Temple of the Jaguar on the other side of the ancient town. I saw a million nameless hands cutting formless rocks into shaped stones. A million nameless priests and politicians send down edicts, and a million nameless peasants ignore them or rise up. And no one knows because the Earth rose and swallowed this whole town, this whole civilization. A thousand years later a man finds it again and we cut it free from jungle. People whose names I will never know cart off barrels and bucket loads of dirt and debris to expose this masterful earthwork project that a million people whose names I will never know had built a thousand years ago by carrying in barrels and bucket loads of dirt and debris.

I looked down at the ground so far away and I took a deep breath.

A grandfather recites his favorite poem and then he dies. A young man skips into his new professional life in a brand new suit, his shirt pressed and starched. The Caribbean is flat and blue like it is pressed under blue cellophane and concentric circles ripple out from a sinking jewel in the Pacific ocean. An exhausted man lowers his head because he cannot go on like this. A couple dances wildly across the stage, or the street, and collapse together embracing and laughing. The father measures his newborn's fingers against his own.

See them all fall in and out of love.

I feel Mabel's heart beating against my leg in a cold tent in a southwestern desert. You write your name on a piece of paper under florescent lights in a florescent office. Men in blue suits smile and wonder what they could do if they only had the time. An attorney fights to slip a snorkel mask over thick tresses of blonde hair and falls with a splash into the sea. The fresh water slams into the salt water. A newborn learns to breathe, and a toddler learns to walk, and an old man learns to drink water. A man lowers the final Stars and Strips out of remarkable skies like the day turning softly into night: And the Moon says Hallelujah!

I am so small and so temporary. It is irrational to care about the consequences of my actions on others; it is irrational to care about the consequences of my actions on future generations. We are all so small, all so temporary.

Biology won't let us live long enough that we should give a damn.

Still, I am inclined to give all that I can.

When a thousand years roll by, they won't recall that I lived.

Or that I died.

But I do not care.

I train my eye on the distant land.

Made in the USA
San Bernardino, CA
17 December 2012